KOYOHARU GOTOUGE

Hi, I'm Gotouge! Volume 17 is out! The fighting is gradually getting more fierce. When a character you like gets injured, you feel bad for them, so reading can be grueling and you may not really want to do it, but the manga is set in a world where they have to engage in deadly combat, so I'm sorry. I'll dedicate myself to it until the end, so please keep reading.

DEMON SLAYER:
KIMETSU NO YAIBA
VOLUME 17
Shonen Jump Edition

Story and Art by
KOYOHARU GOTOUGE

KIMETSU NO YAIBA
© 2016 by Koyoharu Gotouge
All rights reserved. First published in Japan
in 2016 by SHUEISHA Inc., Tokyo. English
translation rights arranged by SHUEISHA Inc.

TRANSLATION John Werry
ENGLISH ADAPTATION Stan!
TOUCH-UP ART & LETTERING Evan Waldinger
DESIGN Jimmy Presler
EDITOR Mike Montesa

Printed in Canada

Published by VIZ Media, LLC
P.O. Box 77010
San Francisco, CA 94107

10 9 8 7 6 5 4 3 2
First printing, October 2020
Second printing, March 2021

VIZ MEDIA
viz.com

SHONEN JUMP

DEMON SLAYER

KIMETSU NO YAIBA

17

SUCCESSORS

**KOYOHARU
GOTOUGE**

CHARACTERS

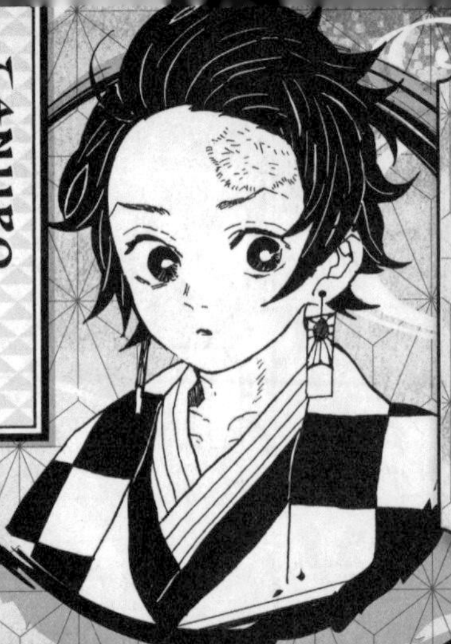

TANJIRO KAMADO

A kind boy who saved his sister when the rest of his family was killed. Now he seeks revenge. He can smell the scent of demons and his opponents' weaknesses.

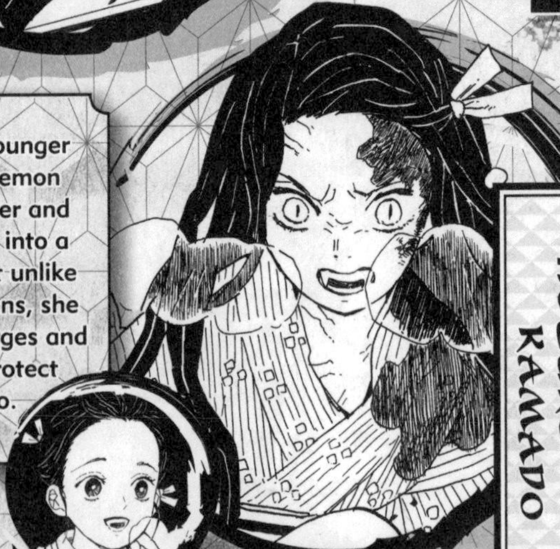

NEZUKO KAMADO

Tanjiro's younger sister. A demon attacked her and turned her into a demon. But unlike other demons, she fights her urges and tries to protect Tanjiro.

STORY

In Taisho-Era Japan, young Tanjiro makes a living selling charcoal. One day, demons kill his family and turn his younger sister Nezuko into a demon. Tanjiro and Nezuko set out to find a way to return Nezuko to human form and defeat Kibutsuji, the demon who killed their family!

After joining the Demon Slayer Corps, Tanjiro meets Tamayo and Yushiro—demons who oppose Kibutsuji—who provide a clue to how Nezuko may regain her humanity. Then, during a fierce battle against the Upper Rank 6 demon, Nezuko manifests the ability to withstand sunlight. When he learns of this, Muzan Kibutsuji attacks Ubuyashiki Mansion, but Kagaya Ubuyashiki used himself as bait in an explosive trap! The Demon Slayers plunge into Infinity Castle in pursuit. Inside, the Insect Hashira Shinobu clashes with Doma—the demon who killed her older sister!!

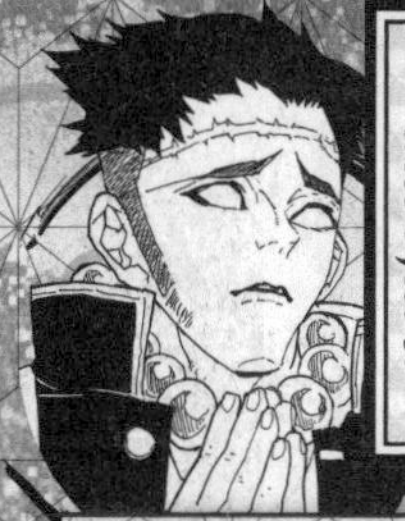

GYOMEI HIMEJIMA

Stone Hashira in the Demon Slayer Corps. He is always clasping a rosary and reciting a Buddhist prayer.

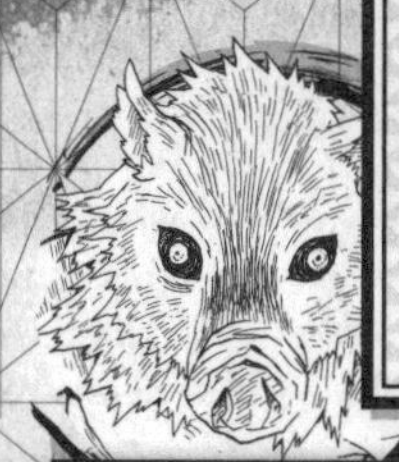

INOSUKE HASHIBIRA

He also went through Final Selection at the same time as Tanjiro. He wears the pelt of a wild boar and is very belligerent.

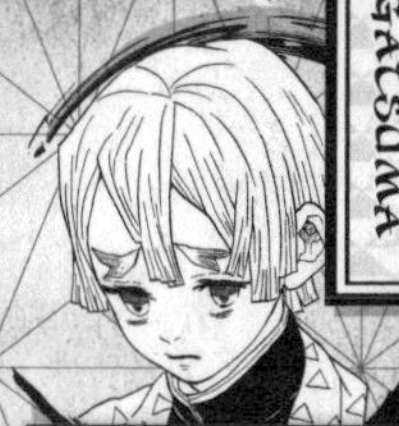

ZENITSU AGATSUMA

He went through Final Selection at the same time as Tanjiro. He's usually cowardly, but when he falls asleep, his true power comes out.

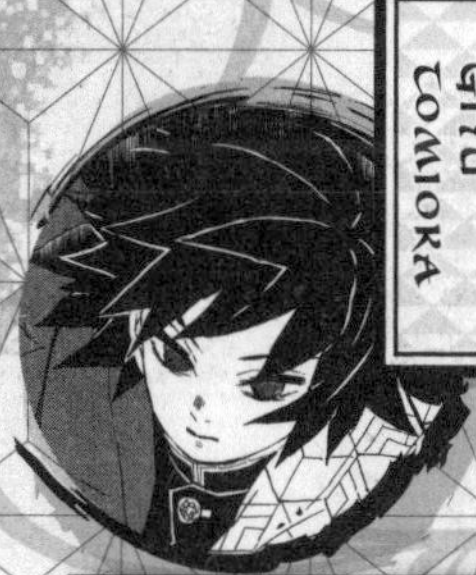

GIYU TOMIOKA

The Hashira who invited Tanjiro to join the Demon Slayer Corps. He has always cared about Tanjiro.

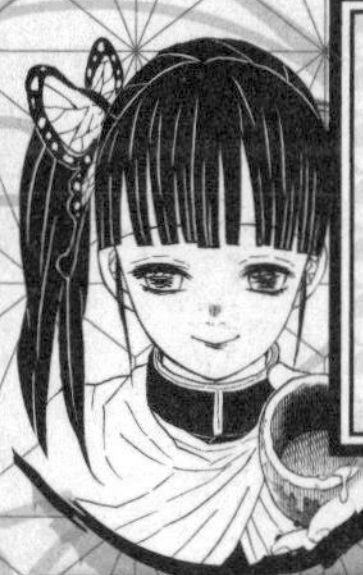

KANAO TSUYURI

Successor to Shinobu. She doesn't talk much and has difficulty making any kind of decision by herself.

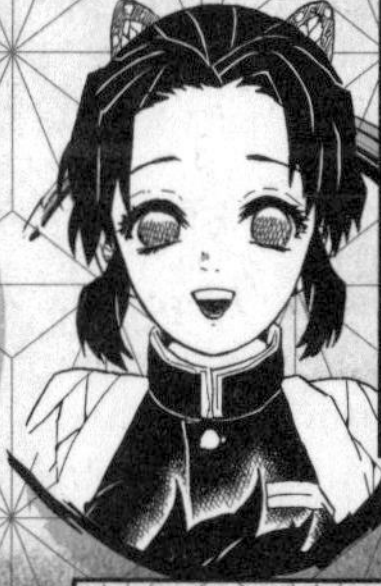

SHINOBU KOCHO

Another Hashira in the Demon Slayer Corps. Familiar with pharmacology, she is a swordswoman who has created a poison that kills demons.

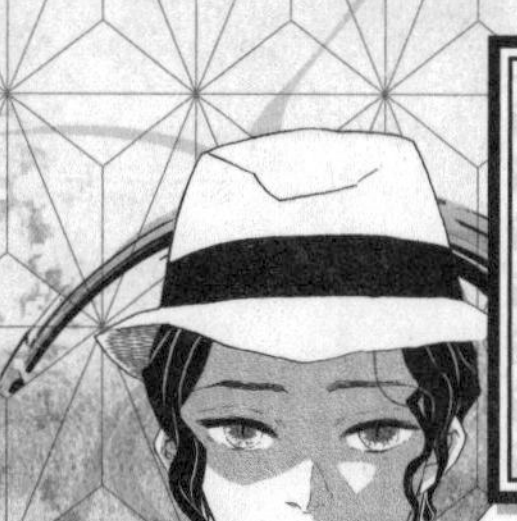

MUZAN KIBUTSUJI

Kibutsuji turned Nezuko into a demon. He is Tanjiro's enemy and hides his nature in order to live among human beings.

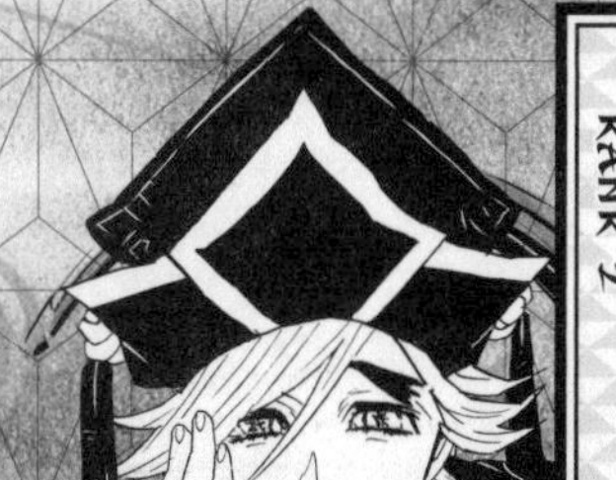

DOMA: UPPER RANK 2

The demon who killed Shinobu Kocho's older sister Kanae and founded the Eternal Paradise Faith.

CONTENTS

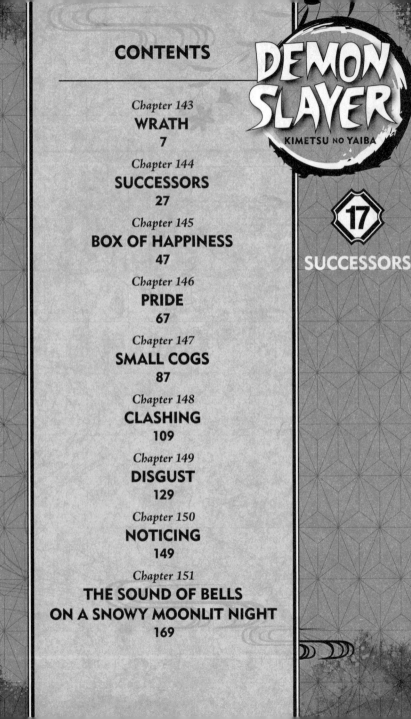

DEMON SLAYER!
KIMETSU NO YAIBA

17

SUCCESSORS

Chapter 143
WRATH
7

Chapter 144
SUCCESSORS
27

Chapter 145
BOX OF HAPPINESS
47

Chapter 146
PRIDE
67

Chapter 147
SMALL COGS
87

Chapter 148
CLASHING
109

Chapter 149
DISGUST
129

Chapter 150
NOTICING
149

Chapter 151
THE SOUND OF BELLS ON A SNOWY MOONLIT NIGHT
169

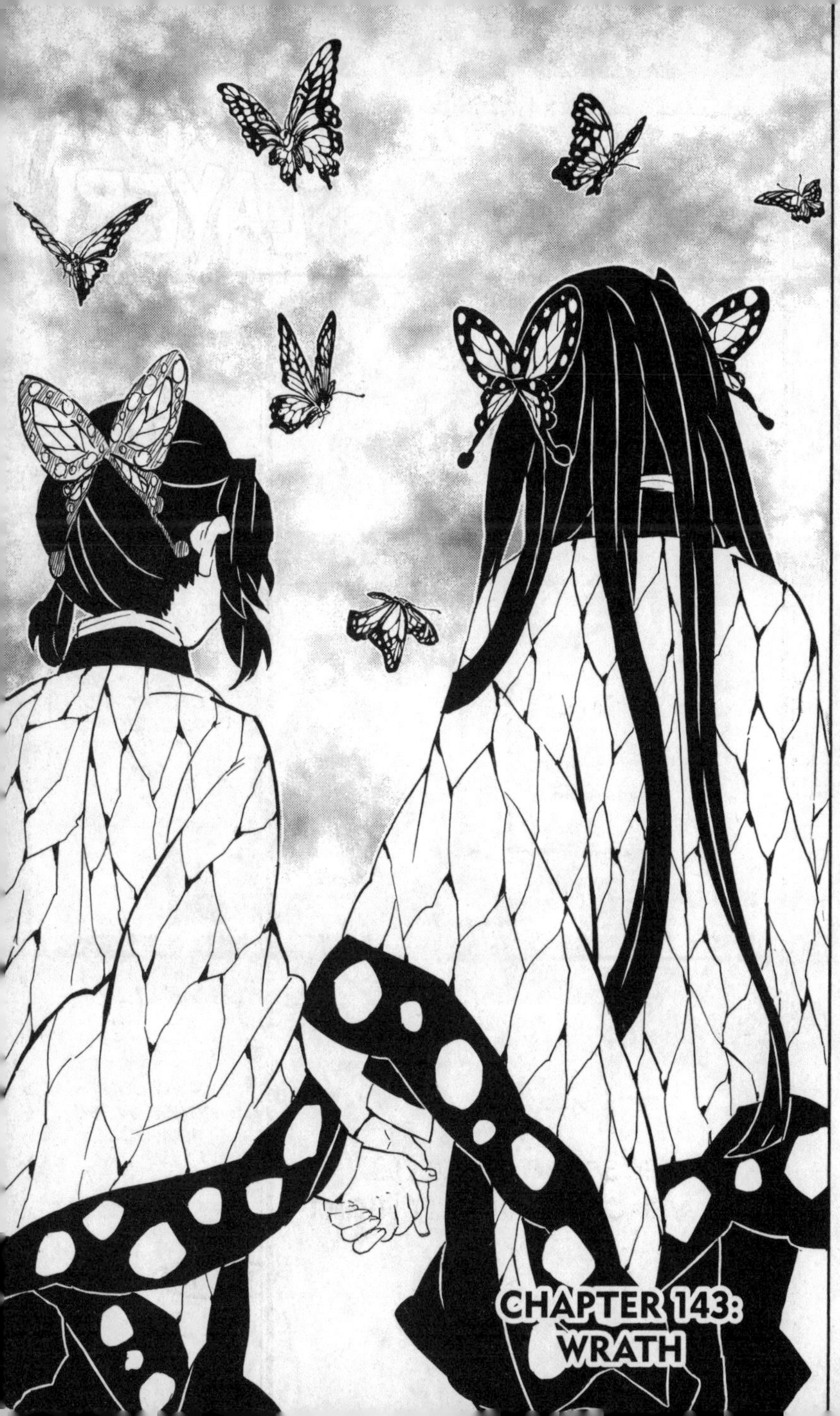
CHAPTER 143:
WRATH

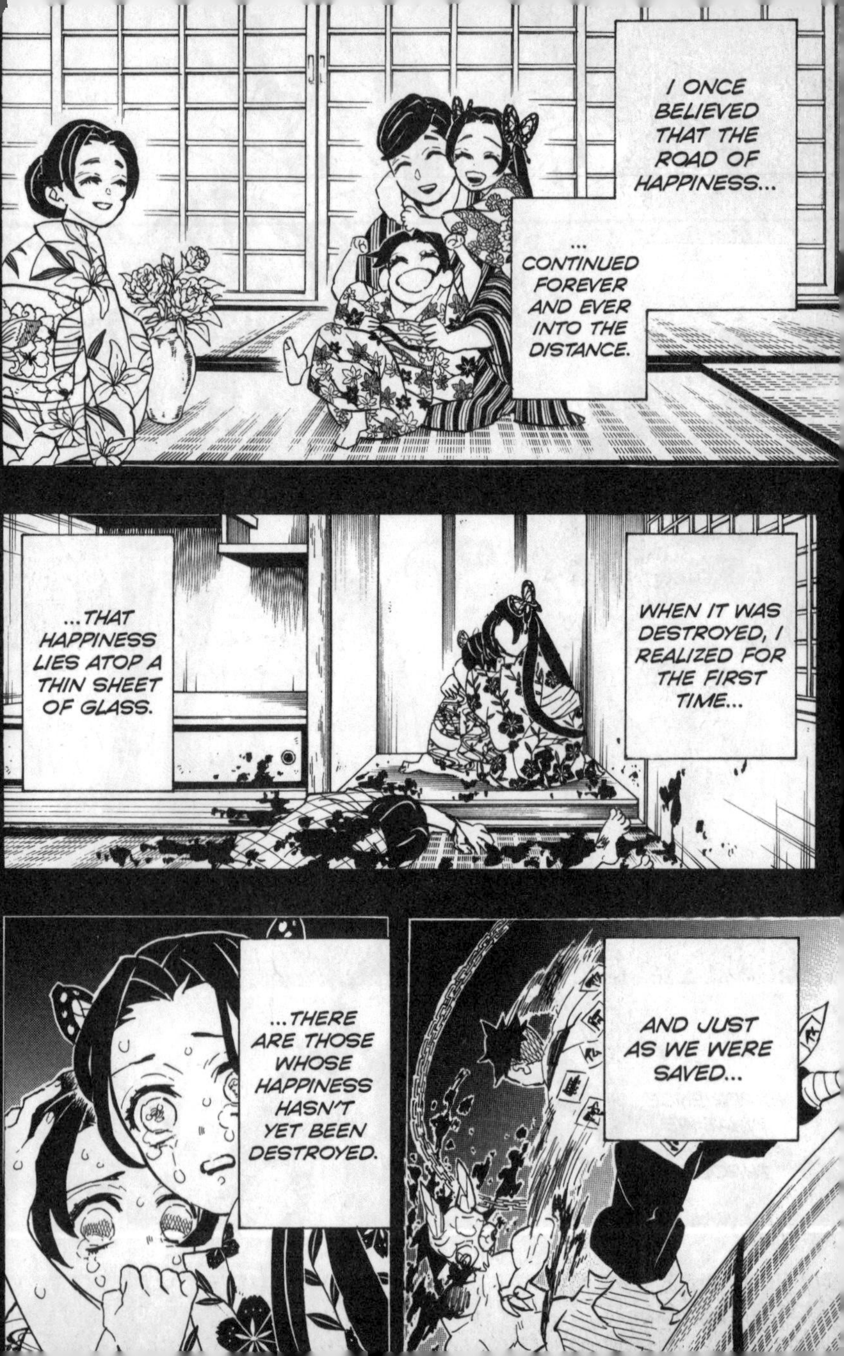
I ONCE BELIEVED THAT THE ROAD OF HAPPINESS...
...CONTINUED FOREVER AND EVER INTO THE DISTANCE.
WHEN IT WAS DESTROYED, I REALIZED FOR THE FIRST TIME...
...THAT HAPPINESS LIES ATOP A THIN SHEET OF GLASS.
AND JUST AS WE WERE SAVED...
...THERE ARE THOSE WHOSE HAPPINESS HASN'T YET BEEN DESTROYED.

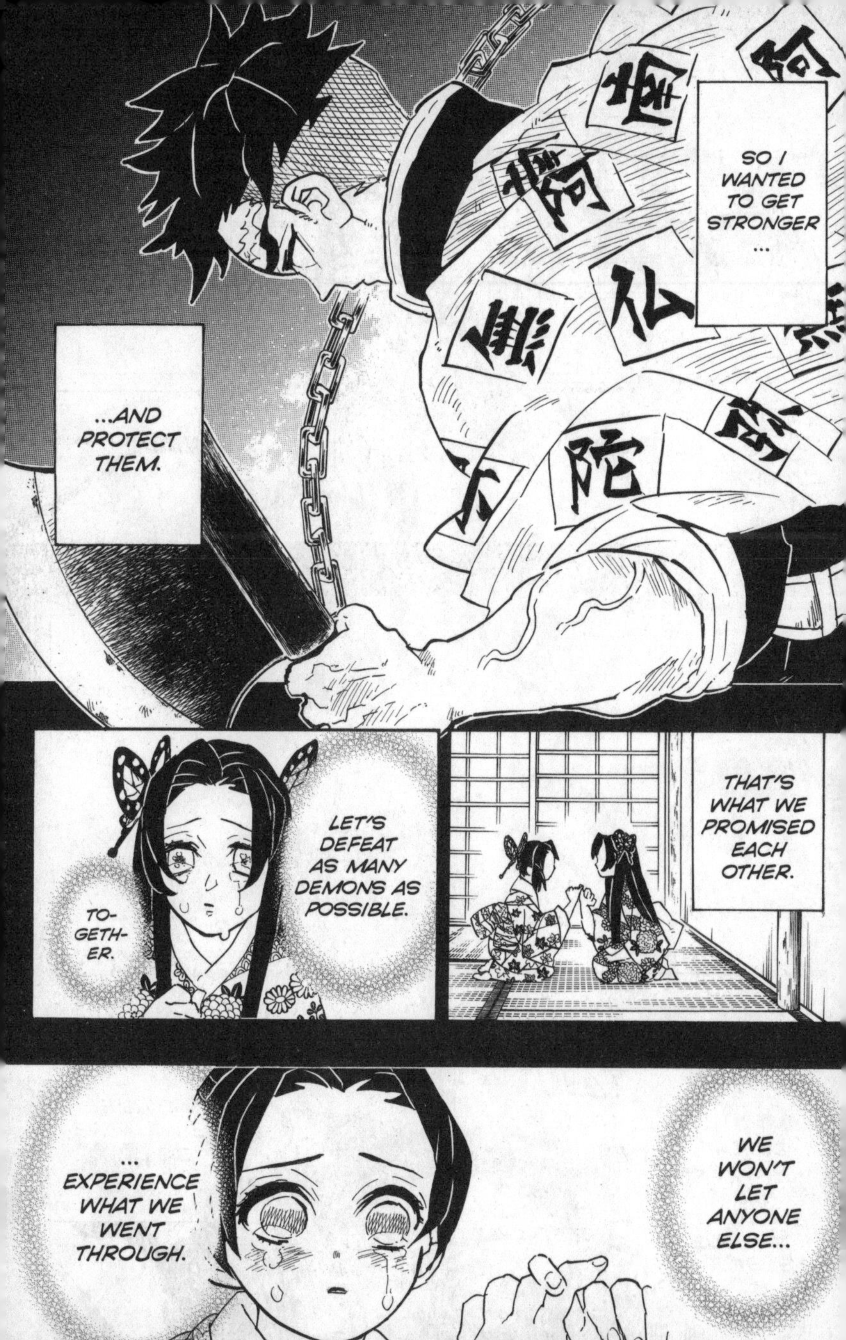
SO I WANTED TO GET STRONGER ...
...AND PROTECT THEM.
THAT'S WHAT WE PROMISED EACH OTHER.
LET'S DEFEAT AS MANY DEMONS AS POSSIBLE.
TO-GETH-ER.
WE WON'T LET ANYONE ELSE...
... EXPERIENCE WHAT WE WENT THROUGH.

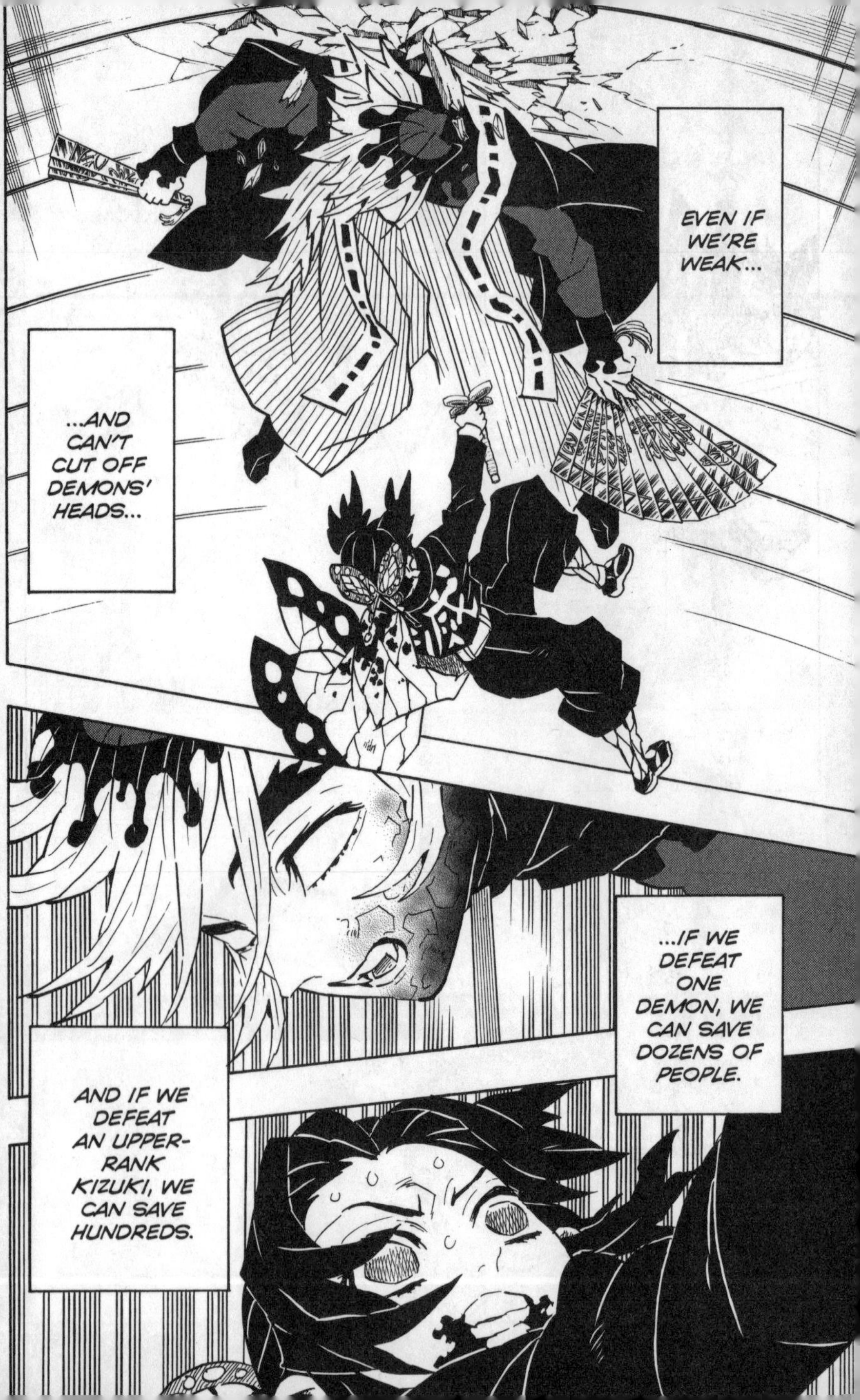
EVEN IF WE'RE WEAK...
...AND CAN'T CUT OFF DEMONS' HEADS...
...IF WE DEFEAT ONE DEMON, WE CAN SAVE DOZENS OF PEOPLE.
AND IF WE DEFEAT AN UPPER-RANK KIZUKI, WE CAN SAVE HUNDREDS.

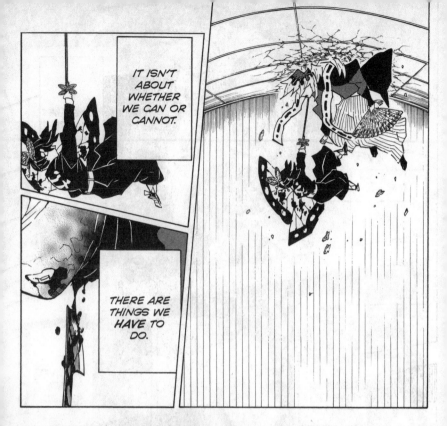

IT ISN'T
ABOUT
WHETHER
WE CAN OR
CANNOT.

THERE ARE
THINGS WE
HAVE TO
DO.

ARE
YOU
ANGRY?

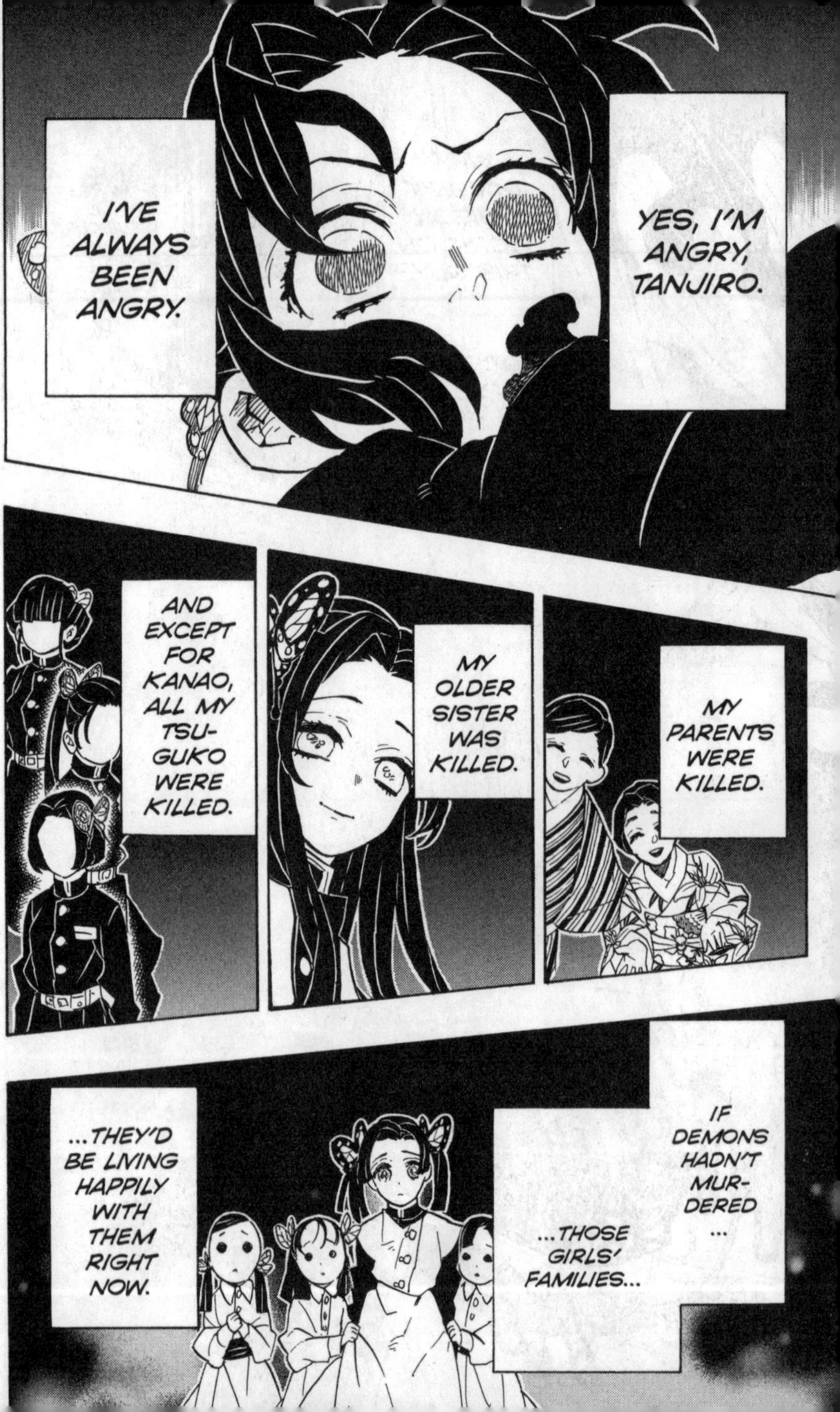
YES, I'M ANGRY, TANJIRO.
I'VE ALWAYS BEEN ANGRY.
MY PARENTS WERE KILLED.
MY OLDER SISTER WAS KILLED.
AND EXCEPT FOR KANAO, ALL MY TSUGUKO WERE KILLED.
IF DEMONS HADN'T MURDERED...
...THOSE GIRLS' FAMILIES...
...THEY'D BE LIVING HAPPILY WITH THEM RIGHT NOW.

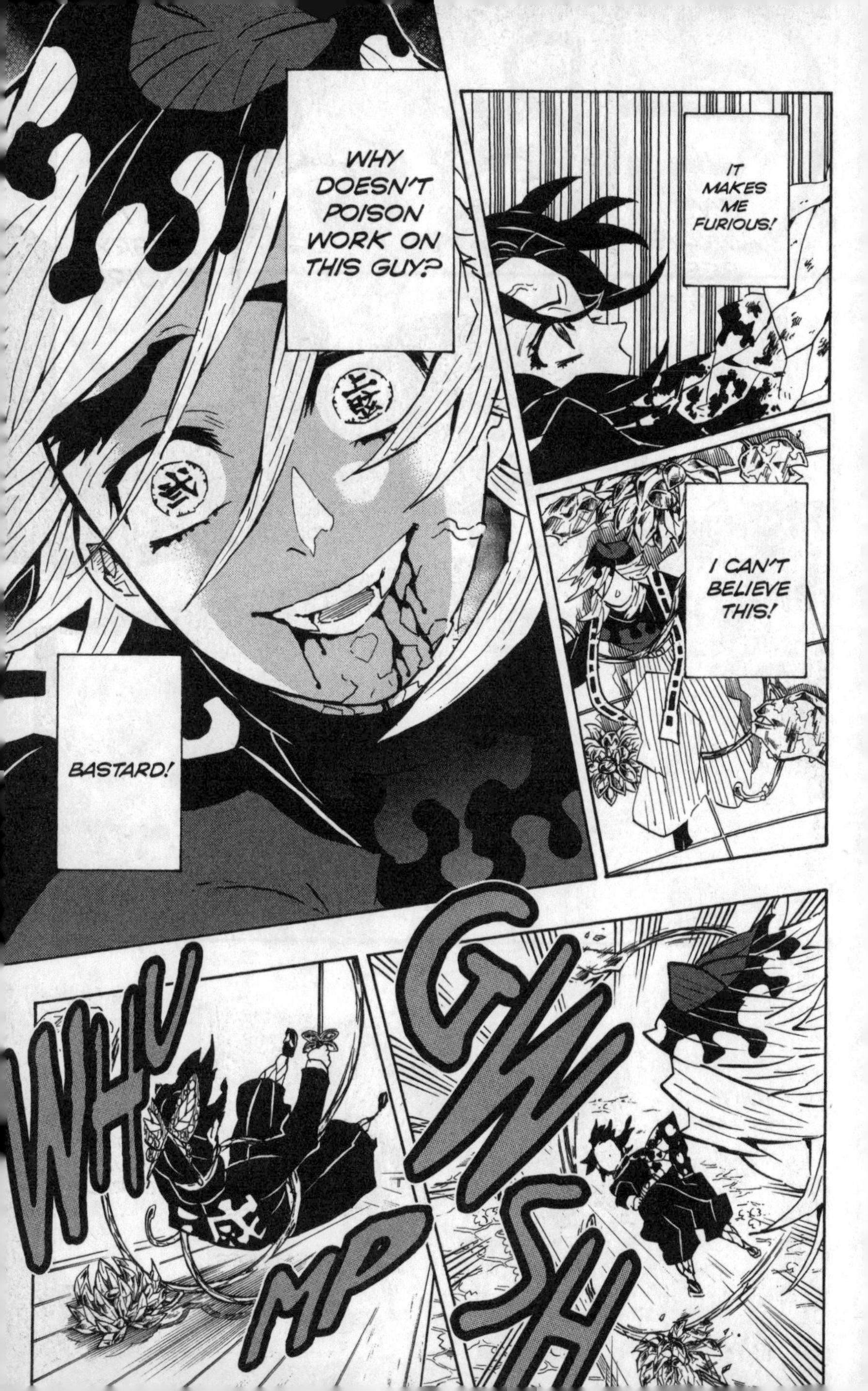
IT MAKES ME FURIOUS!
I CAN'T BELIEVE THIS!
WHY DOESN'T POISON WORK ON THIS GUY?
BASTARD!
GWSH
WHUMP

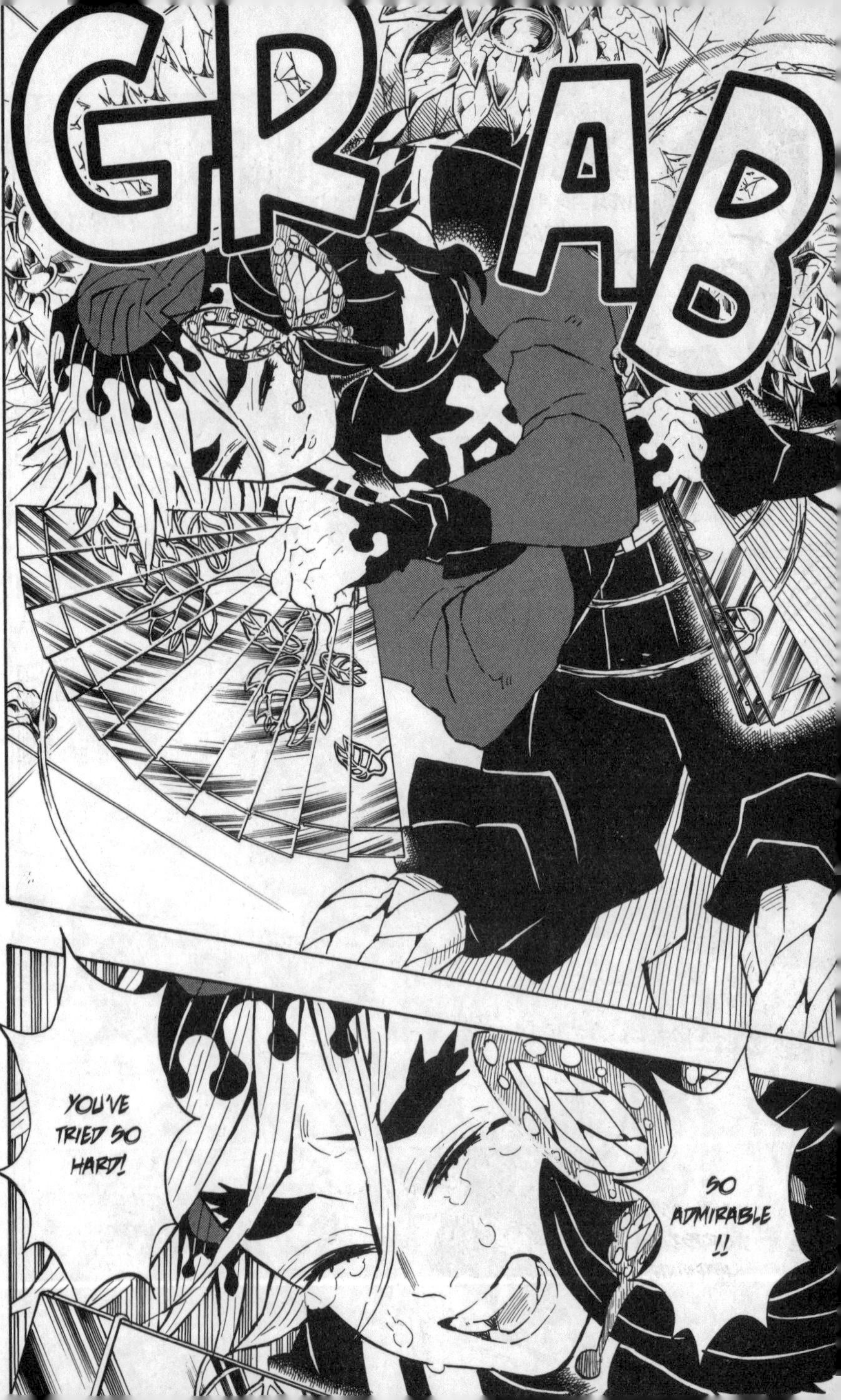
GRAB
SO ADMIRABLE !!
YOU'VE TRIED SO HARD!

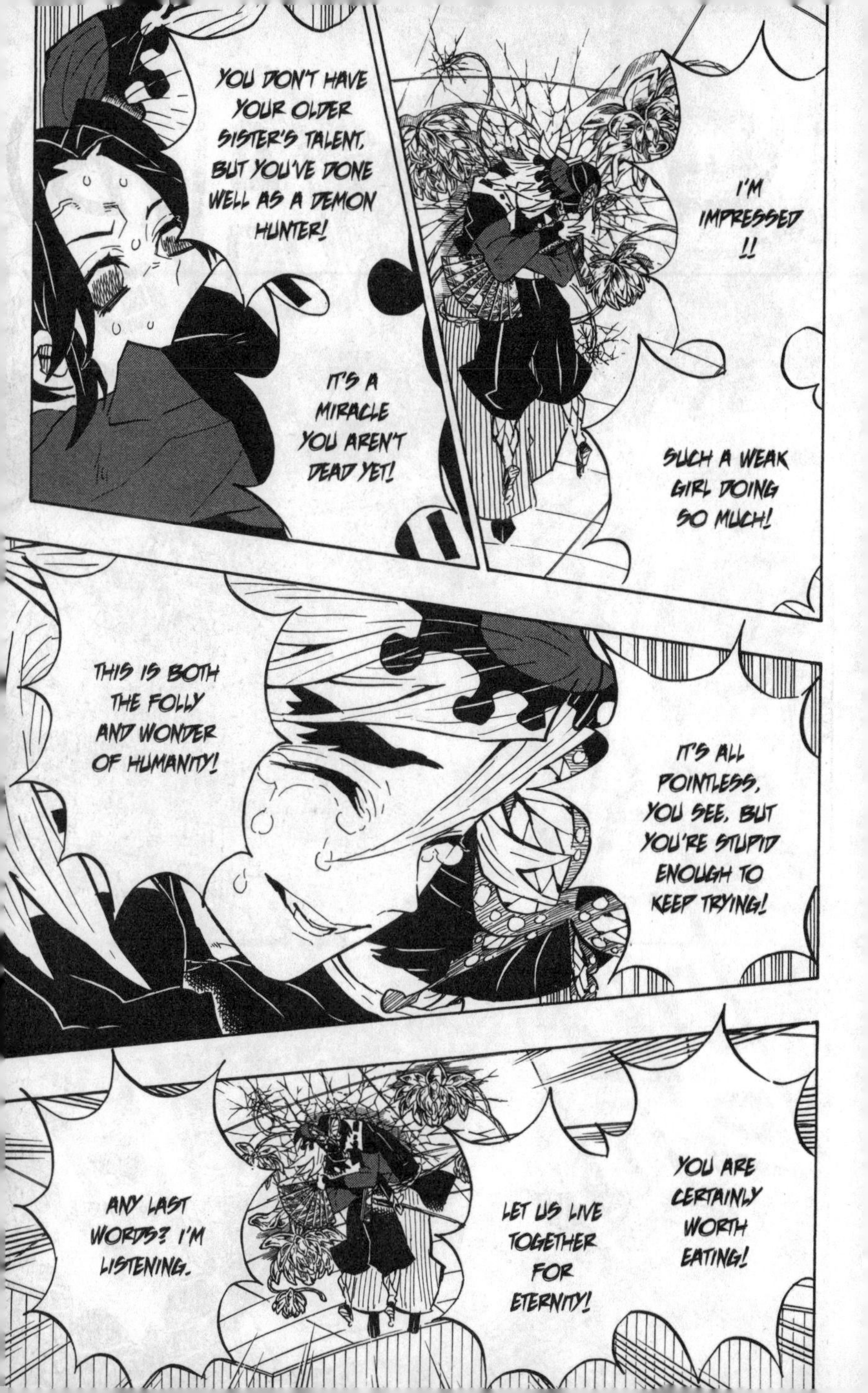
I'M IMPRESSED!!
SUCH A WEAK GIRL DOING SO MUCH!
YOU DON'T HAVE YOUR OLDER SISTER'S TALENT, BUT YOU'VE DONE WELL AS A DEMON HUNTER!
IT'S A MIRACLE YOU AREN'T DEAD YET!
IT'S ALL POINTLESS, YOU SEE, BUT YOU'RE STUPID ENOUGH TO KEEP TRYING!
THIS IS BOTH THE FOLLY AND WONDER OF HUMANITY!
YOU ARE CERTAINLY WORTH EATING!
LET US LIVE TOGETHER FOR ETERNITY!
ANY LAST WORDS? I'M LISTENING.

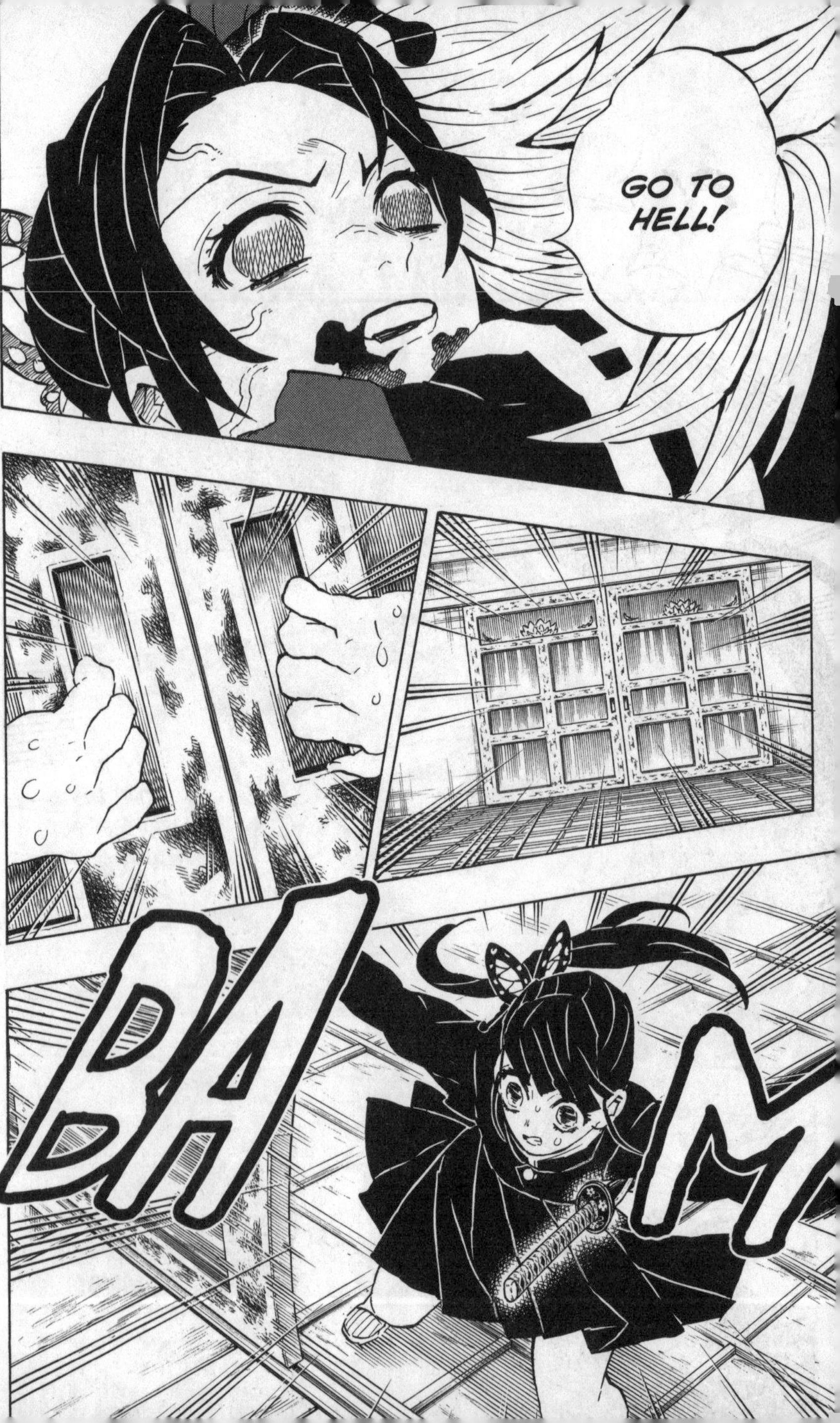
GO TO HELL!
BAM

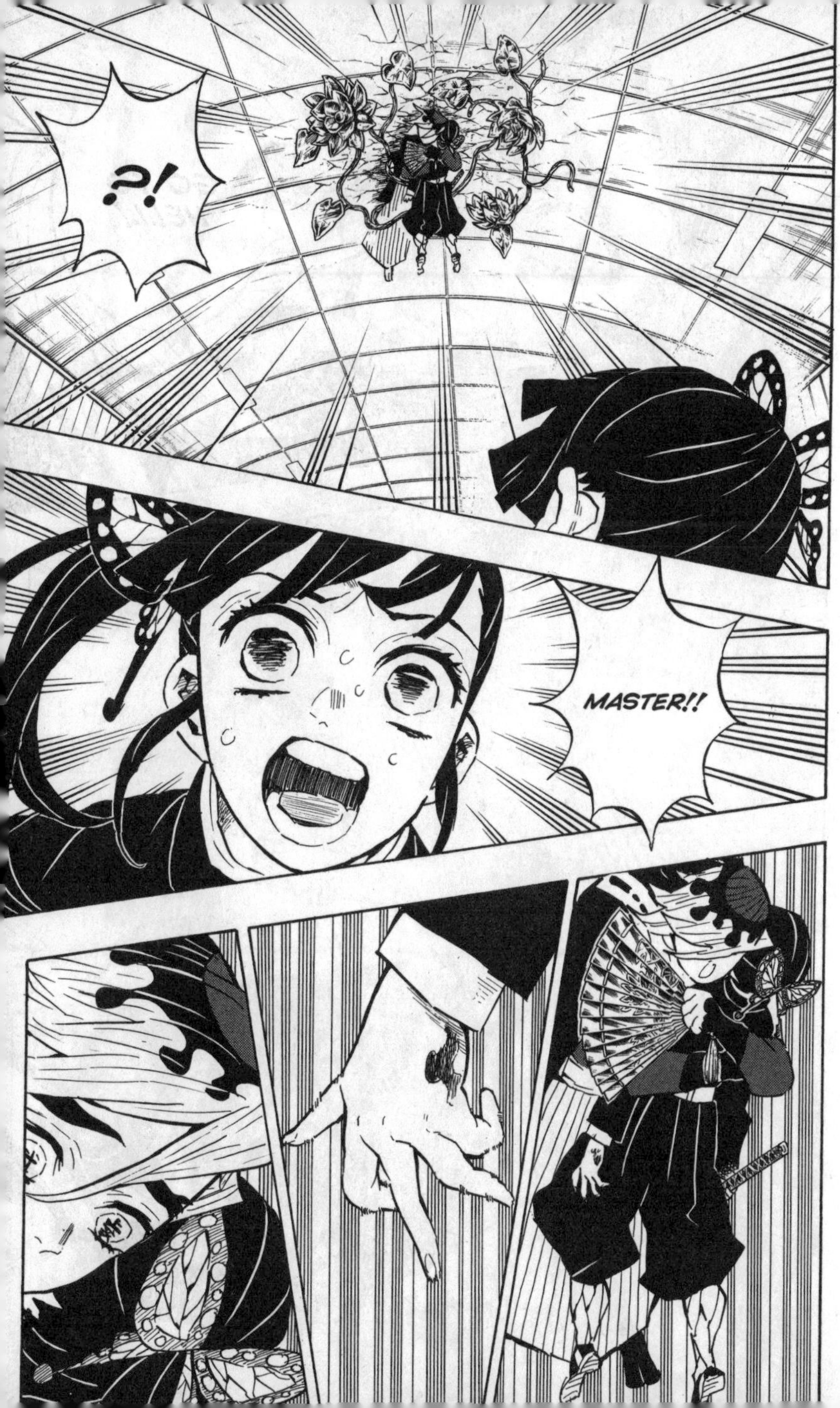
?!
MASTER!!

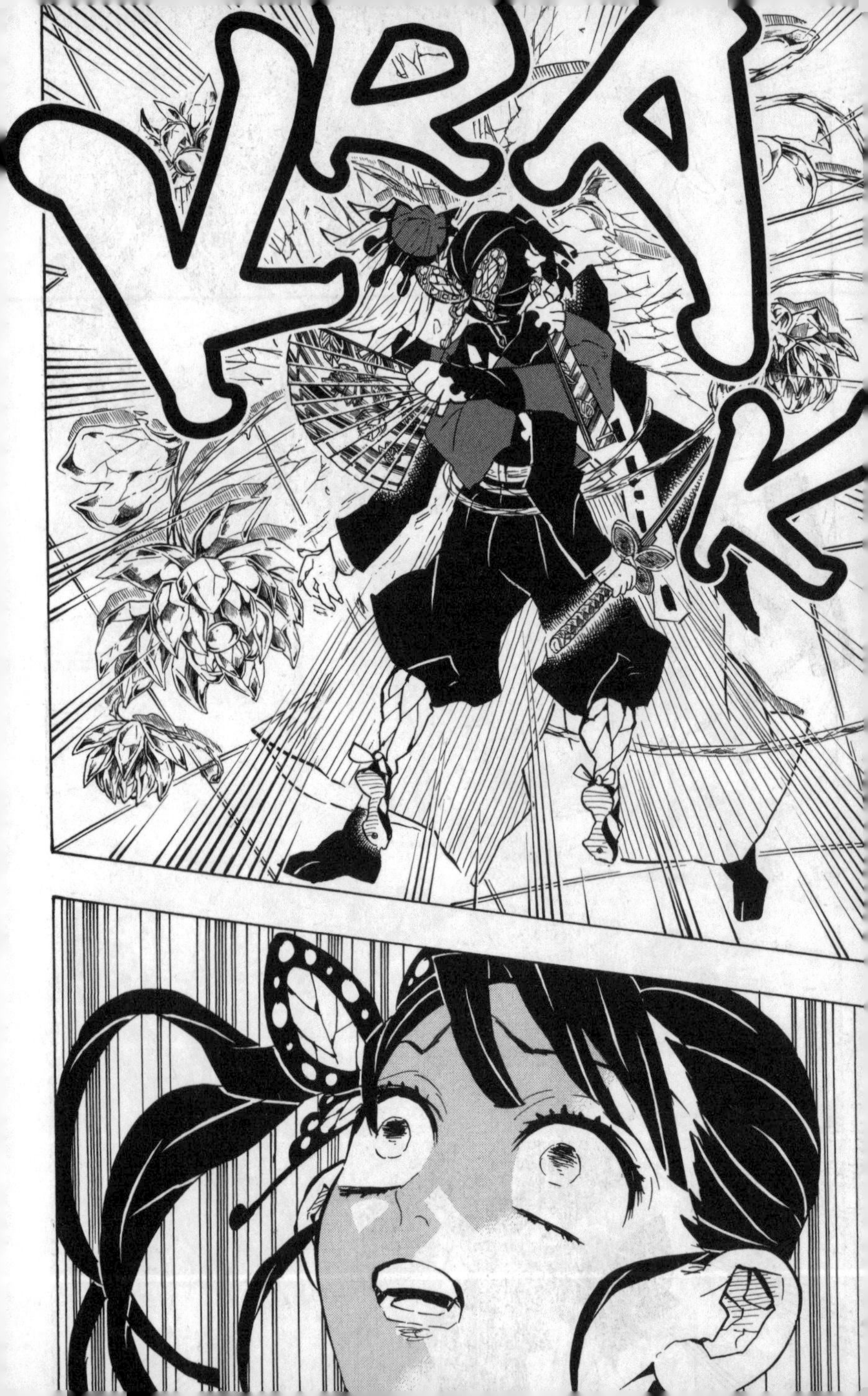
VRAK

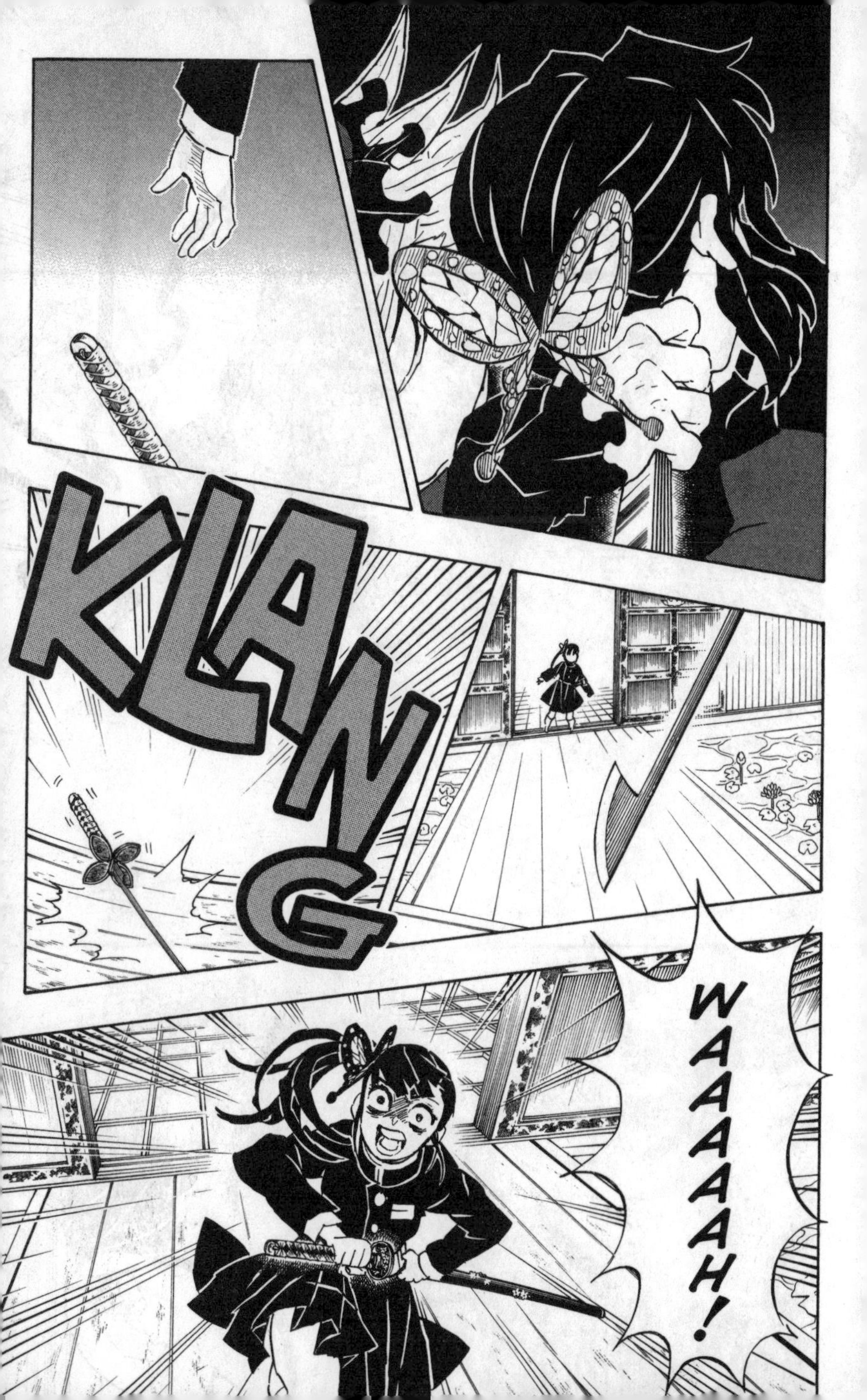
KLANG
WAAAAAAH!

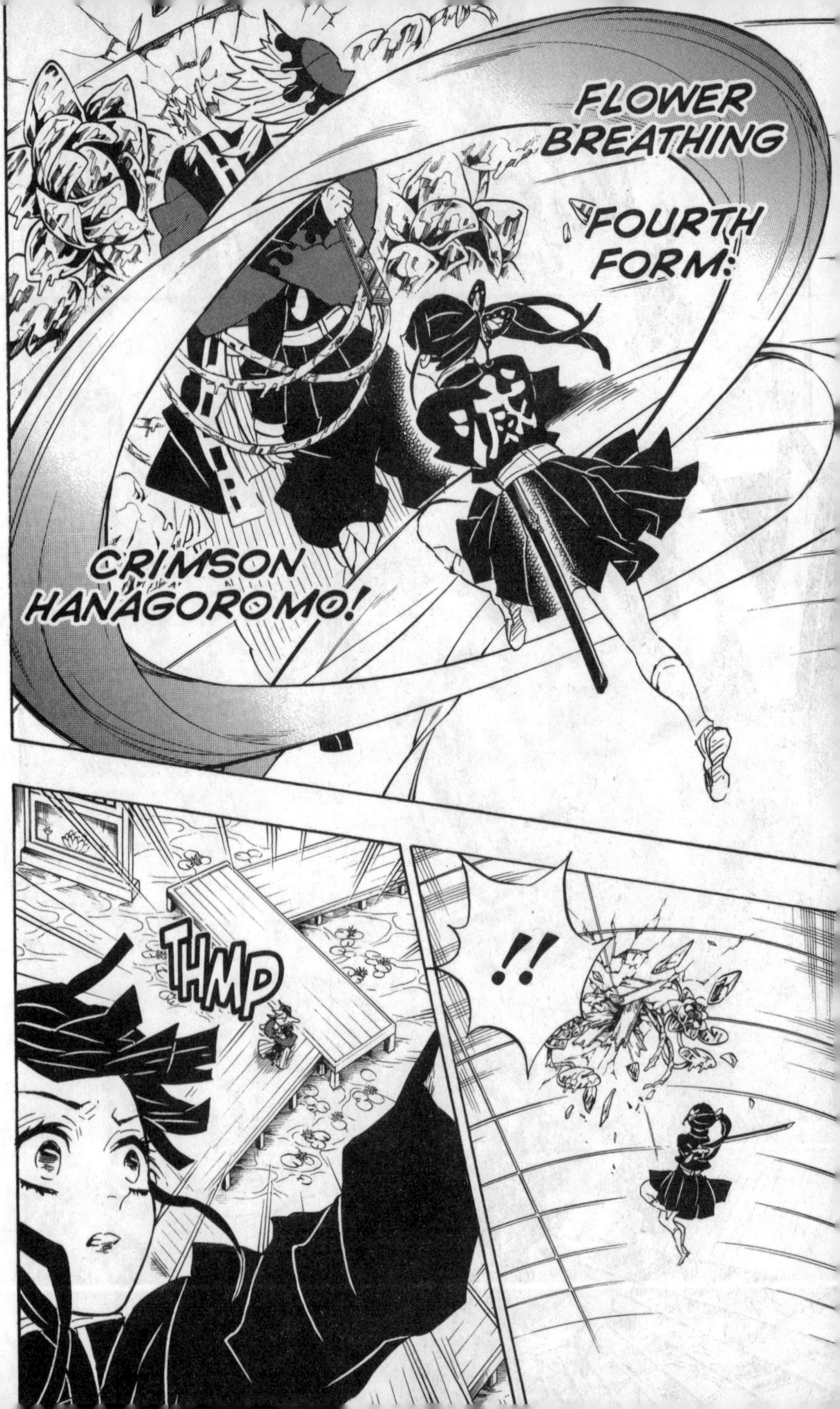
FLOWER BREATHING
FOURTH FORM:
CRIMSON HANAGOROMO!
!!
THMP

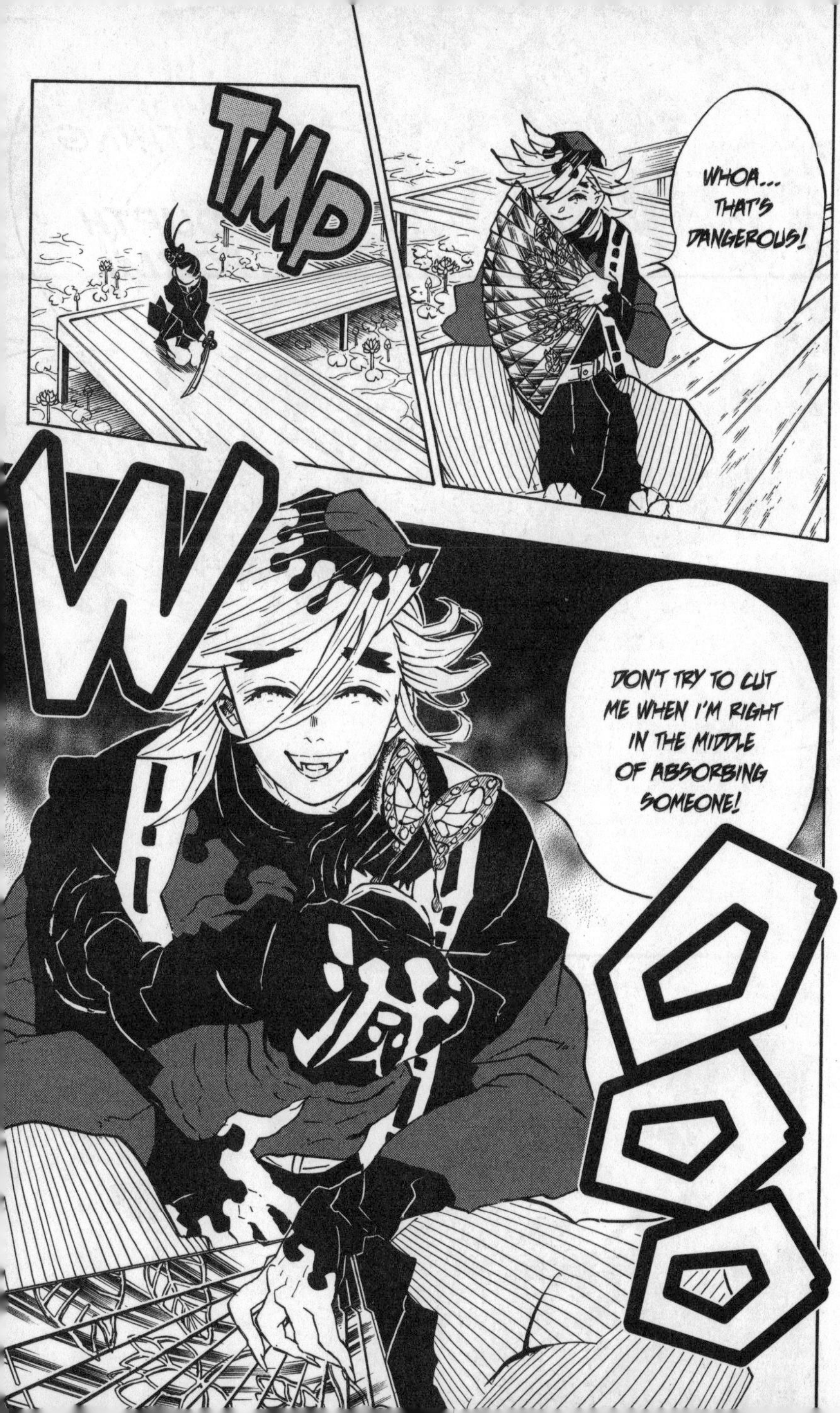
WHOA... THAT'S DANGEROUS!
TMP
DON'T TRY TO CUT ME WHEN I'M RIGHT IN THE MIDDLE OF ABSORBING SOMEONE!
WOOO

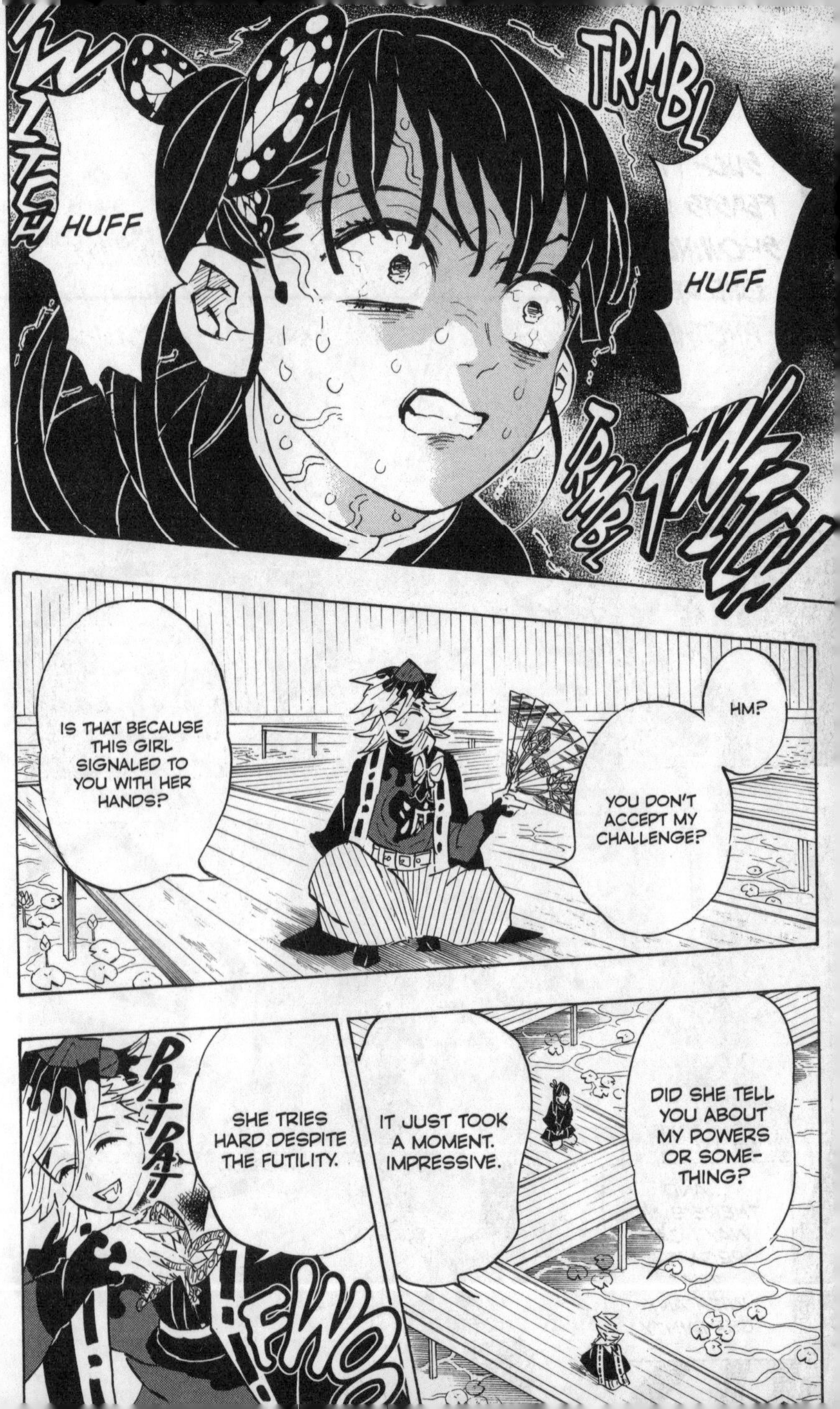
TRMBL
HUFF
TRMBL
TWITCH
HUFF
TWITCH
HM?
YOU DON'T ACCEPT MY CHALLENGE?
IS THAT BECAUSE THIS GIRL SIGNALED TO YOU WITH HER HANDS?
DID SHE TELL YOU ABOUT MY POWERS OR SOME-THING?
IT JUST TOOK A MOMENT. IMPRESSIVE.
SHE TRIES HARD DESPITE THE FUTILITY.
PAT PAT
FWOO

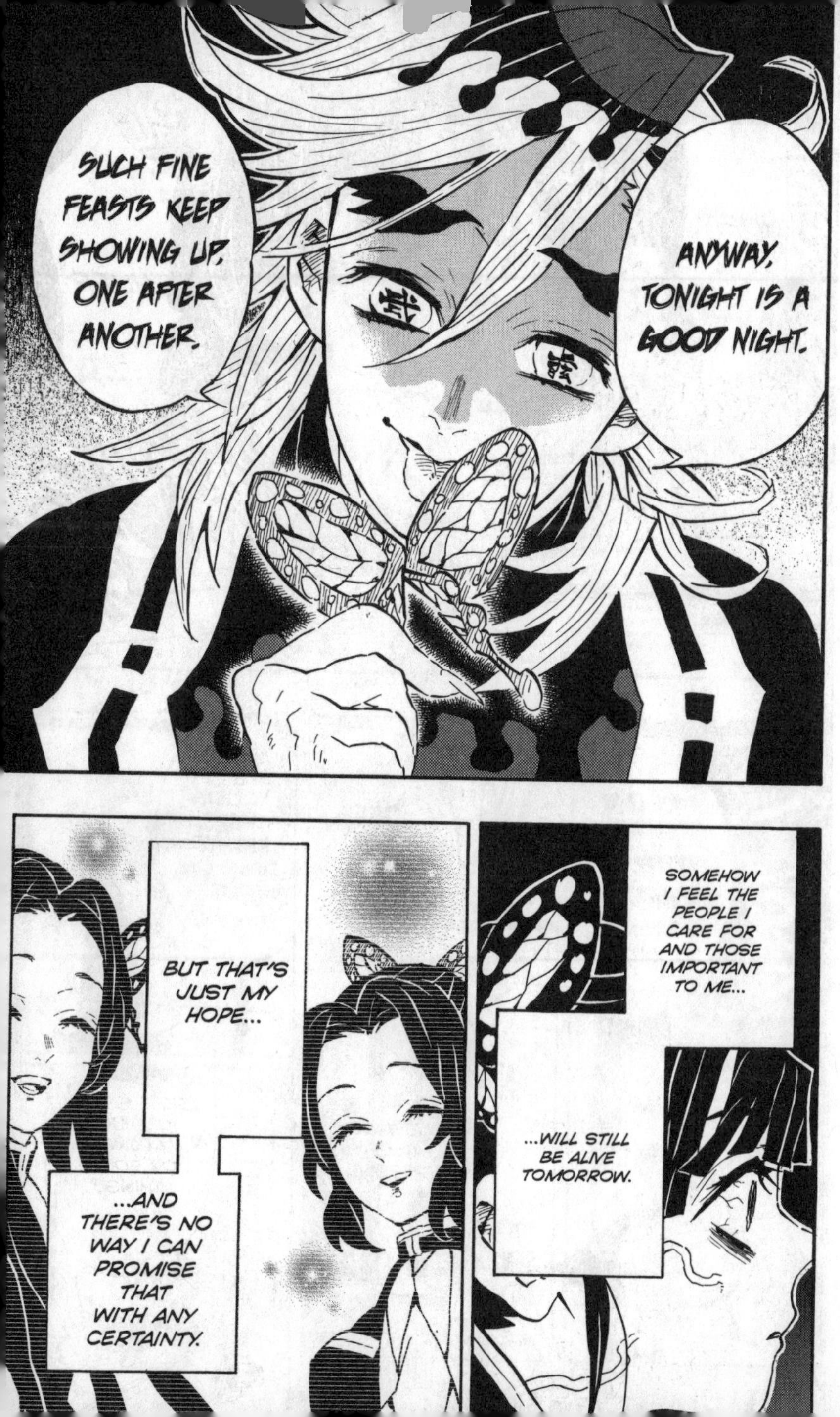
ANYWAY, TONIGHT IS A GOOD NIGHT.
SUCH FINE FEASTS KEEP SHOWING UP, ONE AFTER ANOTHER.
SOMEHOW I FEEL THE PEOPLE I CARE FOR AND THOSE IMPORTANT TO ME...
...WILL STILL BE ALIVE TOMORROW.
BUT THAT'S JUST MY HOPE...
...AND THERE'S NO WAY I CAN PROMISE THAT WITH ANY CERTAINTY.

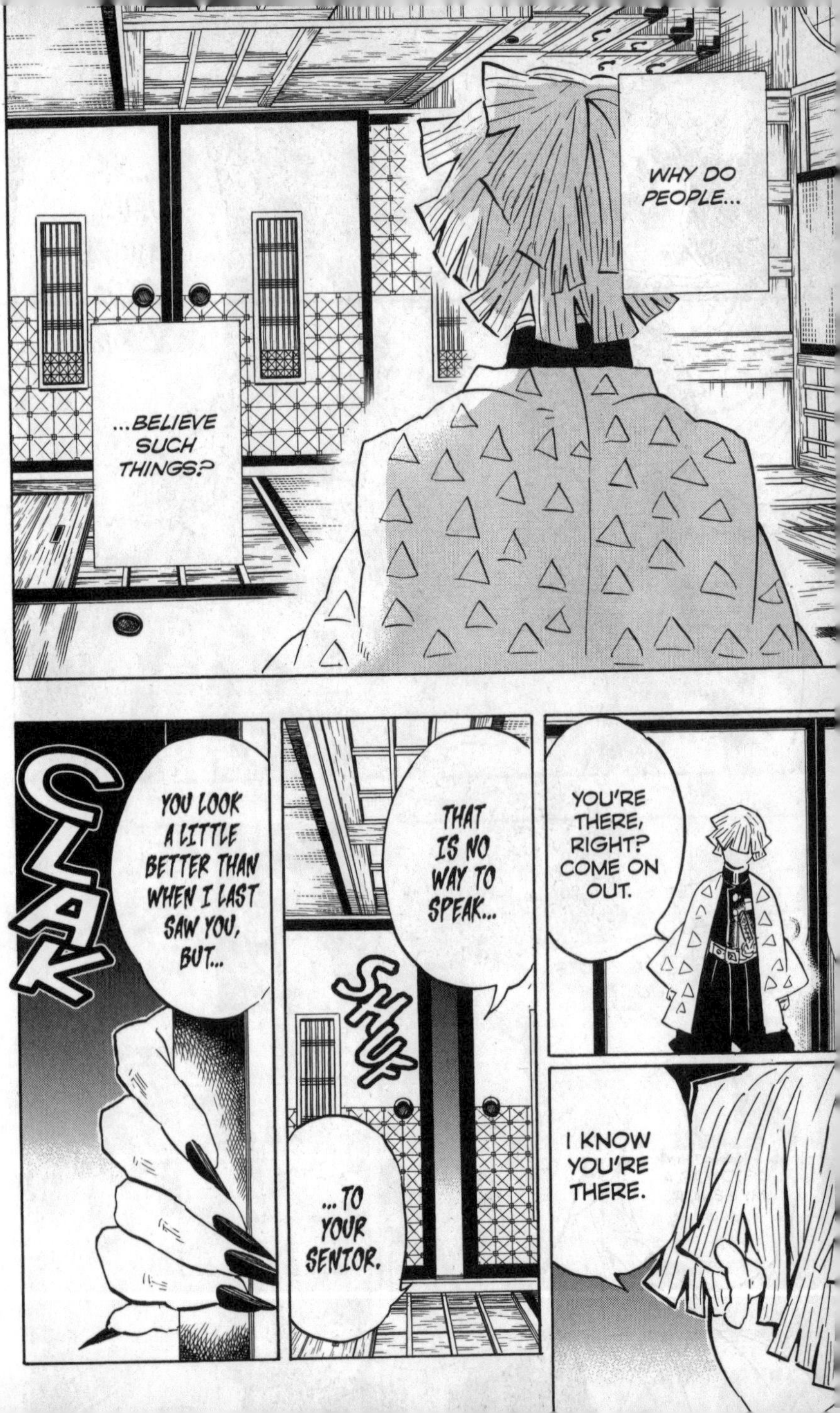
WHY DO PEOPLE...
...BELIEVE SUCH THINGS?
YOU'RE THERE, RIGHT? COME ON OUT.
I KNOW YOU'RE THERE.
THAT IS NO WAY TO SPEAK...
SHUT
...TO YOUR SENIOR.
CLAK
YOU LOOK A LITTLE BETTER THAN WHEN I LAST SAW YOU, BUT...

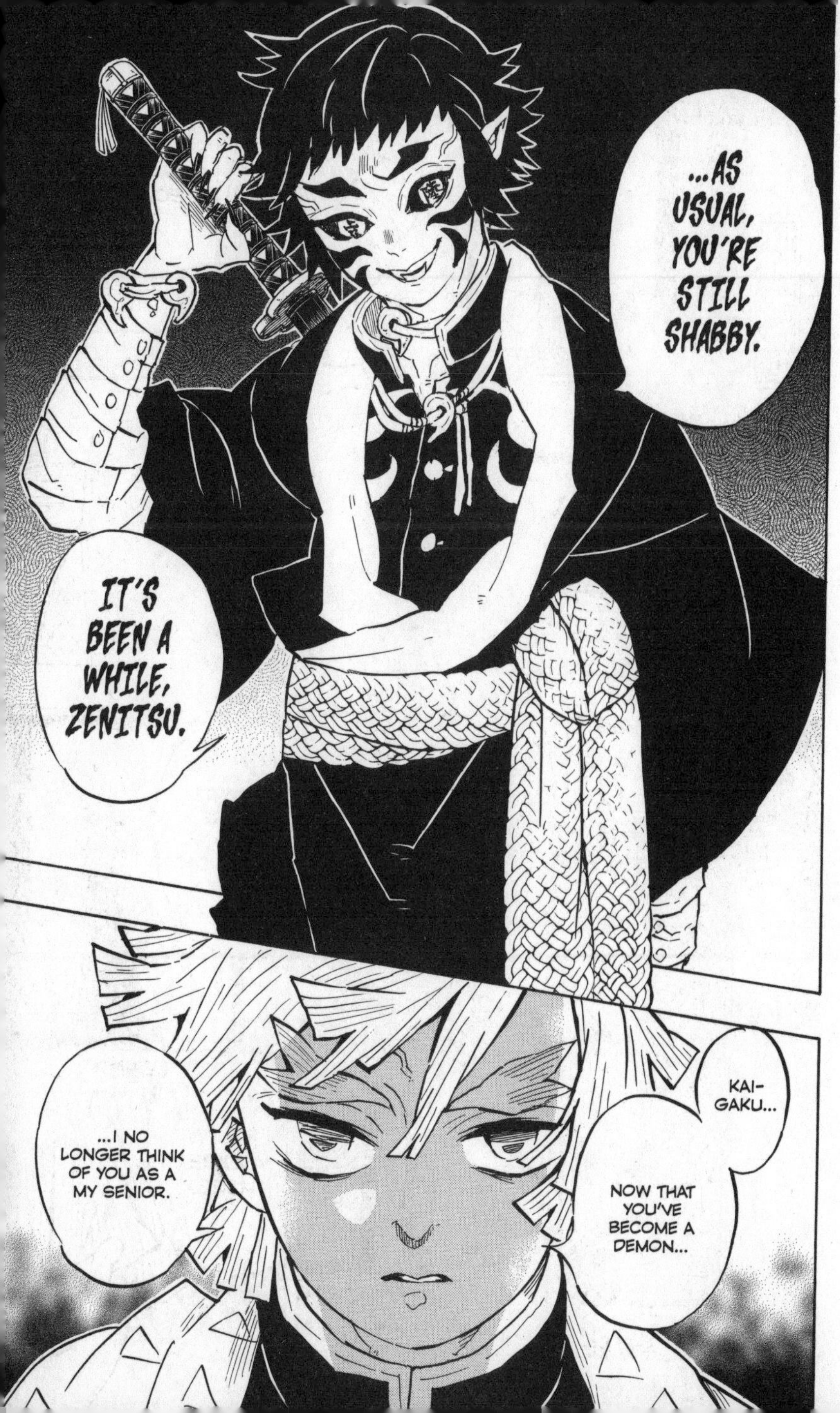
...AS USUAL, YOU'RE STILL SHABBY.
IT'S BEEN A WHILE, ZENITSU.
KAI-GAKU...
NOW THAT YOU'VE BECOME A DEMON...
...I NO LONGER THINK OF YOU AS A MY SENIOR.

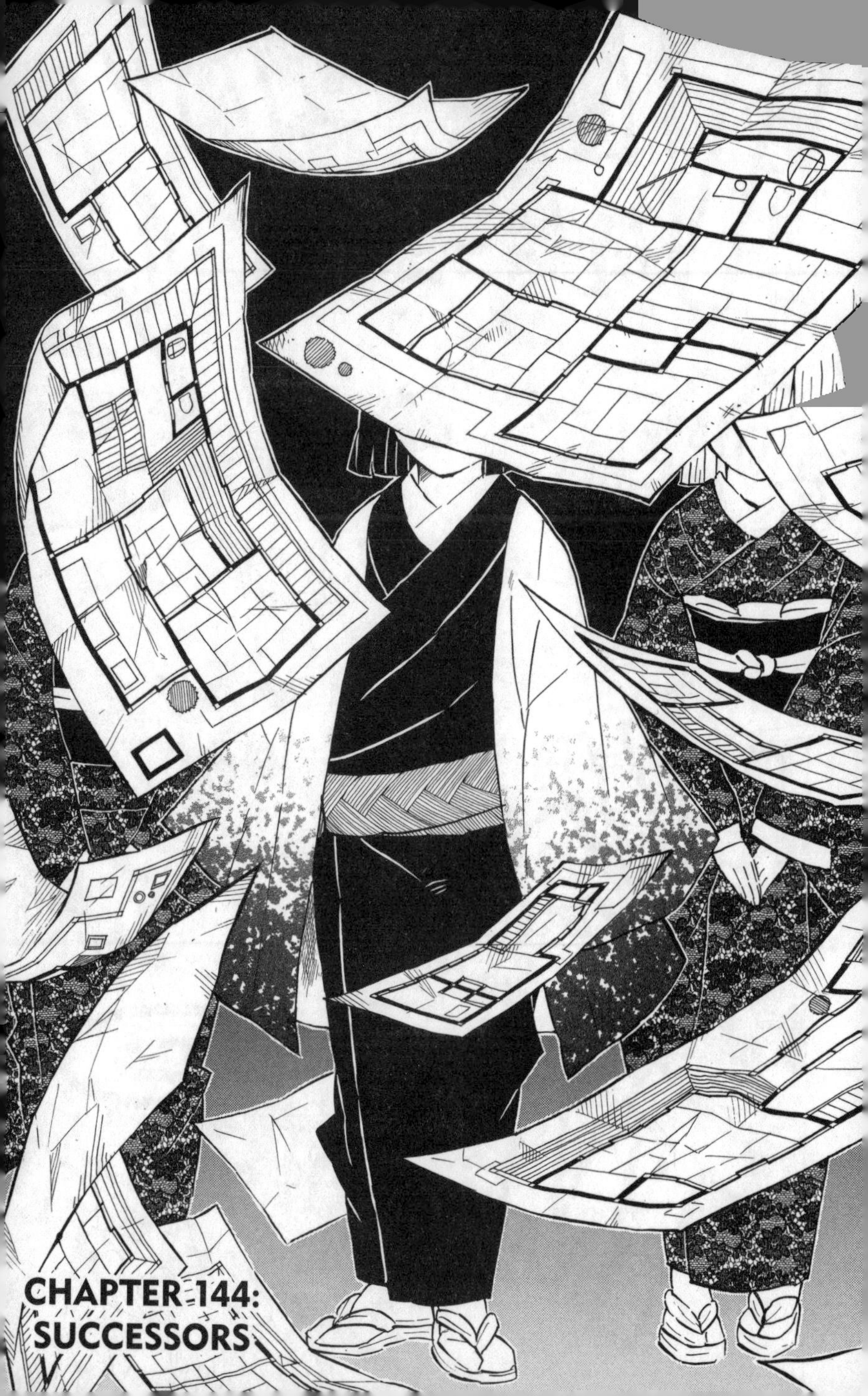
CHAPTER 144:
SUCCESSORS

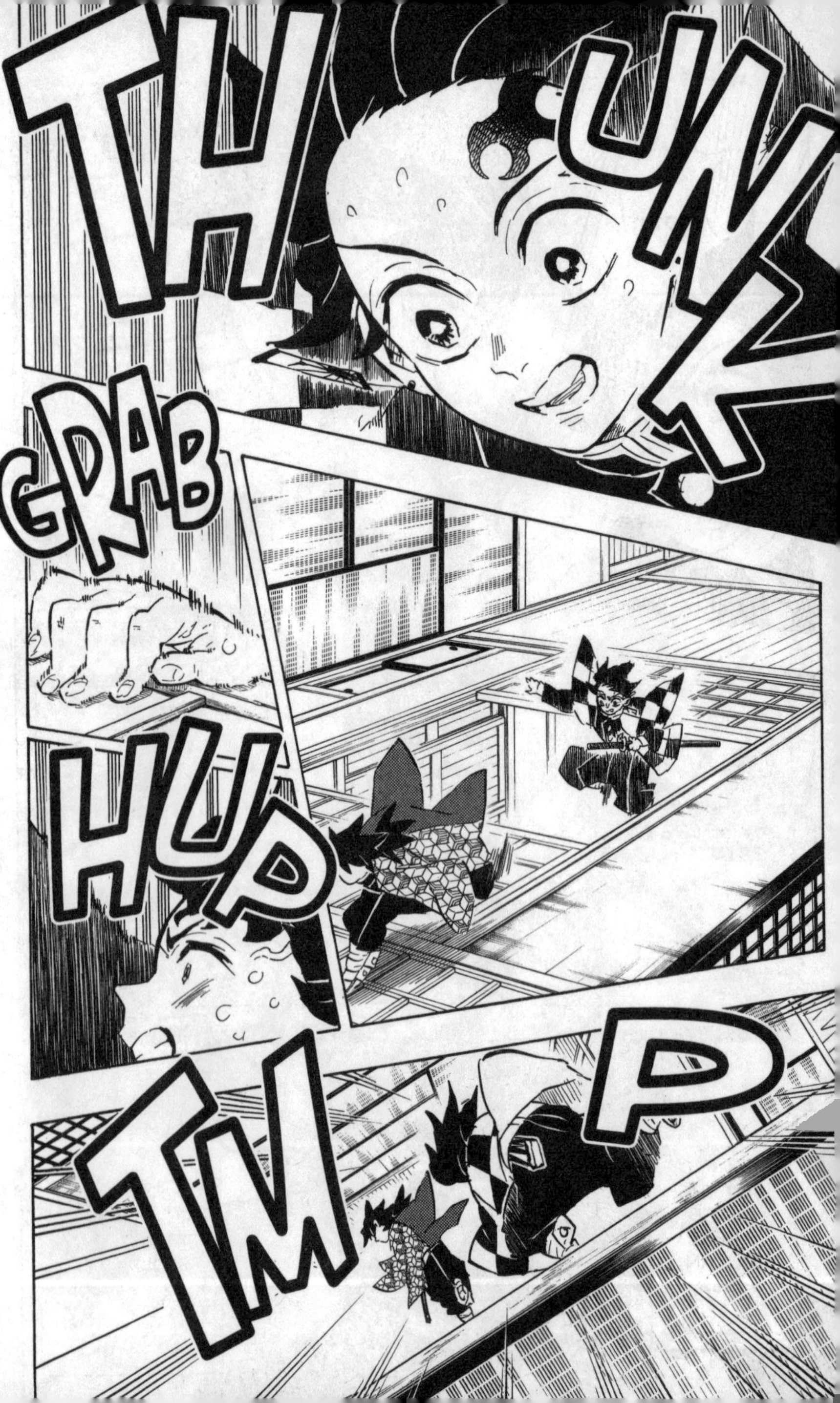
THUNK
GRAB
HUP
TMP

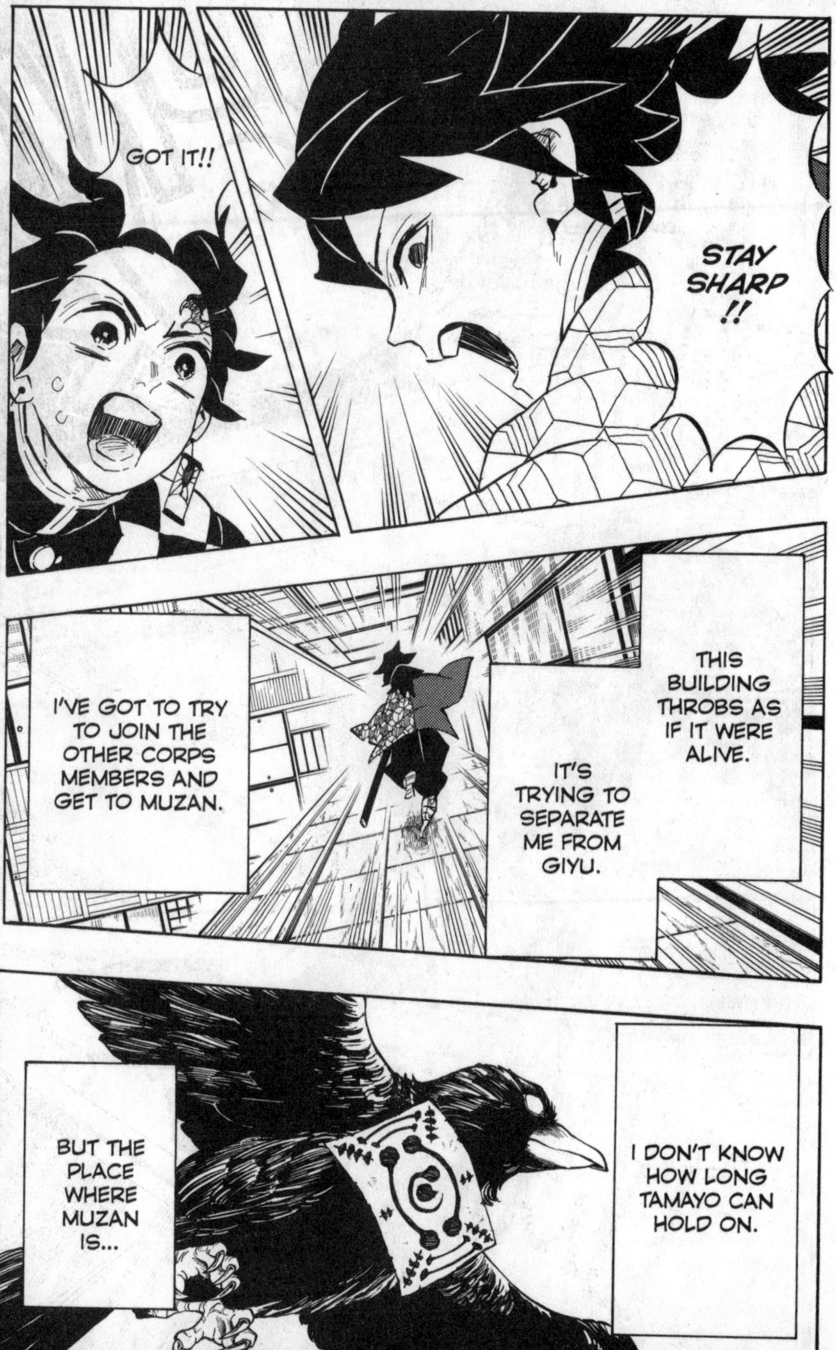
STAY SHARP!!
GOT IT!!
THIS BUILDING THROBS AS IF IT WERE ALIVE.
IT'S TRYING TO SEPARATE ME FROM GIYU.
I'VE GOT TO TRY TO JOIN THE OTHER CORPS MEMBERS AND GET TO MUZAN.
I DON'T KNOW HOW LONG TAMAYO CAN HOLD ON.
BUT THE PLACE WHERE MUZAN IS...

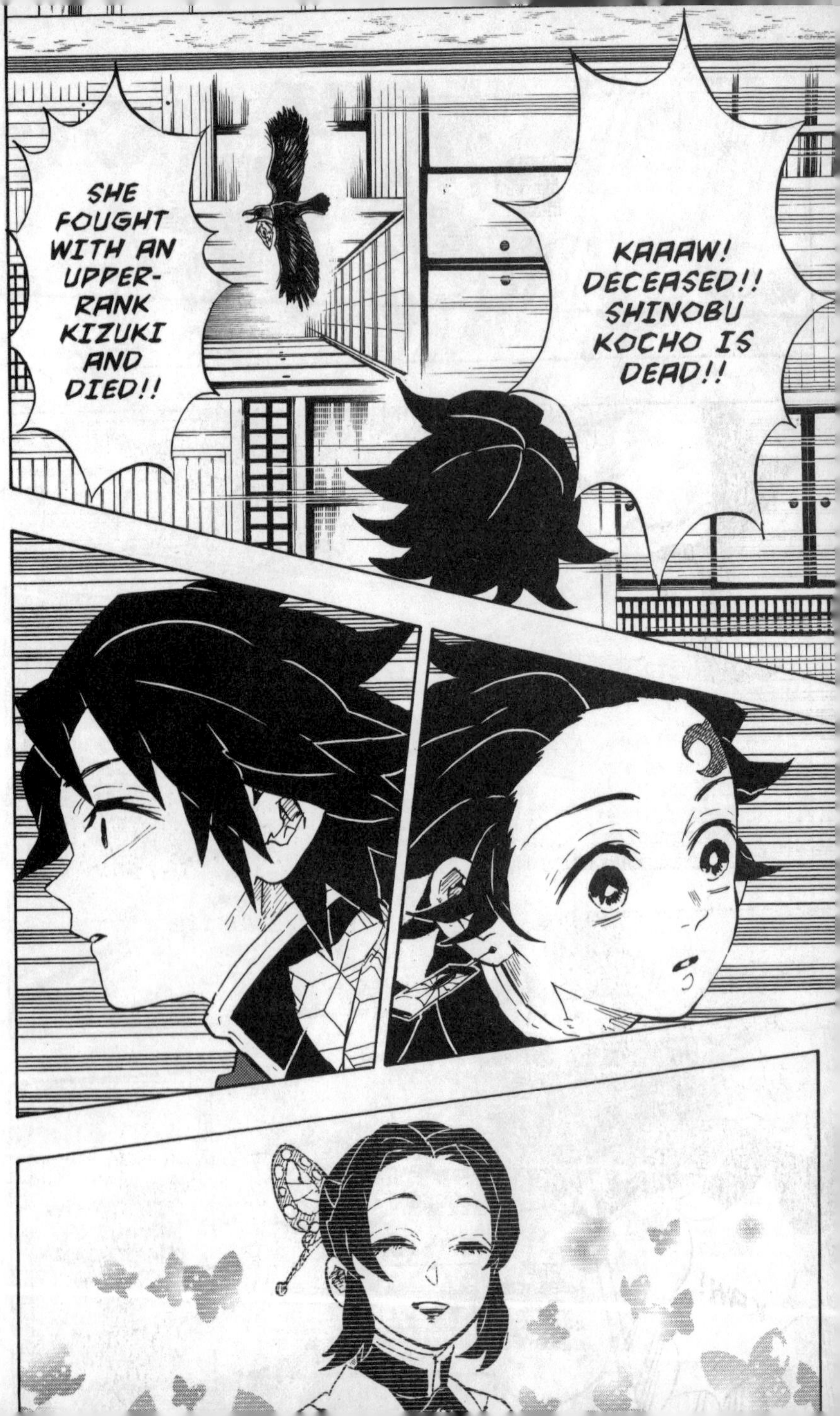
KAAAW! DECEASED!! SHINOBU KOCHO IS DEAD!!
SHE FOUGHT WITH AN UPPER-RANK KIZUKI AND DIED!!

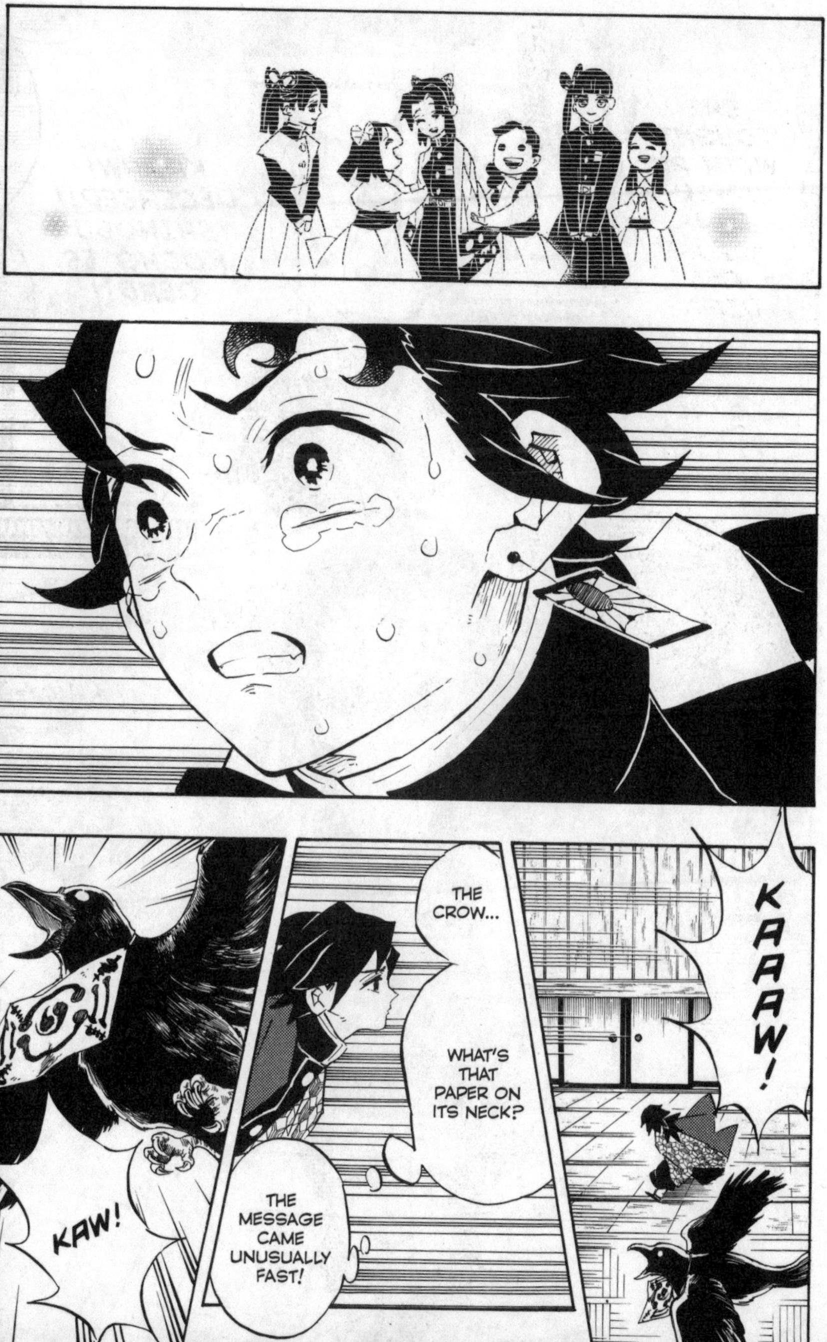
KAAAAW!
THE CROW... WHAT'S THAT PAPER ON ITS NECK?
THE MESSAGE CAME UNUSUALLY FAST!
KAW!

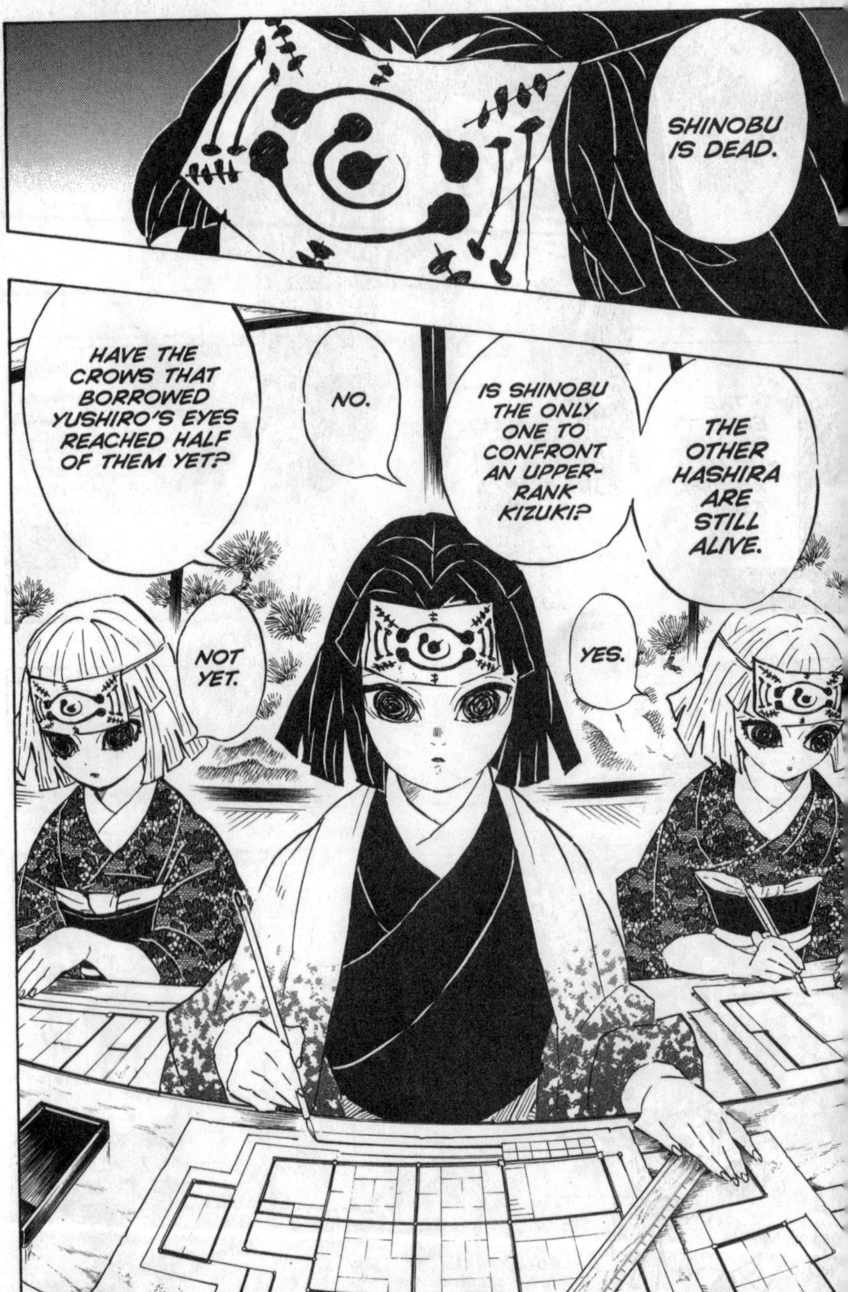
SHINOBU IS DEAD.
THE OTHER HASHIRA ARE STILL ALIVE.
IS SHINOBU THE ONLY ONE TO CONFRONT AN UPPER-RANK KIZUKI?
YES.
NO.
HAVE THE CROWS THAT BORROWED YUSHIRO'S EYES REACHED HALF OF THEM YET?
NOT YET.

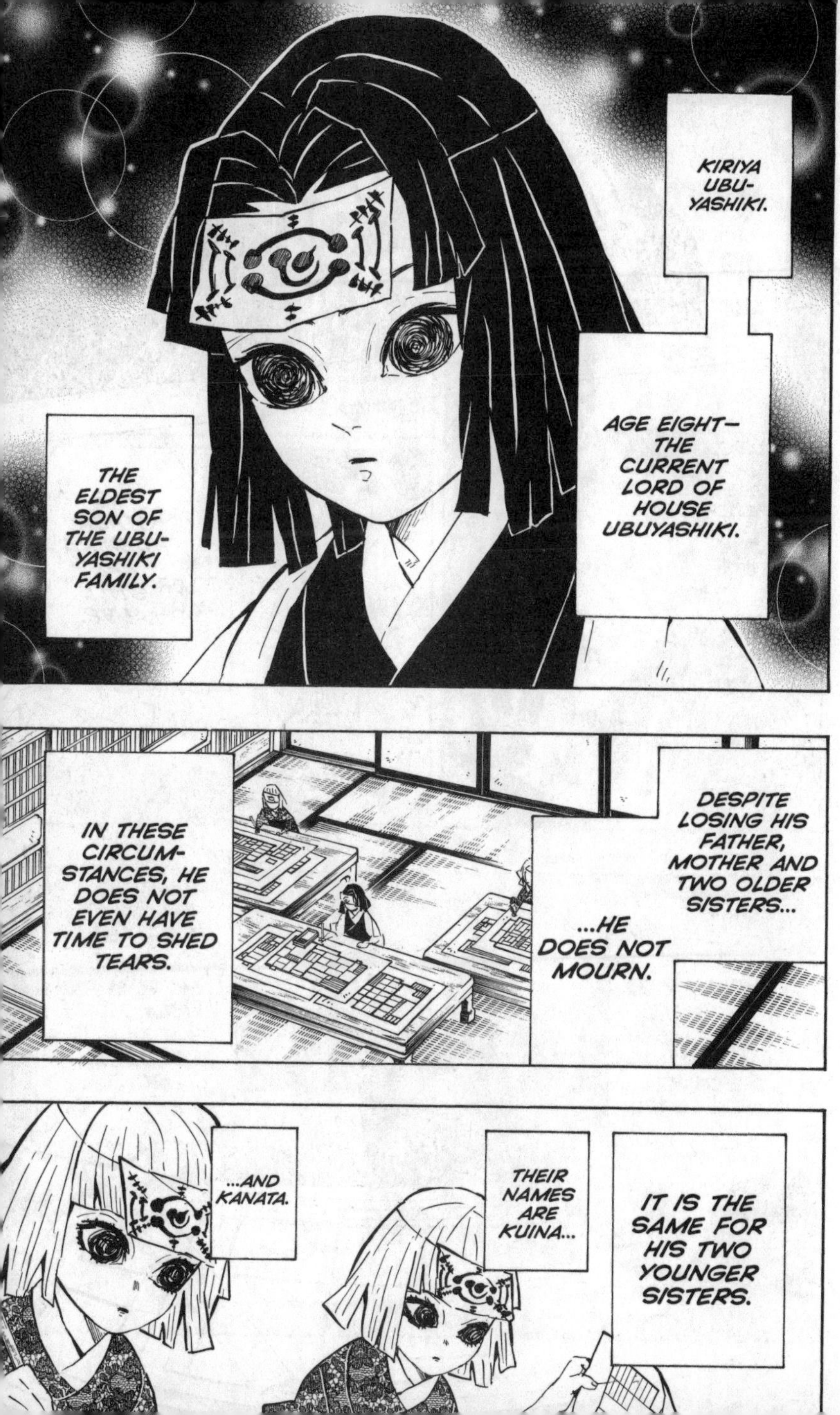

KIRIYA UBU-YASHIKI.
AGE EIGHT—THE CURRENT LORD OF HOUSE UBUYASHIKI.
THE ELDEST SON OF THE UBU-YASHIKI FAMILY.
DESPITE LOSING HIS FATHER, MOTHER AND TWO OLDER SISTERS...
...HE DOES NOT MOURN.
IN THESE CIRCUM-STANCES, HE DOES NOT EVEN HAVE TIME TO SHED TEARS.
IT IS THE SAME FOR HIS TWO YOUNGER SISTERS.
THEIR NAMES ARE KUINA...
...AND KANATA.

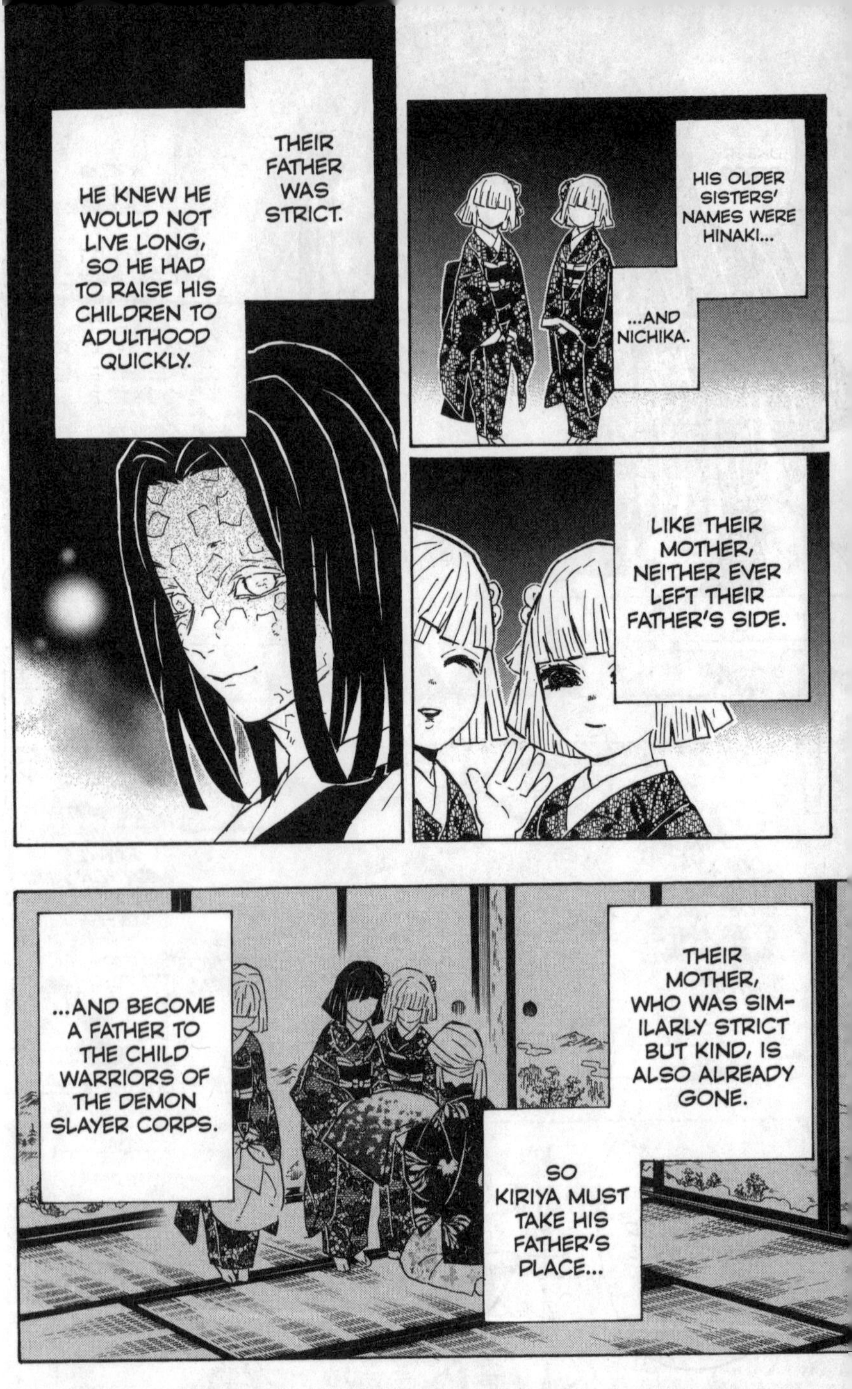
HIS OLDER SISTERS' NAMES WERE HINAKI...
...AND NICHIKA.
LIKE THEIR MOTHER, NEITHER EVER LEFT THEIR FATHER'S SIDE.
THEIR FATHER WAS STRICT.
HE KNEW HE WOULD NOT LIVE LONG, SO HE HAD TO RAISE HIS CHILDREN TO ADULTHOOD QUICKLY.
THEIR MOTHER, WHO WAS SIM-ILARLY STRICT BUT KIND, IS ALSO ALREADY GONE.
SO KIRIYA MUST TAKE HIS FATHER'S PLACE...
...AND BECOME A FATHER TO THE CHILD WARRIORS OF THE DEMON SLAYER CORPS.

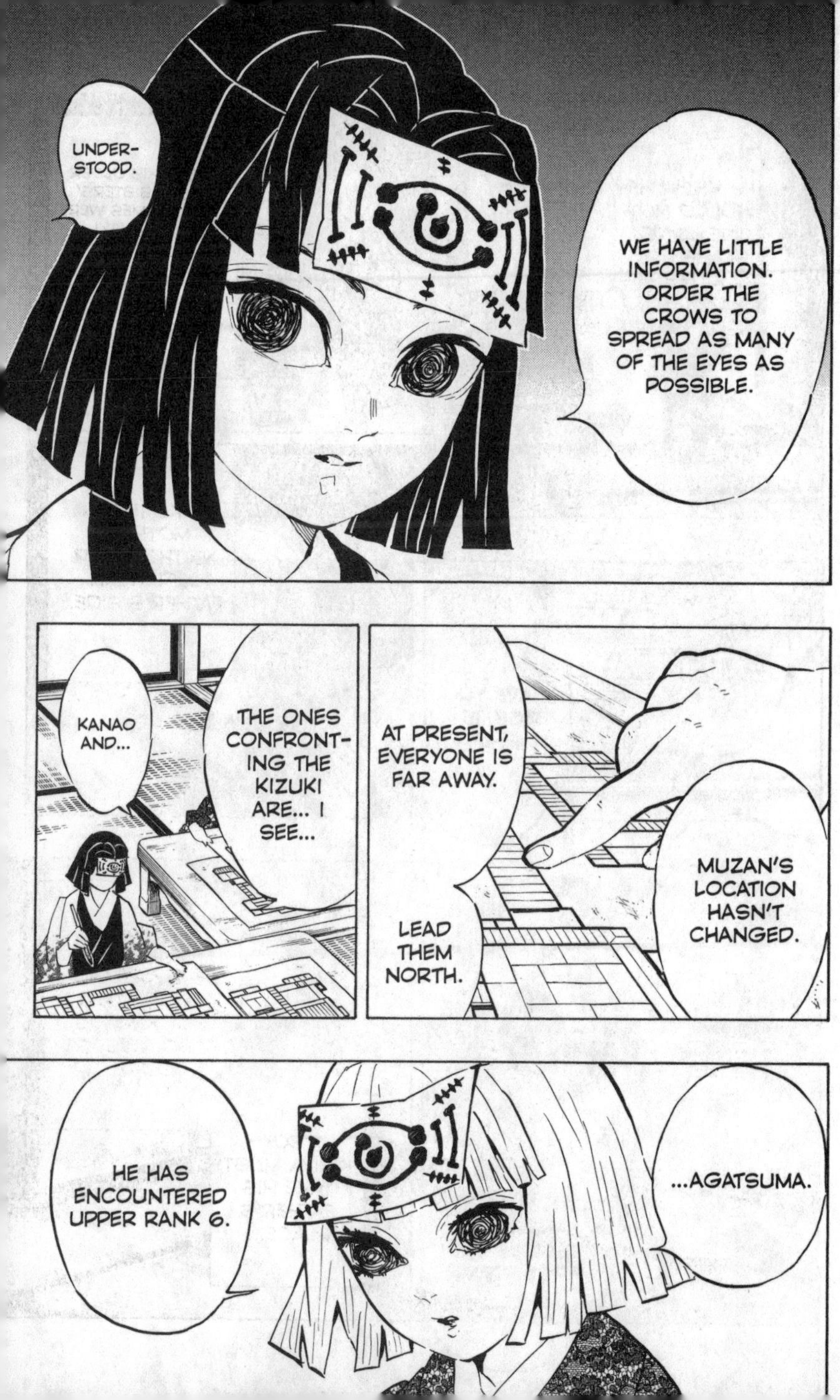
WE HAVE LITTLE INFORMATION. ORDER THE CROWS TO SPREAD AS MANY OF THE EYES AS POSSIBLE.
UNDER-STOOD.
MUZAN'S LOCATION HASN'T CHANGED.
AT PRESENT, EVERYONE IS FAR AWAY.
LEAD THEM NORTH.
THE ONES CONFRONT-ING THE KIZUKI ARE... I SEE...
KANAO AND...
...AGATSUMA.
HE HAS ENCOUNTERED UPPER RANK 6.

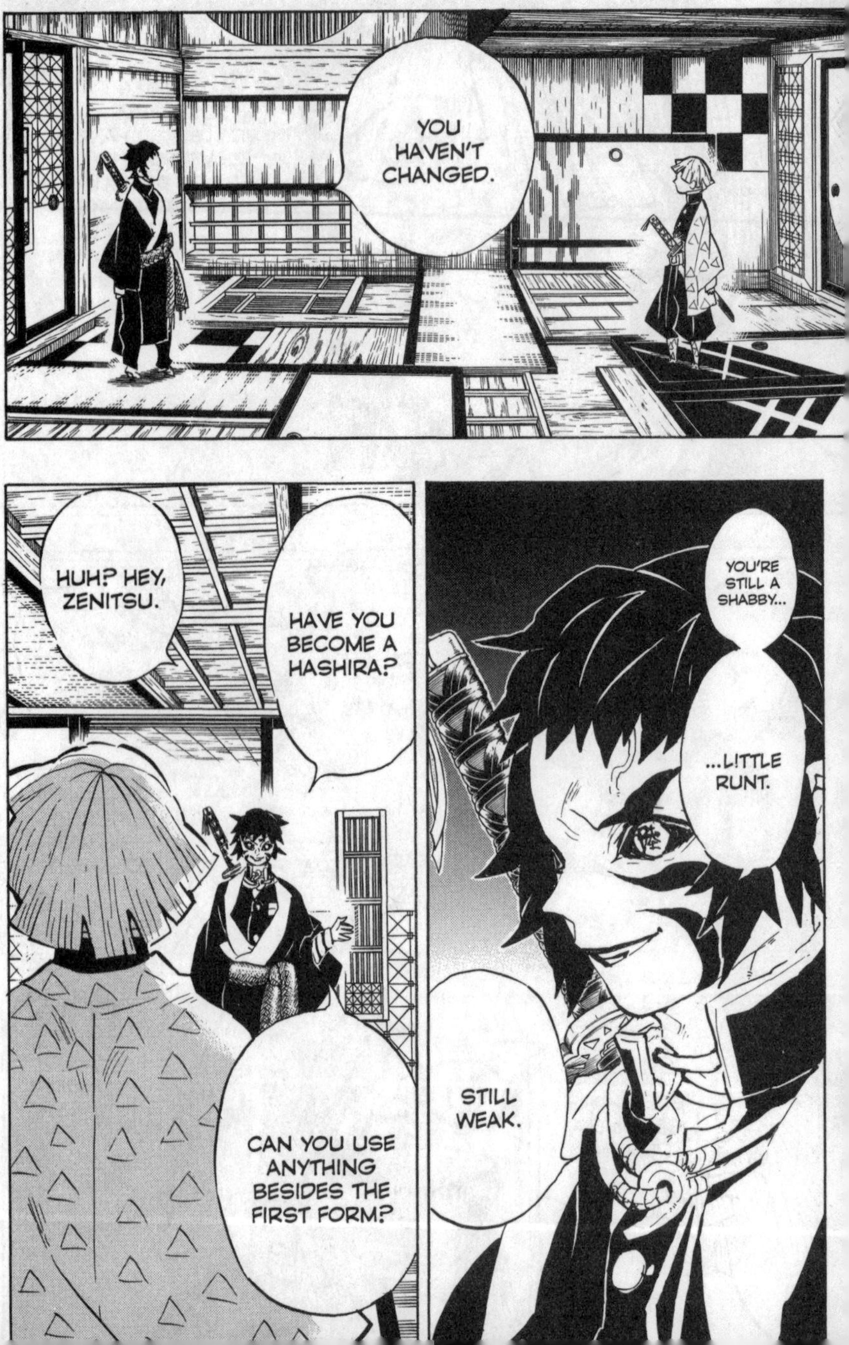
YOU HAVEN'T CHANGED.
YOU'RE STILL A SHABBY...
...LITTLE RUNT.
STILL WEAK.
HUH? HEY, ZENITSU.
HAVE YOU BECOME A HASHIRA?
CAN YOU USE ANYTHING BESIDES THE FIRST FORM?

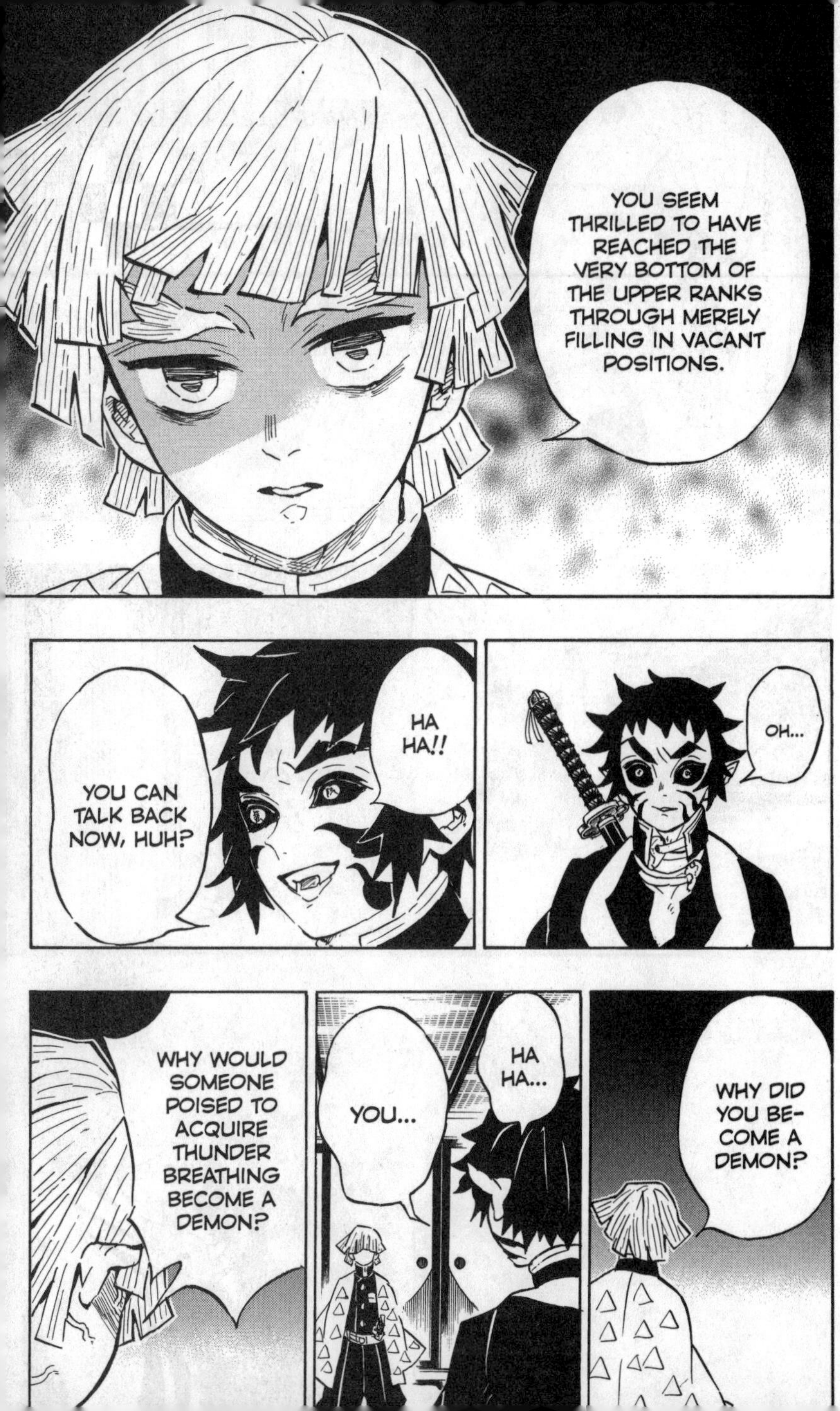
YOU SEEM THRILLED TO HAVE REACHED THE VERY BOTTOM OF THE UPPER RANKS THROUGH MERELY FILLING IN VACANT POSITIONS.
OH...
HA HA!!
YOU CAN TALK BACK NOW, HUH?
WHY DID YOU BE-COME A DEMON?
HA HA...
YOU...
WHY WOULD SOMEONE POISED TO ACQUIRE THUNDER BREATHING BECOME A DEMON?

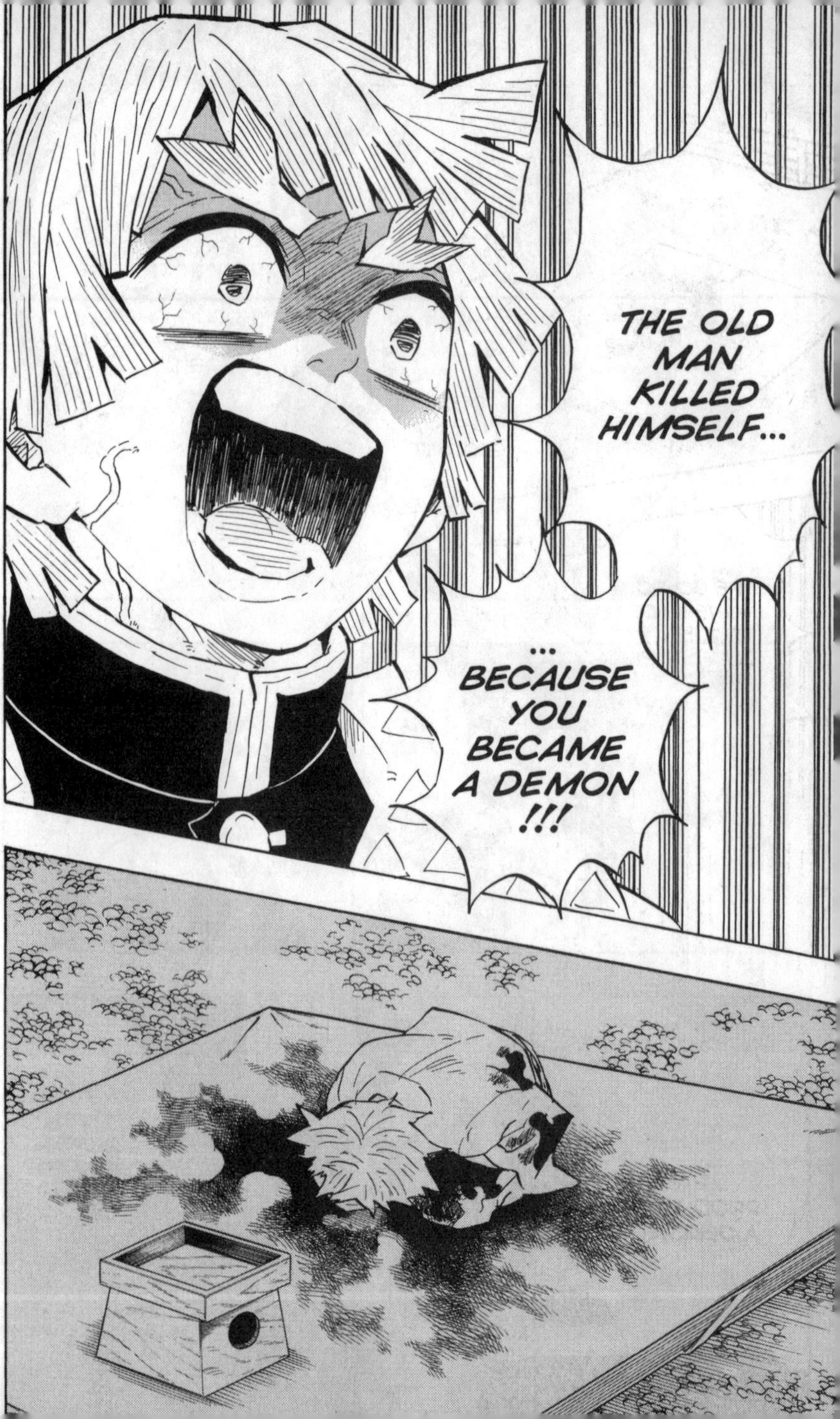
THE OLD MAN KILLED HIMSELF...
...BECAUSE YOU BECAME A DEMON!!!

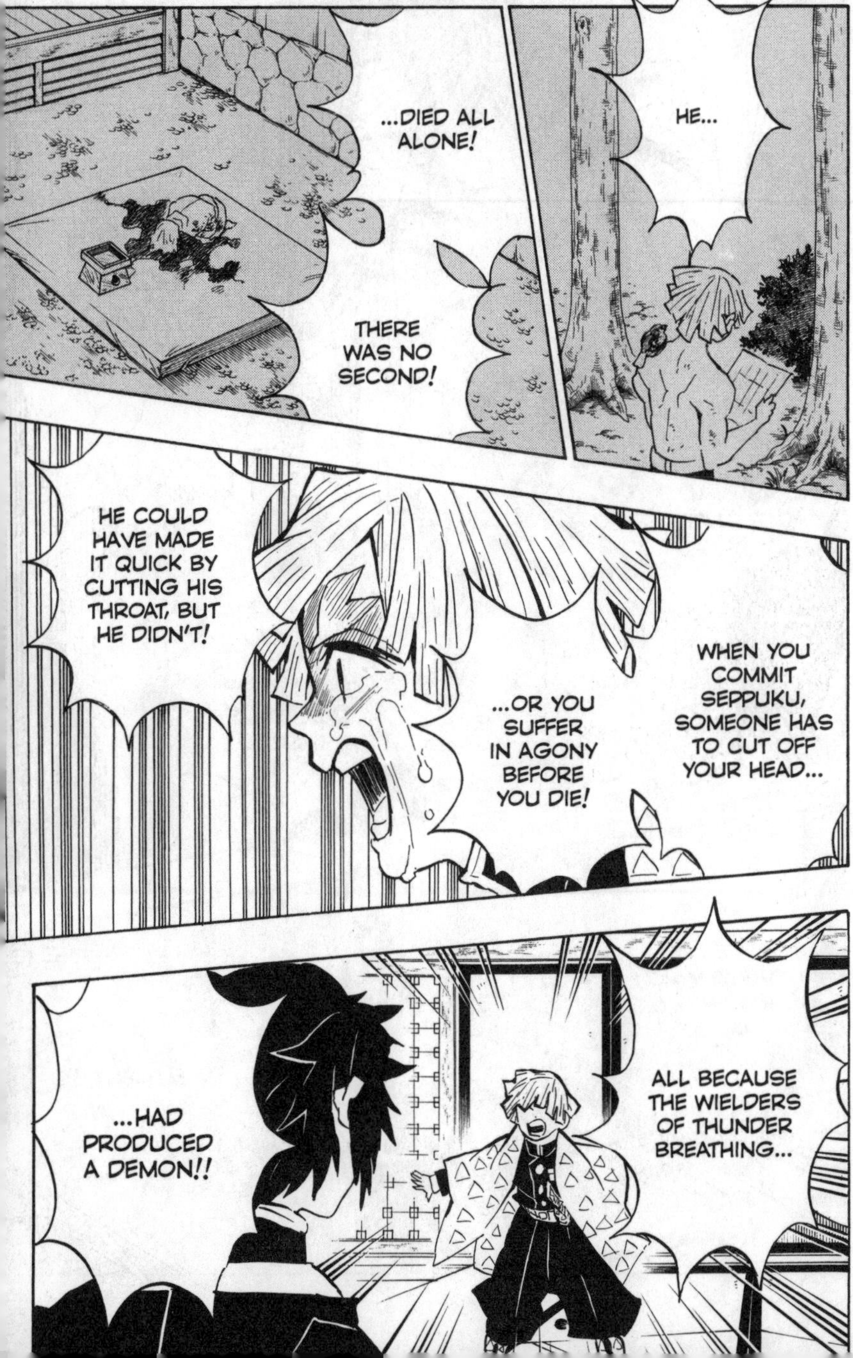
HE...
...DIED ALL ALONE!
THERE WAS NO SECOND!
WHEN YOU COMMIT SEPPUKU, SOMEONE HAS TO CUT OFF YOUR HEAD...
...OR YOU SUFFER IN AGONY BEFORE YOU DIE!
HE COULD HAVE MADE IT QUICK BY CUTTING HIS THROAT, BUT HE DIDN'T!
ALL BECAUSE THE WIELDERS OF THUNDER BREATHING...
...HAD PRODUCED A DEMON!!

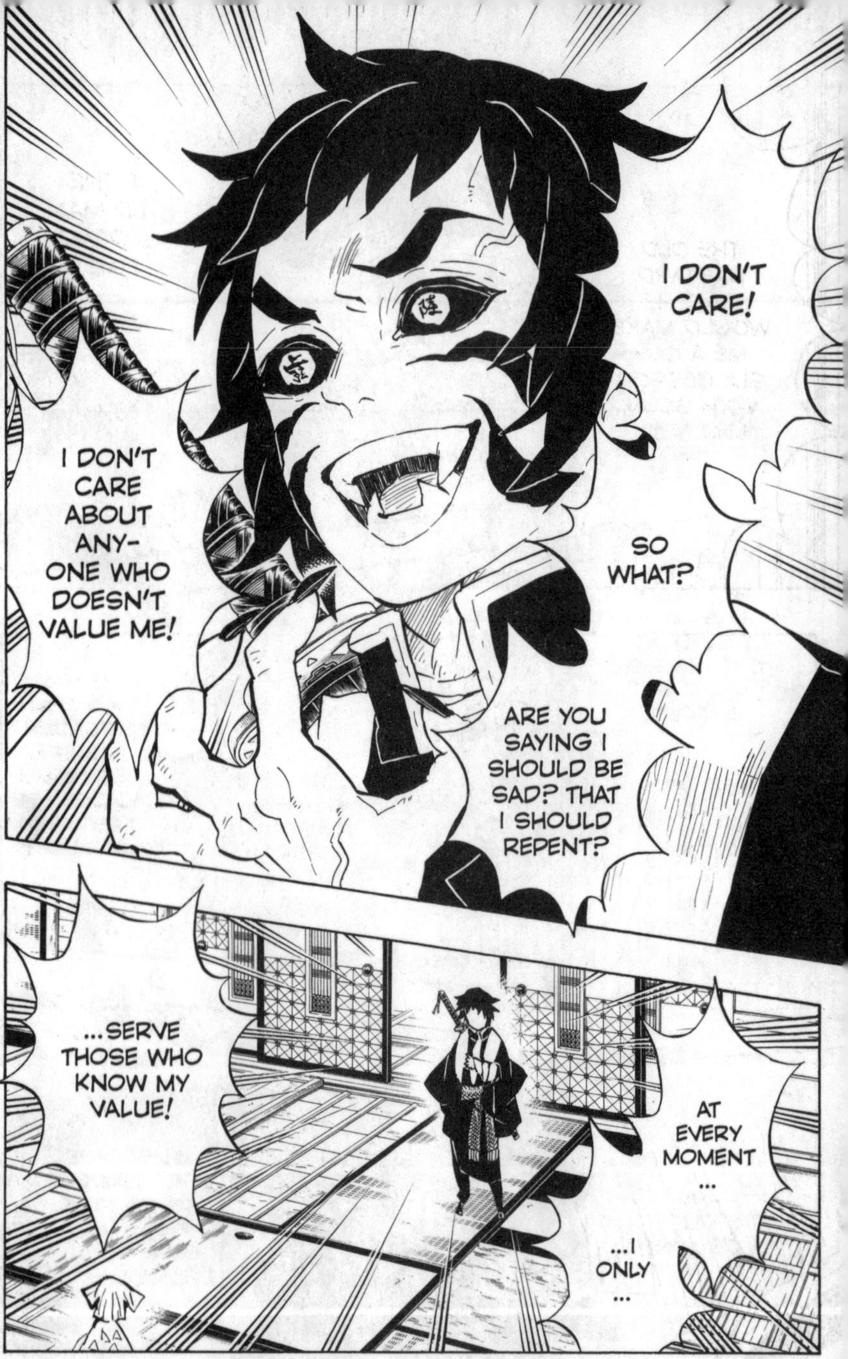
I DON'T CARE!
SO WHAT?
ARE YOU SAYING I SHOULD BE SAD? THAT I SHOULD REPENT?
I DON'T CARE ABOUT ANY-ONE WHO DOESN'T VALUE ME!
AT EVERY MOMENT ...
...I ONLY ...
...SERVE THOSE WHO KNOW MY VALUE!

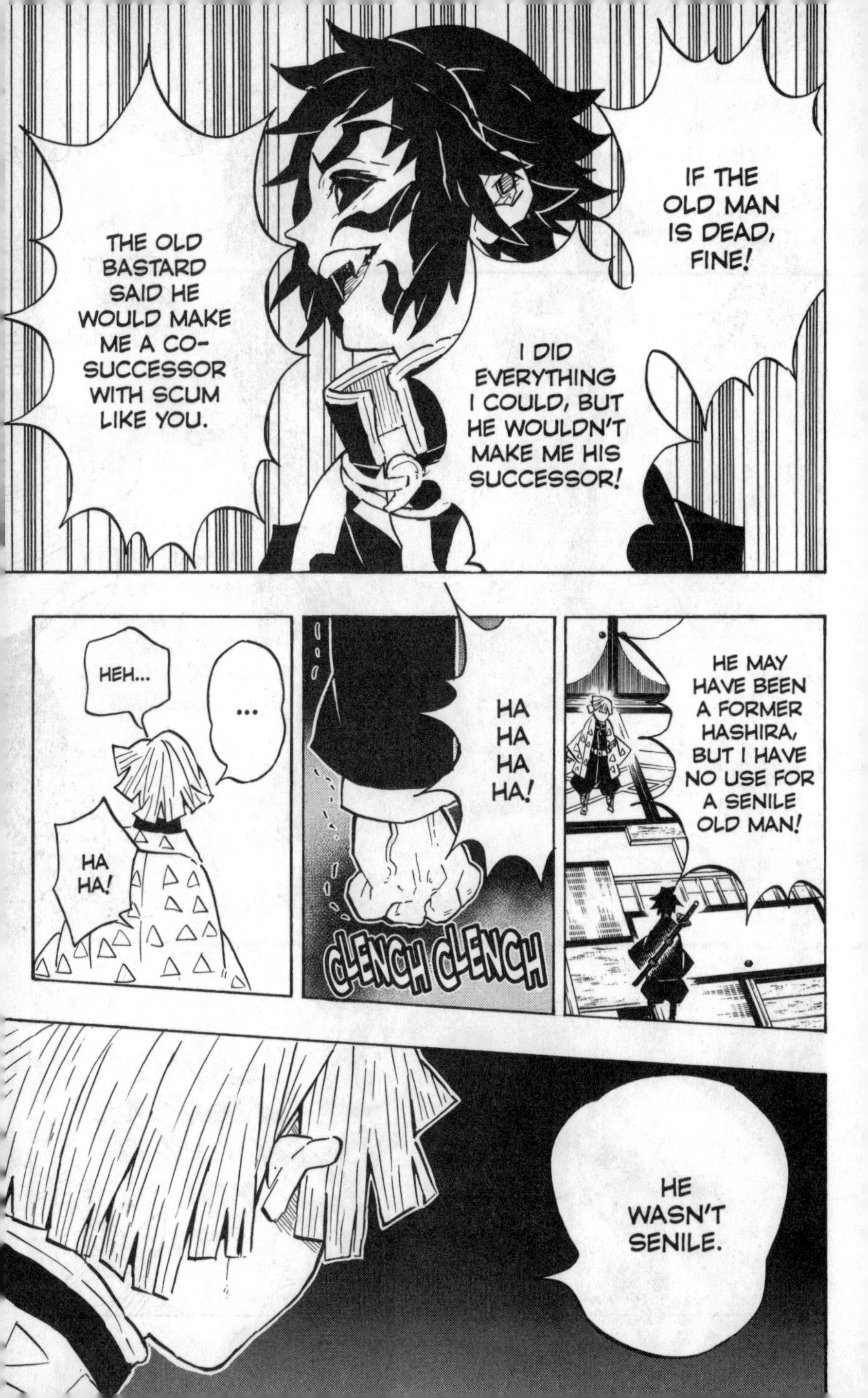
IF THE OLD MAN IS DEAD, FINE!
I DID EVERYTHING I COULD, BUT HE WOULDN'T MAKE ME HIS SUCCESSOR!
THE OLD BASTARD SAID HE WOULD MAKE ME A CO-SUCCESSOR WITH SCUM LIKE YOU.
HE MAY HAVE BEEN A FORMER HASHIRA, BUT I HAVE NO USE FOR A SENILE OLD MAN!
HA HA HA HA!
CLENCH CLENCH
HEH...
...
HA HA!
HE WASN'T SENILE.

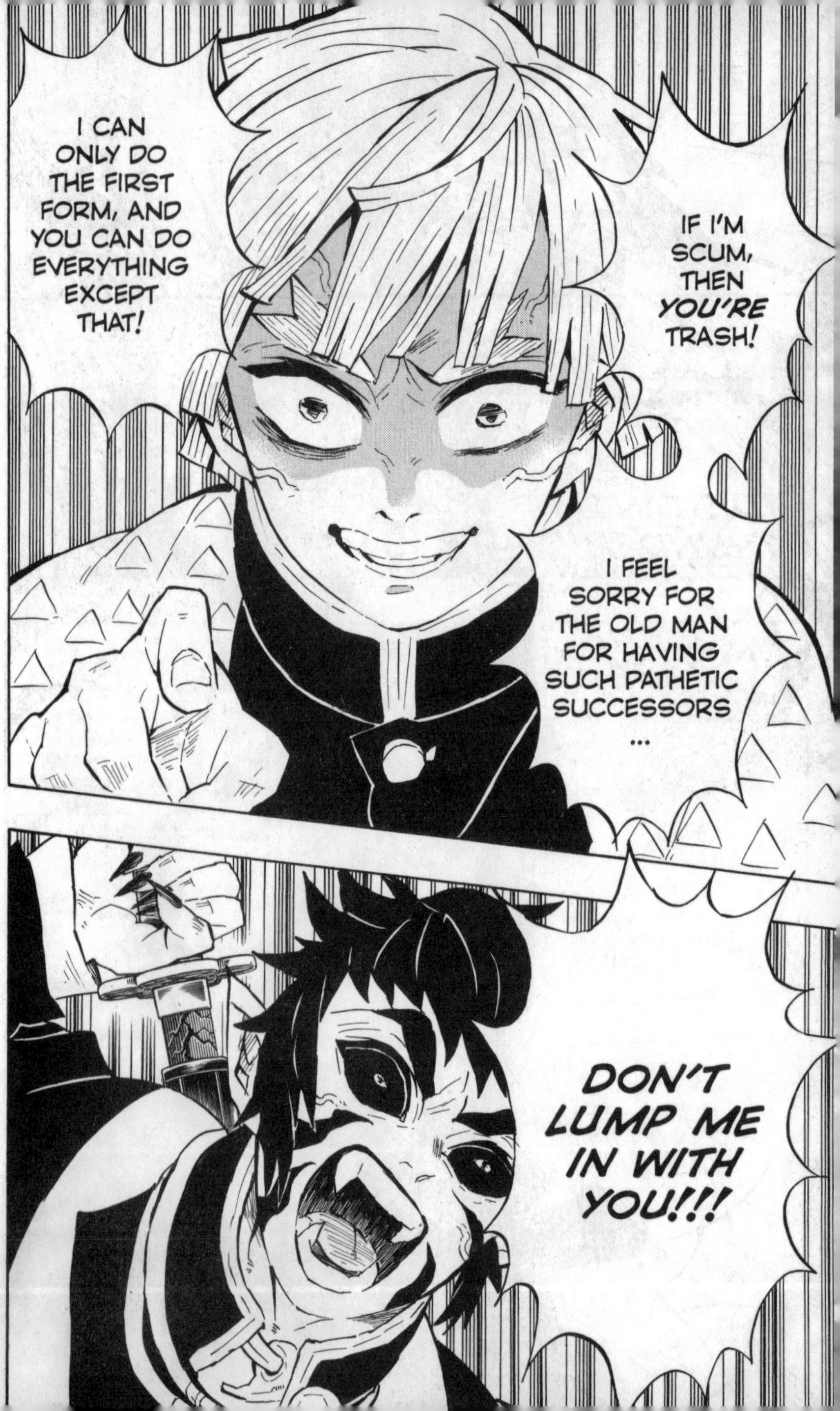
IF I'M SCUM, THEN *YOU'RE* TRASH!
I CAN ONLY DO THE FIRST FORM, AND YOU CAN DO EVERYTHING EXCEPT THAT!
I FEEL SORRY FOR THE OLD MAN FOR HAVING SUCH PATHETIC SUCCESSORS ...
DON'T LUMP ME IN WITH YOU!!!

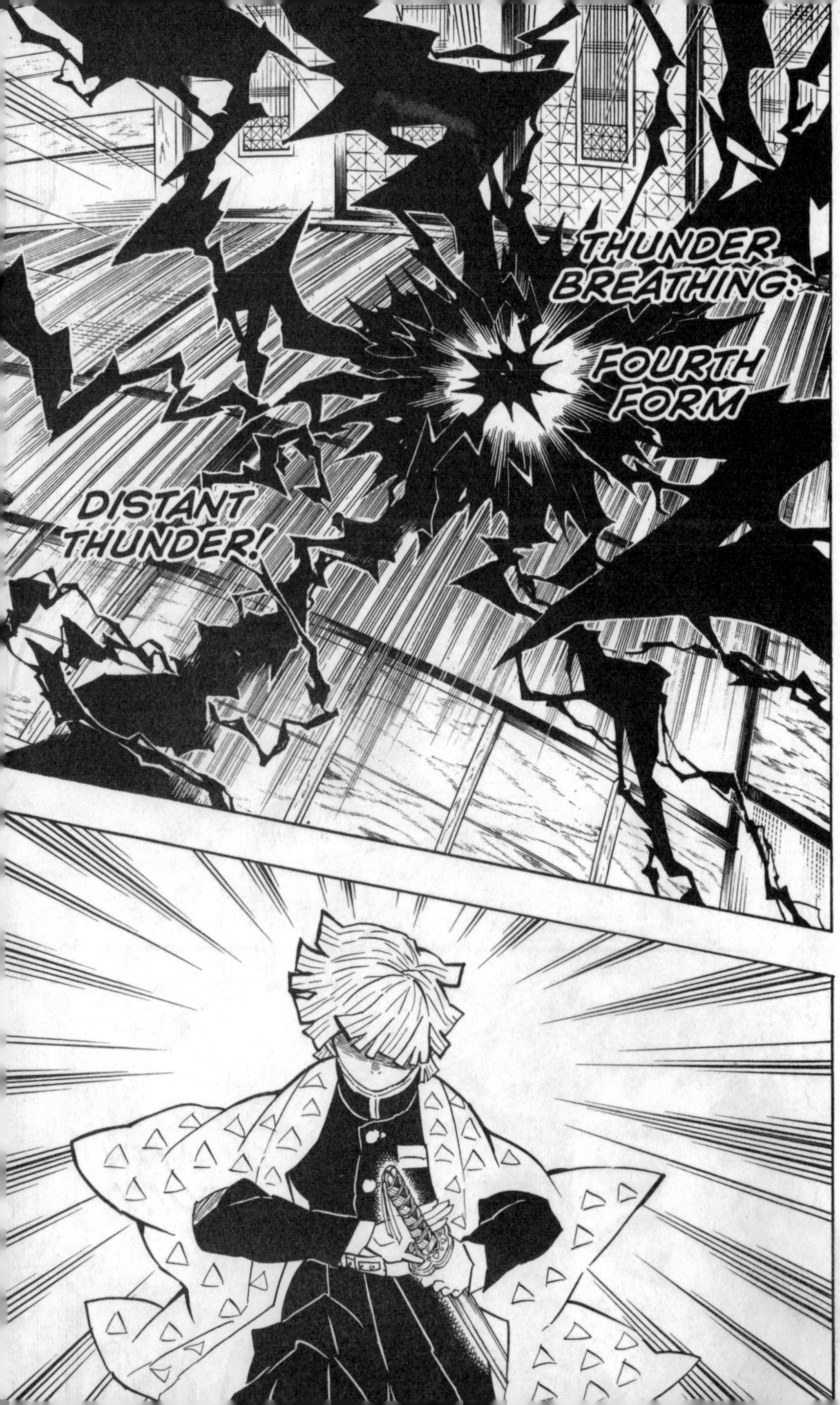
THUNDER BREATHING:
FOURTH FORM
DISTANT THUNDER!

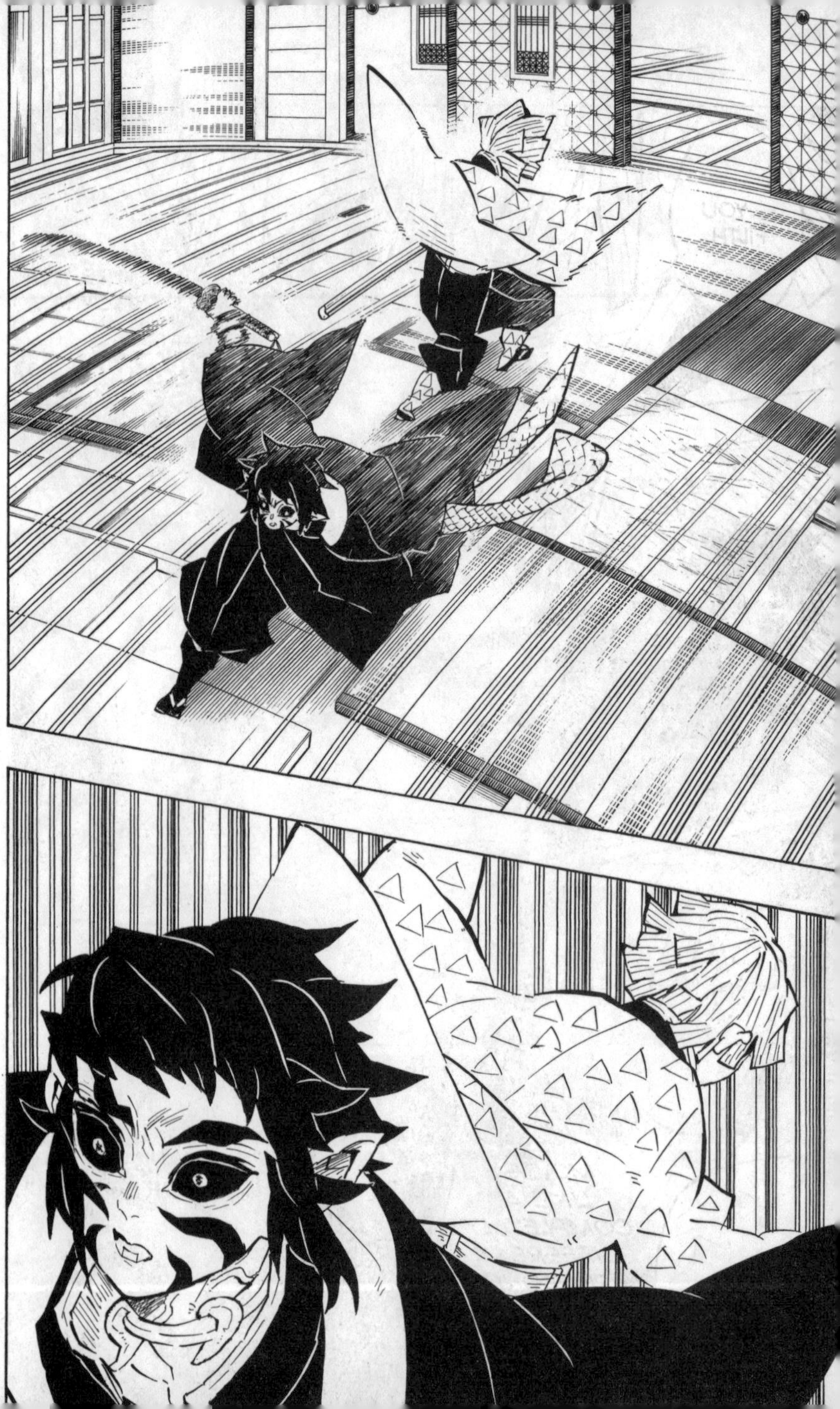

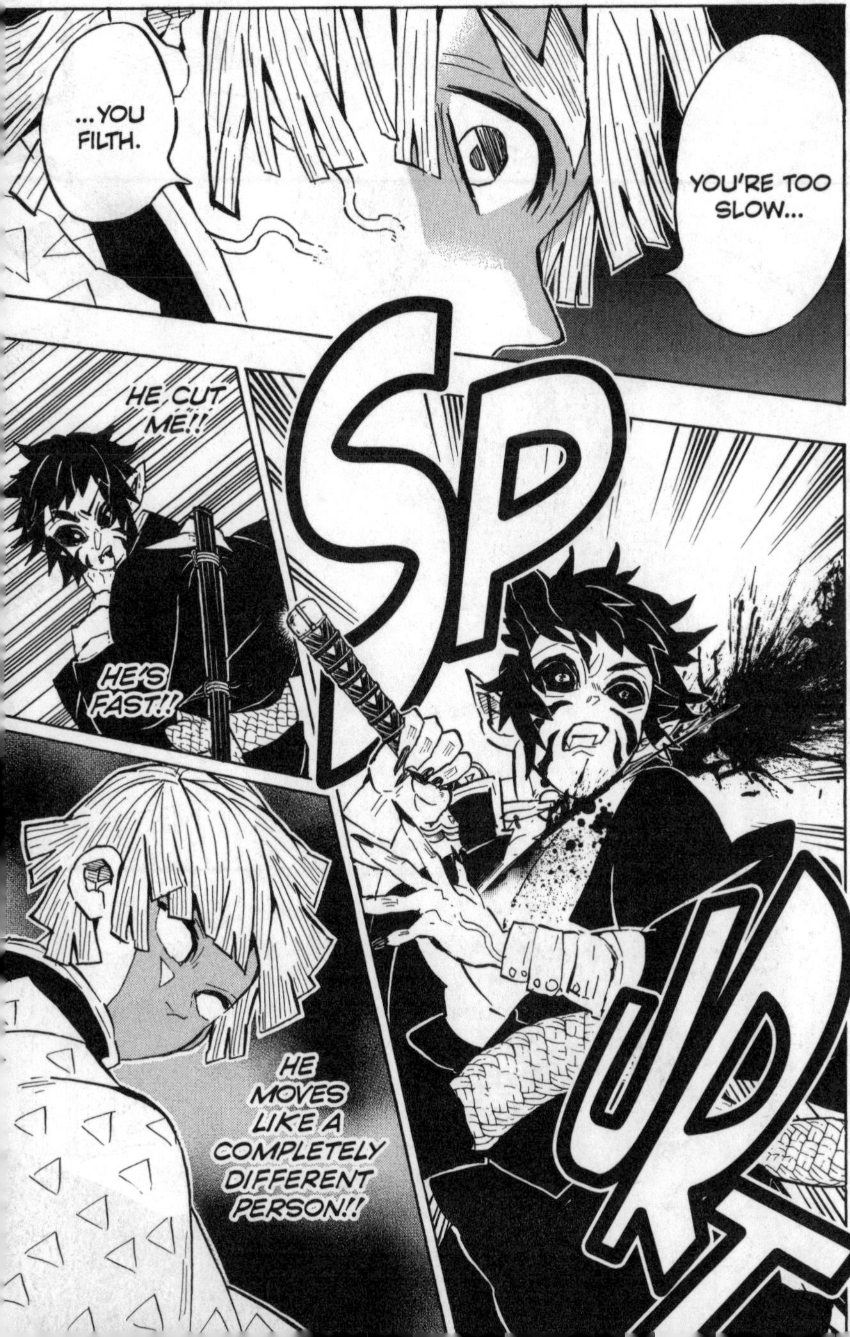
YOU'RE TOO SLOW...
...YOU FILTH.
SPURT
HE CUT ME!!
HE'S FAST!!
HE MOVES LIKE A COMPLETELY DIFFERENT PERSON!!

Zenitsu's trainer, Jigoro Kuwajima, was the Rumble Hashira. (That's what it's called when a user of Thunder Breathing becomes a Hashira.) Kaigaku became his student first, but Kuwajima valued Zenitsu equally even though he became a student later. However, Kaigaku didn't like that he wasn't the only special one anymore and held a grudge. He gave Kaigaku a kimono with the same pattern as his, but the boy never wore it.

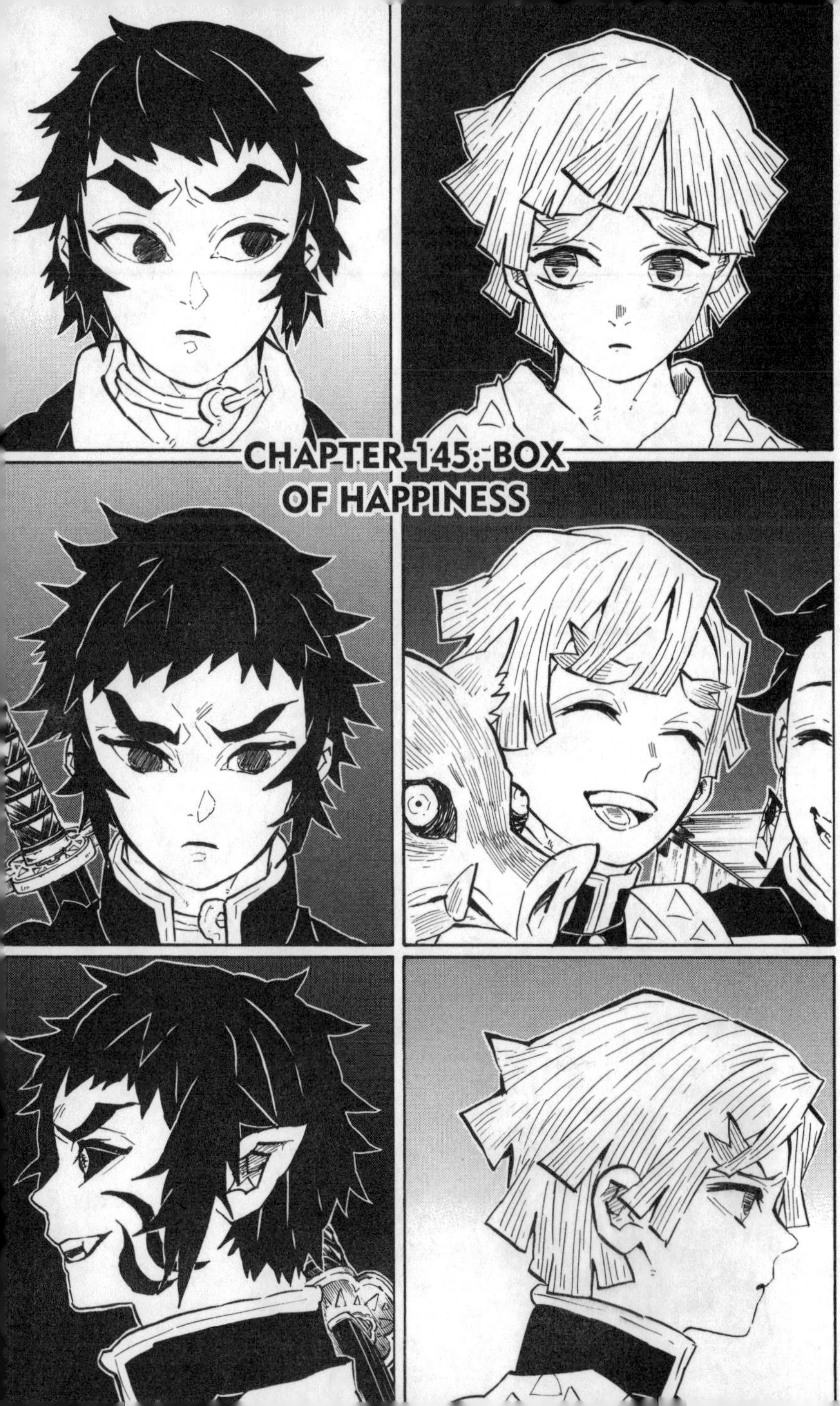
CHAPTER 145: BOX OF HAPPINESS

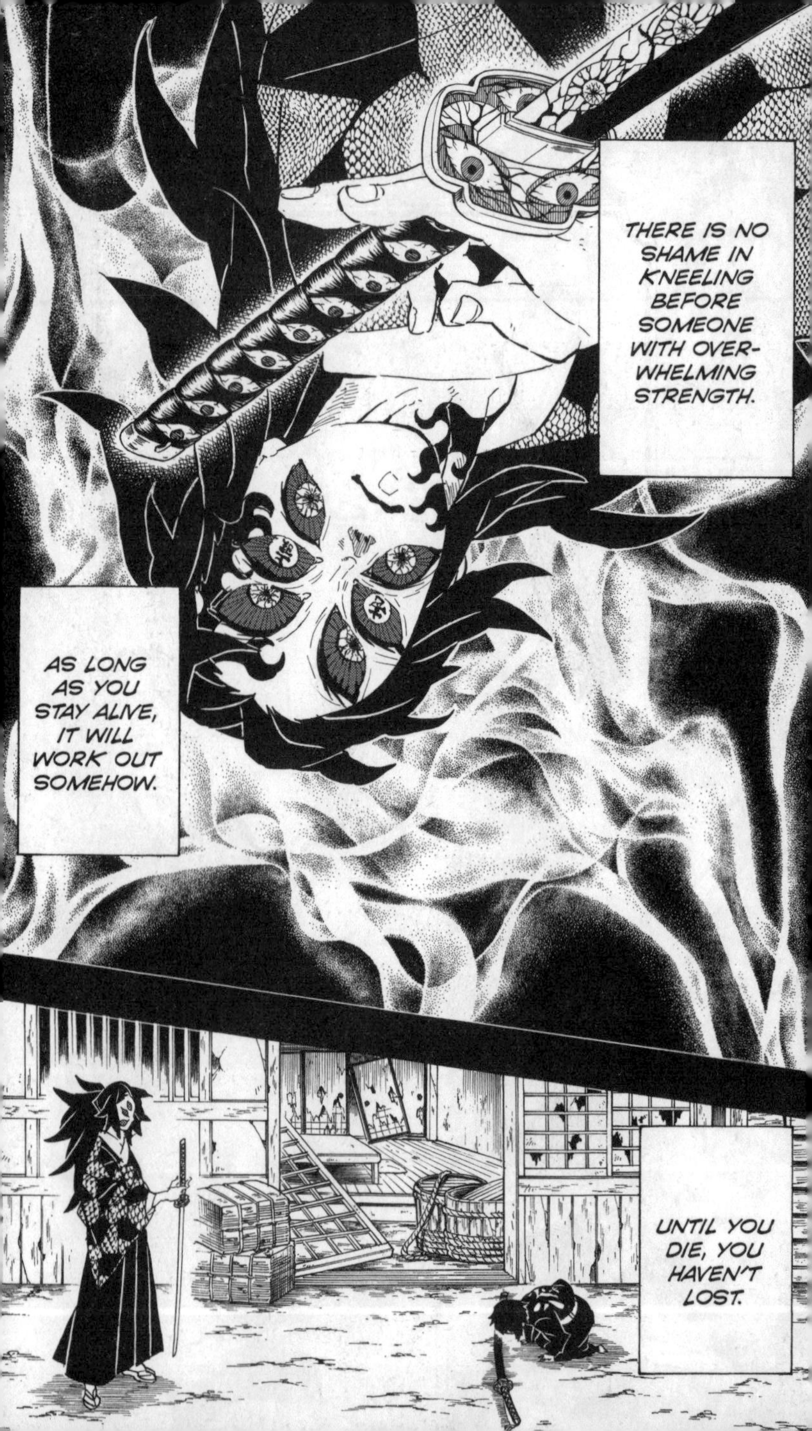

THERE IS NO SHAME IN KNEELING BEFORE SOMEONE WITH OVER-WHELMING STRENGTH.
AS LONG AS YOU STAY ALIVE, IT WILL WORK OUT SOMEHOW.
UNTIL YOU DIE, YOU HAVEN'T LOST.

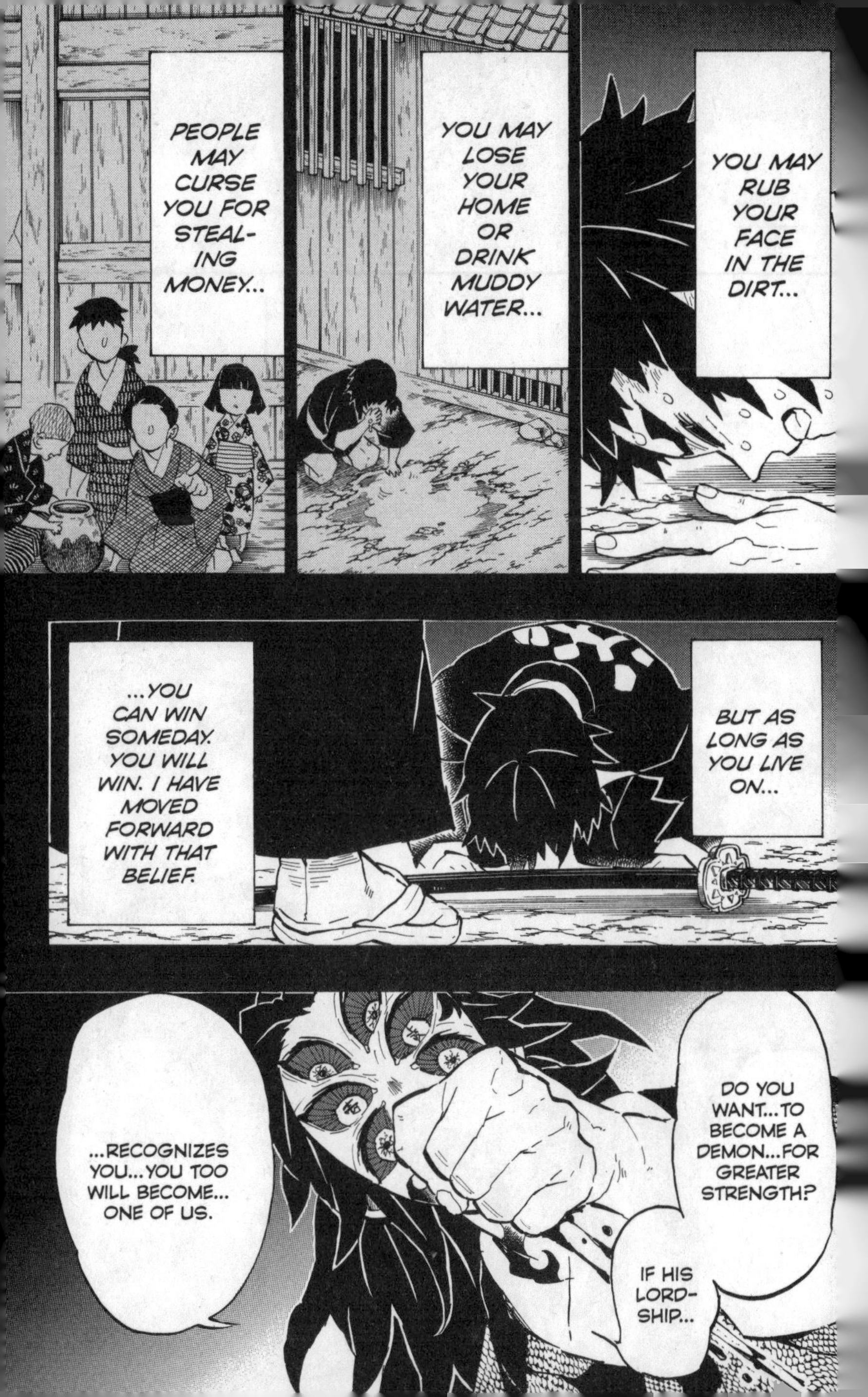
YOU MAY RUB YOUR FACE IN THE DIRT...
YOU MAY LOSE YOUR HOME OR DRINK MUDDY WATER...
PEOPLE MAY CURSE YOU FOR STEAL-ING MONEY...
BUT AS LONG AS YOU LIVE ON...
...YOU CAN WIN SOMEDAY. YOU WILL WIN. I HAVE MOVED FORWARD WITH THAT BELIEF.
DO YOU WANT...TO BECOME A DEMON...FOR GREATER STRENGTH?
IF HIS LORD-SHIP...
...RECOGNIZES YOU...YOU TOO WILL BECOME... ONE OF US.

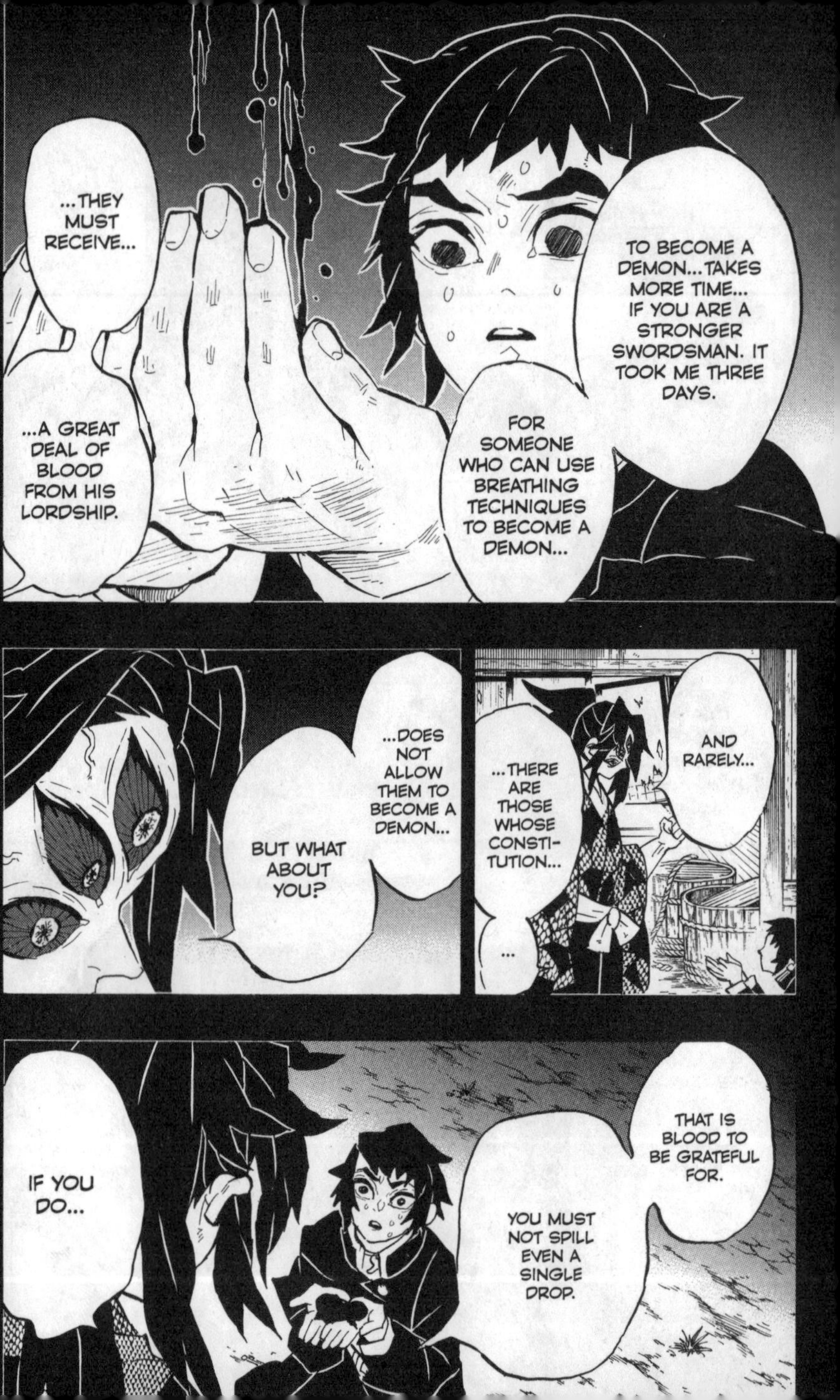

TO BECOME A DEMON...TAKES MORE TIME... IF YOU ARE A STRONGER SWORDSMAN. IT TOOK ME THREE DAYS.
FOR SOMEONE WHO CAN USE BREATHING TECHNIQUES TO BECOME A DEMON...
...THEY MUST RECEIVE...
...A GREAT DEAL OF BLOOD FROM HIS LORDSHIP.
AND RARELY...
...THERE ARE THOSE WHOSE CONSTI-TUTION...
...
...DOES NOT ALLOW THEM TO BECOME A DEMON...
BUT WHAT ABOUT YOU?
THAT IS BLOOD TO BE GRATEFUL FOR.
YOU MUST NOT SPILL EVEN A SINGLE DROP.
IF YOU DO...

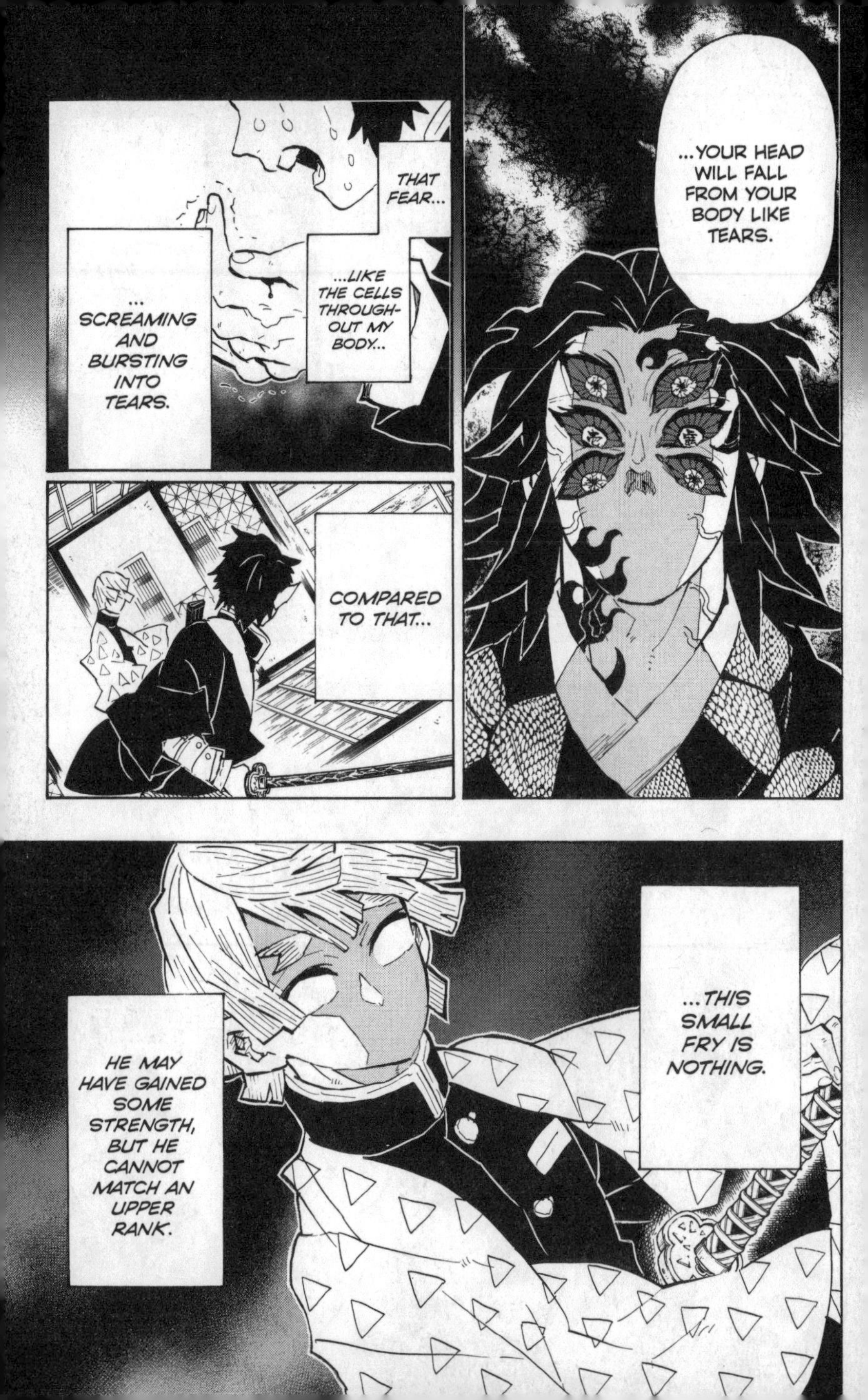
...YOUR HEAD WILL FALL FROM YOUR BODY LIKE TEARS.
THAT FEAR...
...LIKE THE CELLS THROUGH-OUT MY BODY...
... SCREAMING AND BURSTING INTO TEARS.
COMPARED TO THAT...
...THIS SMALL FRY IS NOTHING.
HE MAY HAVE GAINED SOME STRENGTH, BUT HE CANNOT MATCH AN UPPER RANK.

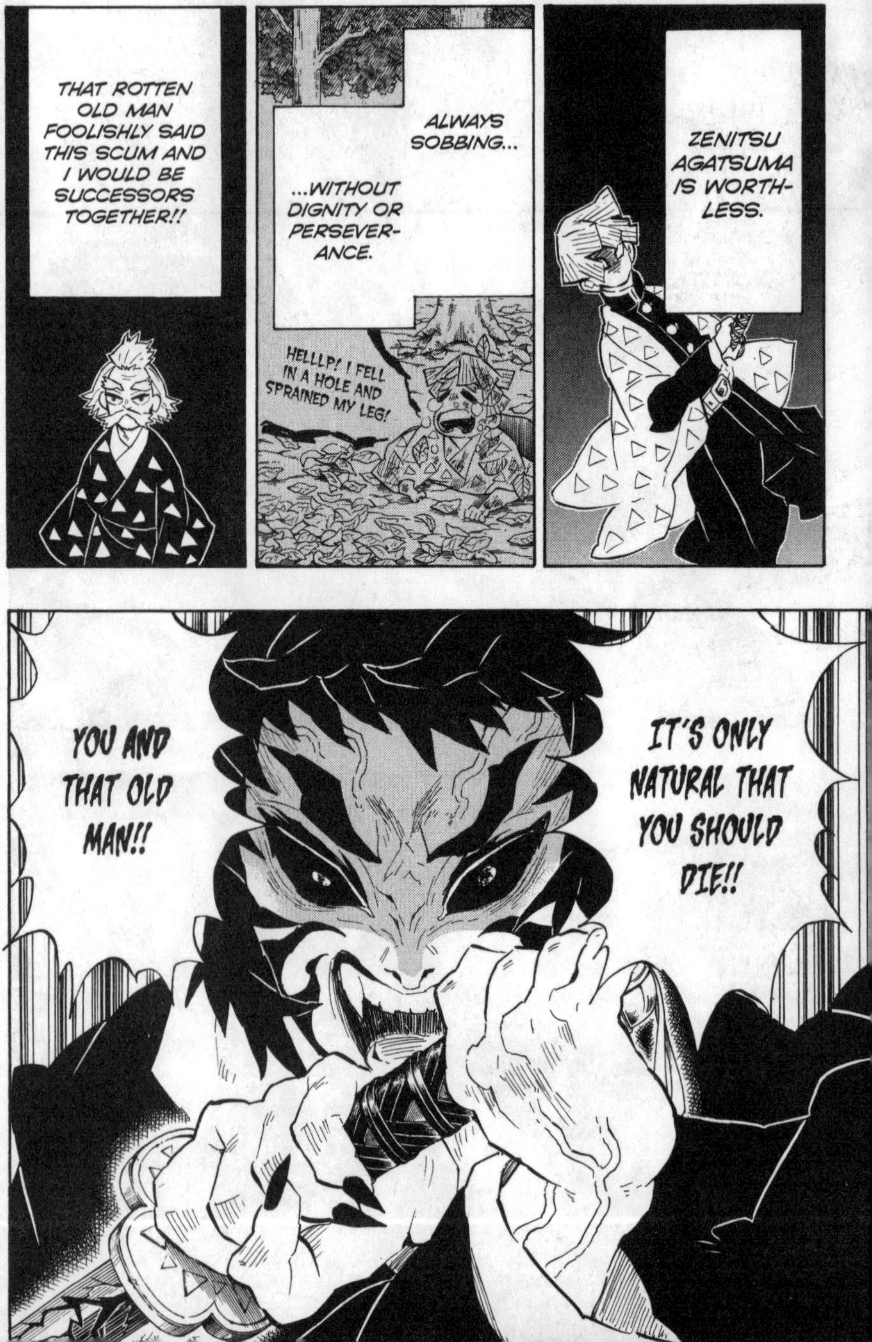
ZENITSU AGATSUMA IS WORTHLESS.
ALWAYS SOBBING...
...WITHOUT DIGNITY OR PERSEVERANCE.
HELLLP! I FELL IN A HOLE AND SPRAINED MY LEG!
THAT ROTTEN OLD MAN FOOLISHLY SAID THIS SCUM AND I WOULD BE SUCCESSORS TOGETHER!!
IT'S ONLY NATURAL THAT YOU SHOULD DIE!!
YOU AND THAT OLD MAN!!

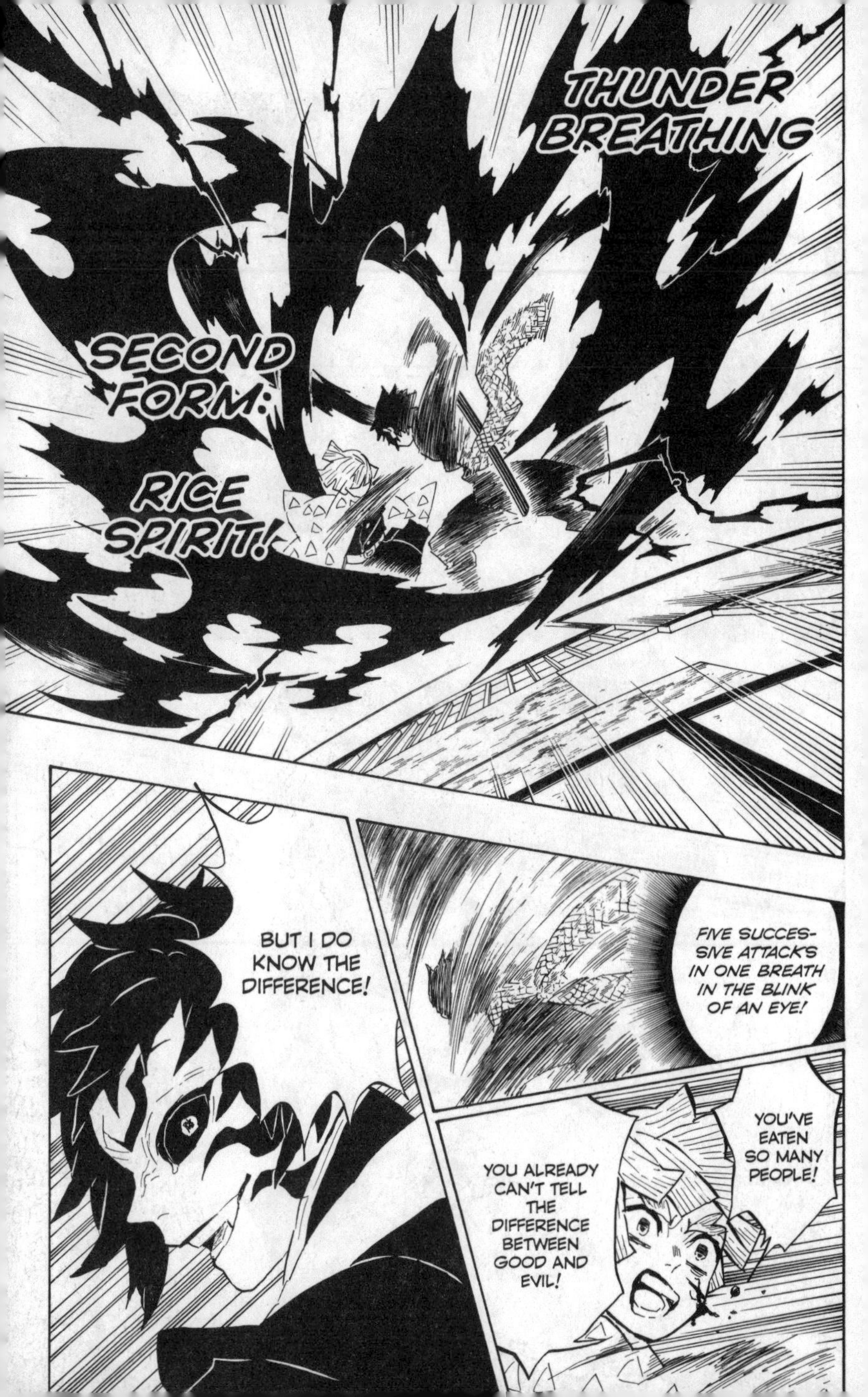
THUNDER BREATHING
SECOND FORM:
RICE SPIRIT!
FIVE SUCCES-SIVE ATTACKS IN ONE BREATH IN THE BLINK OF AN EYE!
YOU'VE EATEN SO MANY PEOPLE!
YOU ALREADY CAN'T TELL THE DIFFERENCE BETWEEN GOOD AND EVIL!
BUT I DO KNOW THE DIFFERENCE!

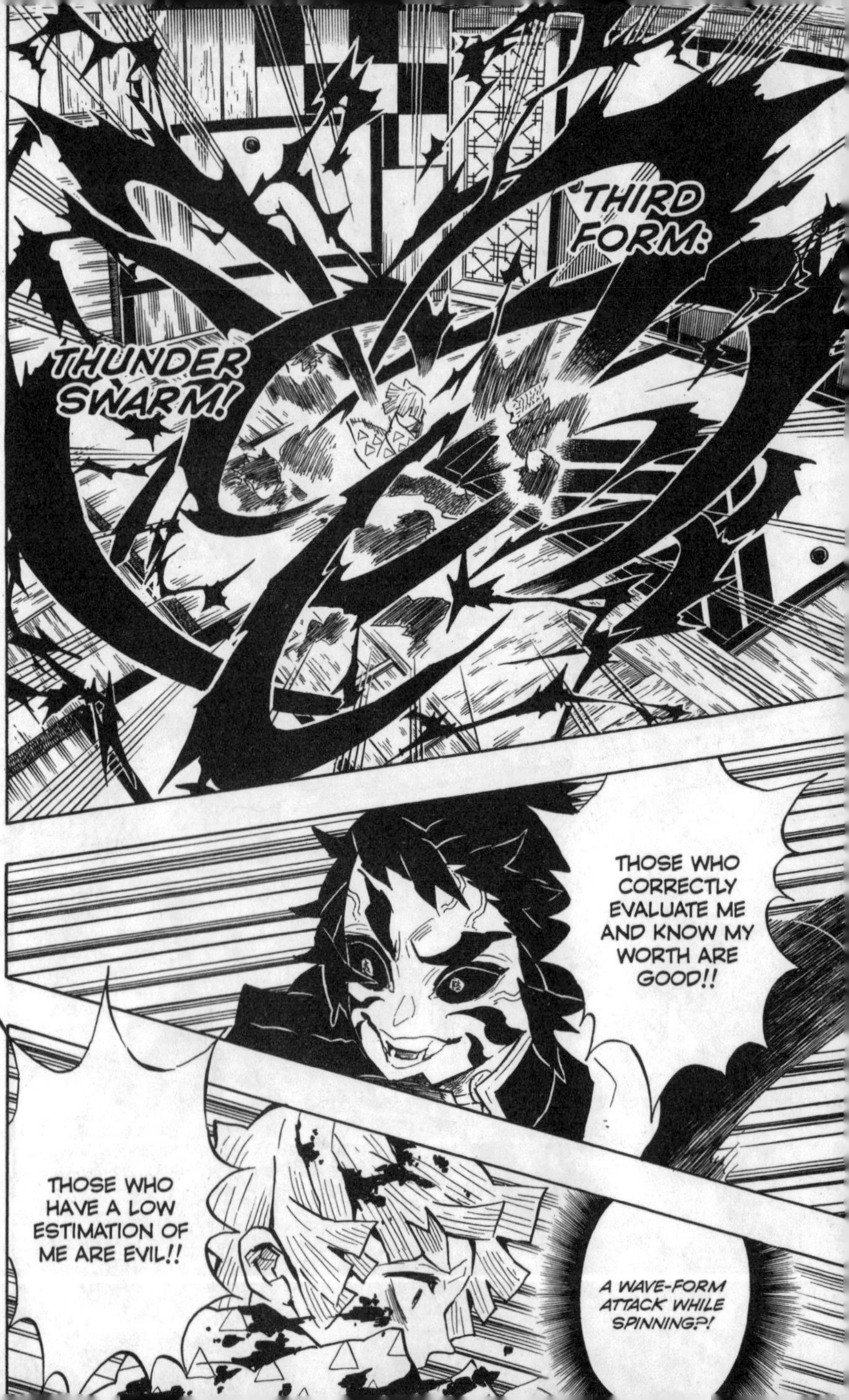
THIRD FORM:
THUNDER SWARM!
THOSE WHO CORRECTLY EVALUATE ME AND KNOW MY WORTH ARE GOOD!!
THOSE WHO HAVE A LOW ESTIMATION OF ME ARE EVIL!!
A WAVE-FORM ATTACK WHILE SPINNING?!

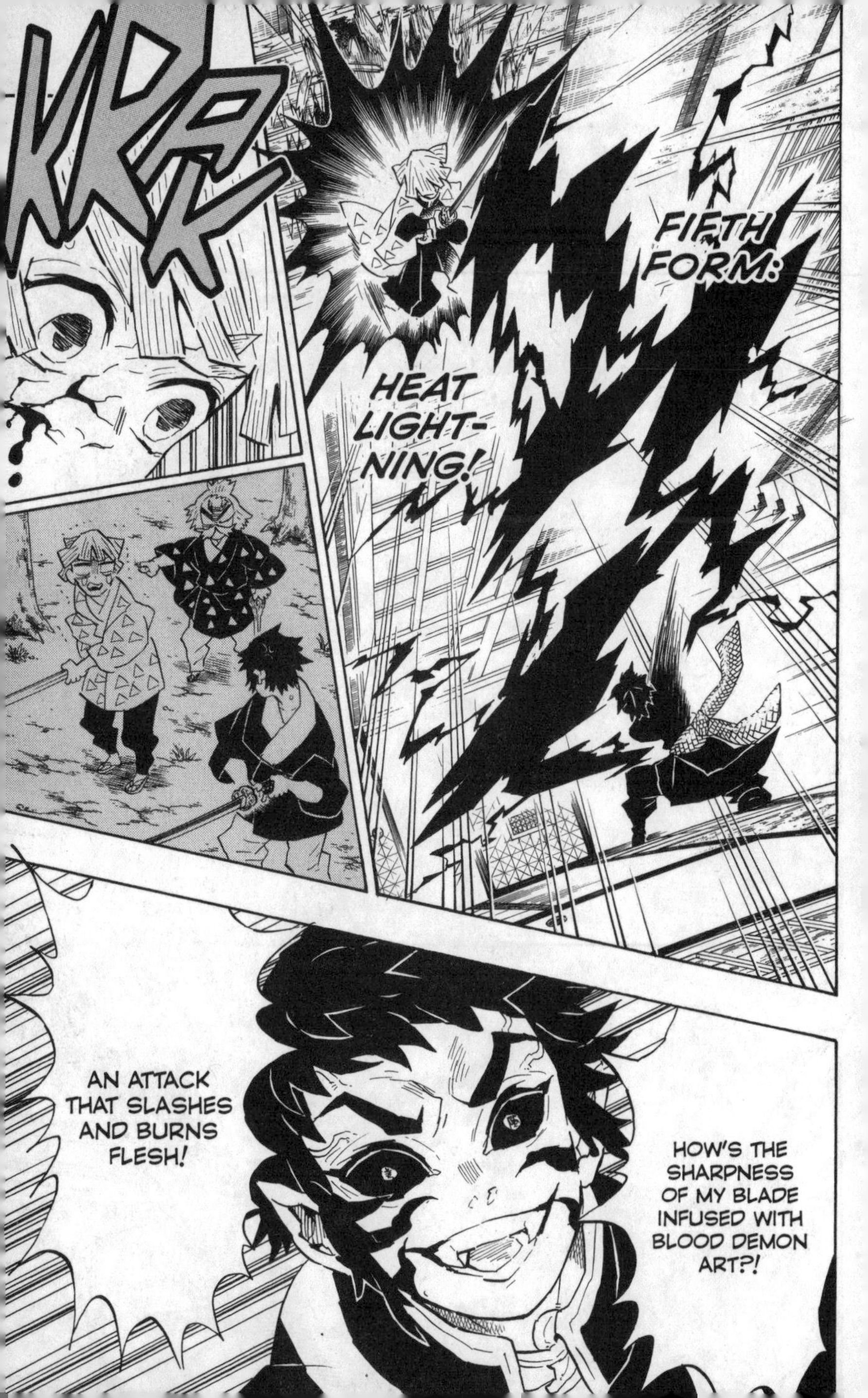
FIFTH FORM:
HEAT LIGHTNING!
HOW'S THE SHARPNESS OF MY BLADE INFUSED WITH BLOOD DEMON ART?!
AN ATTACK THAT SLASHES AND BURNS FLESH!

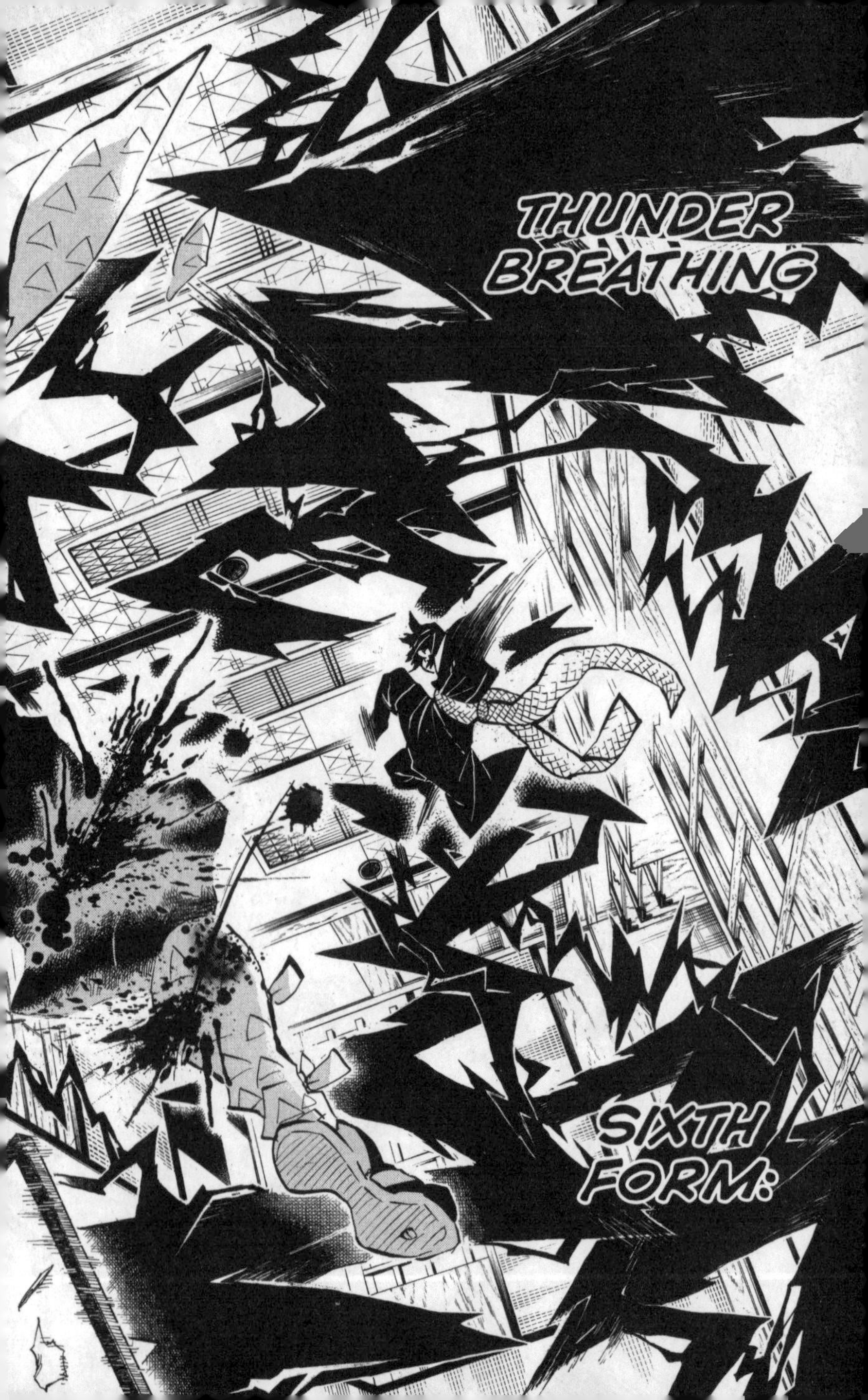
THUNDER BREATHING
SIXTH FORM:

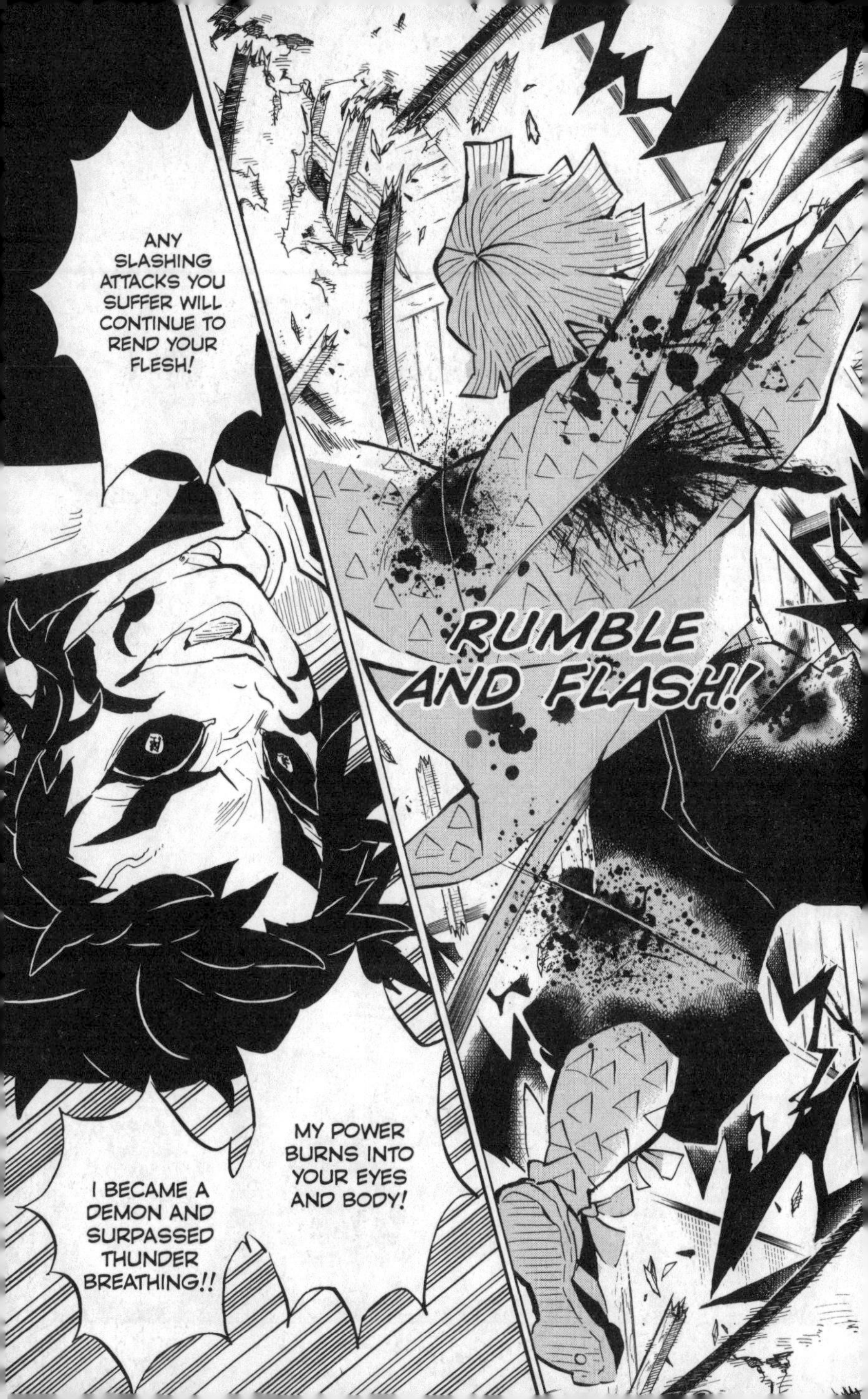
RUMBLE AND FLASH!
ANY SLASHING ATTACKS YOU SUFFER WILL CONTINUE TO REND YOUR FLESH!
MY POWER BURNS INTO YOUR EYES AND BODY!
I BECAME A DEMON AND SURPASSED THUNDER BREATHING!!

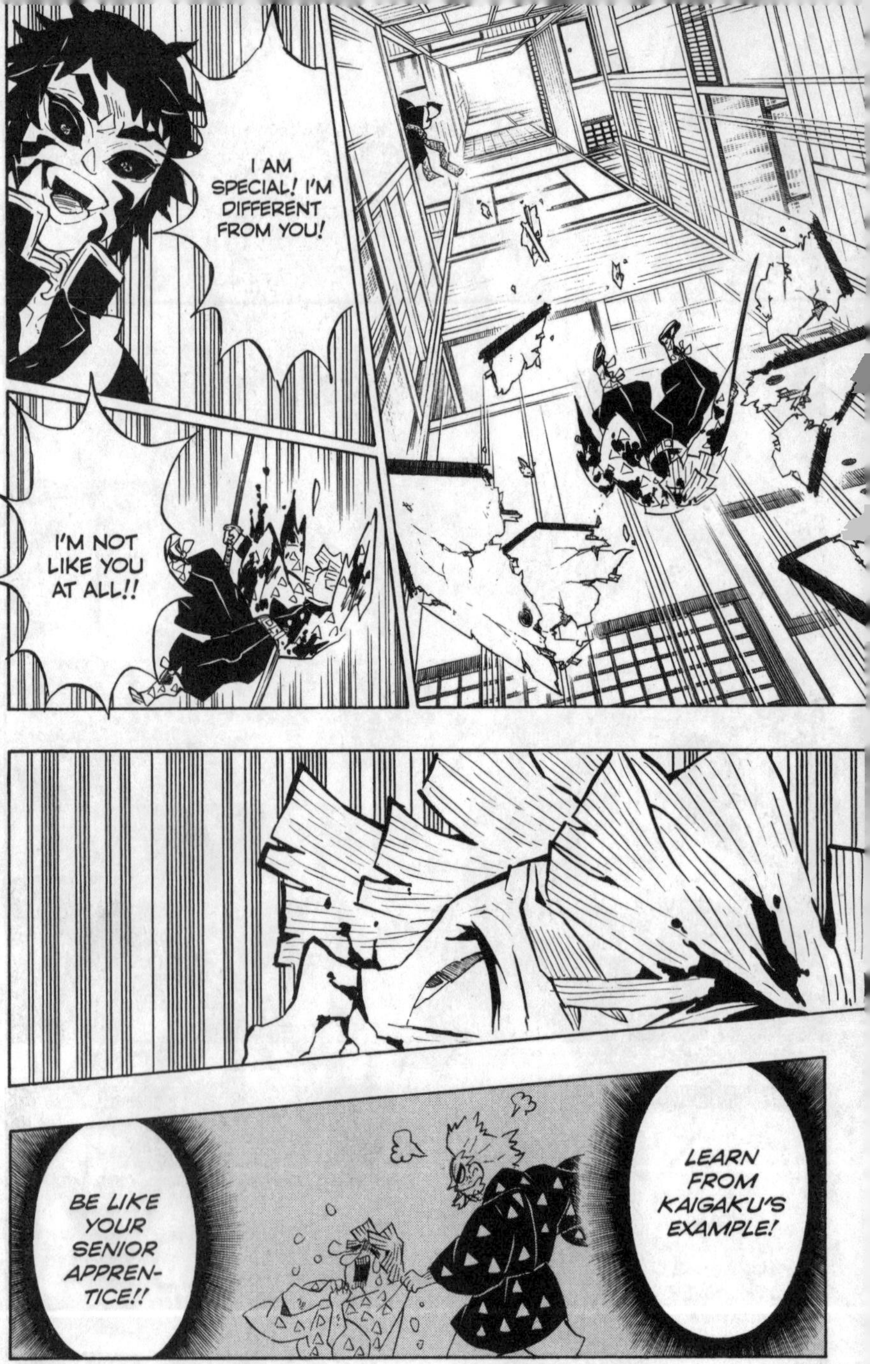
I AM SPECIAL! I'M DIFFERENT FROM YOU!
I'M NOT LIKE YOU AT ALL!!
LEARN FROM KAIGAKU'S EXAMPLE!
BE LIKE YOUR SENIOR APPREN-TICE!!

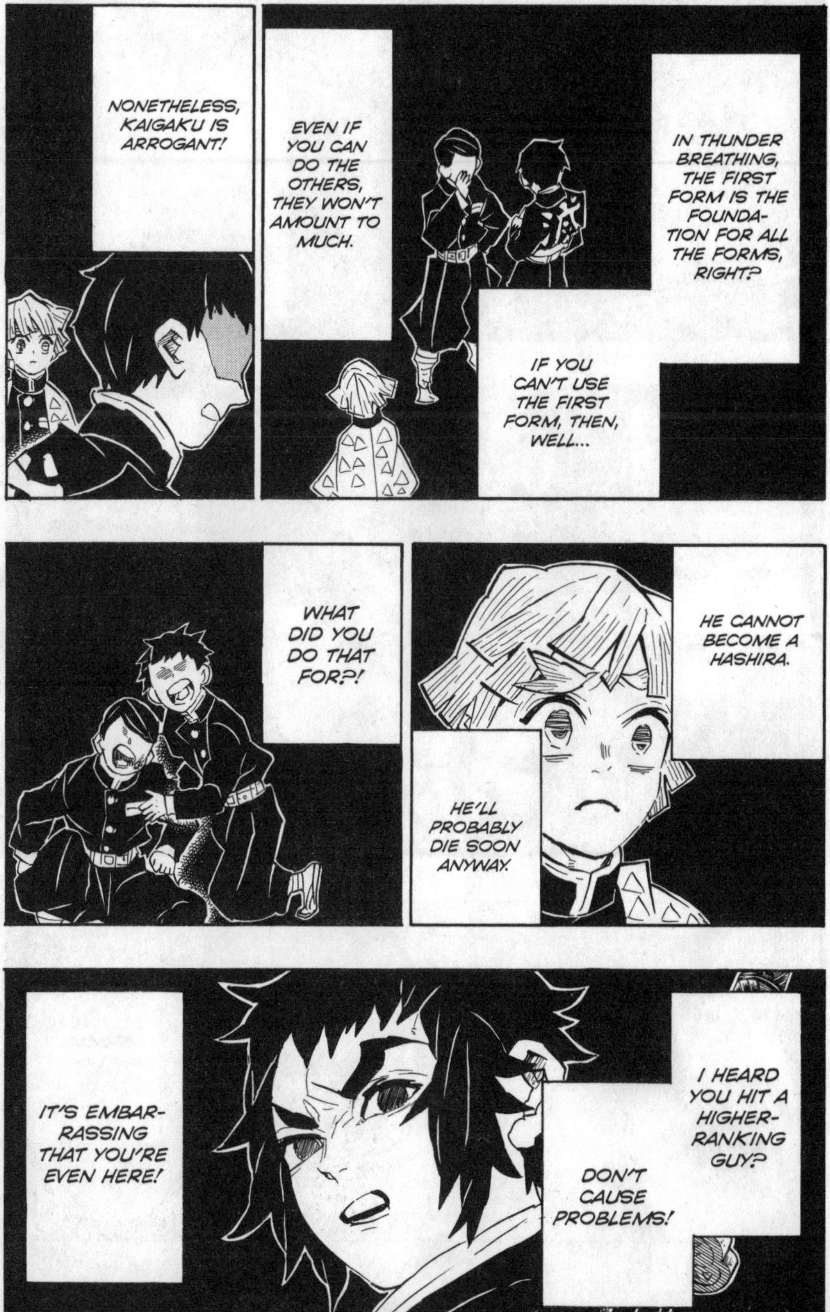

IN THUNDER BREATHING, THE FIRST FORM IS THE FOUNDATION FOR ALL THE FORMS, RIGHT?
IF YOU CAN'T USE THE FIRST FORM, THEN, WELL...
EVEN IF YOU CAN DO THE OTHERS, THEY WON'T AMOUNT TO MUCH.
NONETHELESS, KAIGAKU IS ARROGANT!
HE CANNOT BECOME A HASHIRA.
HE'LL PROBABLY DIE SOON ANYWAY.
WHAT DID YOU DO THAT FOR?!
I HEARD YOU HIT A HIGHER-RANKING GUY?
DON'T CAUSE PROBLEMS!
IT'S EMBARRASSING THAT YOU'RE EVEN HERE!

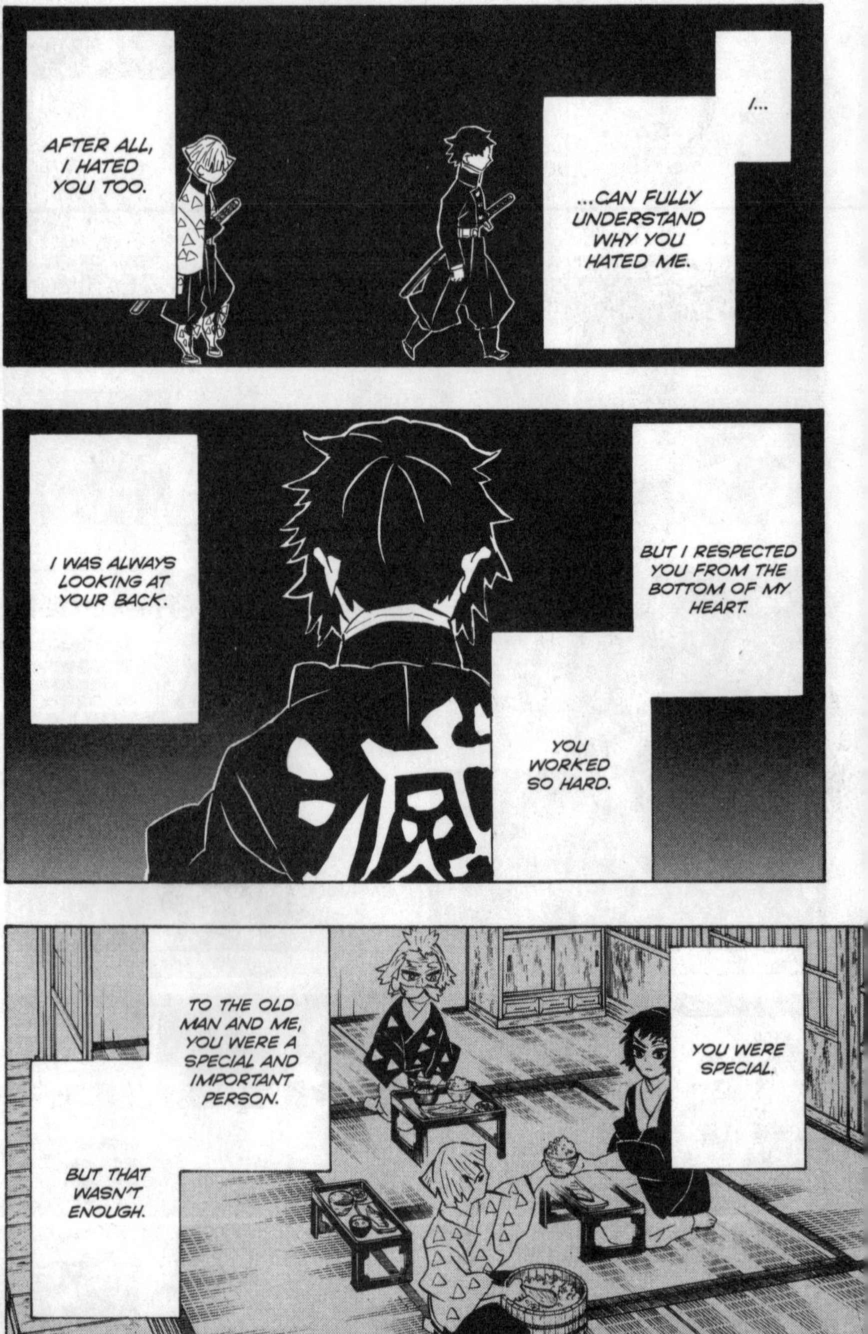
I...
...CAN FULLY UNDERSTAND WHY YOU HATED ME.
AFTER ALL, I HATED YOU TOO.
BUT I RESPECTED YOU FROM THE BOTTOM OF MY HEART.
YOU WORKED SO HARD.
I WAS ALWAYS LOOKING AT YOUR BACK.
YOU WERE SPECIAL.
TO THE OLD MAN AND ME, YOU WERE A SPECIAL AND IMPORTANT PERSON.
BUT THAT WASN'T ENOUGH.

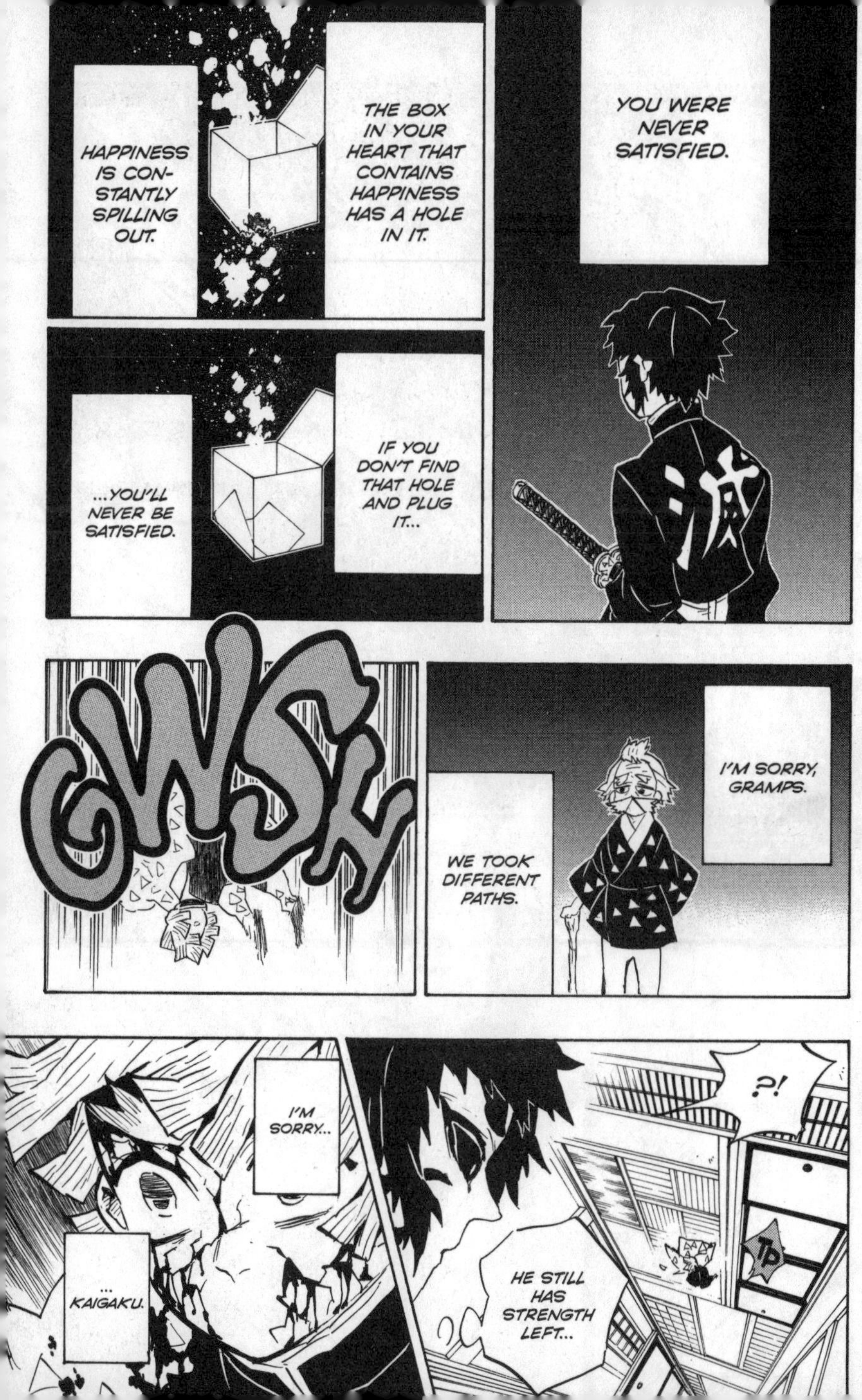
YOU WERE NEVER SATISFIED.
THE BOX IN YOUR HEART THAT CONTAINS HAPPINESS HAS A HOLE IN IT.
HAPPINESS IS CONSTANTLY SPILLING OUT.
IF YOU DON'T FIND THAT HOLE AND PLUG IT...
...YOU'LL NEVER BE SATISFIED.
I'M SORRY, GRAMPS.
WE TOOK DIFFERENT PATHS.
GWSH
?!
TP
HE STILL HAS STRENGTH LEFT...
I'M SORRY...
... KAIGAKU.

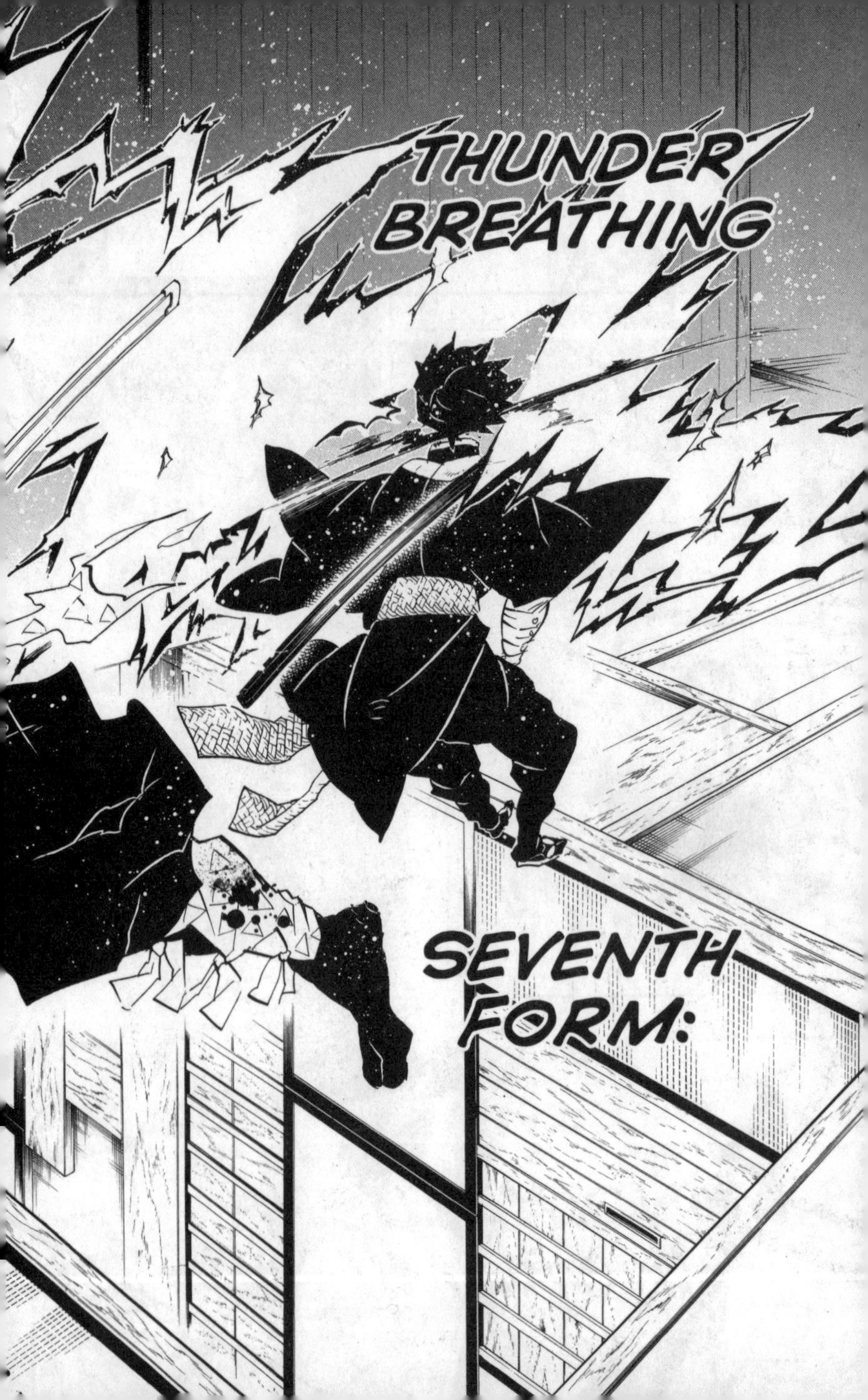
THUNDER BREATHING
SEVENTH FORM:

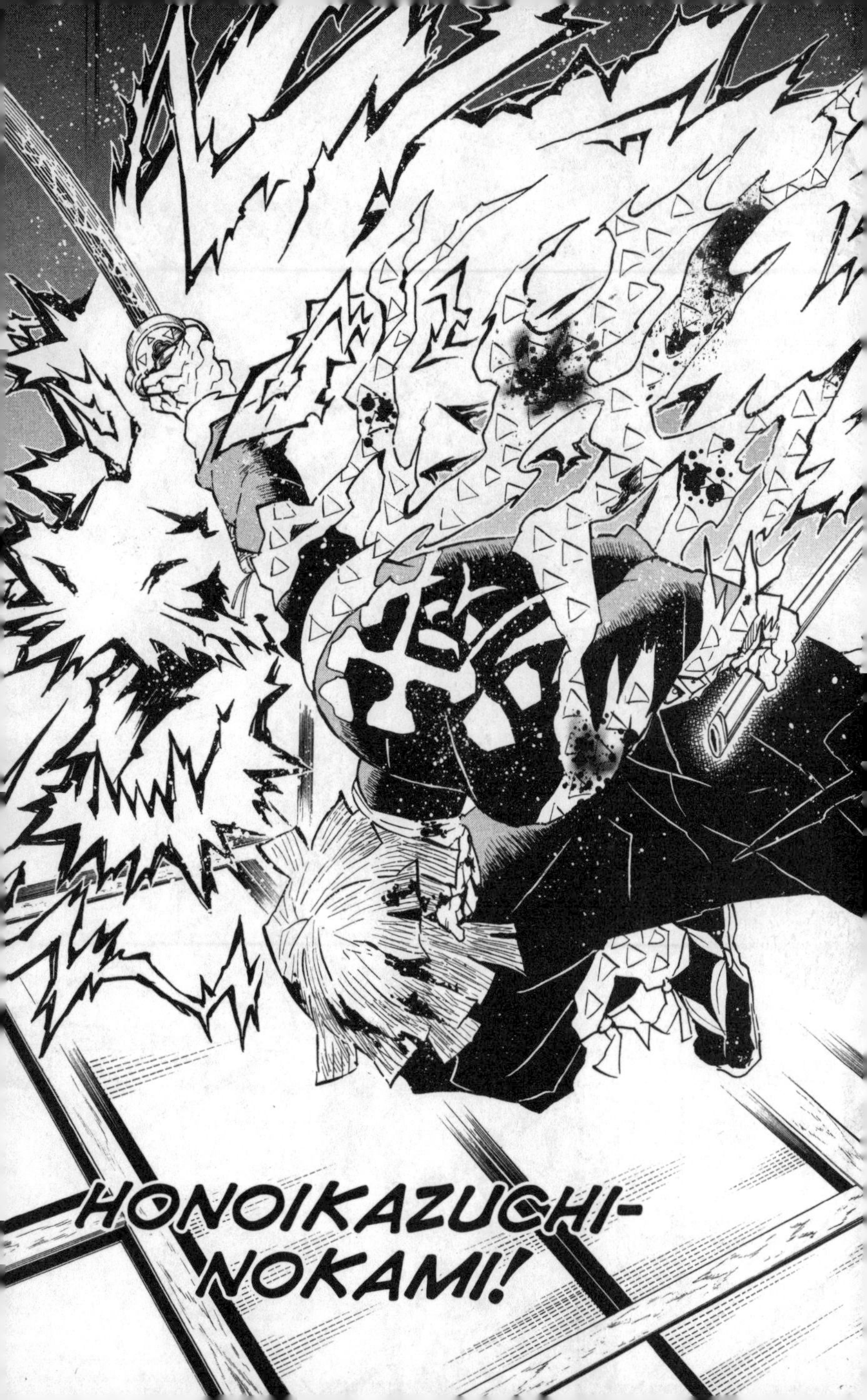
HONOIKAZUCHI-NOKAMI!

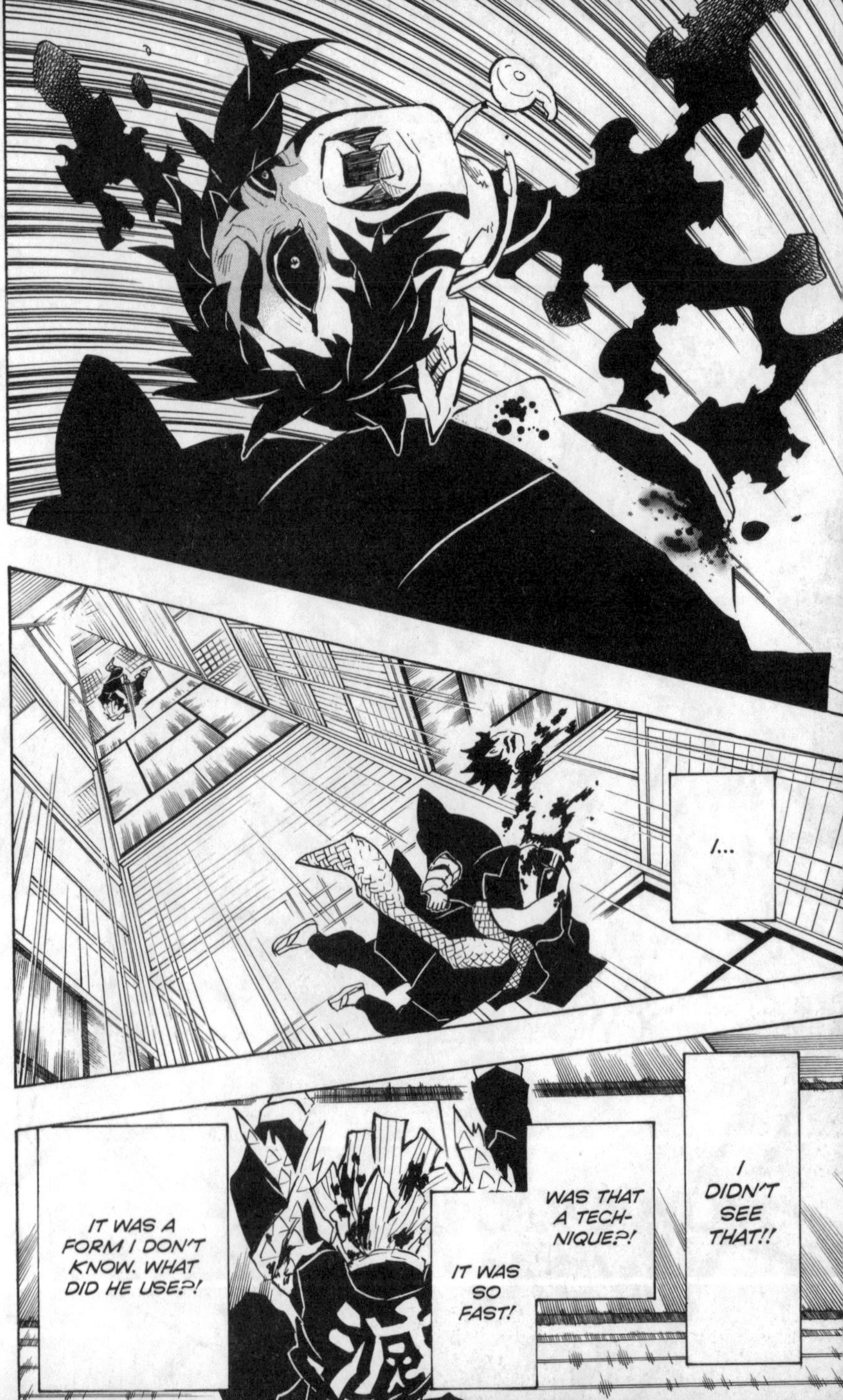
I...
I DIDN'T SEE THAT!!
WAS THAT A TECH-NIQUE?!
IT WAS SO FAST!
IT WAS A FORM I DON'T KNOW. WHAT DID HE USE?!

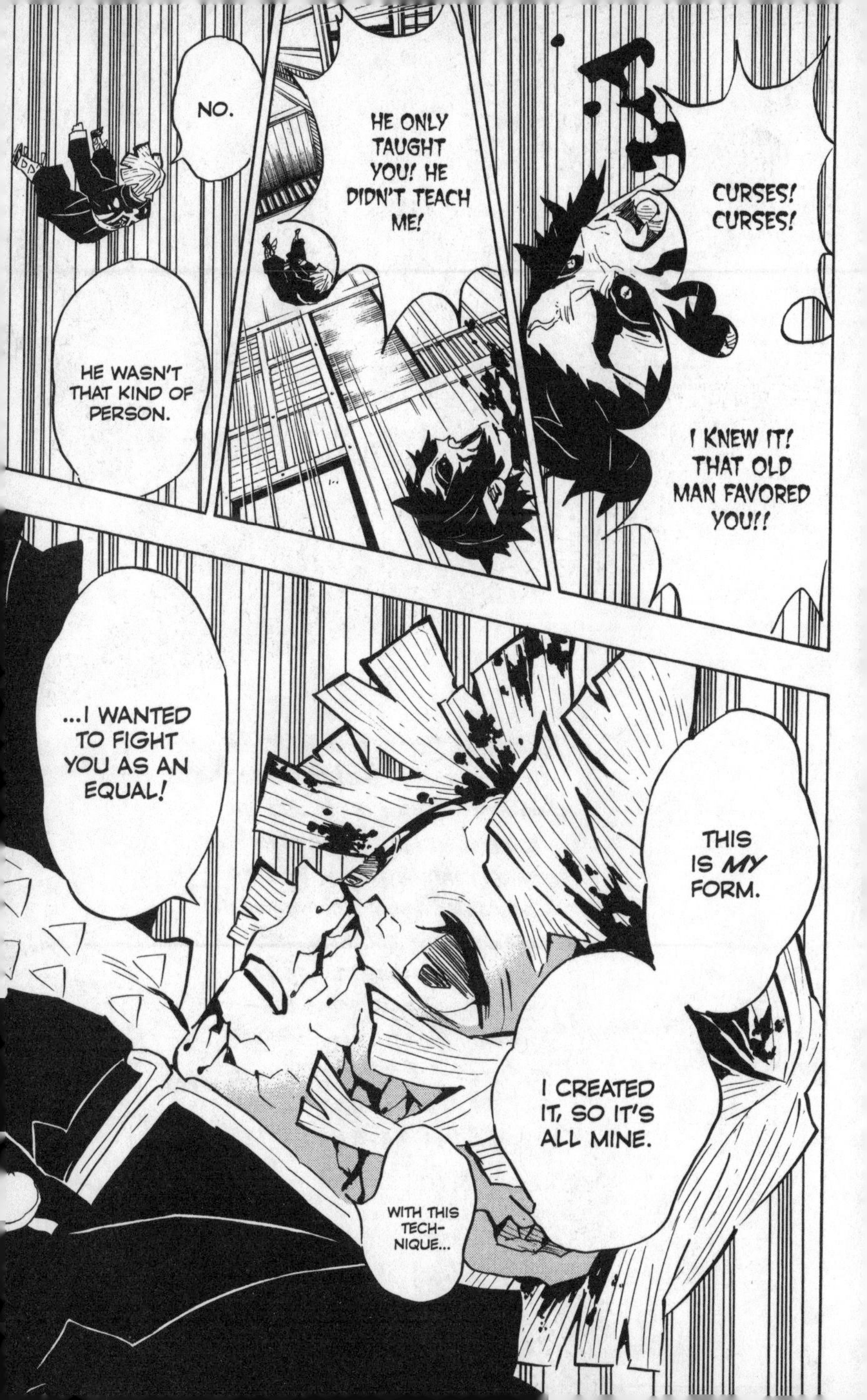

CURSES! CURSES!
I KNEW IT! THAT OLD MAN FAVORED YOU!!
HE ONLY TAUGHT YOU! HE DIDN'T TEACH ME!
NO.
HE WASN'T THAT KIND OF PERSON.
THIS IS *MY* FORM.
I CREATED IT, SO IT'S ALL MINE.
WITH THIS TECHNIQUE...
...I WANTED TO FIGHT YOU AS AN EQUAL!

Kaigaku is the boy who invited in the demon who attacked Hime-jima's temple. The other children had discovered that he stole money from the temple, so they confronted him and drove him outside that night. Himejima's blindness is one reason he never knew Kaigaku was missing until the attacking demon mentioned it. Another reason is that the other children lied and said Kaigaku was sleeping.

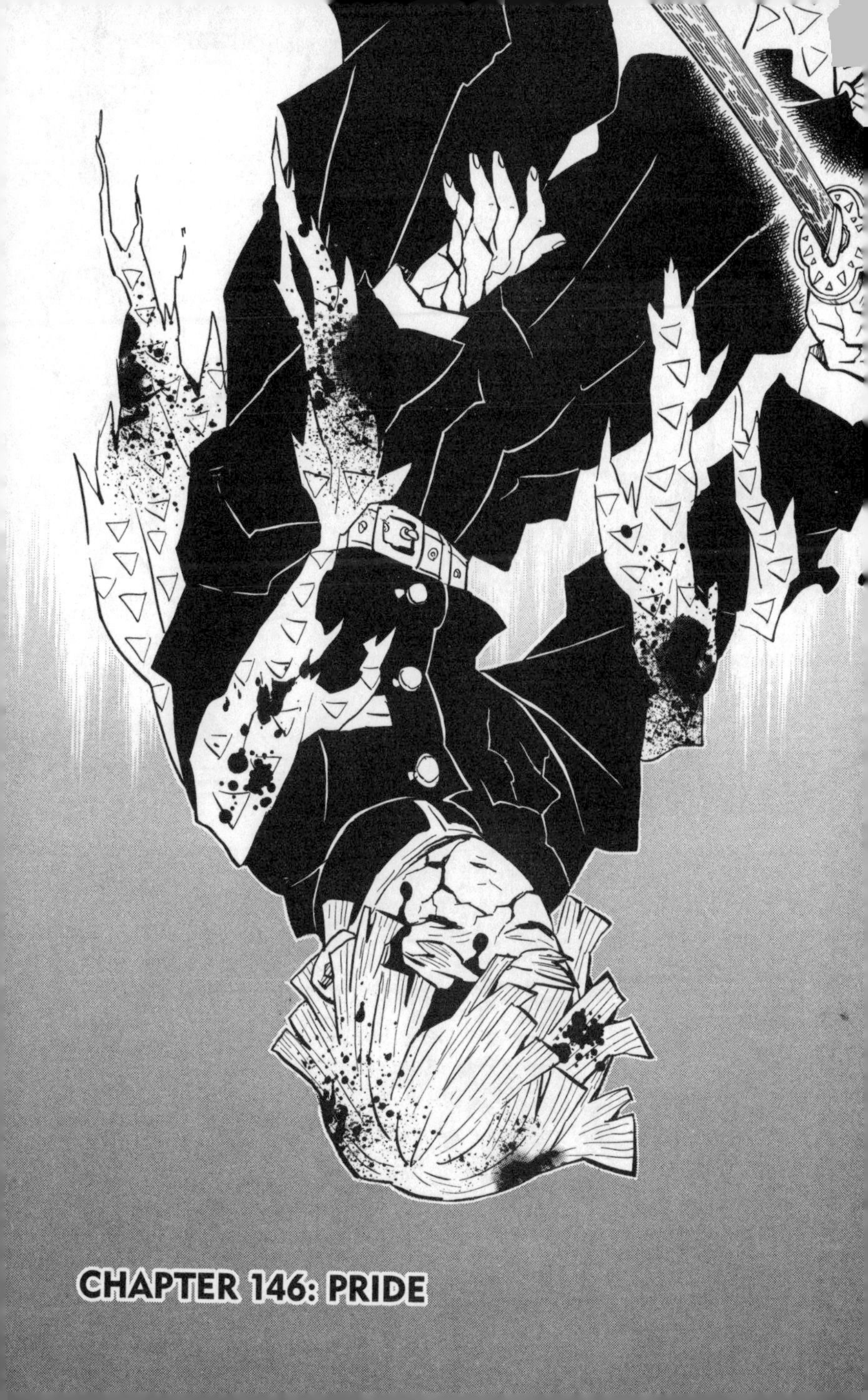

CHAPTER 146: PRIDE

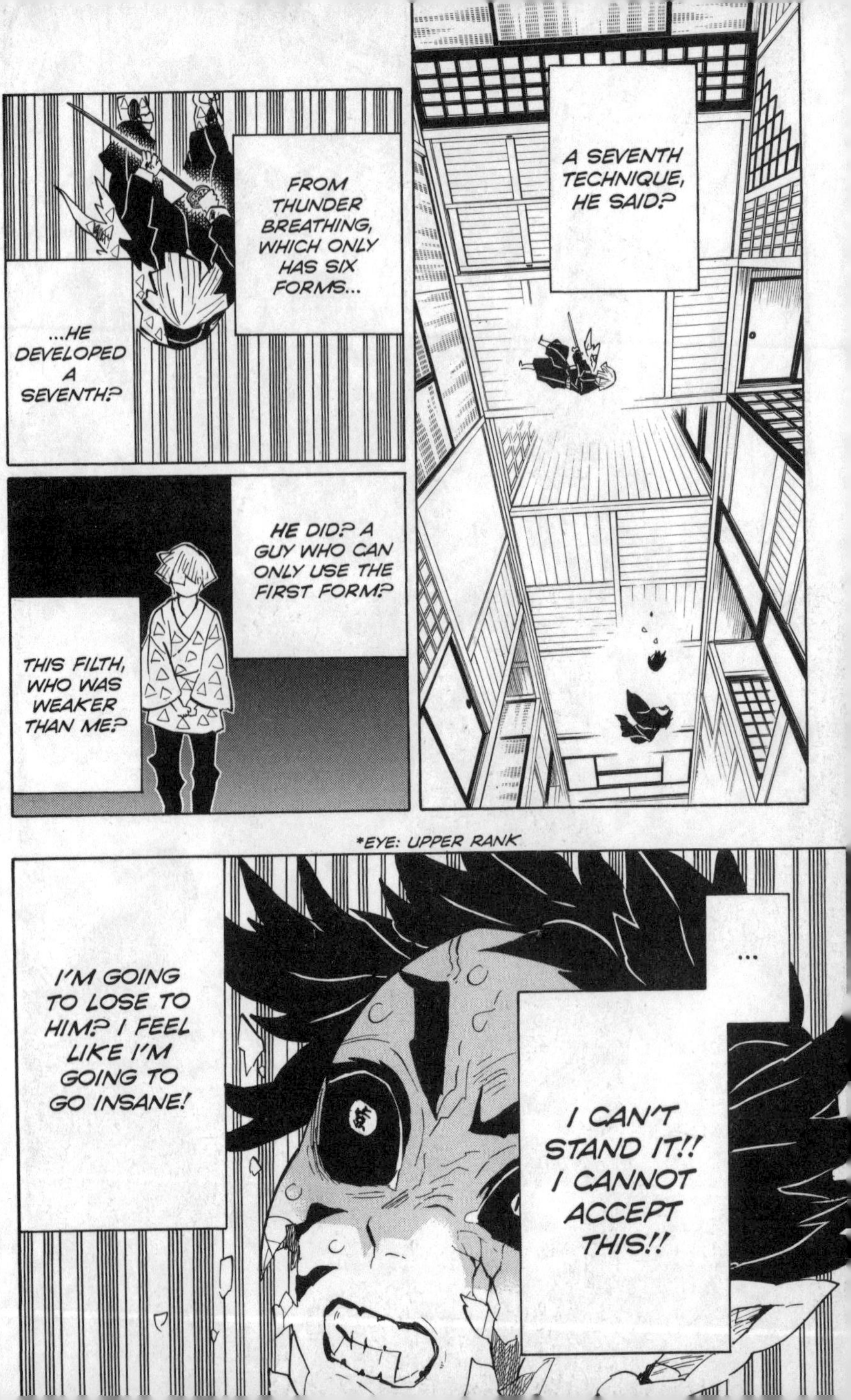
A SEVENTH TECHNIQUE, HE SAID?
FROM THUNDER BREATHING, WHICH ONLY HAS SIX FORMS...
...HE DEVELOPED A SEVENTH?
HE DID? A GUY WHO CAN ONLY USE THE FIRST FORM?
THIS FILTH, WHO WAS WEAKER THAN ME?
*EYE: UPPER RANK
...
I CAN'T STAND IT!! I CANNOT ACCEPT THIS!!
I'M GOING TO LOSE TO HIM? I FEEL LIKE I'M GOING TO GO INSANE!

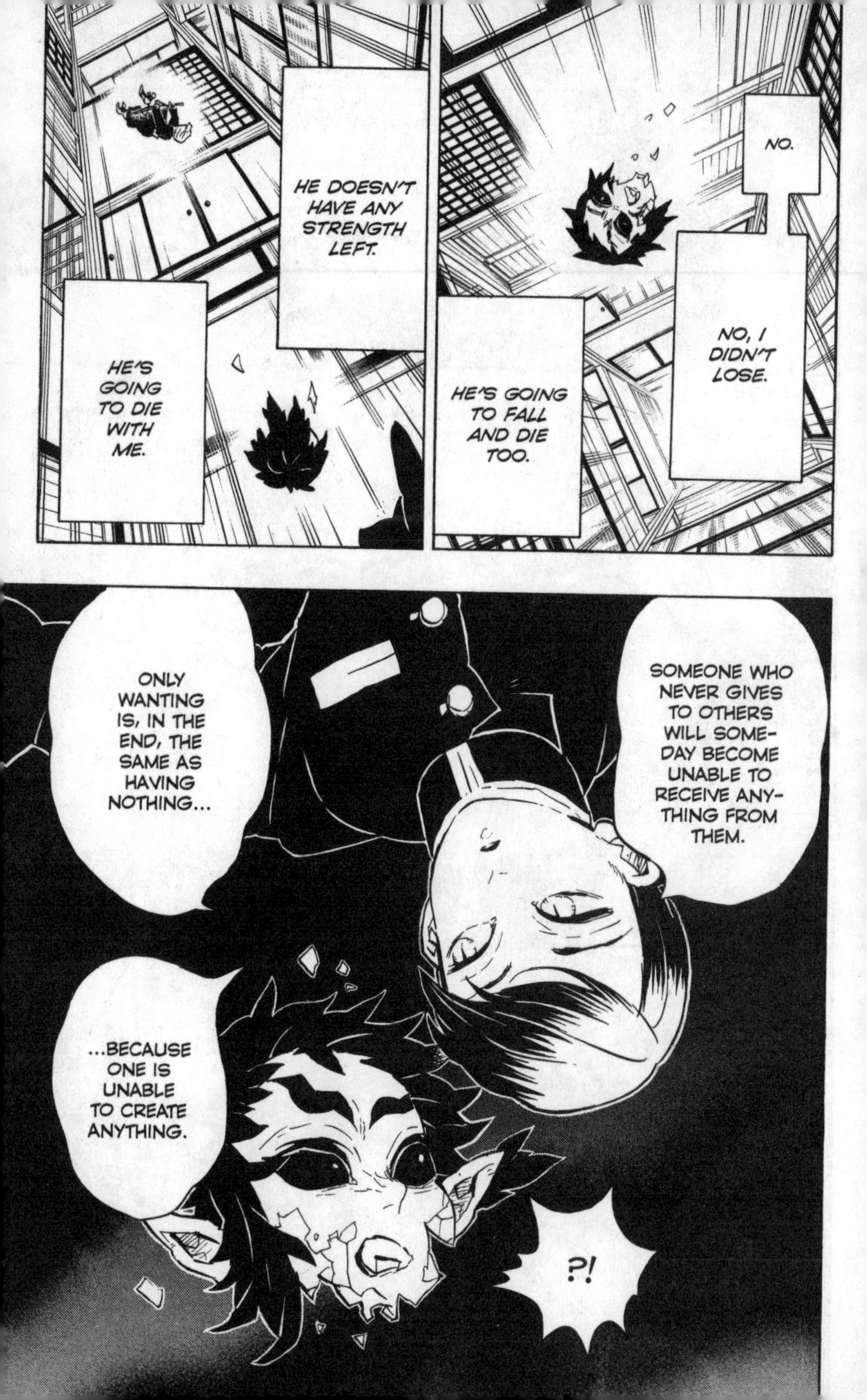
NO.
NO, I DIDN'T LOSE.
HE'S GOING TO FALL AND DIE TOO.
HE DOESN'T HAVE ANY STRENGTH LEFT.
HE'S GOING TO DIE WITH ME.
SOMEONE WHO NEVER GIVES TO OTHERS WILL SOMEDAY BECOME UNABLE TO RECEIVE ANYTHING FROM THEM.
ONLY WANTING IS, IN THE END, THE SAME AS HAVING NOTHING...
...BECAUSE ONE IS UNABLE TO CREATE ANYTHING.
?!

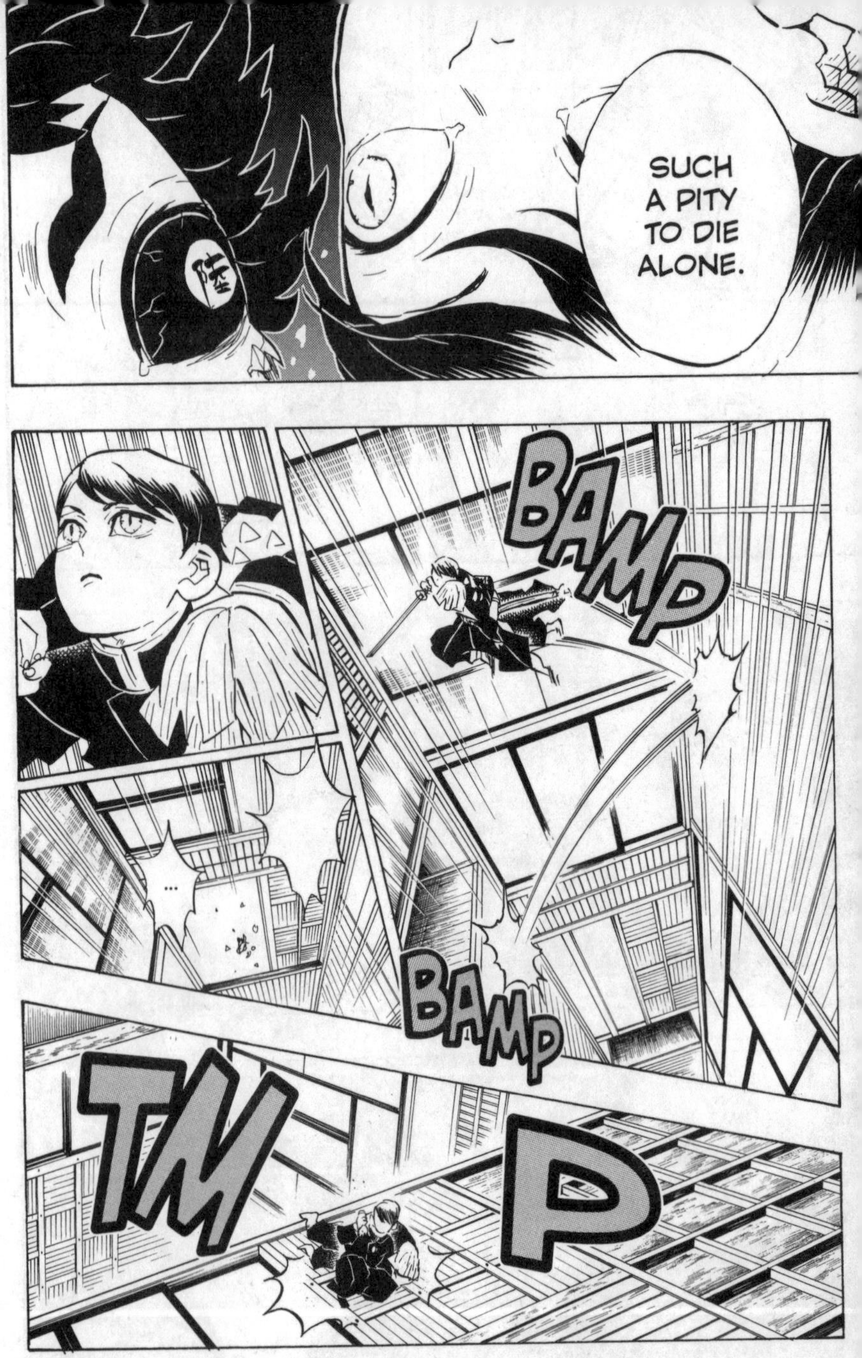
SUCH A PITY TO DIE ALONE.
BAMP
BAMP
...
TMP

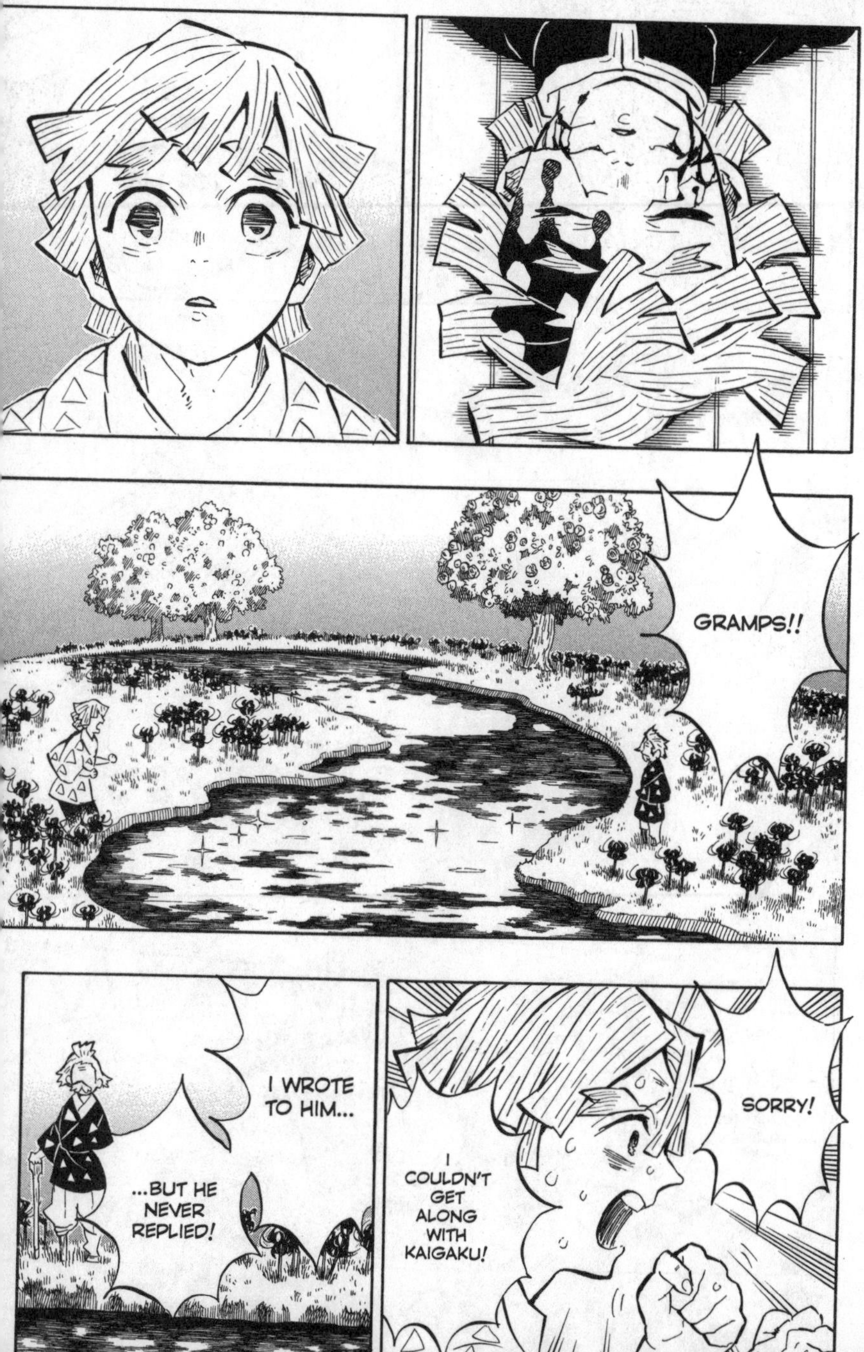
GRAMPS!!
SORRY!
I COULDN'T GET ALONG WITH KAIGAKU!
I WROTE TO HIM...
...BUT HE NEVER REPLIED!

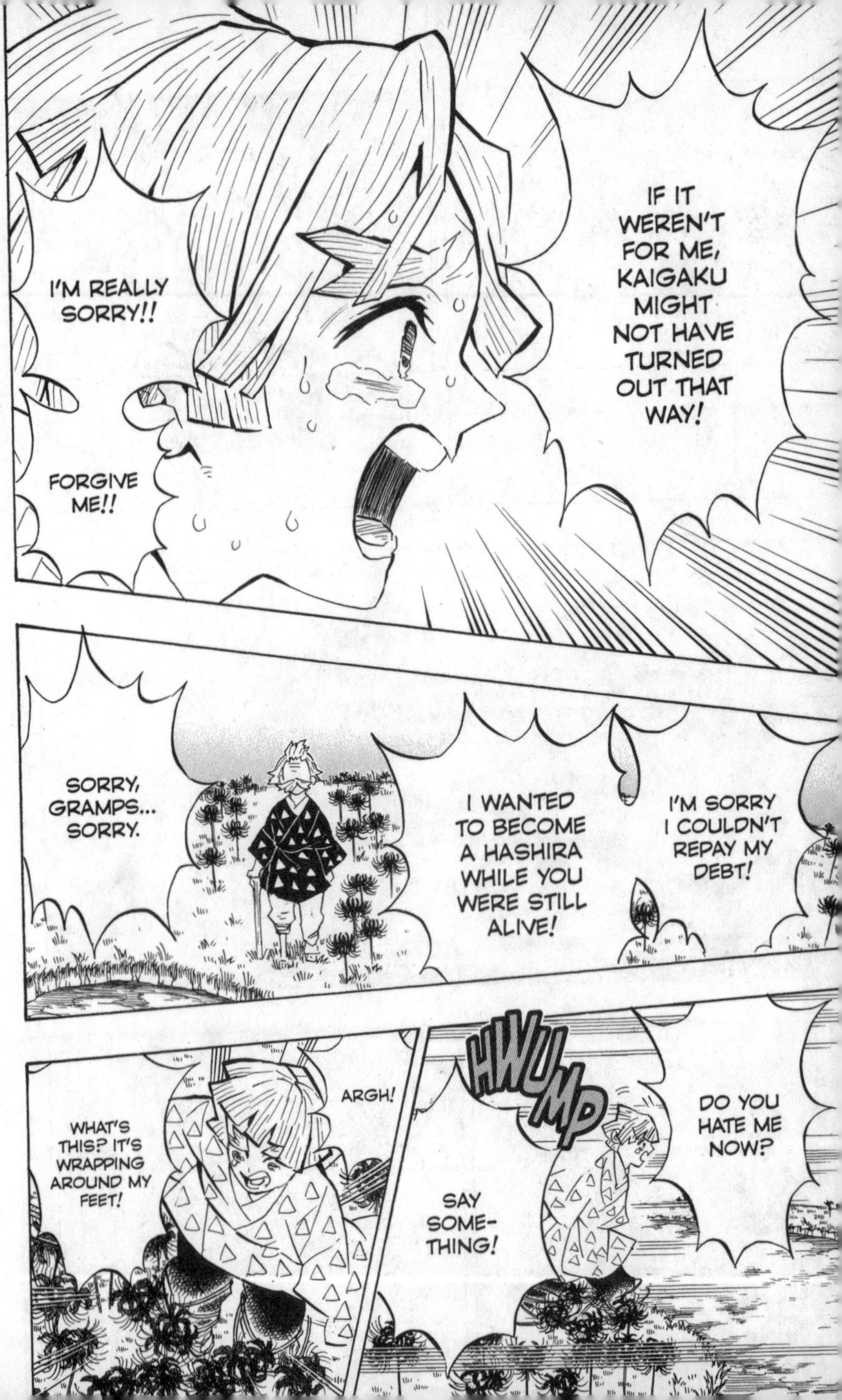
IF IT WEREN'T FOR ME, KAIGAKU MIGHT NOT HAVE TURNED OUT THAT WAY!
I'M REALLY SORRY!!
FORGIVE ME!!
I'M SORRY I COULDN'T REPAY MY DEBT!
I WANTED TO BECOME A HASHIRA WHILE YOU WERE STILL ALIVE!
SORRY, GRAMPS... SORRY.
DO YOU HATE ME NOW?
HWUMP
SAY SOME-THING!
ARGH!
WHAT'S THIS? IT'S WRAPPING AROUND MY FEET!

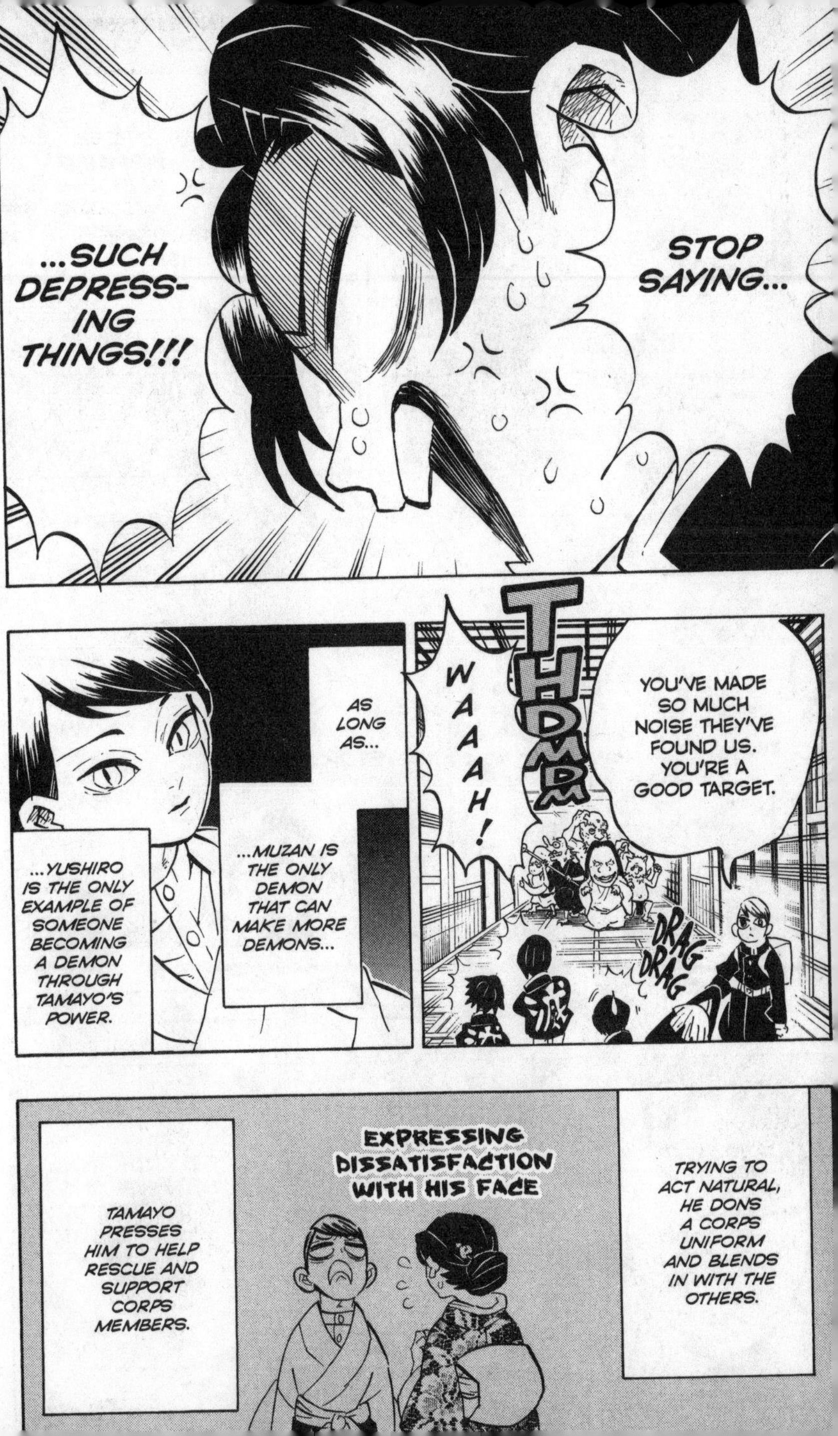
STOP SAYING...
...SUCH DEPRESSING THINGS!!!
THDMDM
WAAAAH!
YOU'VE MADE SO MUCH NOISE THEY'VE FOUND US. YOU'RE A GOOD TARGET.
DRAG DRAG
AS LONG AS...
...MUZAN IS THE ONLY DEMON THAT CAN MAKE MORE DEMONS...
...YUSHIRO IS THE ONLY EXAMPLE OF SOMEONE BECOMING A DEMON THROUGH TAMAYO'S POWER.
EXPRESSING DISSATISFACTION WITH HIS FACE
TRYING TO ACT NATURAL, HE DONS A CORPS UNIFORM AND BLENDS IN WITH THE OTHERS.
TAMAYO PRESSES HIM TO HELP RESCUE AND SUPPORT CORPS MEMBERS.

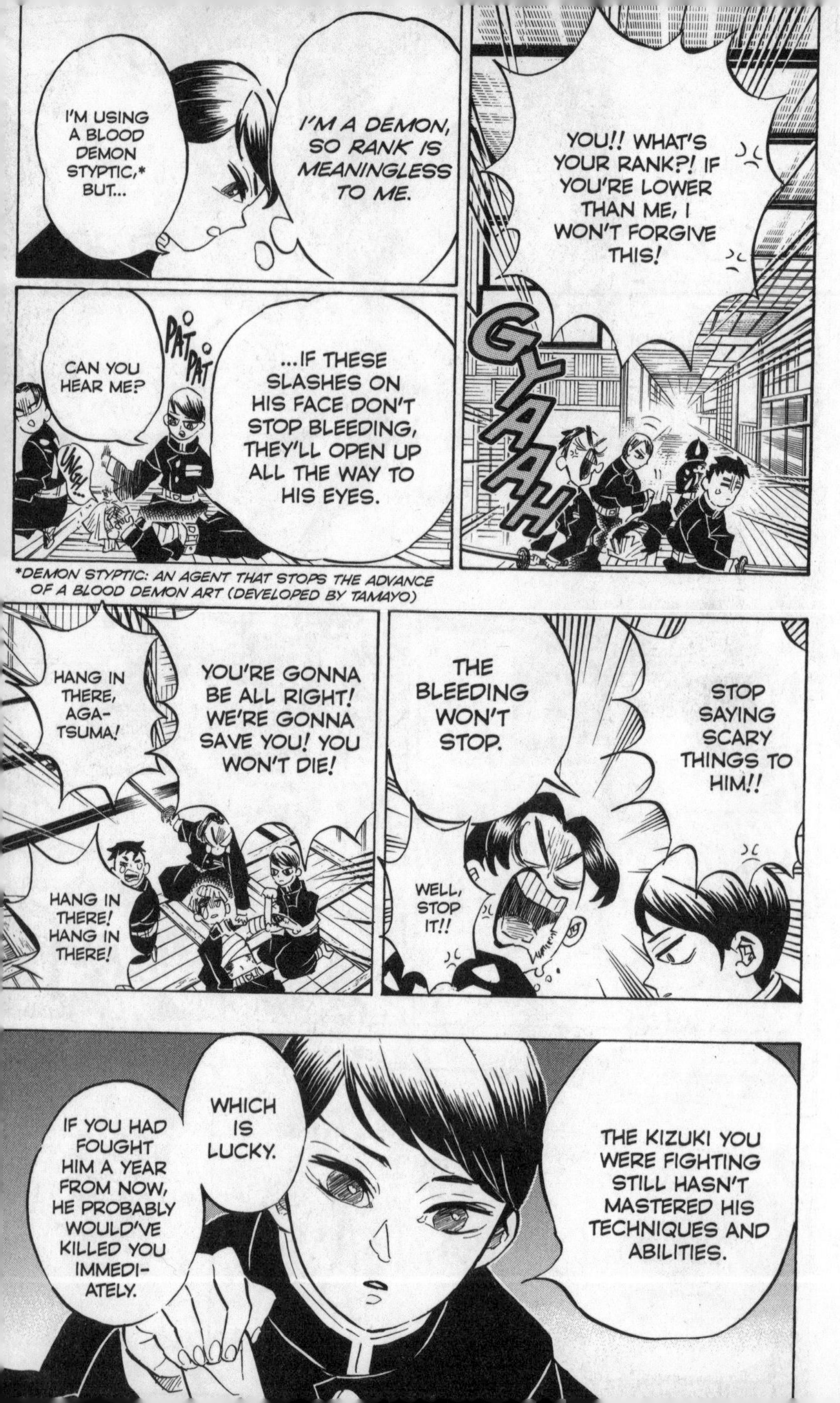
YOU!! WHAT'S YOUR RANK?! IF YOU'RE LOWER THAN ME, I WON'T FORGIVE THIS!
GYAAAH
I'M A DEMON, SO RANK IS MEANINGLESS TO ME.
I'M USING A BLOOD DEMON STYPTIC,* BUT...
...IF THESE SLASHES ON HIS FACE DON'T STOP BLEEDING, THEY'LL OPEN UP ALL THE WAY TO HIS EYES.
PAT PAT
CAN YOU HEAR ME?
UNGH...
*DEMON STYPTIC: AN AGENT THAT STOPS THE ADVANCE OF A BLOOD DEMON ART (DEVELOPED BY TAMAYO)
STOP SAYING SCARY THINGS TO HIM!!
THE BLEEDING WON'T STOP.
WELL, STOP IT!!
YOU'RE GONNA BE ALL RIGHT! WE'RE GONNA SAVE YOU! YOU WON'T DIE!
HANG IN THERE, AGA-TSUMA!
HANG IN THERE! HANG IN THERE!
THE KIZUKI YOU WERE FIGHTING STILL HASN'T MASTERED HIS TECHNIQUES AND ABILITIES.
WHICH IS LUCKY.
IF YOU HAD FOUGHT HIM A YEAR FROM NOW, HE PROBABLY WOULD'VE KILLED YOU IMMEDI-ATELY.

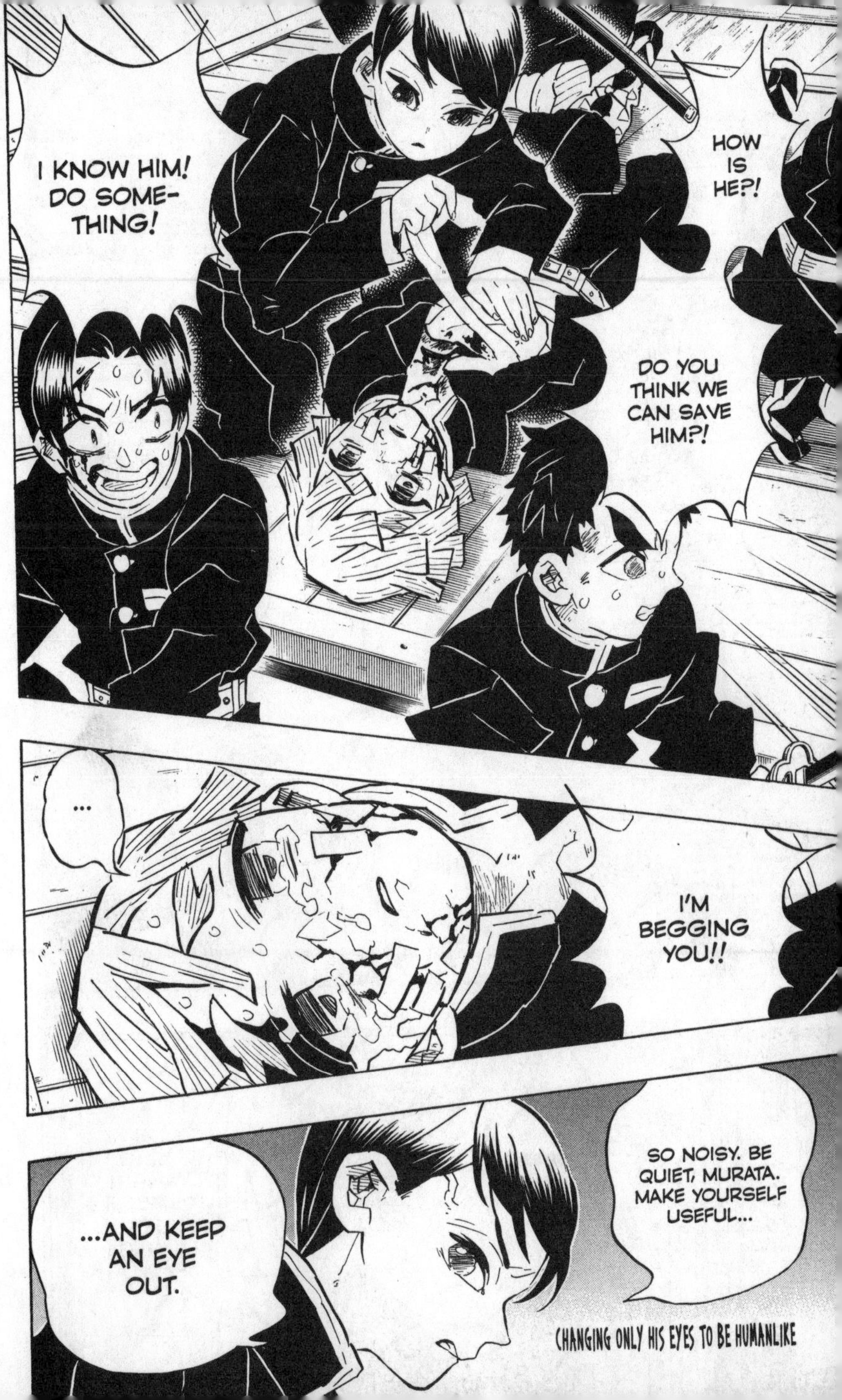
HOW IS HE?!
DO YOU THINK WE CAN SAVE HIM?!
I KNOW HIM! DO SOME-THING!
I'M BEGGING YOU!!
...
SO NOISY. BE QUIET, MURATA. MAKE YOURSELF USEFUL...
...AND KEEP AN EYE OUT.
CHANGING ONLY HIS EYES TO BE HUMANLIKE

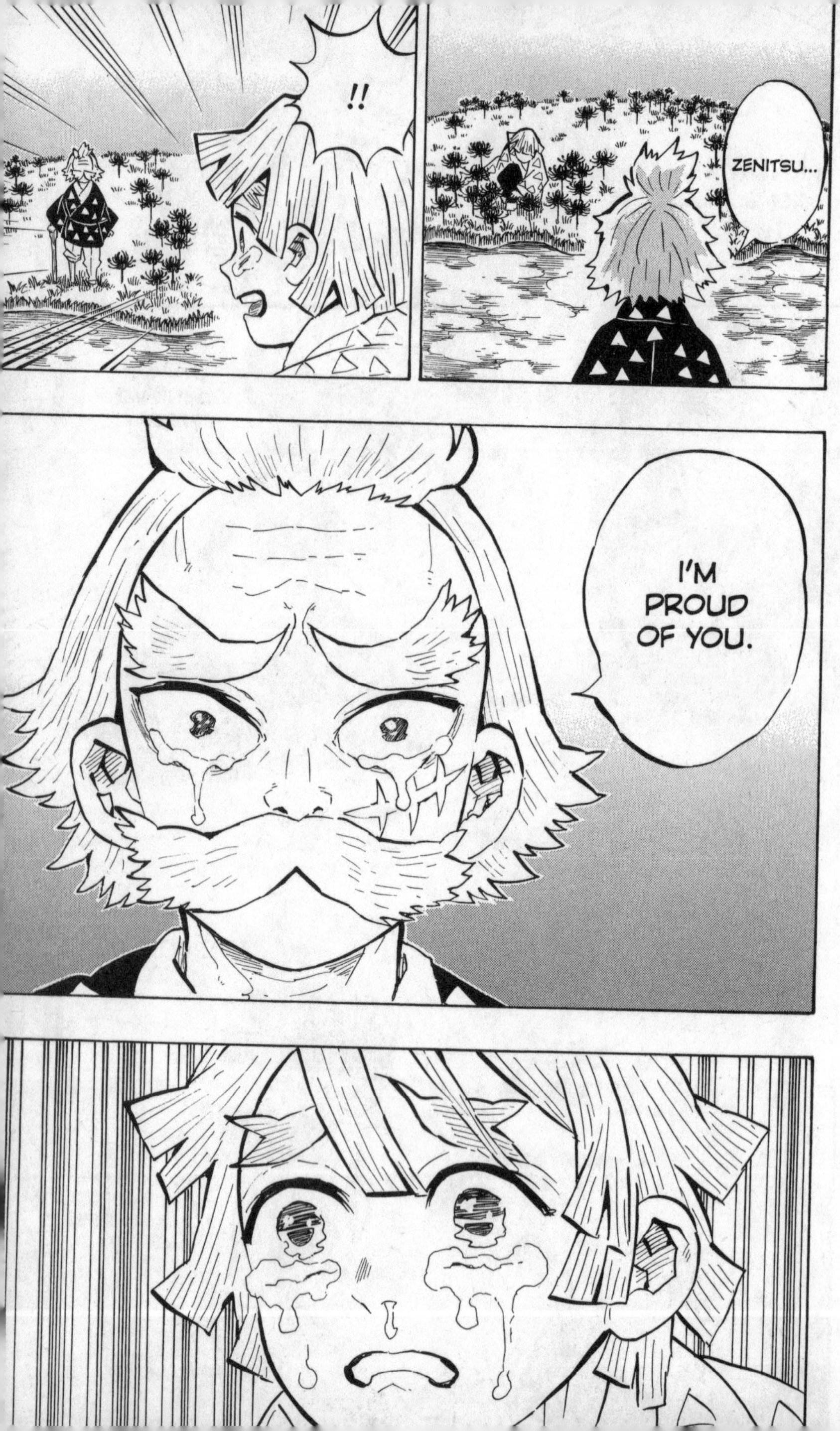
ZENITSU...
!!
I'M PROUD OF YOU.

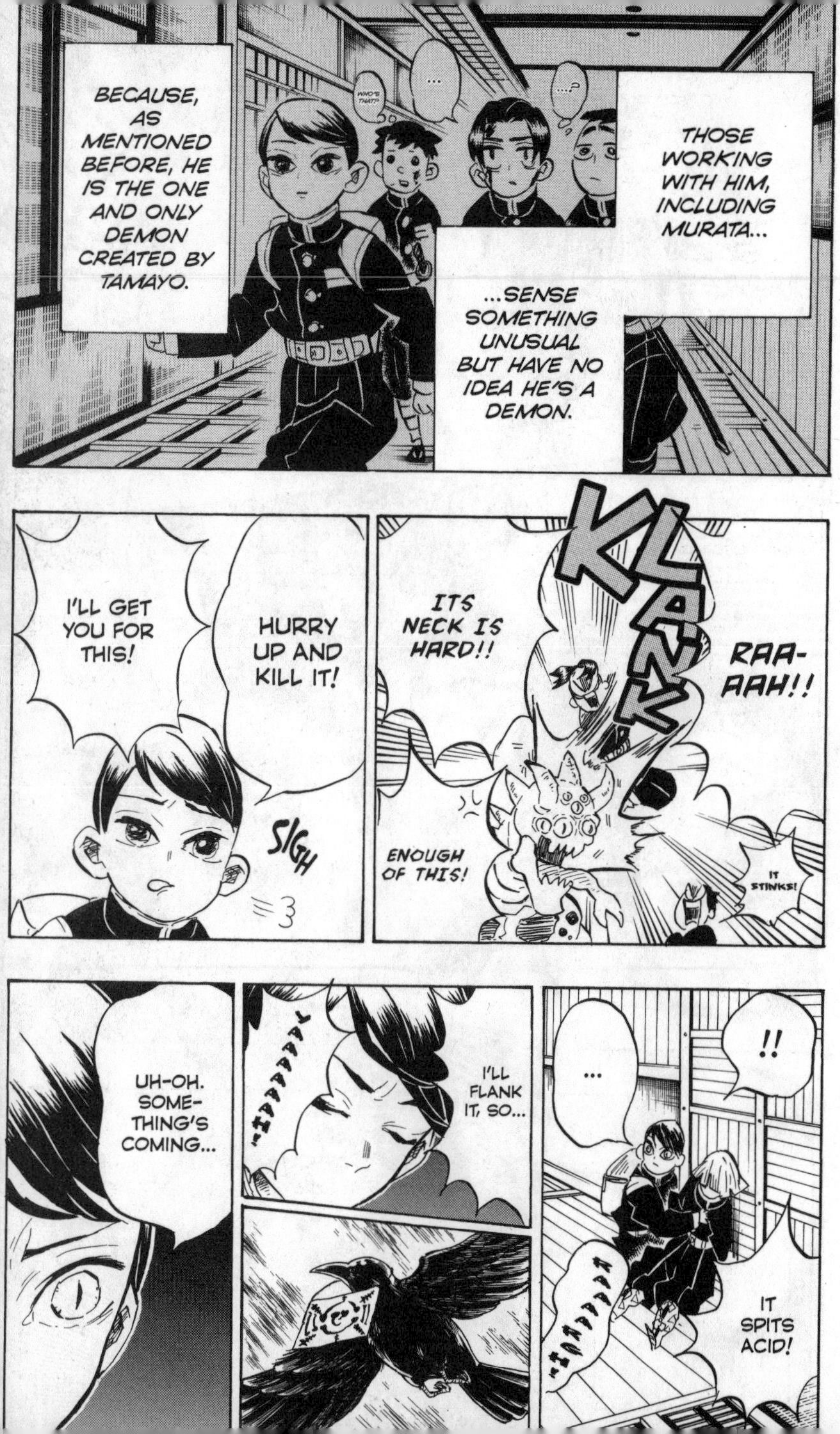
THOSE WORKING WITH HIM, INCLUDING MURATA...
...SENSE SOMETHING UNUSUAL BUT HAVE NO IDEA HE'S A DEMON.
...?
...
WHO'S THAT?
BECAUSE, AS MENTIONED BEFORE, HE IS THE ONE AND ONLY DEMON CREATED BY TAMAYO.
RAAAAH!!
KLANK
ITS NECK IS HARD!!
IT STINKS!
ENOUGH OF THIS!
HURRY UP AND KILL IT!
I'LL GET YOU FOR THIS!
SIGH
!!
...
IT SPITS ACID!
I'LL FLANK IT, SO...
YAAAAAAH!
UH-OH. SOME-THING'S COMING...

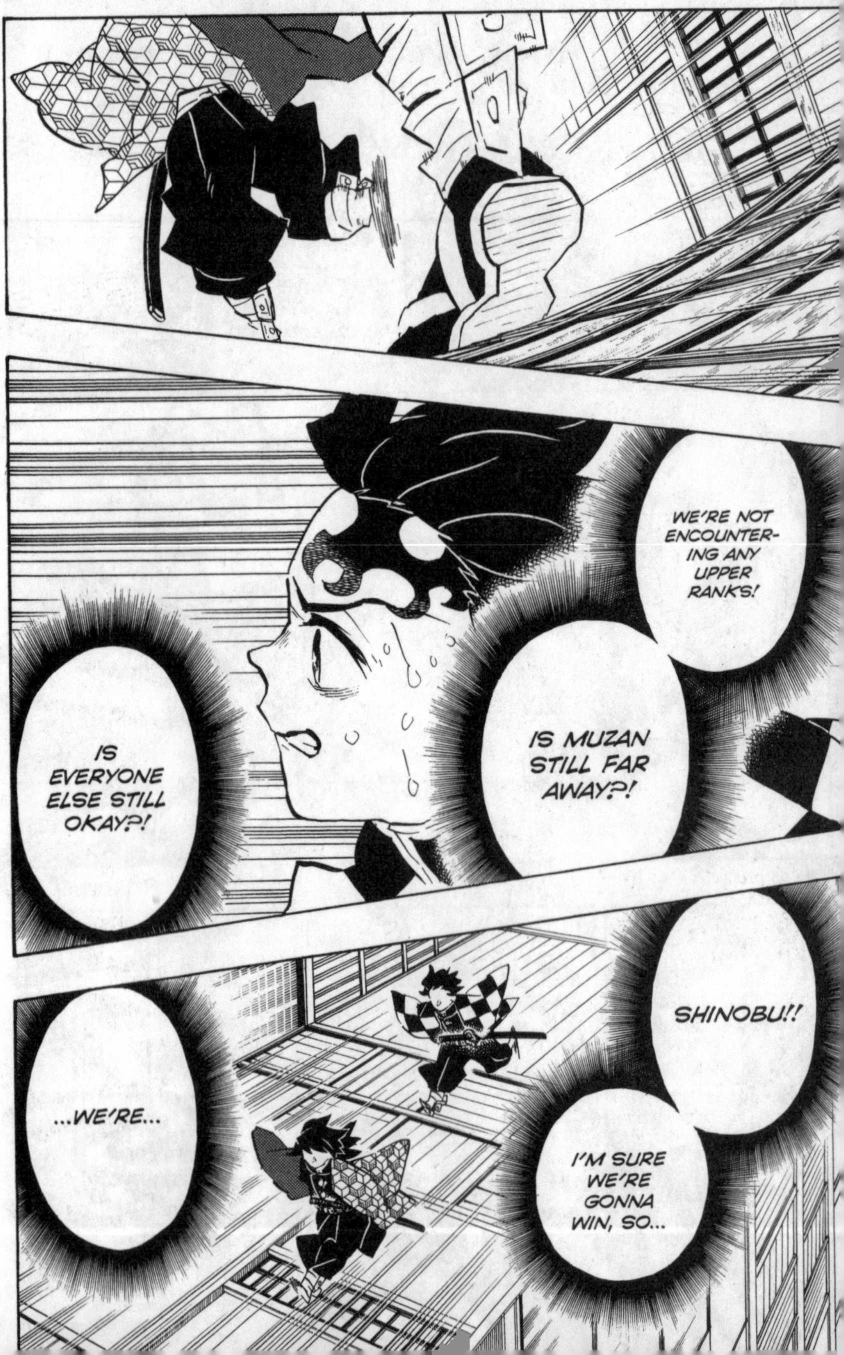
WE'RE NOT ENCOUNTER-ING ANY UPPER RANKS!
IS MUZAN STILL FAR AWAY?!
IS EVERYONE ELSE STILL OKAY?!
SHINOBU!!
I'M SURE WE'RE GONNA WIN, SO...
...WE'RE...

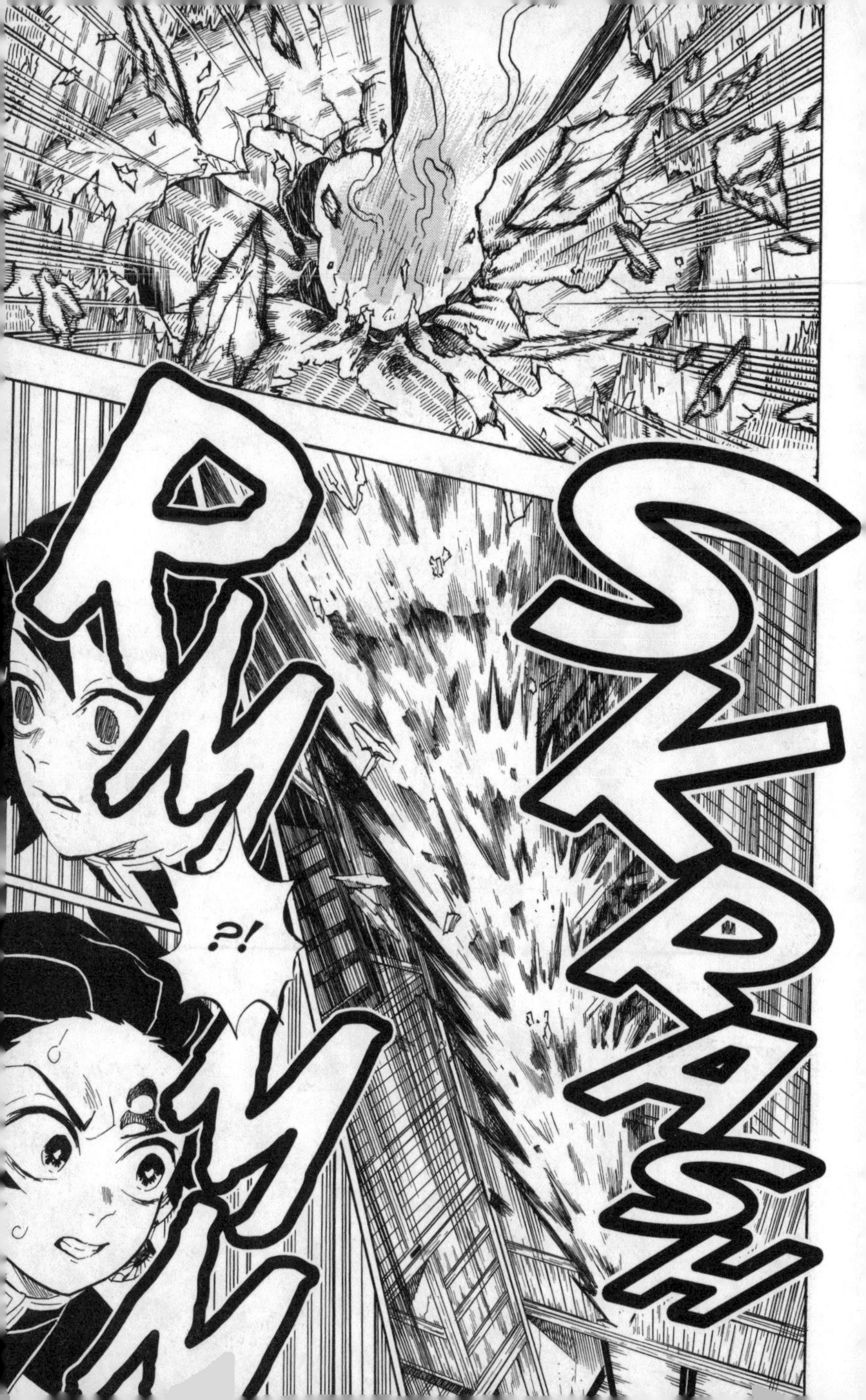
SMASH
?!

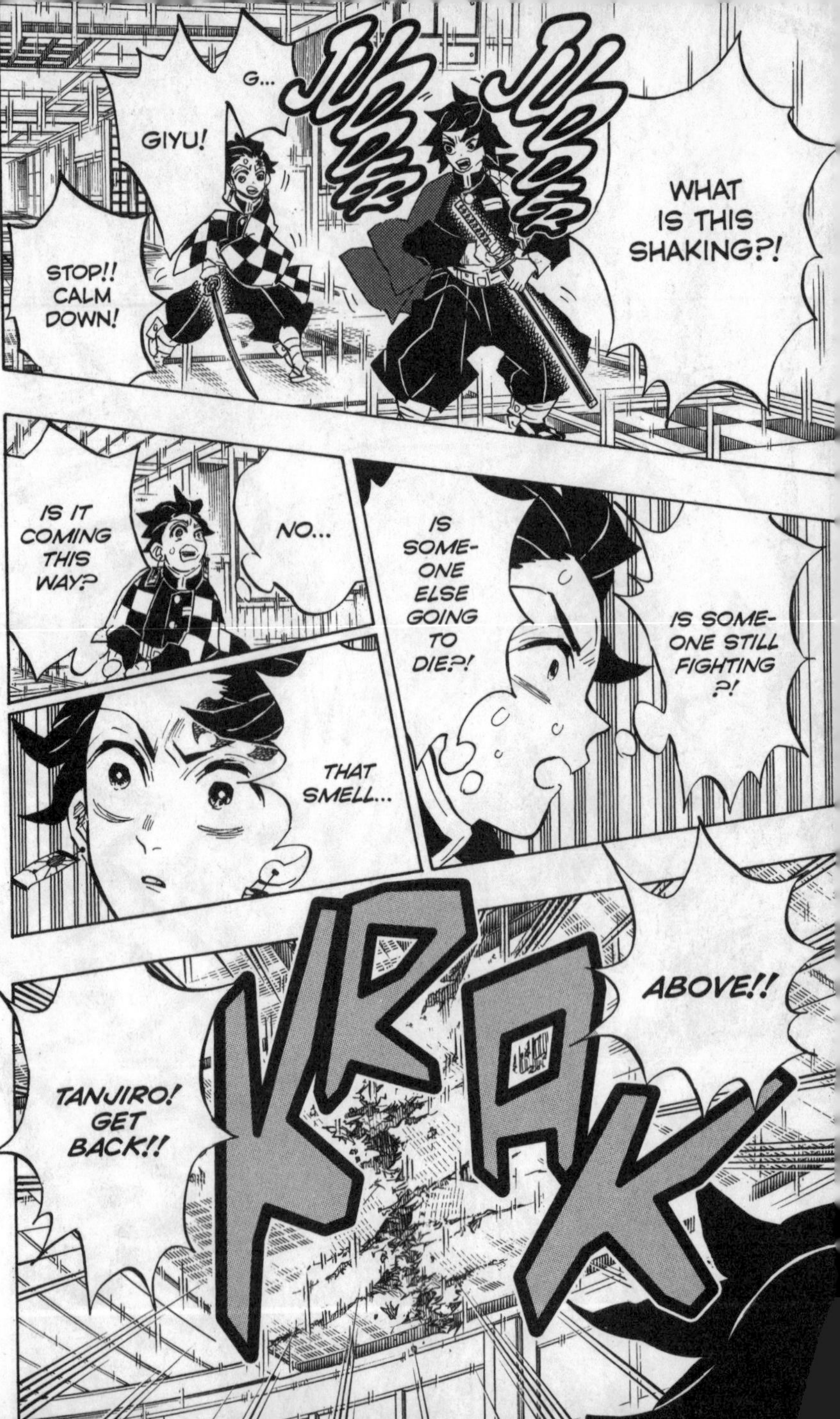
WHAT IS THIS SHAKING?!
G...
GIYU!
STOP!! CALM DOWN!
IS SOME-ONE STILL FIGHTING ?!
IS SOME-ONE ELSE GOING TO DIE?!
NO...
IS IT COMING THIS WAY?
THAT SMELL...
ABOVE!!
TANJIRO! GET BACK!!

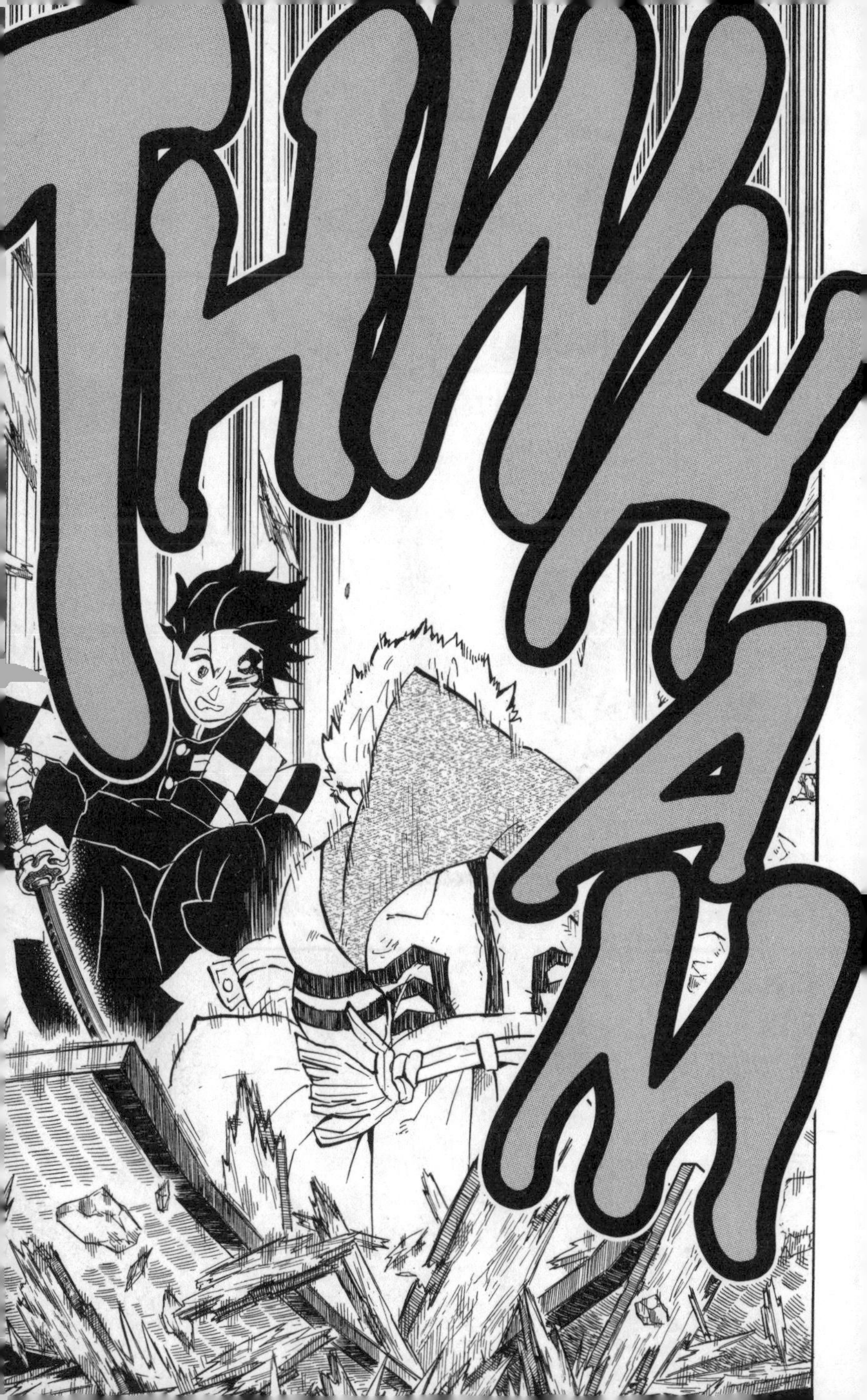

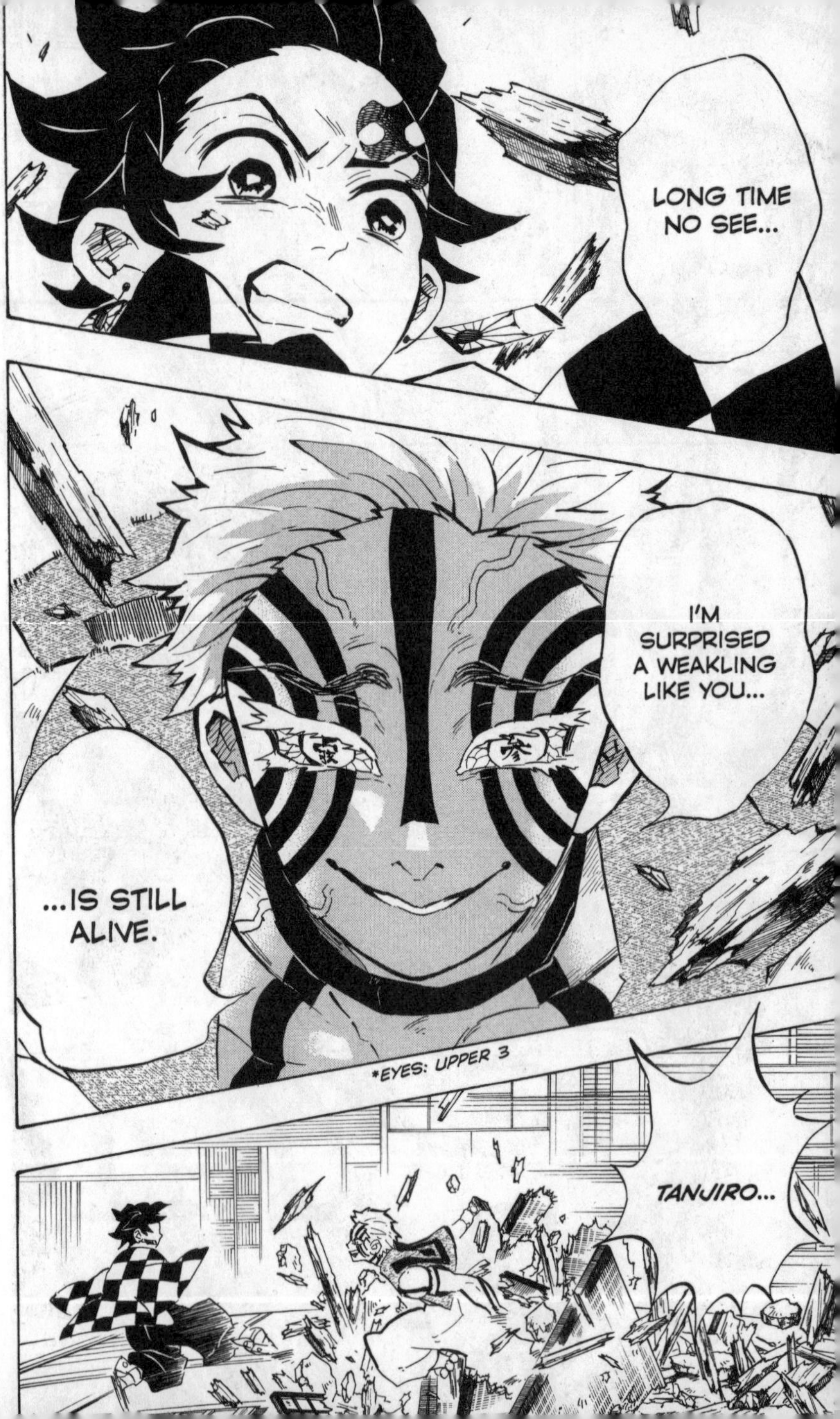
LONG TIME NO SEE...
I'M SURPRISED A WEAKLING LIKE YOU...
...IS STILL ALIVE.
*EYES: UPPER 3
TANJIRO...

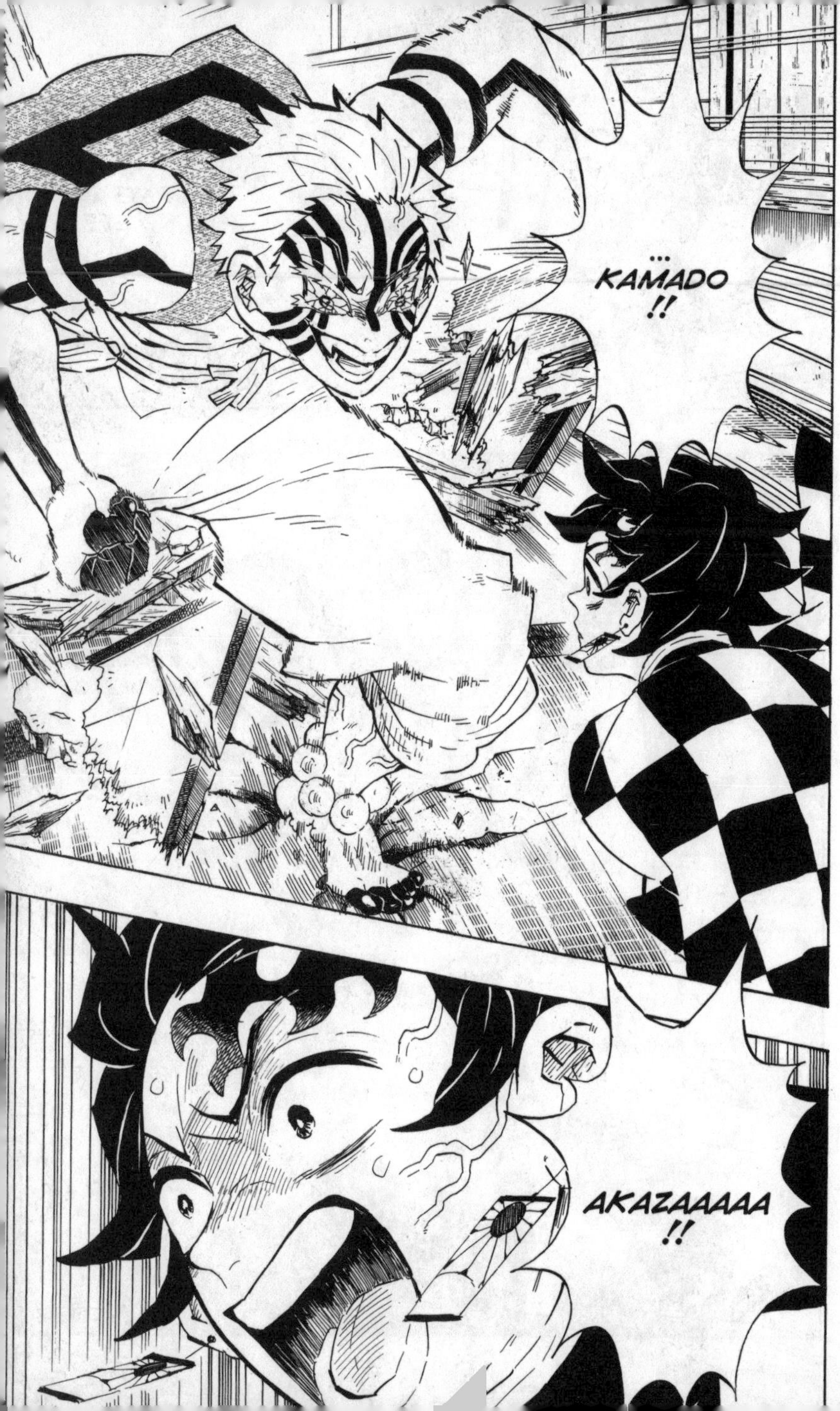
...KAMADO !!
AKAZAAAAA !!

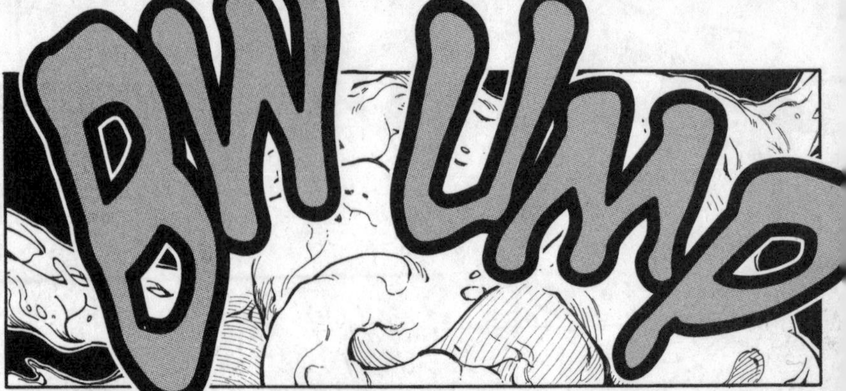
BWUMP
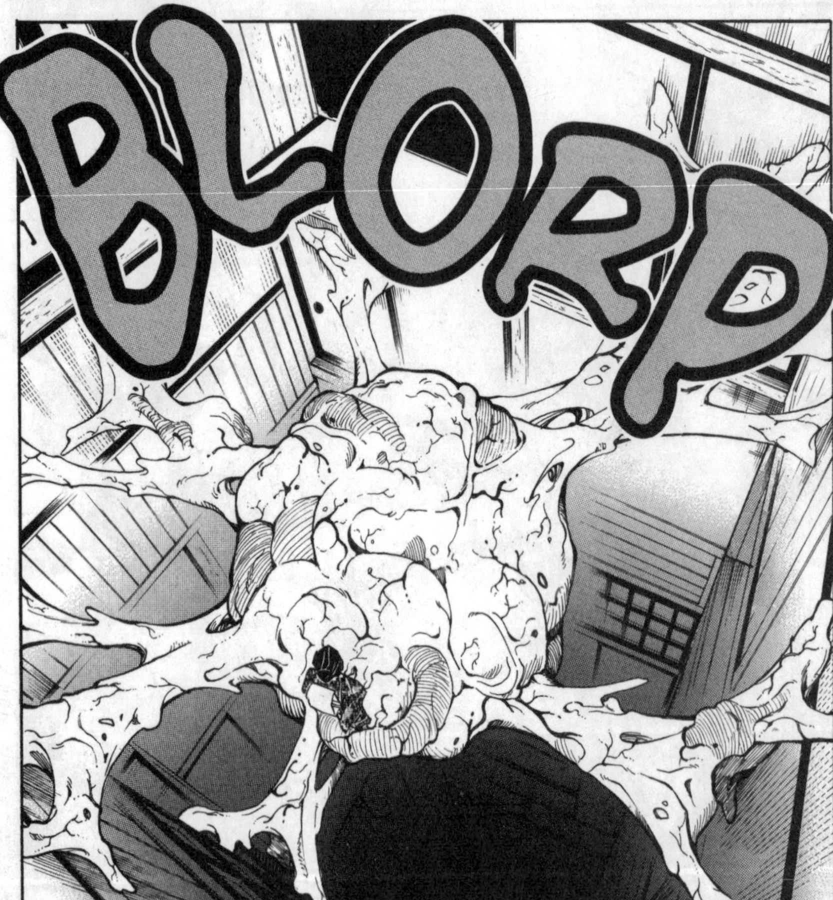
BLORP

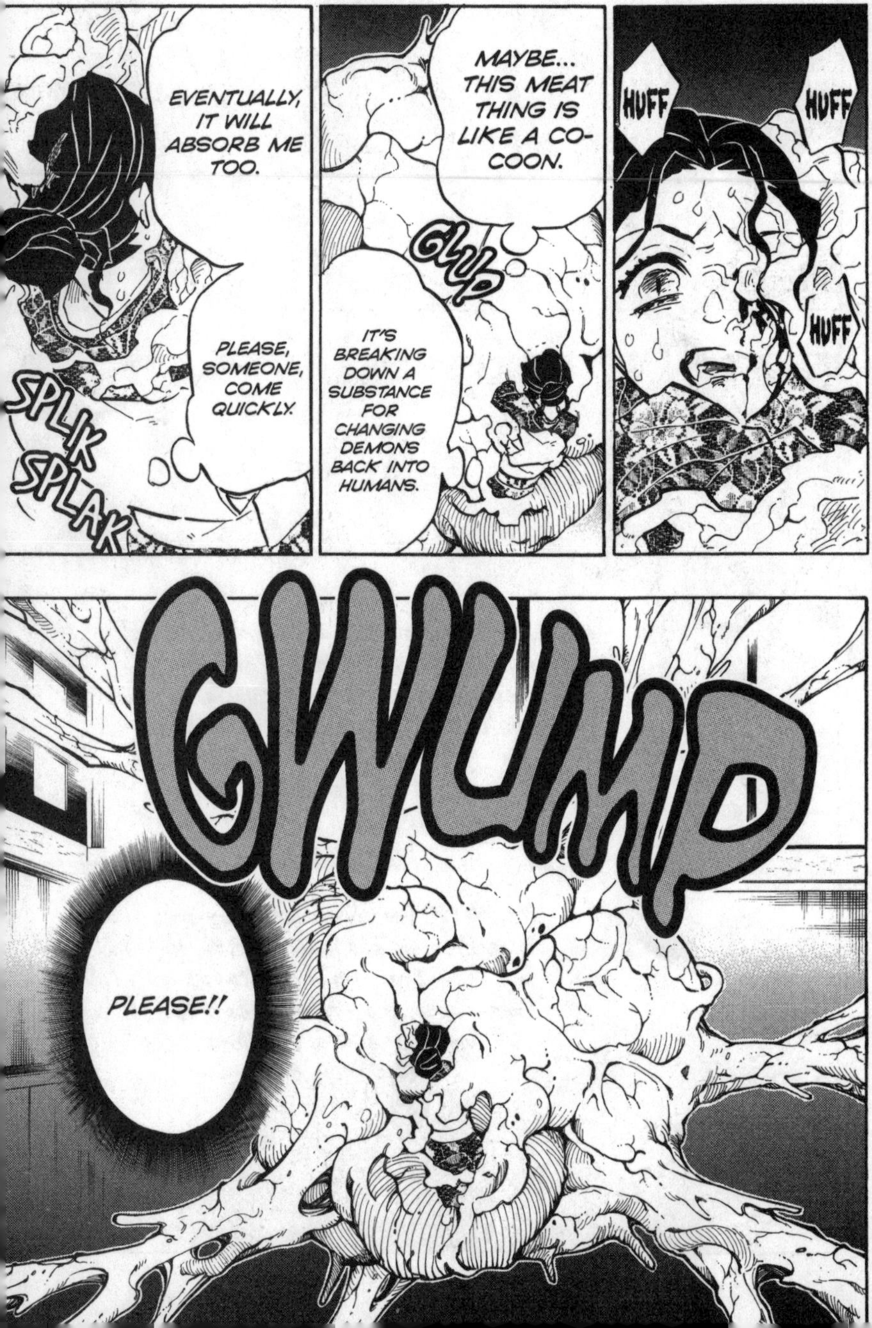
HUFF
HUFF
HUFF
MAYBE... THIS MEAT THING IS LIKE A CO-COON.
GLUP
IT'S BREAKING DOWN A SUBSTANCE FOR CHANGING DEMONS BACK INTO HUMANS.
EVENTUALLY, IT WILL ABSORB ME TOO.
PLEASE, SOMEONE, COME QUICKLY.
SPLIK SPLAK
GWUMP
PLEASE!!

Murata was all alone after demons killed his family, so he joined the Demon Slayer Corps. He uses Water Breathing, but he's so weak that he can't see any water.

(Note) The swordsmen don't actually produce water, but it looks that way to people watching.

(Note) Besides Urokodaki, there are other trainers who teach Water Breathing. Water Breathing is easy for beginners, so more swordsmen use it than any other style of breathing.

I work hard, so don't call me weak!

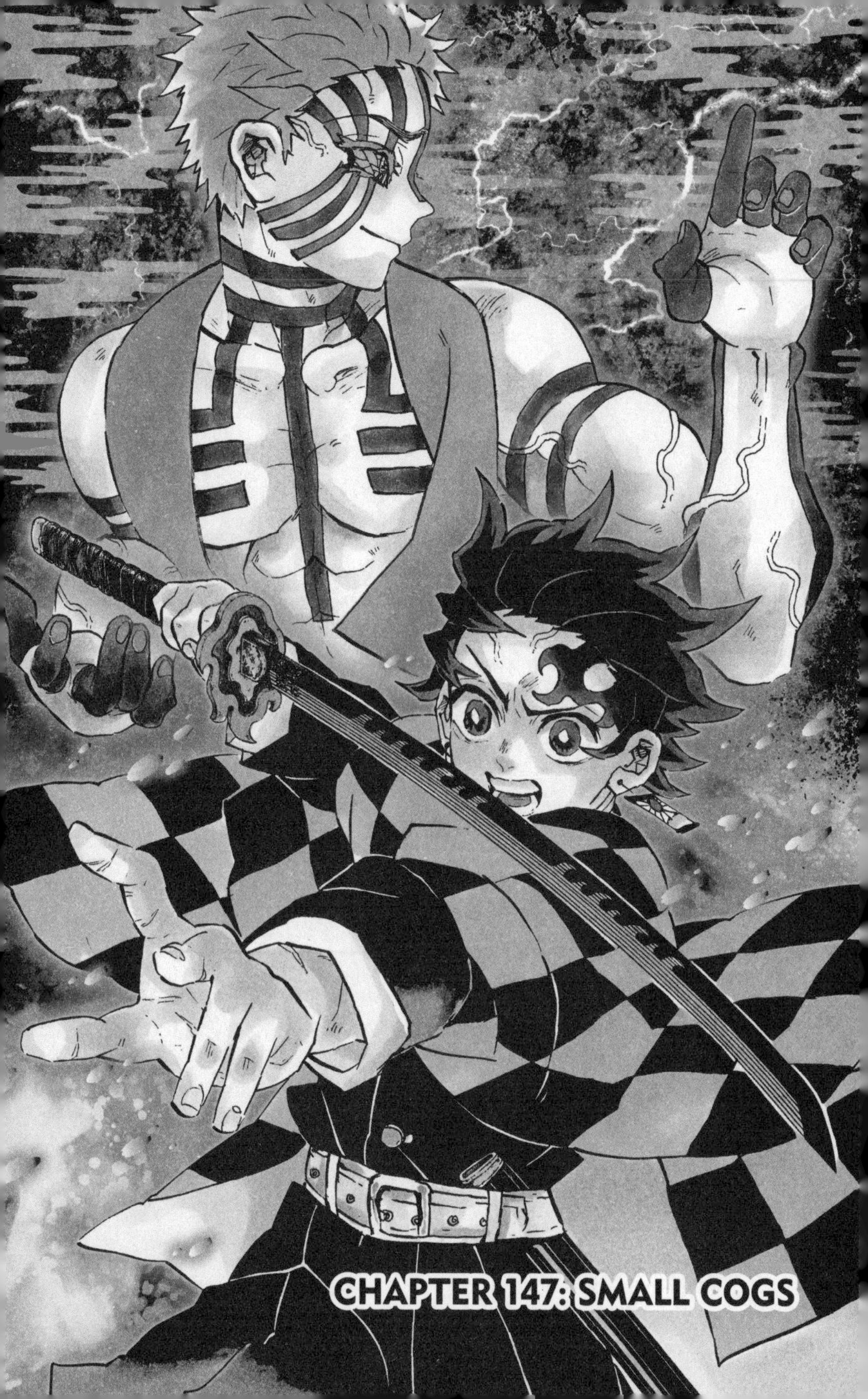
CHAPTER 147: SMALL COGS

At Final Selection in volume 1, the black-haired child holding a lantern was Kiriya. He's the only boy among the five children, so he became the new head of the household in place of his father.

Same person

↔

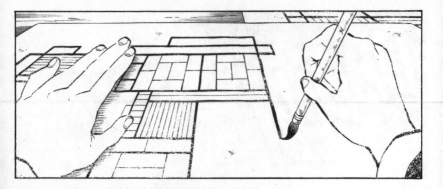

DEFINITELY DO NOT STOP YOUR HANDS.

DON'T CRY.

UNDER-STOOD.

WE WILL NOT LOSE.

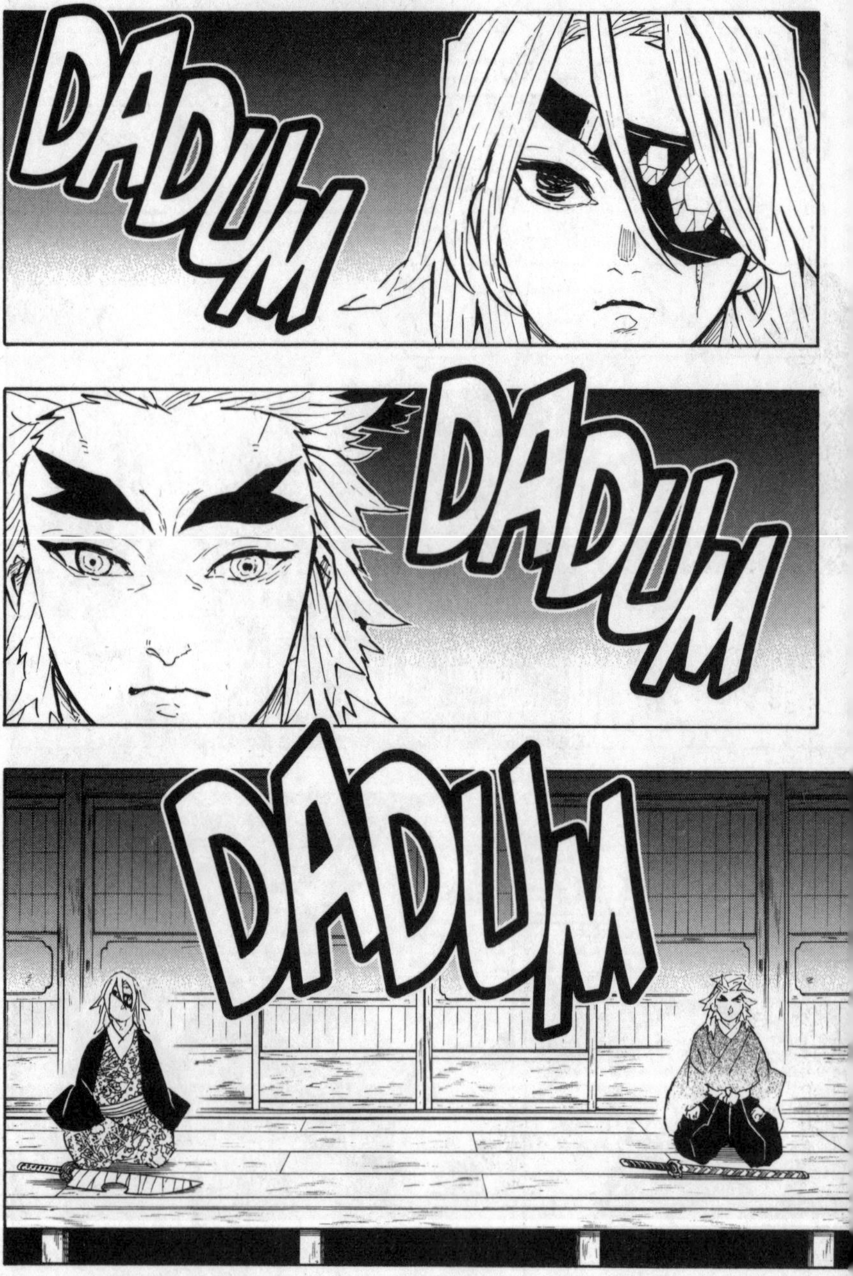
DADUM
DADUM
DADUM

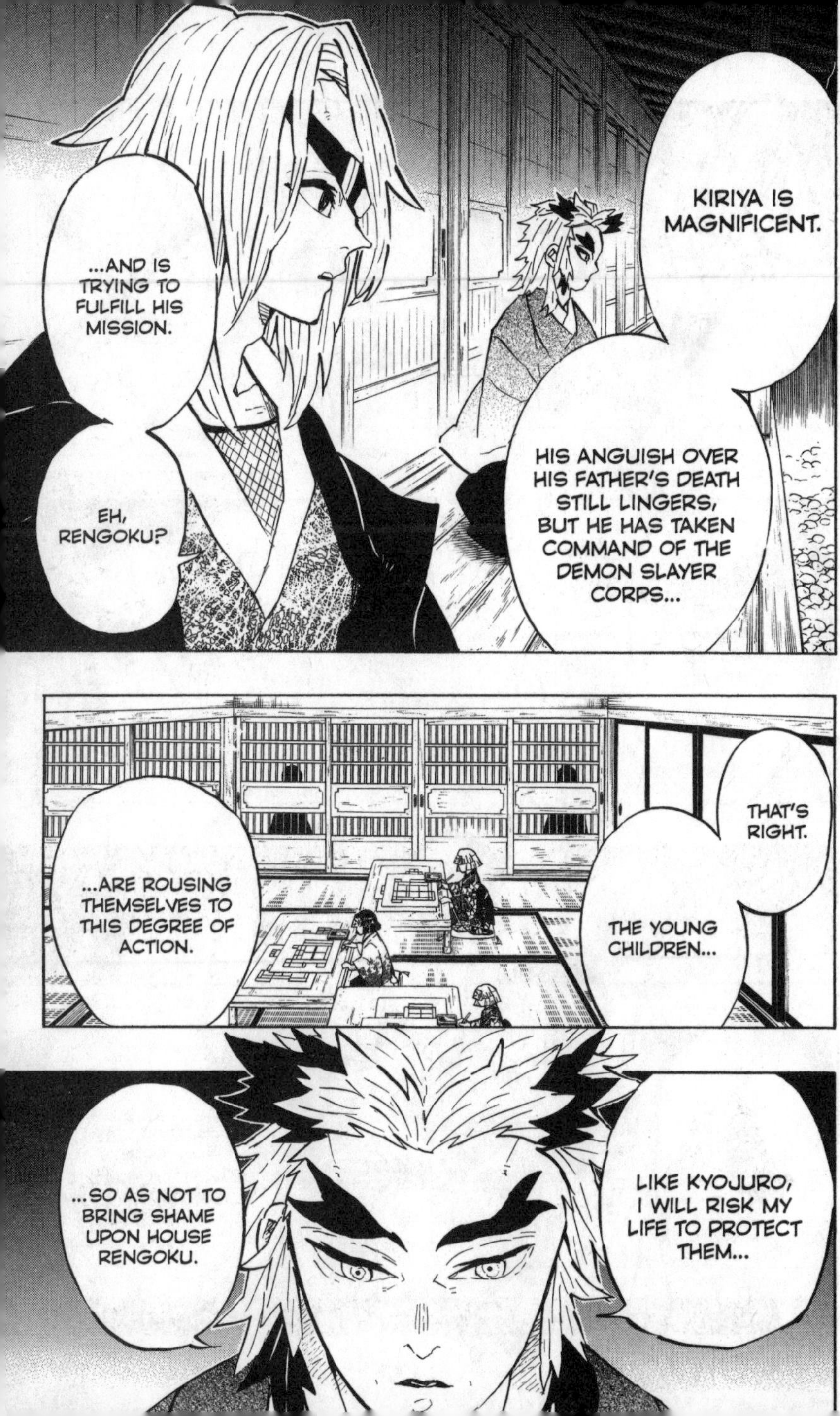
KIRIYA IS MAGNIFICENT.
HIS ANGUISH OVER HIS FATHER'S DEATH STILL LINGERS, BUT HE HAS TAKEN COMMAND OF THE DEMON SLAYER CORPS...
...AND IS TRYING TO FULFILL HIS MISSION.
EH, RENGOKU?
THAT'S RIGHT.
THE YOUNG CHILDREN...
...ARE ROUSING THEMSELVES TO THIS DEGREE OF ACTION.
LIKE KYOJURO, I WILL RISK MY LIFE TO PROTECT THEM...
...SO AS NOT TO BRING SHAME UPON HOUSE RENGOKU.

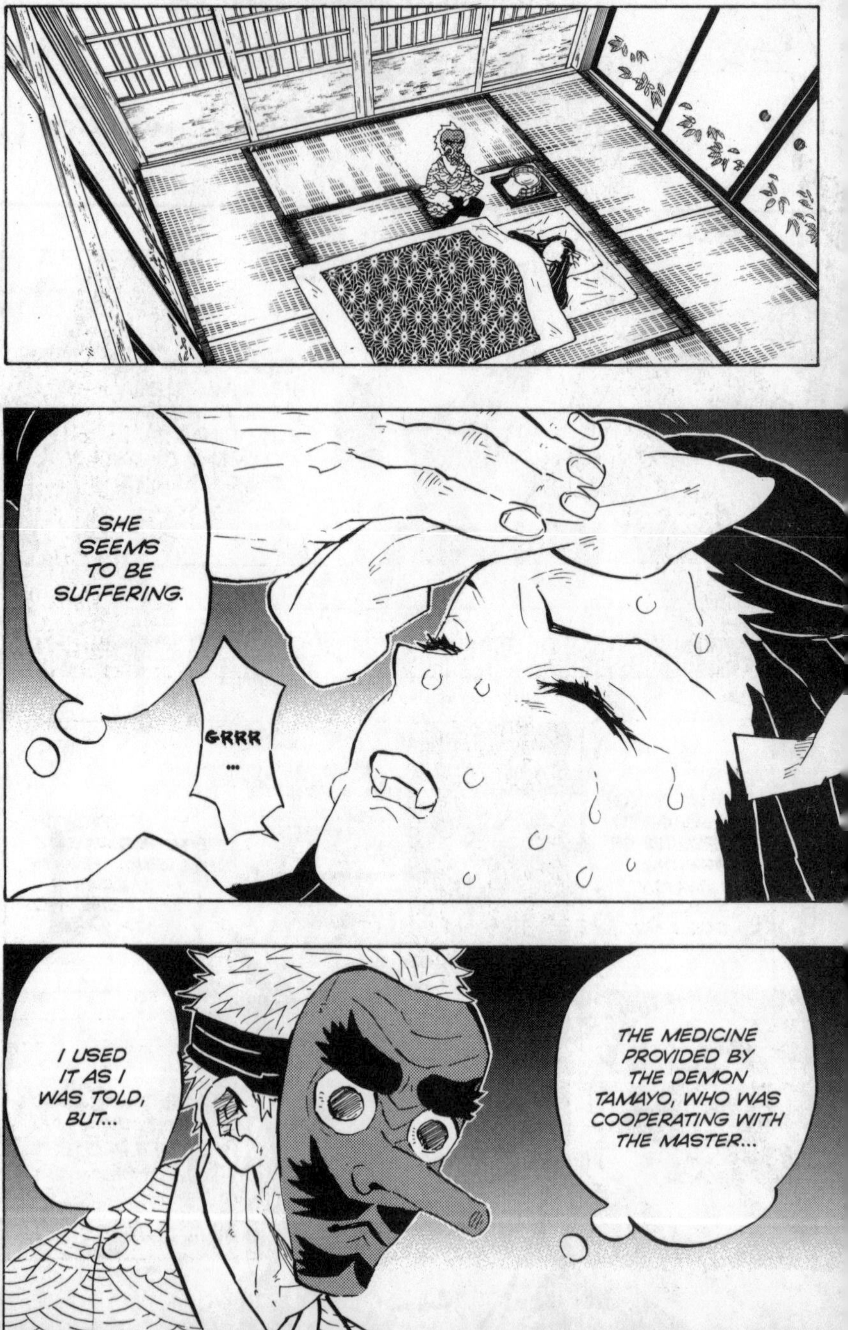
SHE SEEMS TO BE SUFFERING.
GRRR...
THE MEDICINE PROVIDED BY THE DEMON TAMAYO, WHO WAS COOPERATING WITH THE MASTER...
I USED IT AS I WAS TOLD, BUT...

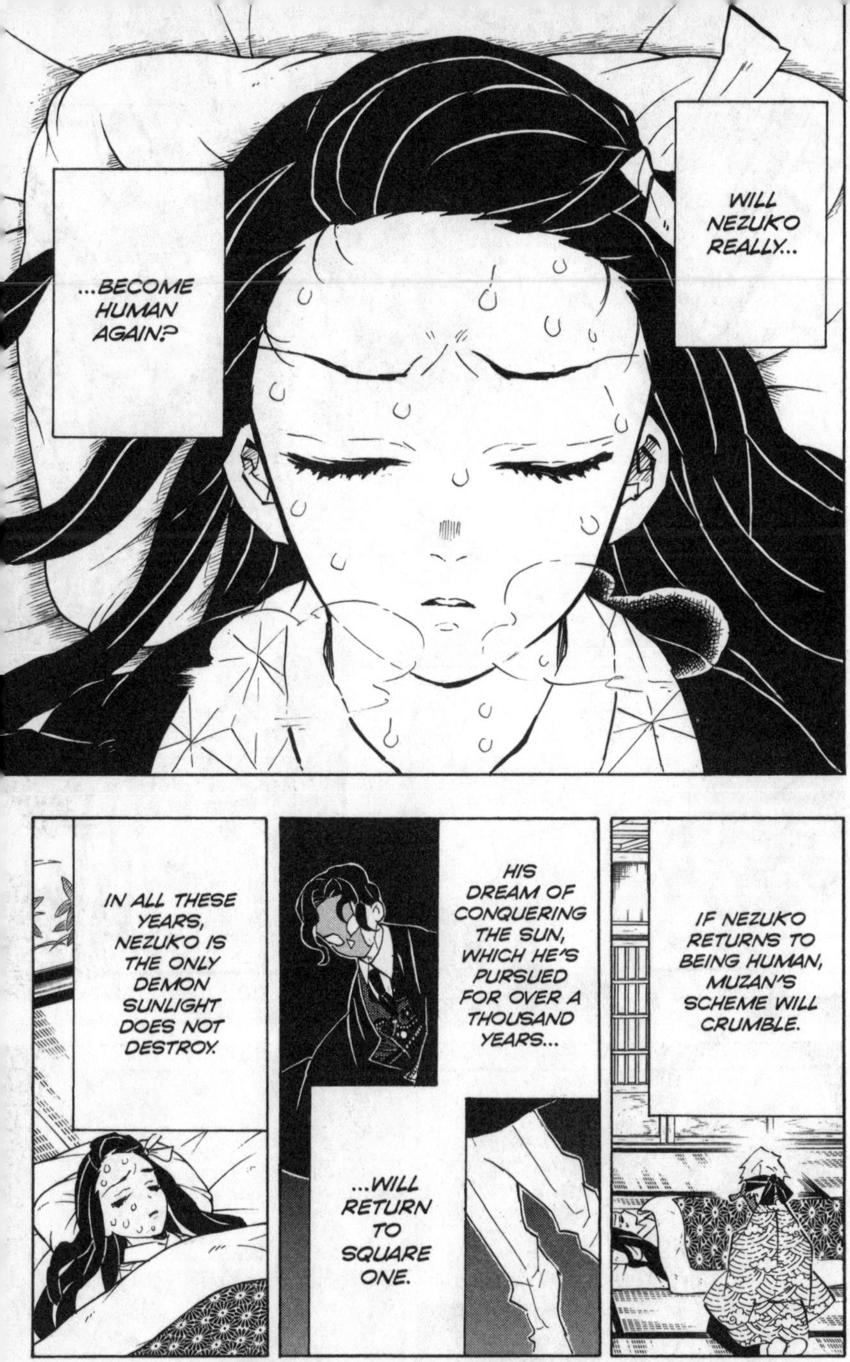
WILL NEZUKO REALLY...
...BECOME HUMAN AGAIN?
IF NEZUKO RETURNS TO BEING HUMAN, MUZAN'S SCHEME WILL CRUMBLE.
HIS DREAM OF CONQUERING THE SUN, WHICH HE'S PURSUED FOR OVER A THOUSAND YEARS...
...WILL RETURN TO SQUARE ONE.
IN ALL THESE YEARS, NEZUKO IS THE ONLY DEMON SUNLIGHT DOES NOT DESTROY.

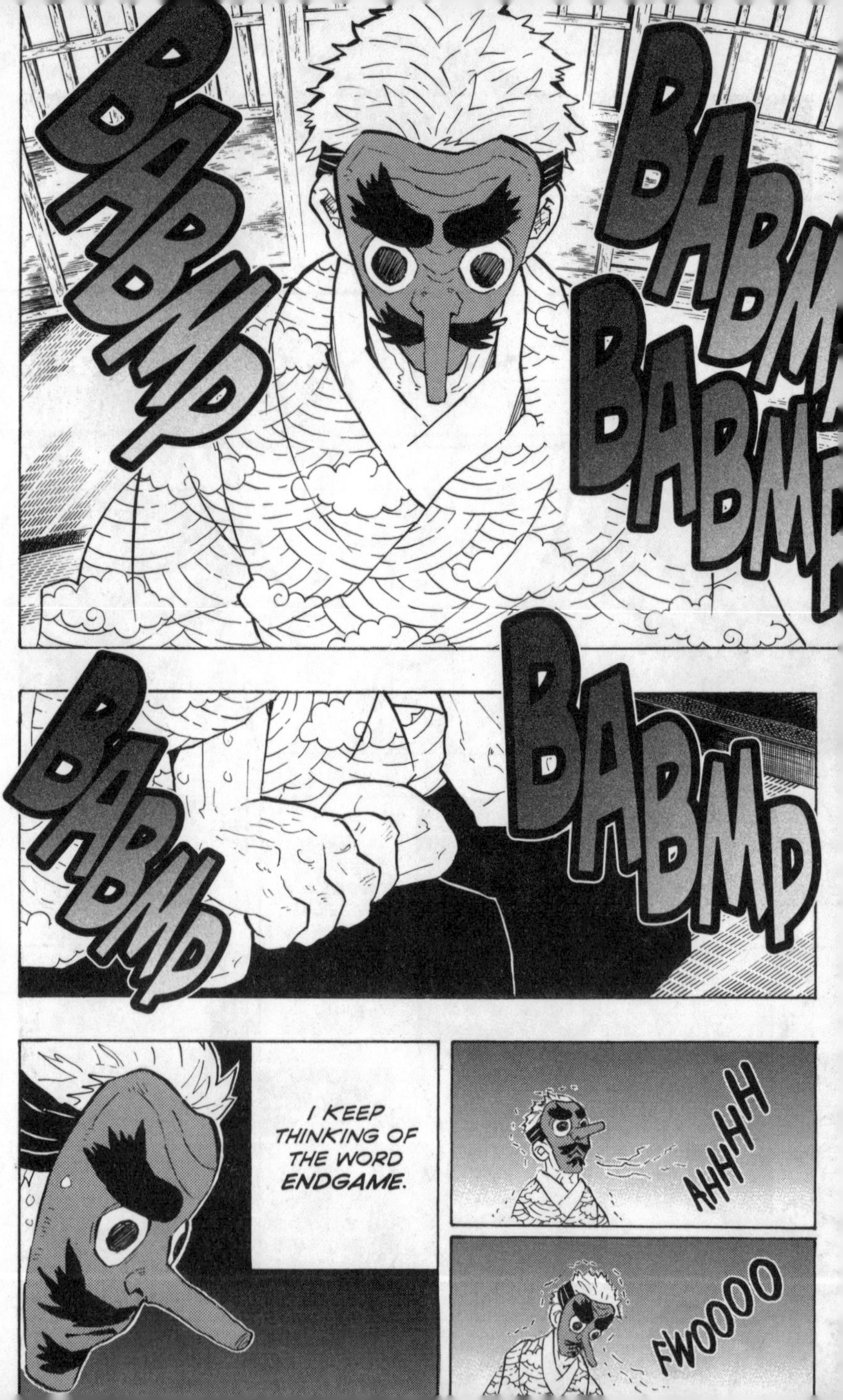
BABM
BABM
BABMP
BABMD
BABMD
AHHHH
FWOOOO
I KEEP THINKING OF THE WORD ENDGAME.

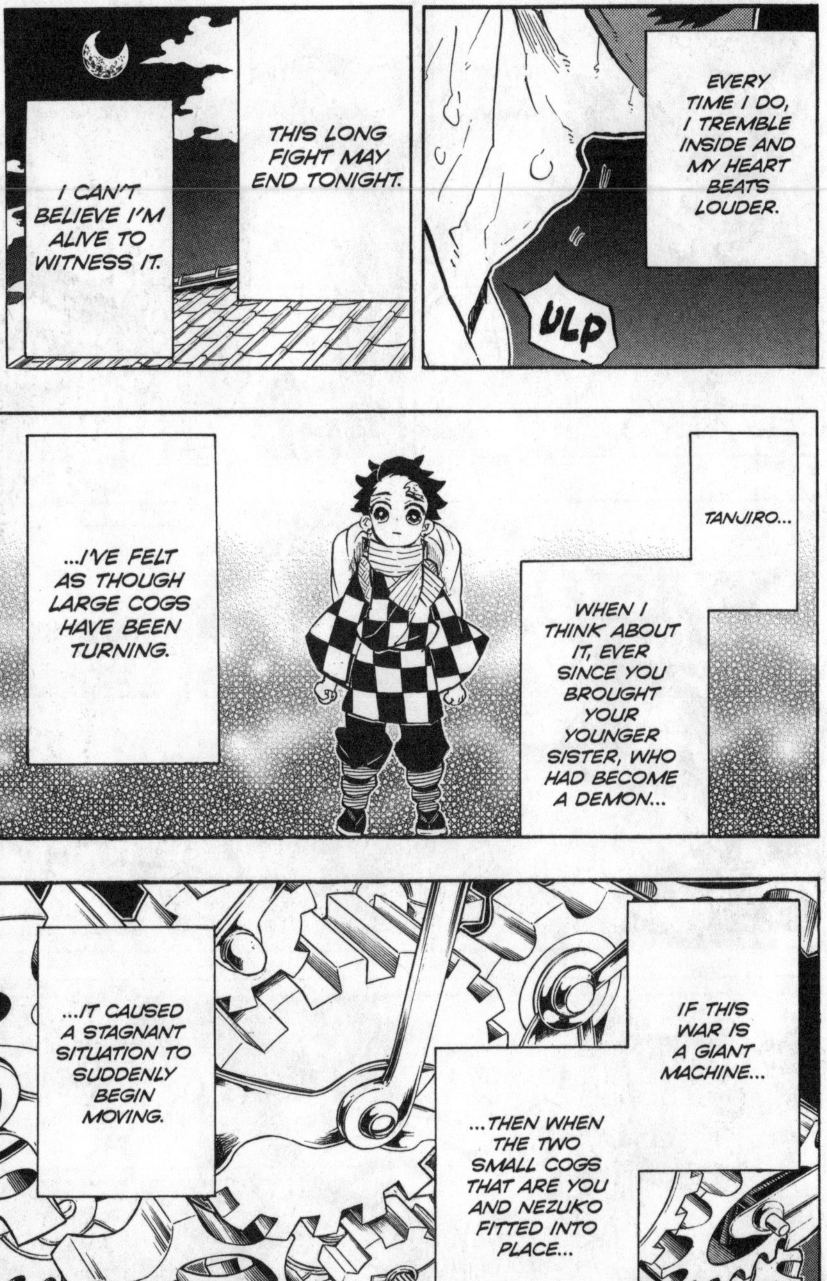
EVERY TIME I DO, I TREMBLE INSIDE AND MY HEART BEATS LOUDER.
ULP
THIS LONG FIGHT MAY END TONIGHT.
I CAN'T BELIEVE I'M ALIVE TO WITNESS IT.
TANJIRO...
WHEN I THINK ABOUT IT, EVER SINCE YOU BROUGHT YOUR YOUNGER SISTER, WHO HAD BECOME A DEMON...
...I'VE FELT AS THOUGH LARGE COGS HAVE BEEN TURNING.
IF THIS WAR IS A GIANT MACHINE...
...THEN WHEN THE TWO SMALL COGS THAT ARE YOU AND NEZUKO FITTED INTO PLACE...
...IT CAUSED A STAGNANT SITUATION TO SUDDENLY BEGIN MOVING.

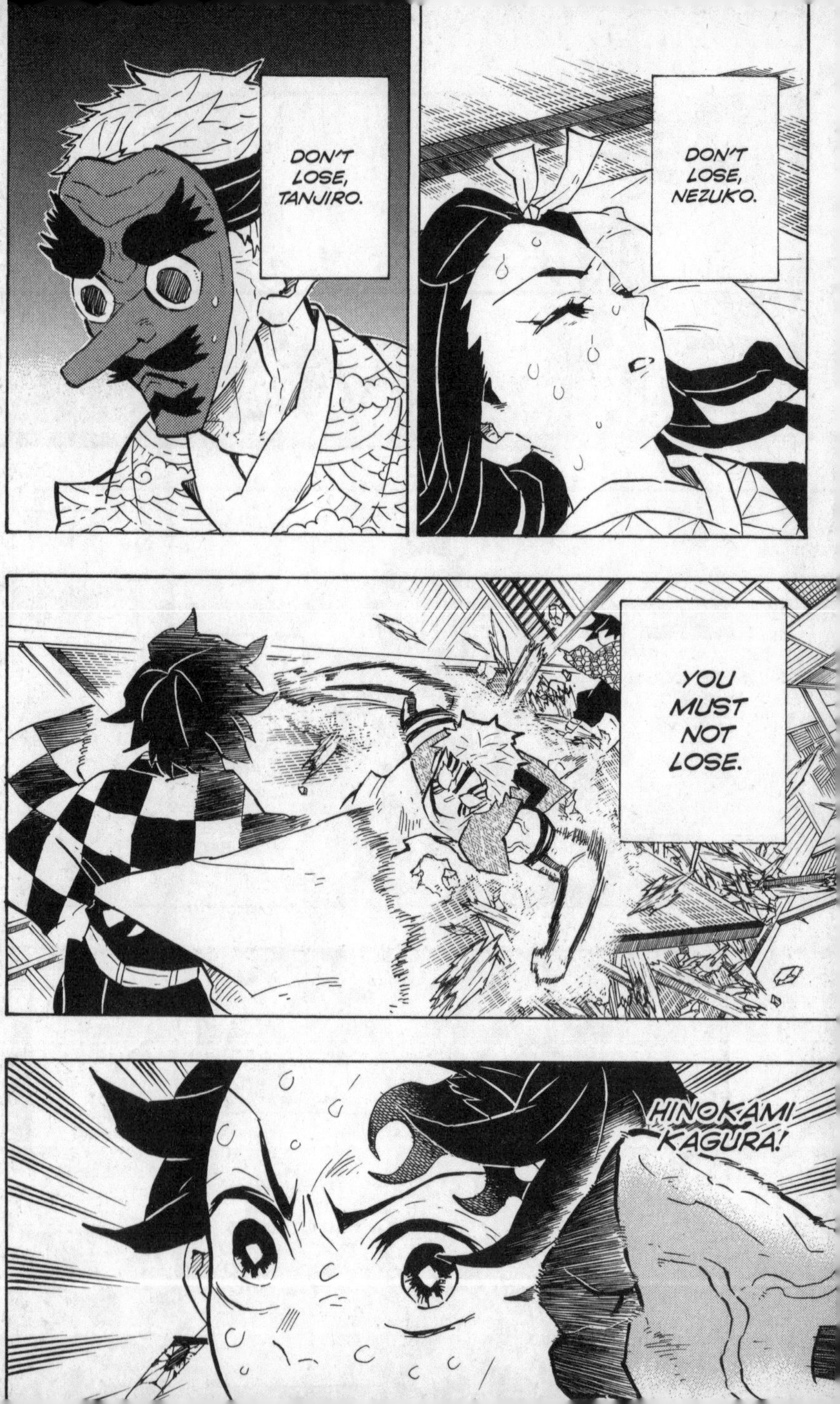
DON'T LOSE, NEZUKO.
DON'T LOSE, TANJIRO.
YOU MUST NOT LOSE.
HINOKAMI KAGURA!

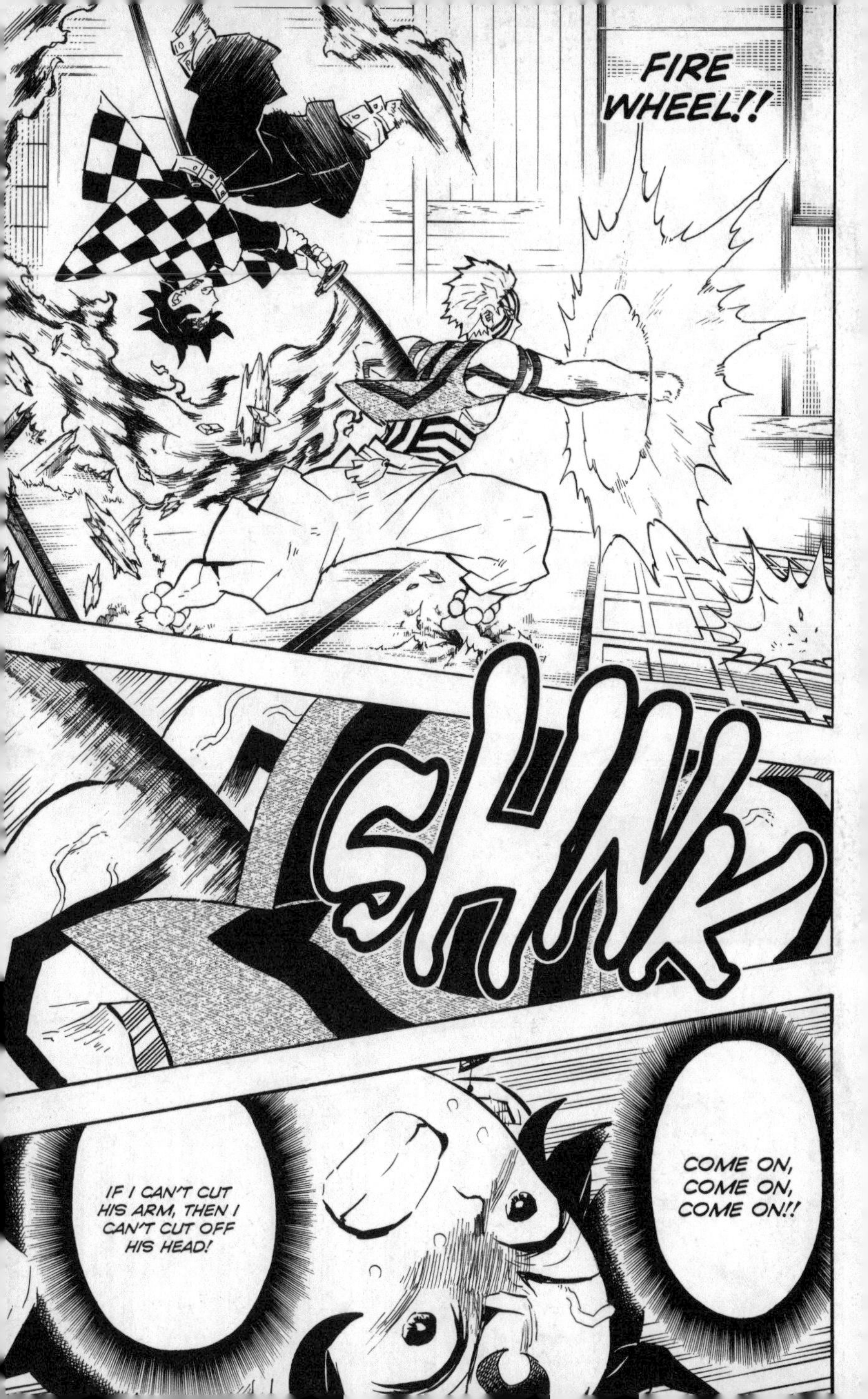
FIRE WHEEL!!
SHLK
COME ON, COME ON, COME ON!!
IF I CAN'T CUT HIS ARM, THEN I CAN'T CUT OFF HIS HEAD!

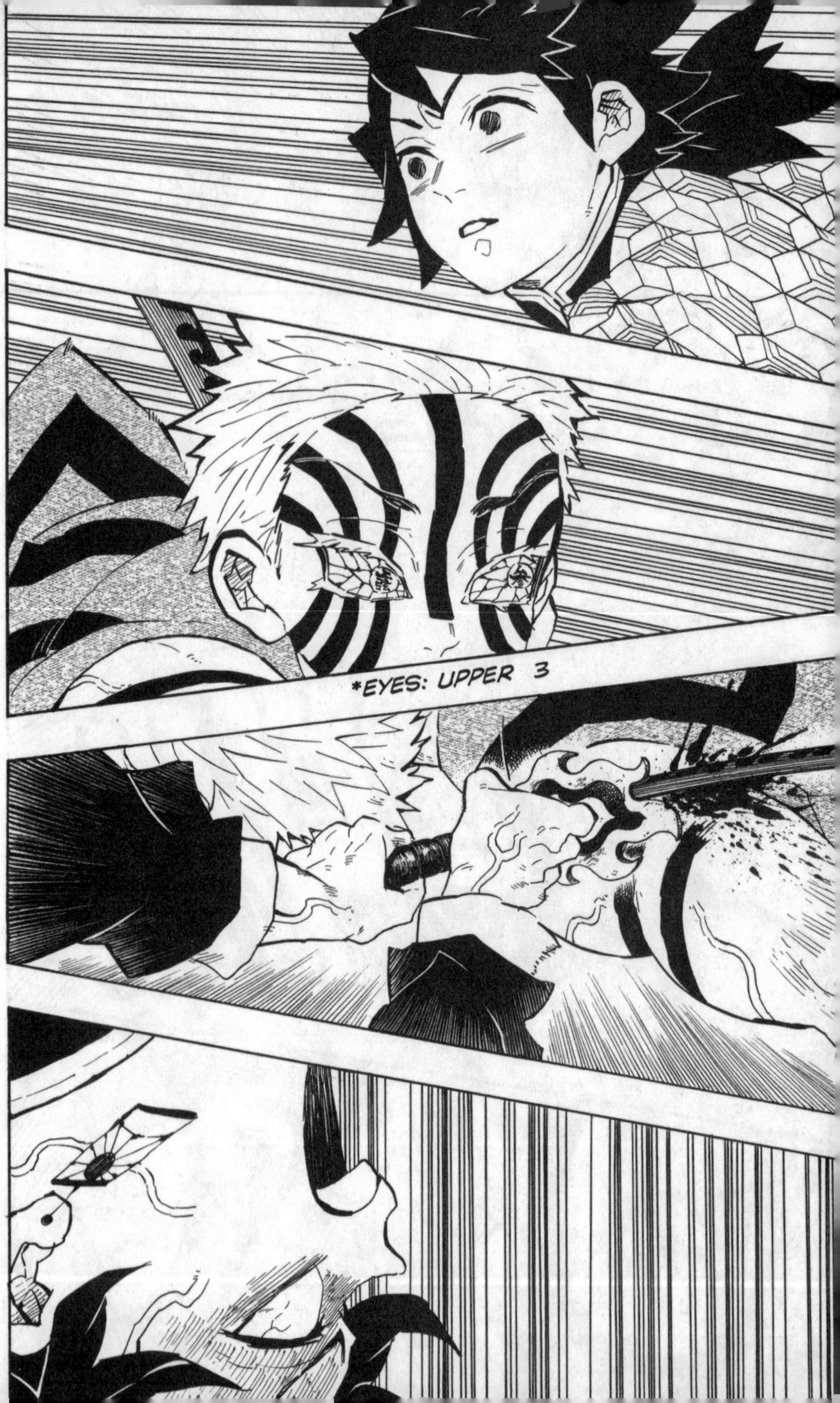
*EYES: UPPER 3

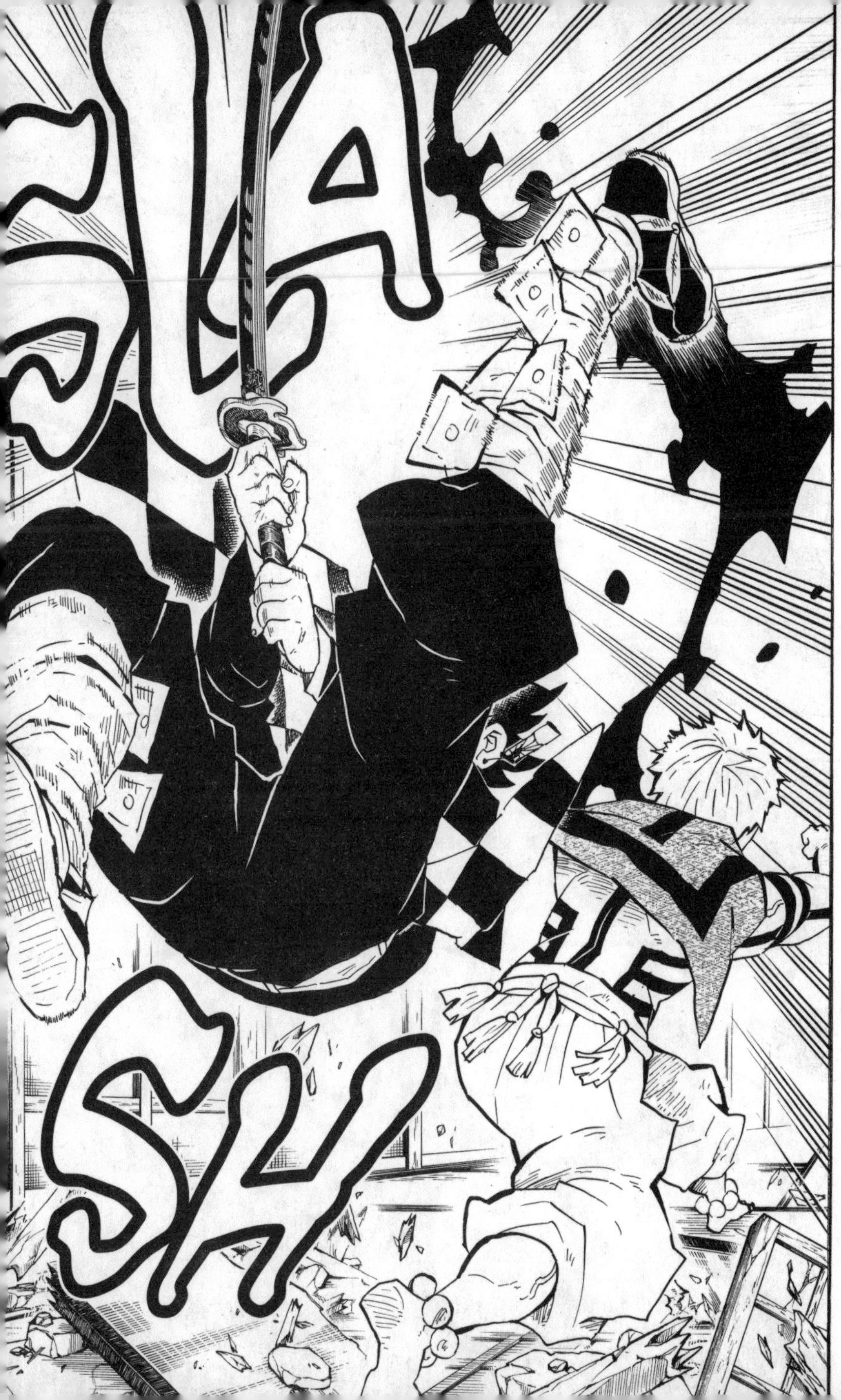
SLA
SH

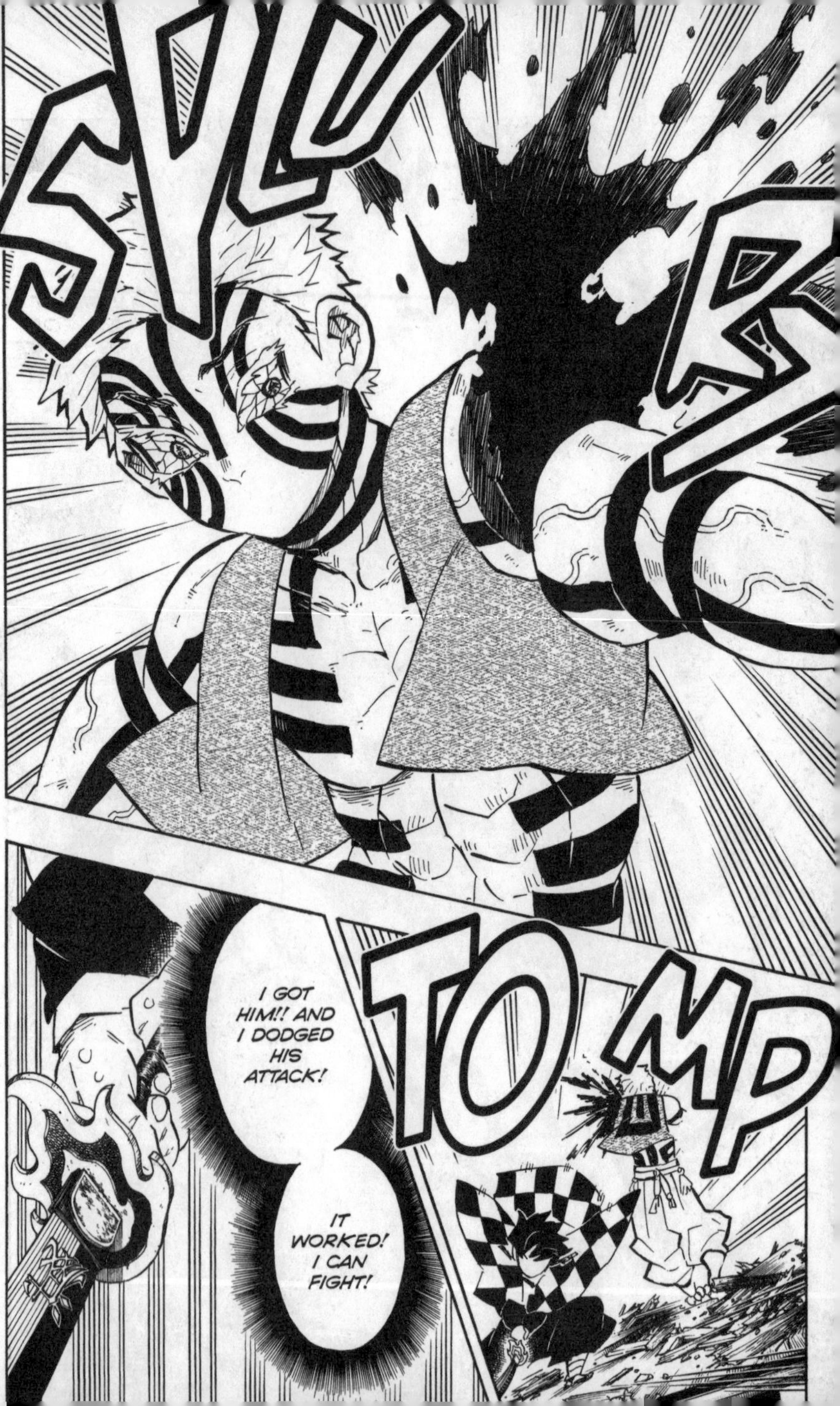
TOMP
I GOT HIM!! AND I DODGED HIS ATTACK!
IT WORKED! I CAN FIGHT!

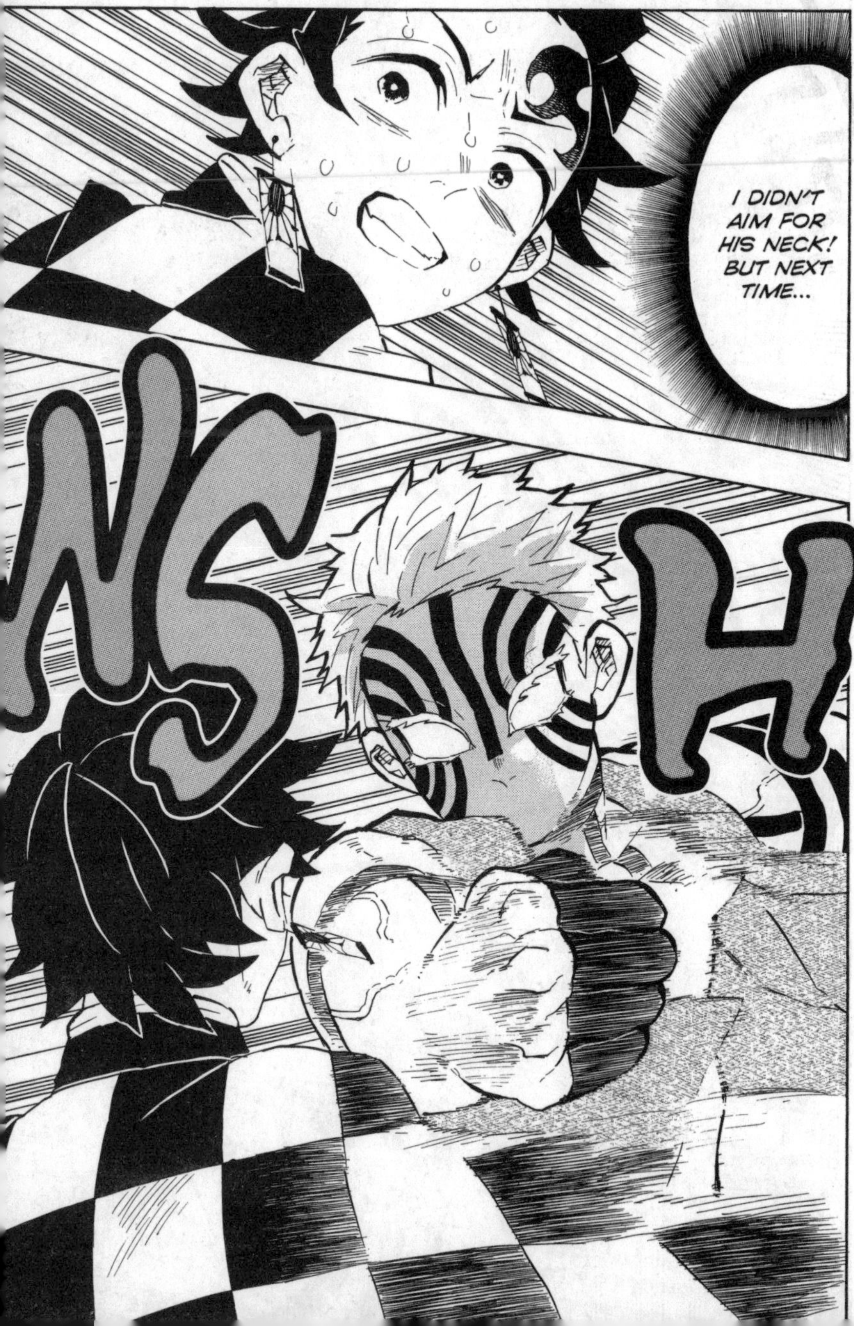
I DIDN'T AIM FOR HIS NECK! BUT NEXT TIME...
WNSH

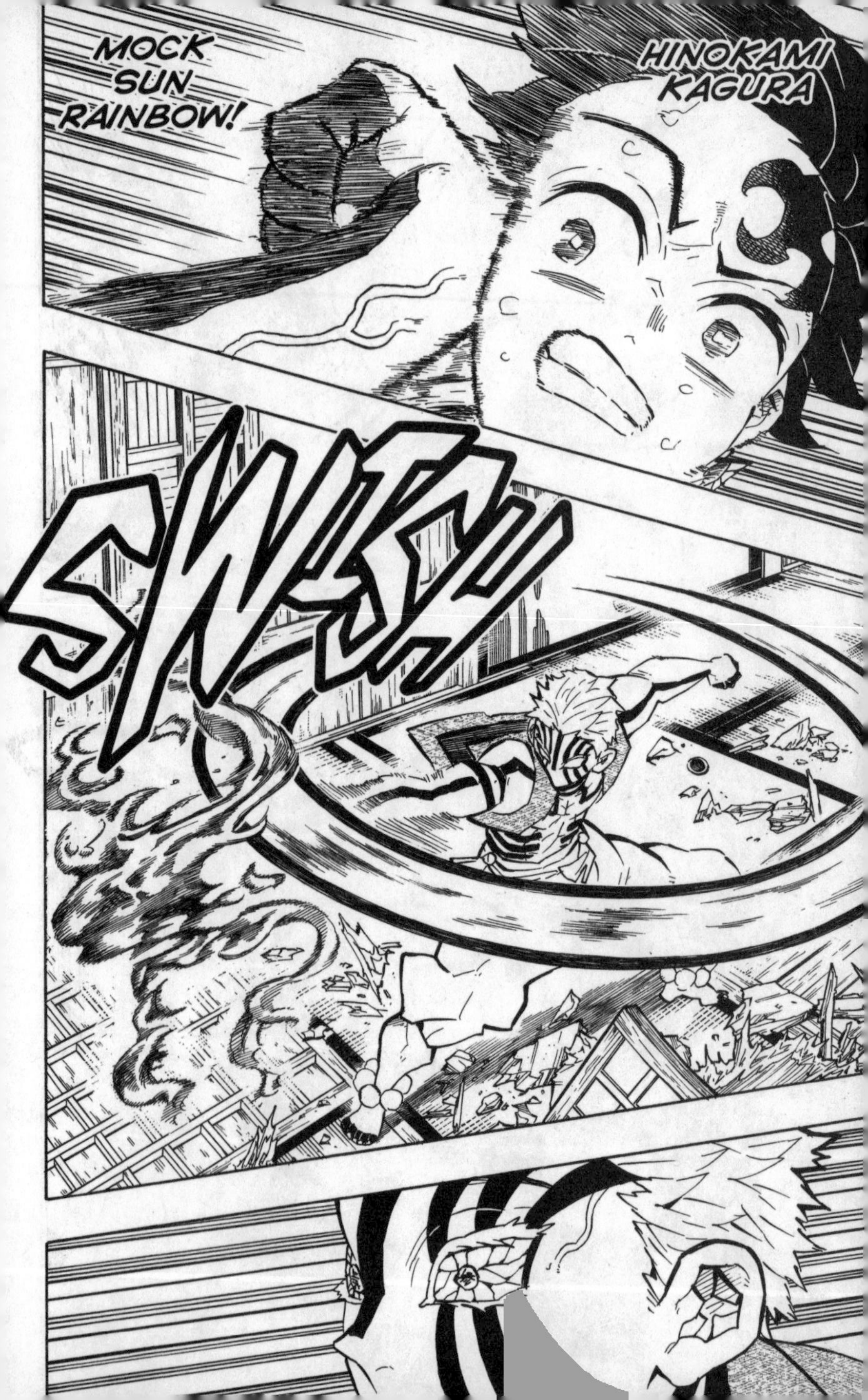
HINOKAMI KAGURA
MOCK SUN RAINBOW!
SWISH

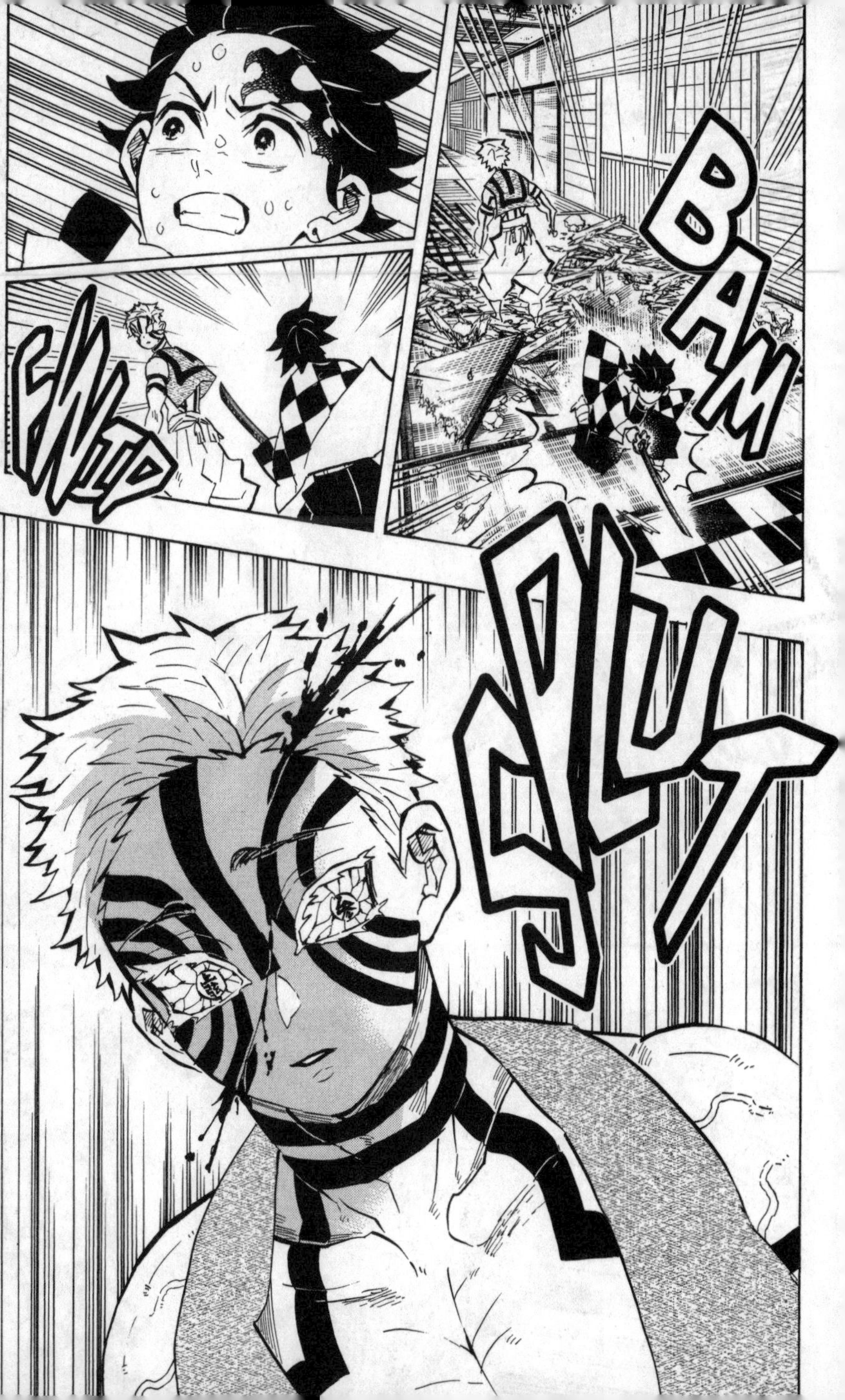
BAM
CHUD
SPLUT

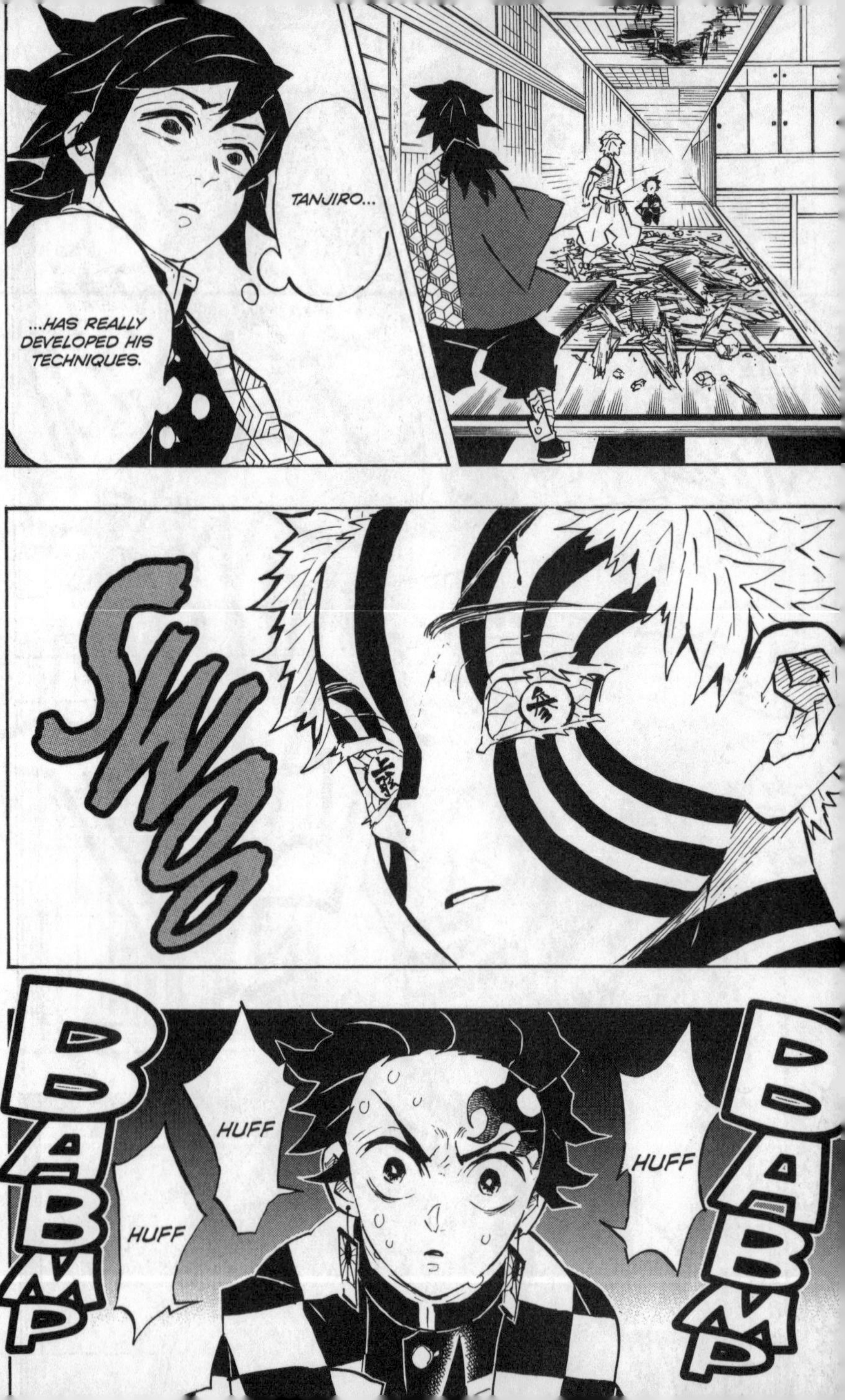
TANJIRO...
...HAS REALLY DEVELOPED HIS TECHNIQUES.
SWOOSH
BABMP
HUFF
HUFF
HUFF
BABMP

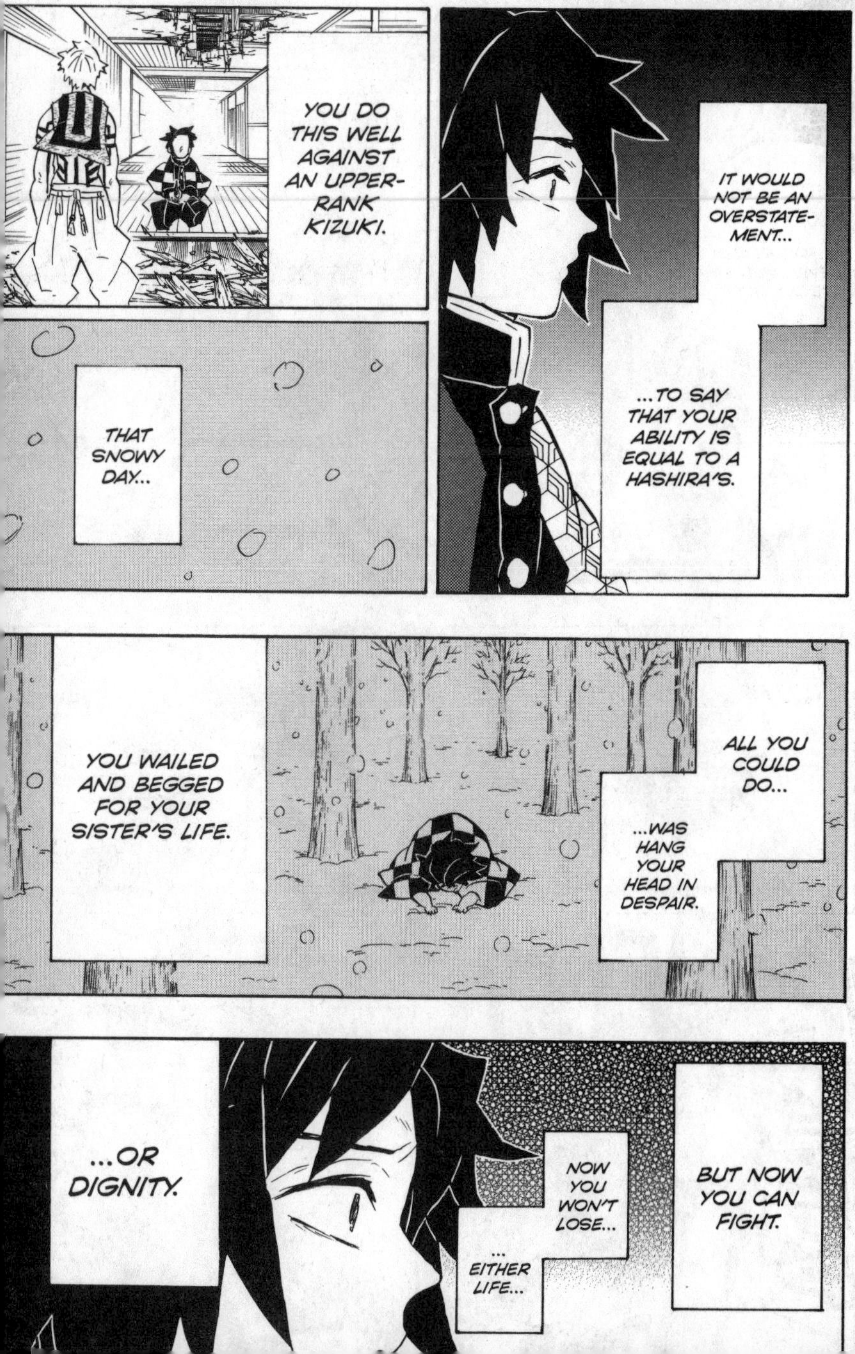

IT WOULD NOT BE AN OVERSTATEMENT...
...TO SAY THAT YOUR ABILITY IS EQUAL TO A HASHIRA'S.
YOU DO THIS WELL AGAINST AN UPPER-RANK KIZUKI.
THAT SNOWY DAY...
ALL YOU COULD DO...
...WAS HANG YOUR HEAD IN DESPAIR.
YOU WAILED AND BEGGED FOR YOUR SISTER'S LIFE.
BUT NOW YOU CAN FIGHT.
NOW YOU WON'T LOSE...
...EITHER LIFE...
...OR DIGNITY.

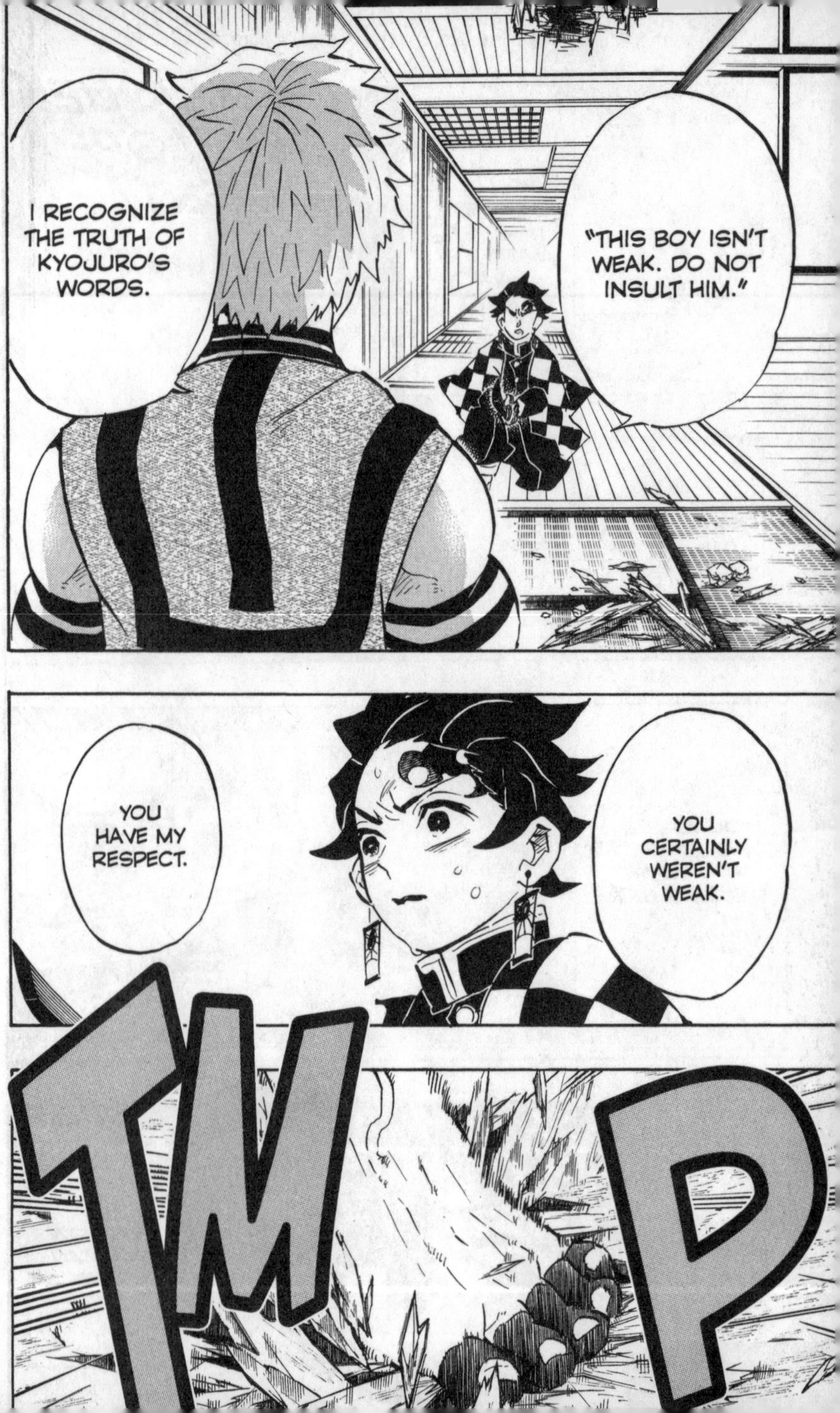
"THIS BOY ISN'T WEAK. DO NOT INSULT HIM."
I RECOGNIZE THE TRUTH OF KYOJURO'S WORDS.
YOU CERTAINLY WEREN'T WEAK.
YOU HAVE MY RESPECT.
TMP

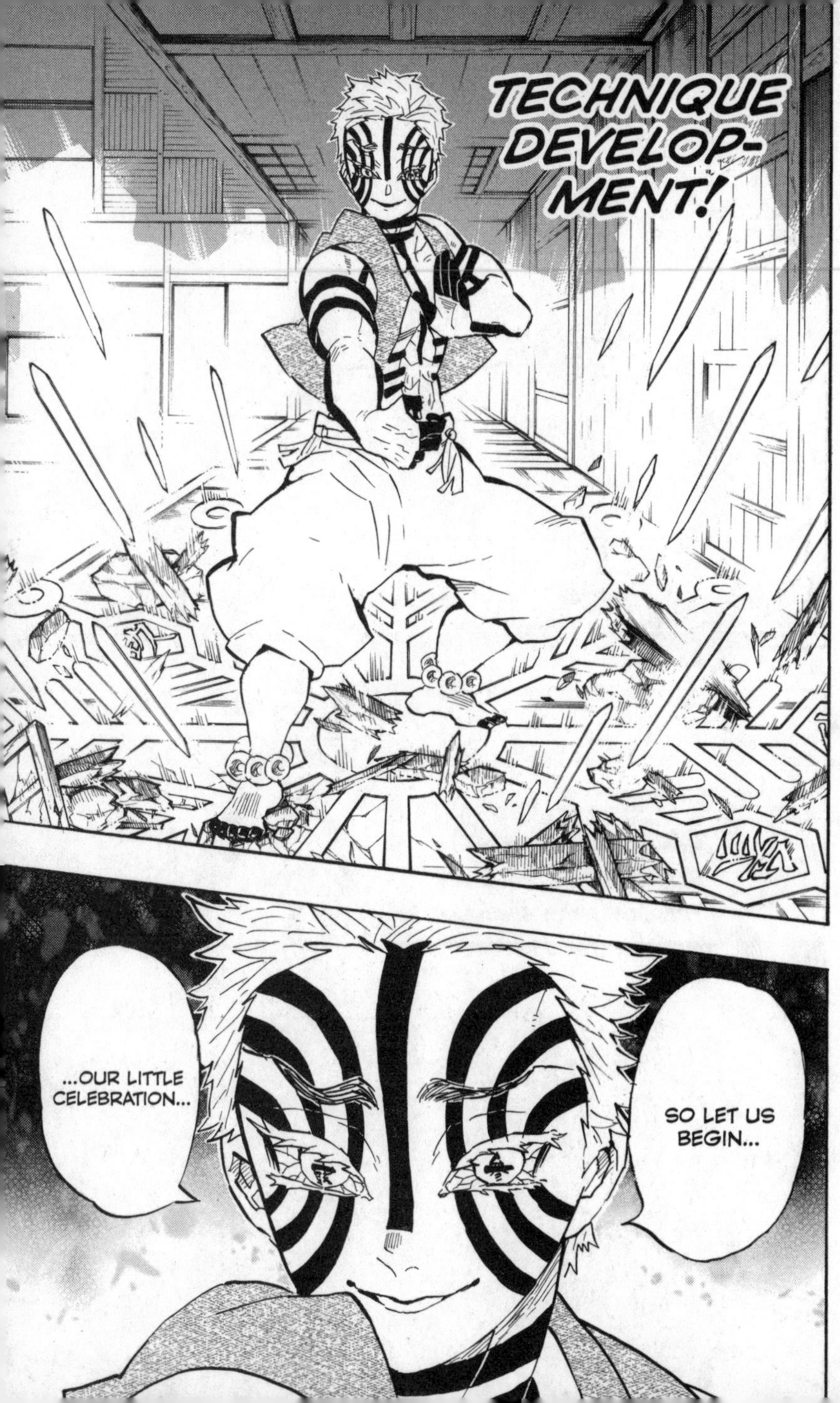
TECHNIQUE DEVELOP-MENT!
SO LET US BEGIN...
...OUR LITTLE CELEBRATION...

Before taking her medicine, Nezuko is delighted to see Urokodaki, whom she hasn't seen for a while.

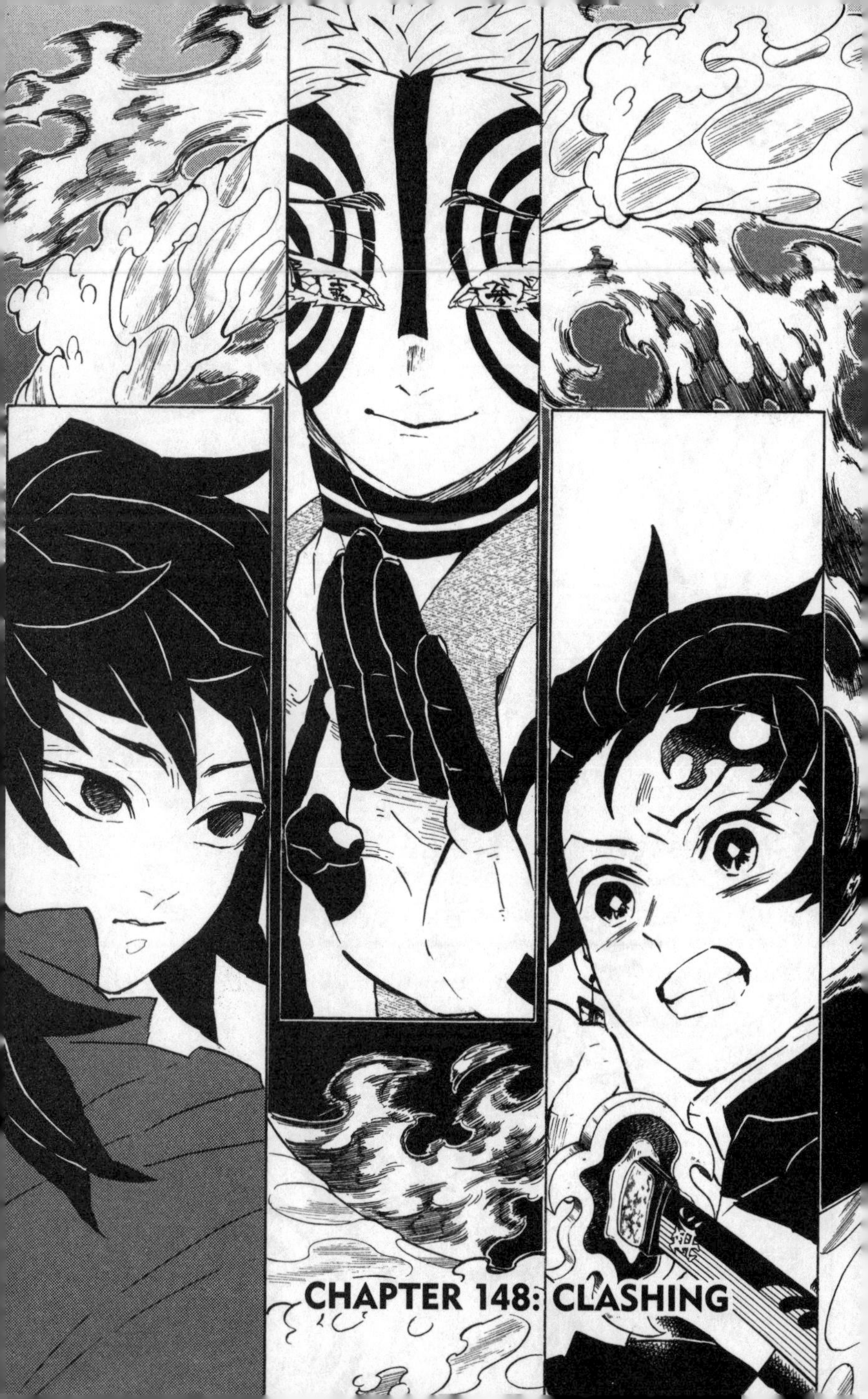
CHAPTER 148: CLASHING

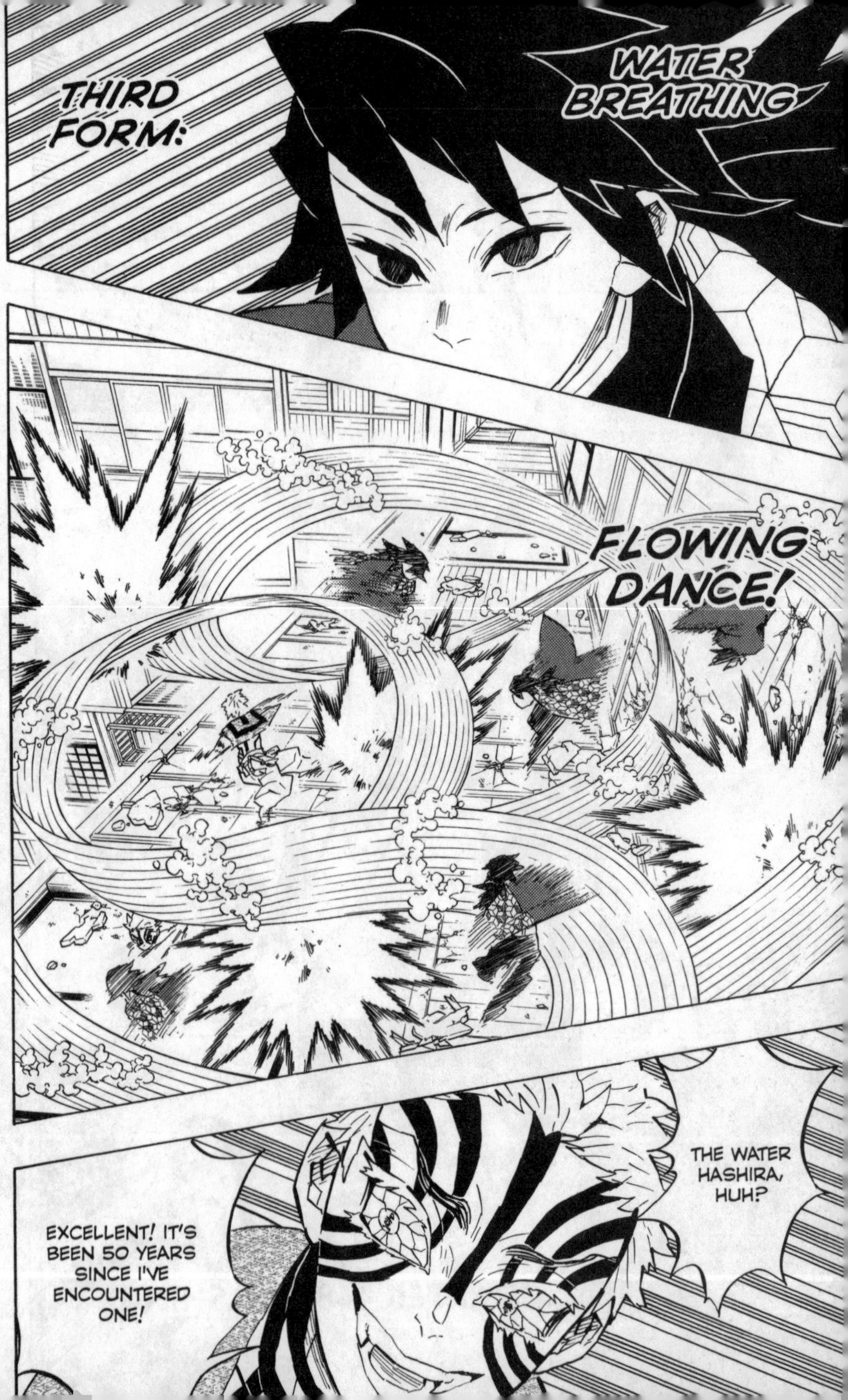
WATER BREATHING
THIRD FORM:
FLOWING DANCE!
THE WATER HASHIRA, HUH?
EXCELLENT! IT'S BEEN 50 YEARS SINCE I'VE ENCOUNTERED ONE!

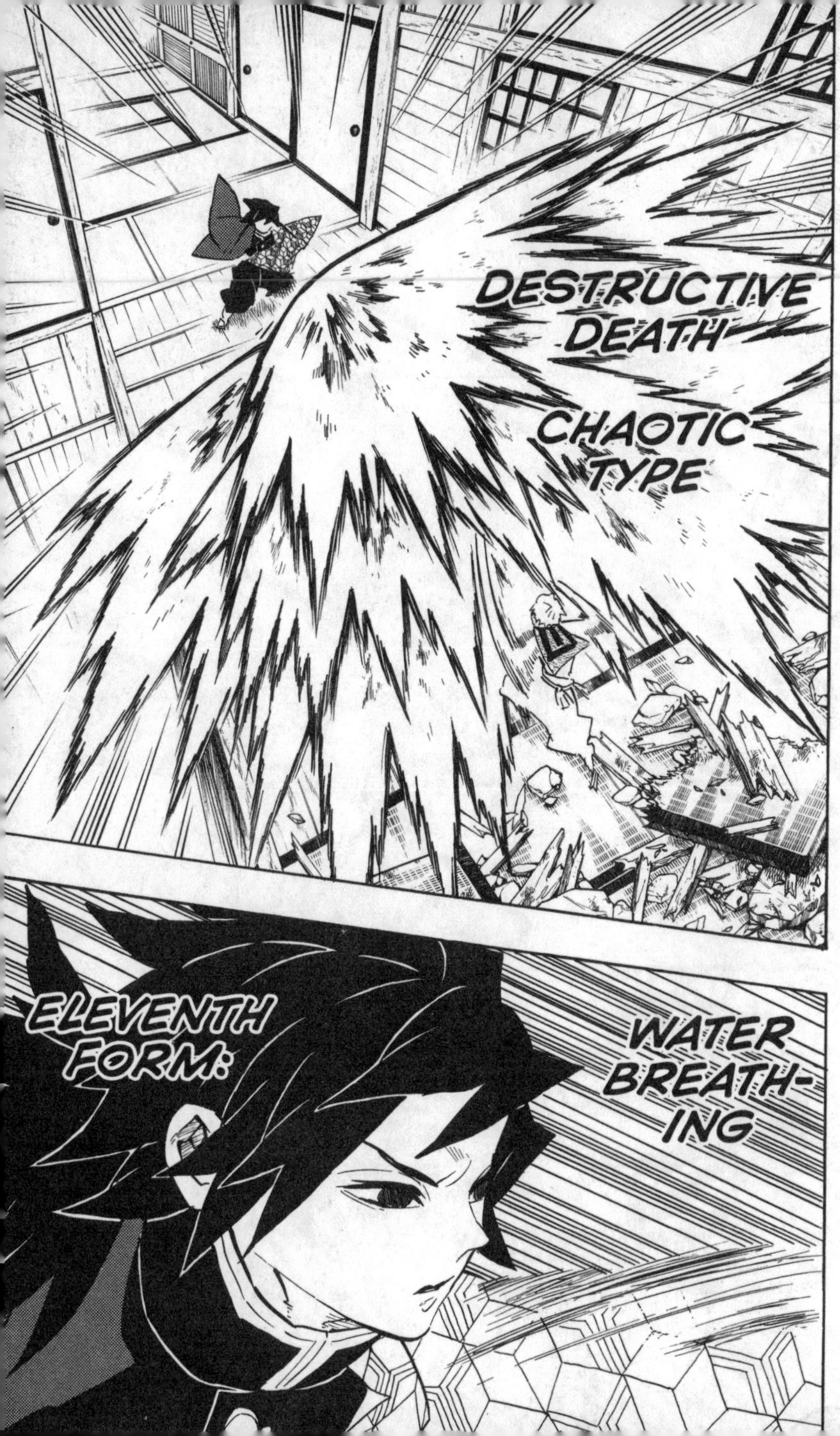
DESTRUCTIVE DEATH
CHAOTIC TYPE
WATER BREATH-ING
ELEVENTH FORM:

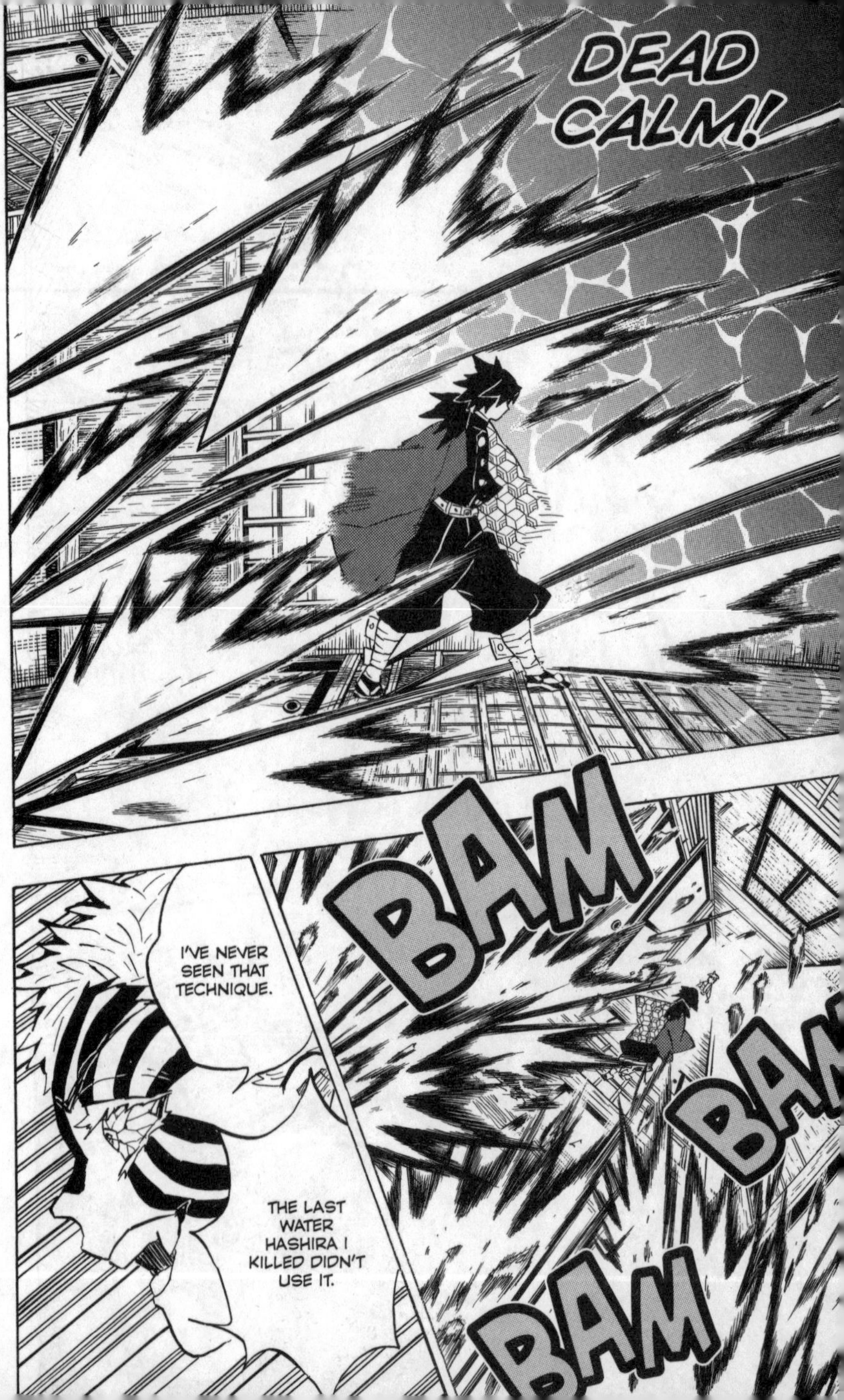
DEAD CALM!
BAM
BAM
I'VE NEVER SEEN THAT TECHNIQUE.
THE LAST WATER HASHIRA I KILLED DIDN'T USE IT.

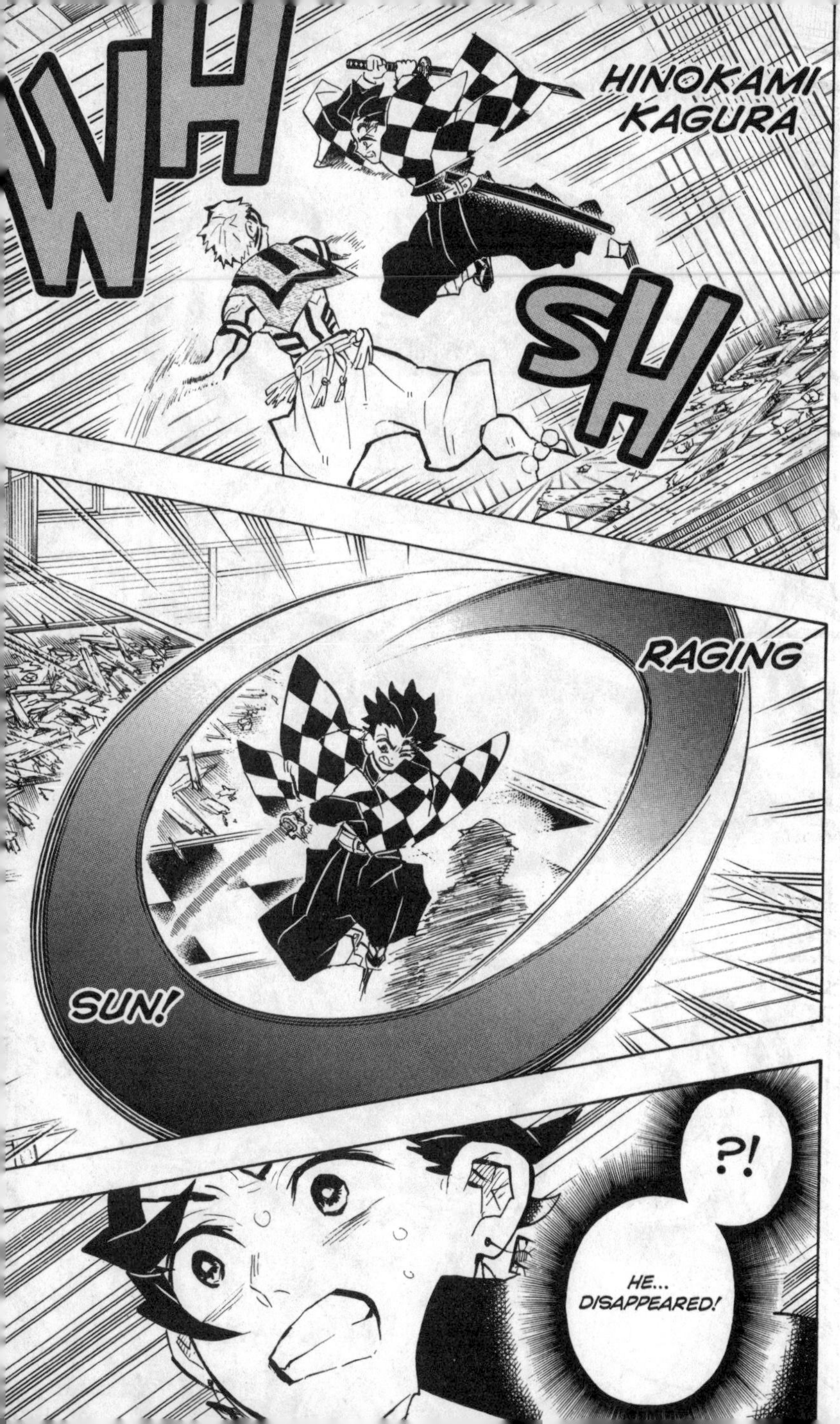
HINOKAMI KAGURA
WH
SH
RAGING
SUN!
?!
HE... DISAPPEARED!

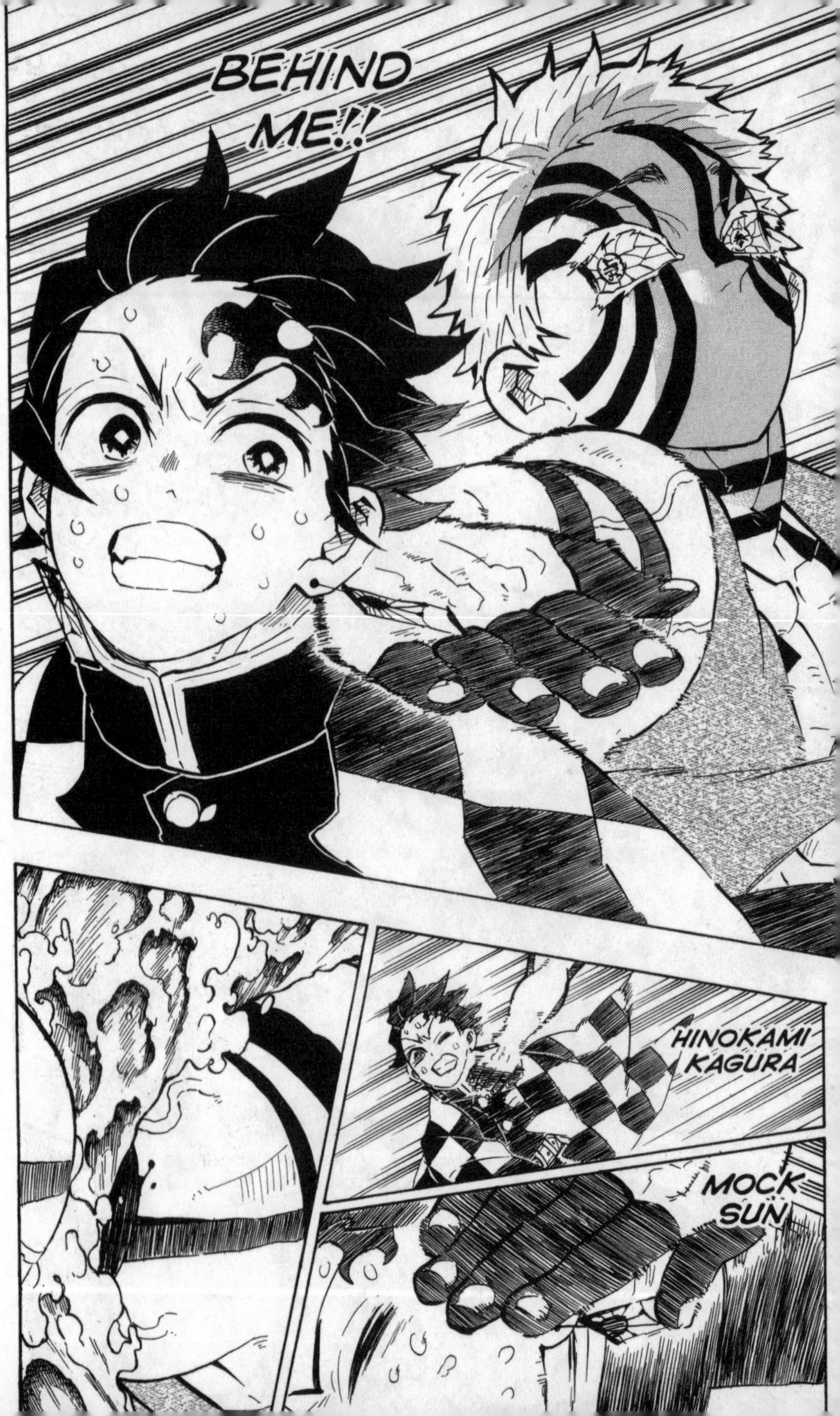
BEHIND ME!!
HINOKAMI KAGURA
MOCK SUN

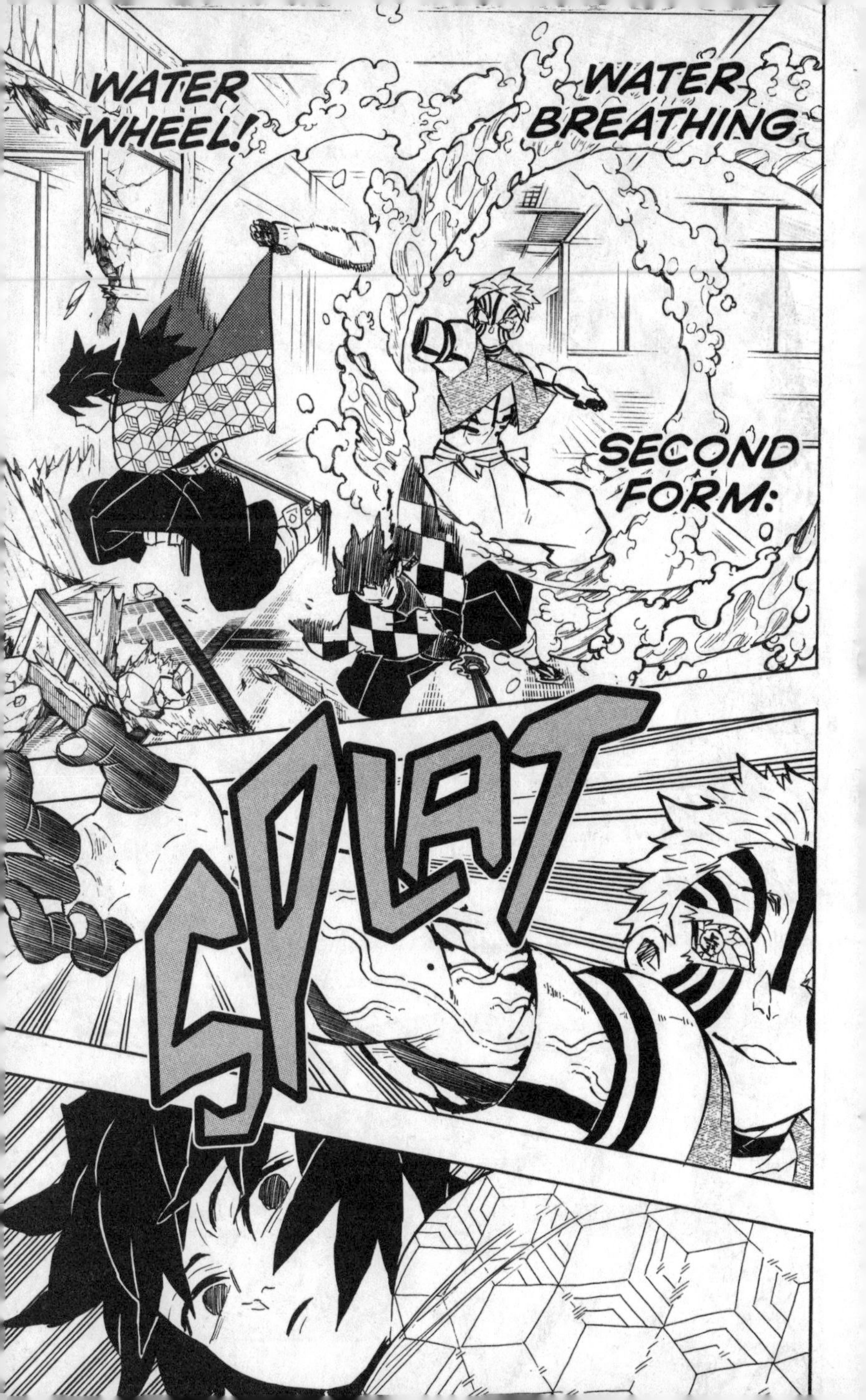
WATER BREATHING
SECOND FORM:
WATER WHEEL!
SPLAT

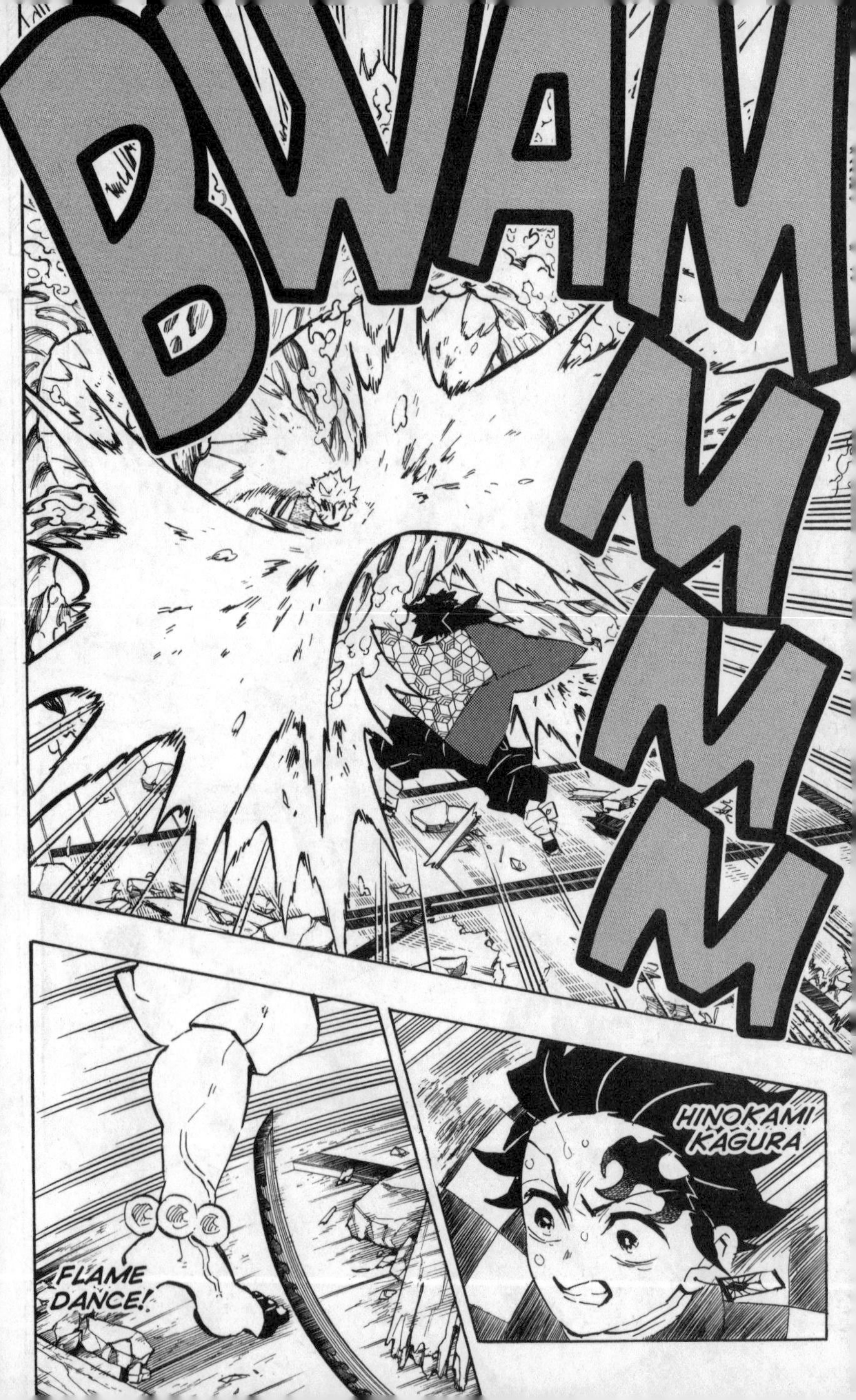
BWAMMMM
HINOKAMI KAGURA
FLAME DANCE!

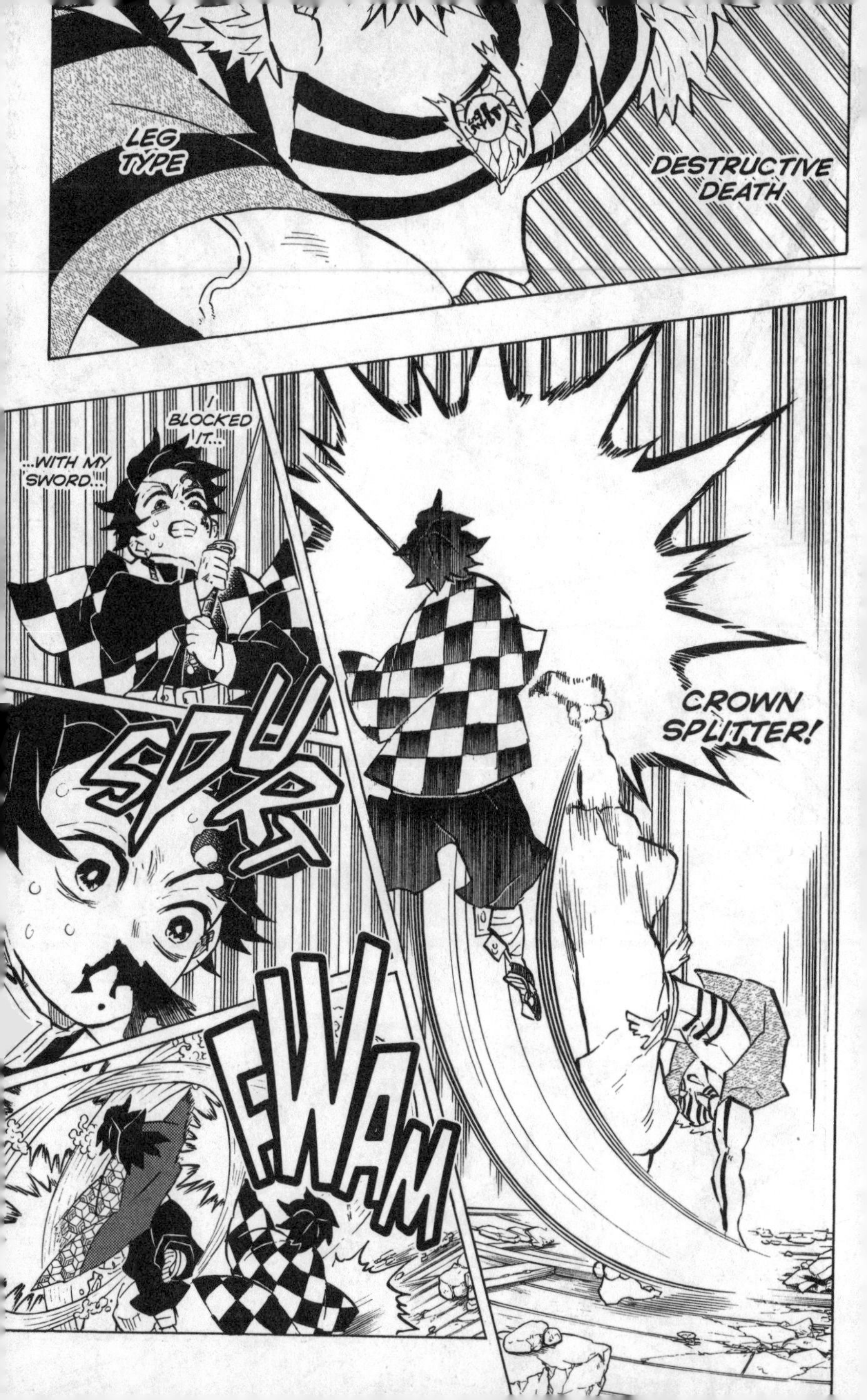
DESTRUCTIVE DEATH
LEG TYPE
CROWN SPLITTER!
I BLOCKED IT...
...WITH MY SWORD...
SPURT
FWAM

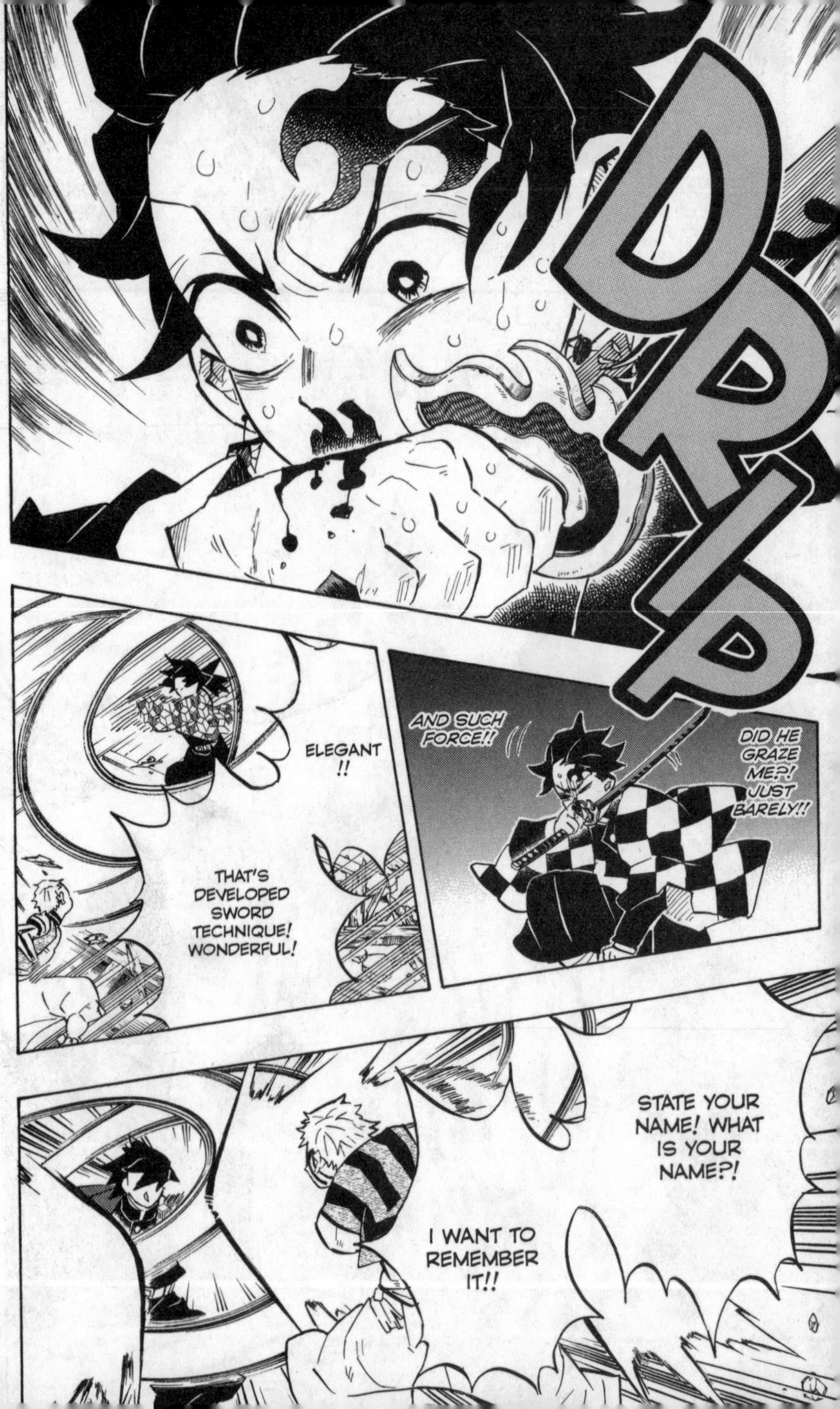
DRIP
DID HE GRAZE ME?! JUST BARELY!!
AND SUCH FORCE!!
ELEGANT!!
THAT'S DEVELOPED SWORD TECHNIQUE! WONDERFUL!
STATE YOUR NAME! WHAT IS YOUR NAME?!
I WANT TO REMEMBER IT!!

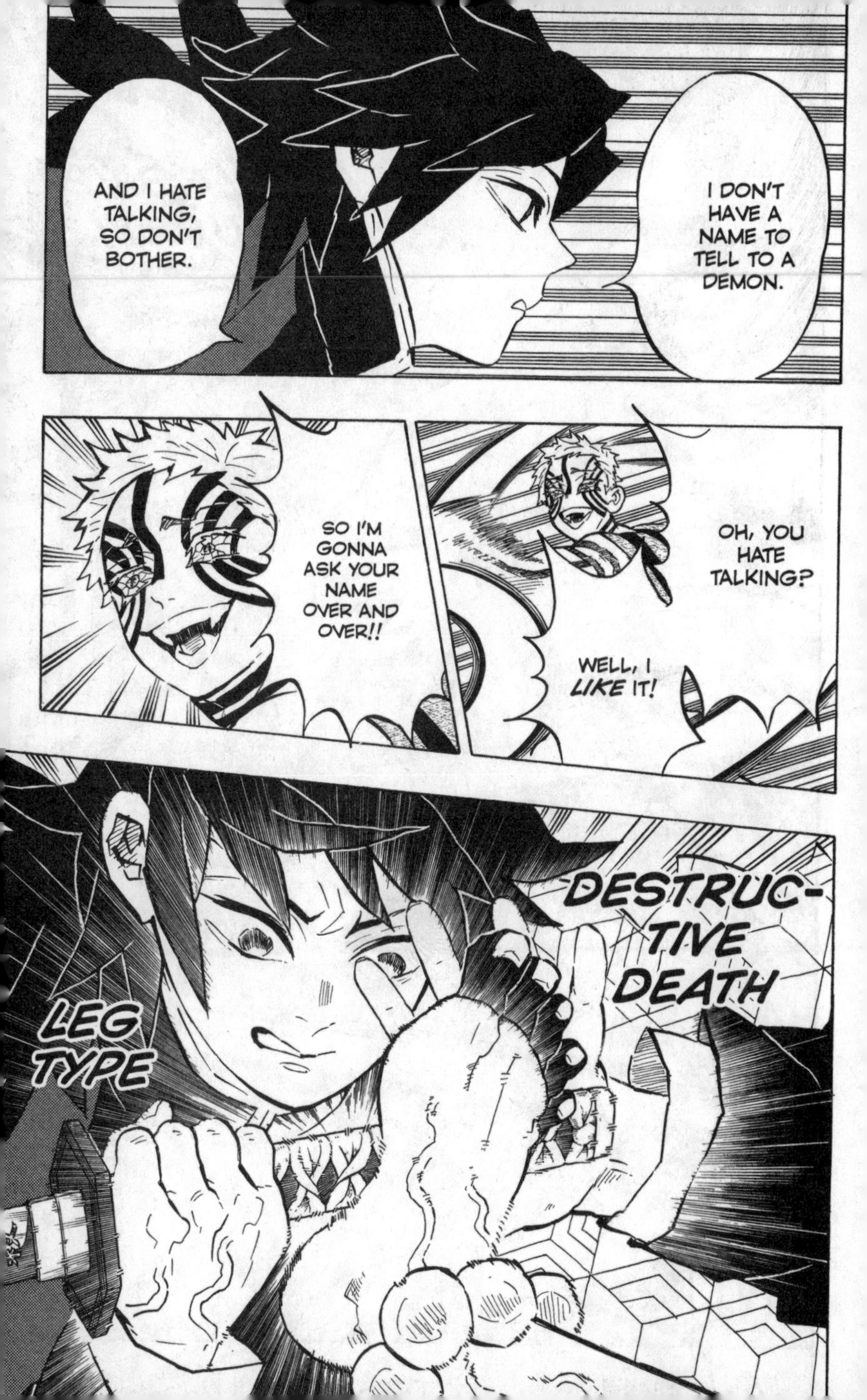
I DON'T HAVE A NAME TO TELL TO A DEMON.
AND I HATE TALKING, SO DON'T BOTHER.
OH, YOU HATE TALKING?
WELL, I *LIKE* IT!
SO I'M GONNA ASK YOUR NAME OVER AND OVER!!
DESTRUC-TIVE DEATH
LEG TYPE

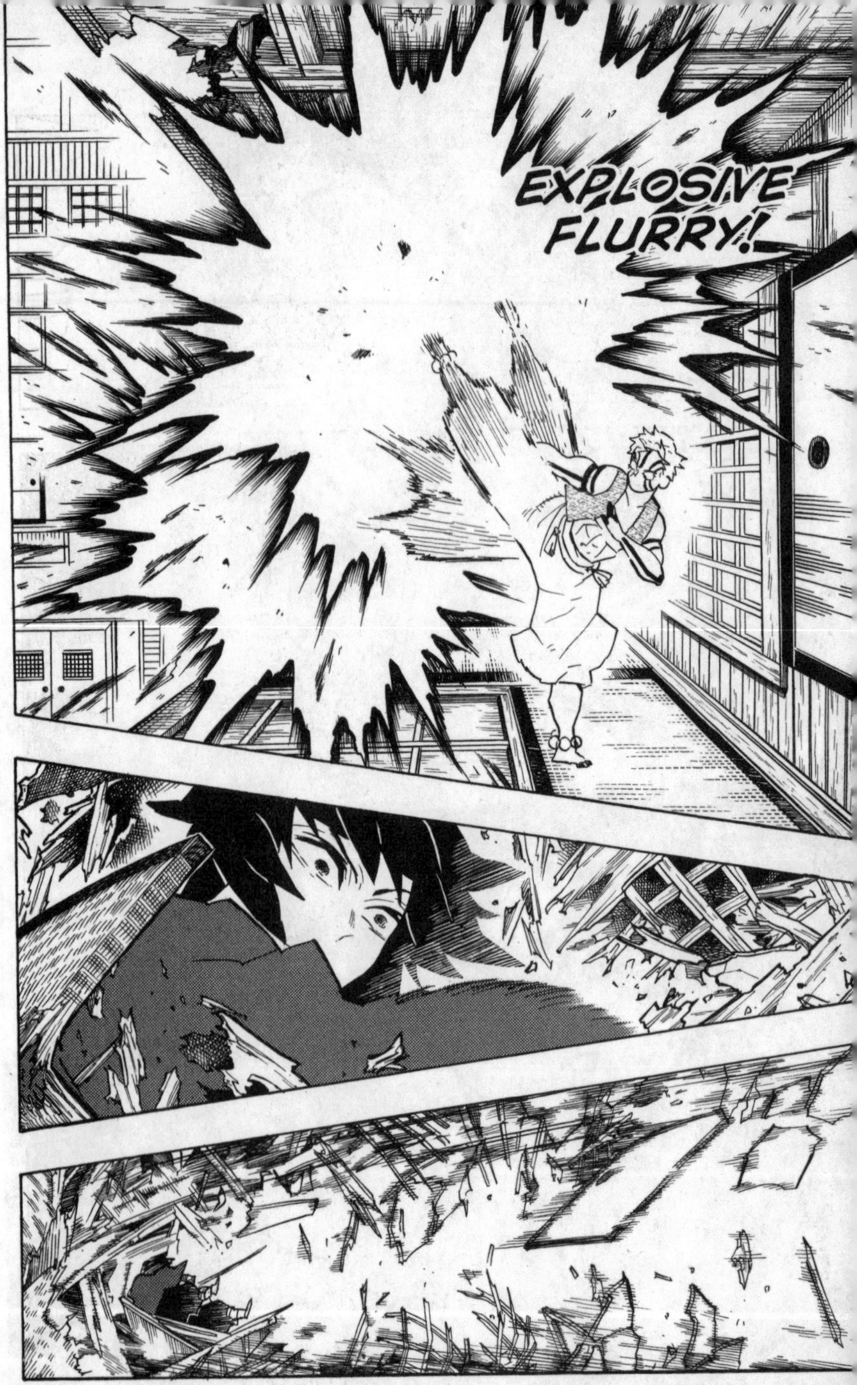
EXPLOSIVE FLURRY!

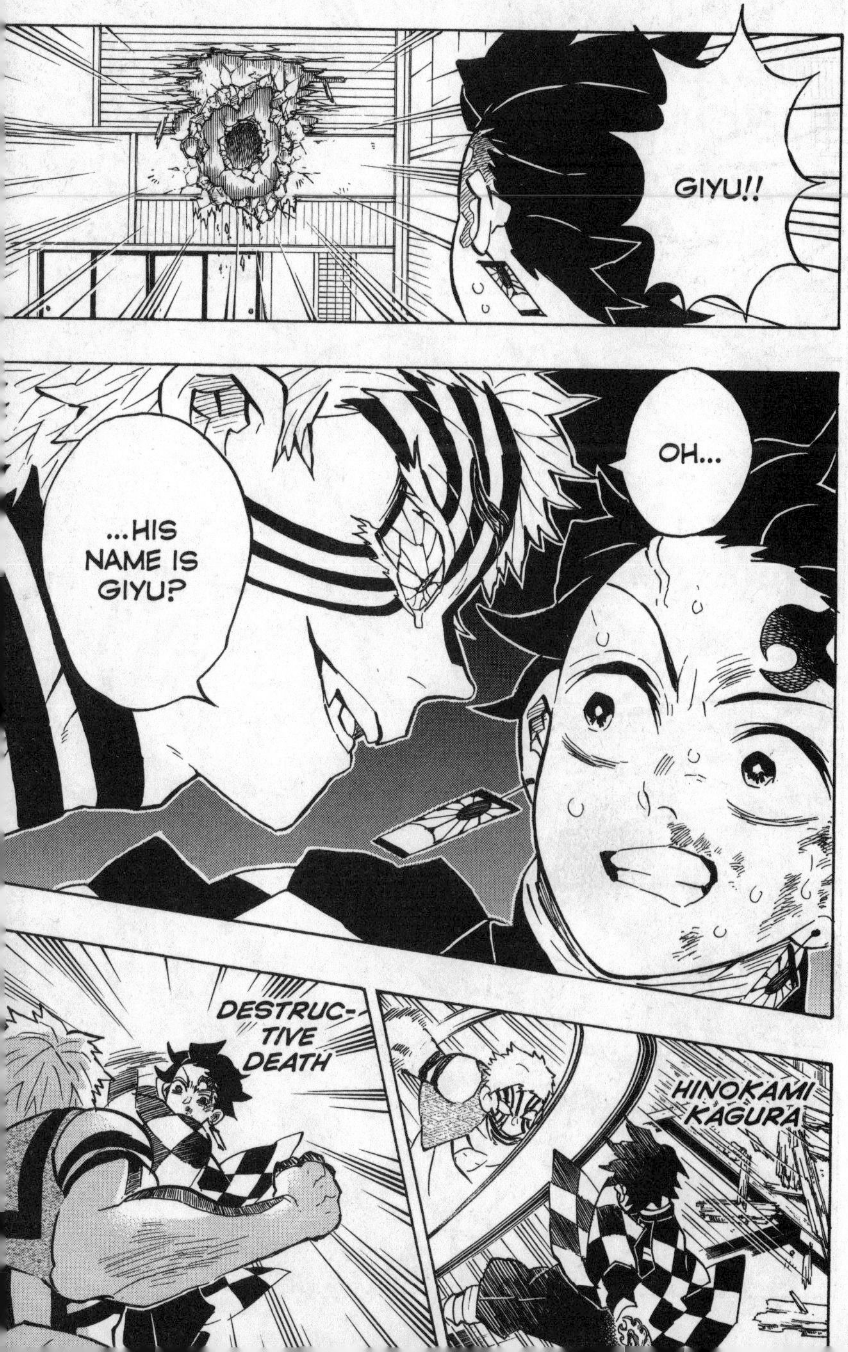
GIYU!!
OH...
...HIS NAME IS GIYU?
HINOKAMI KAGURA
DESTRUC-TIVE DEATH

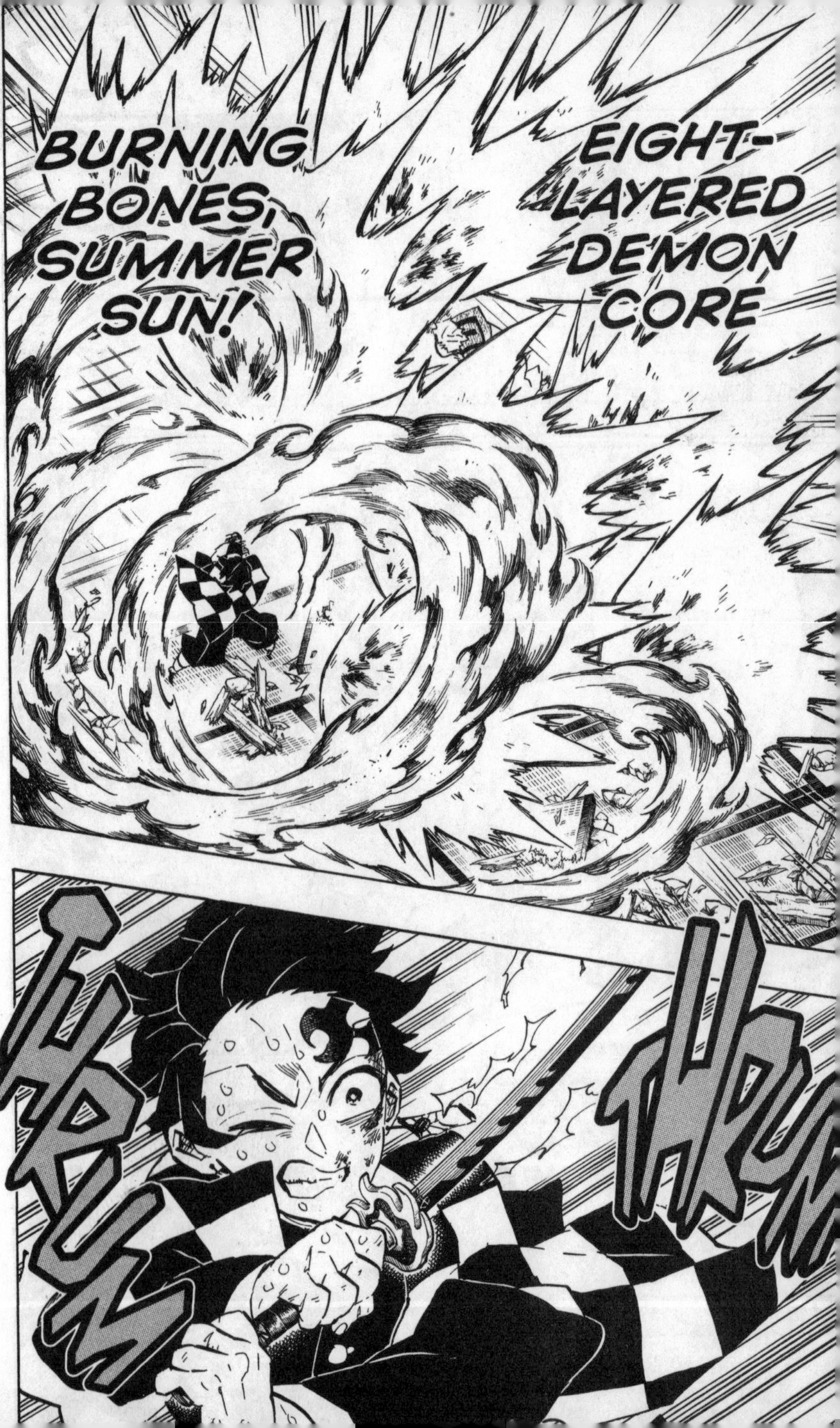
EIGHT-LAYERED DEMON CORE
BURNING BONES, SUMMER SUN!
THRU
THRUM

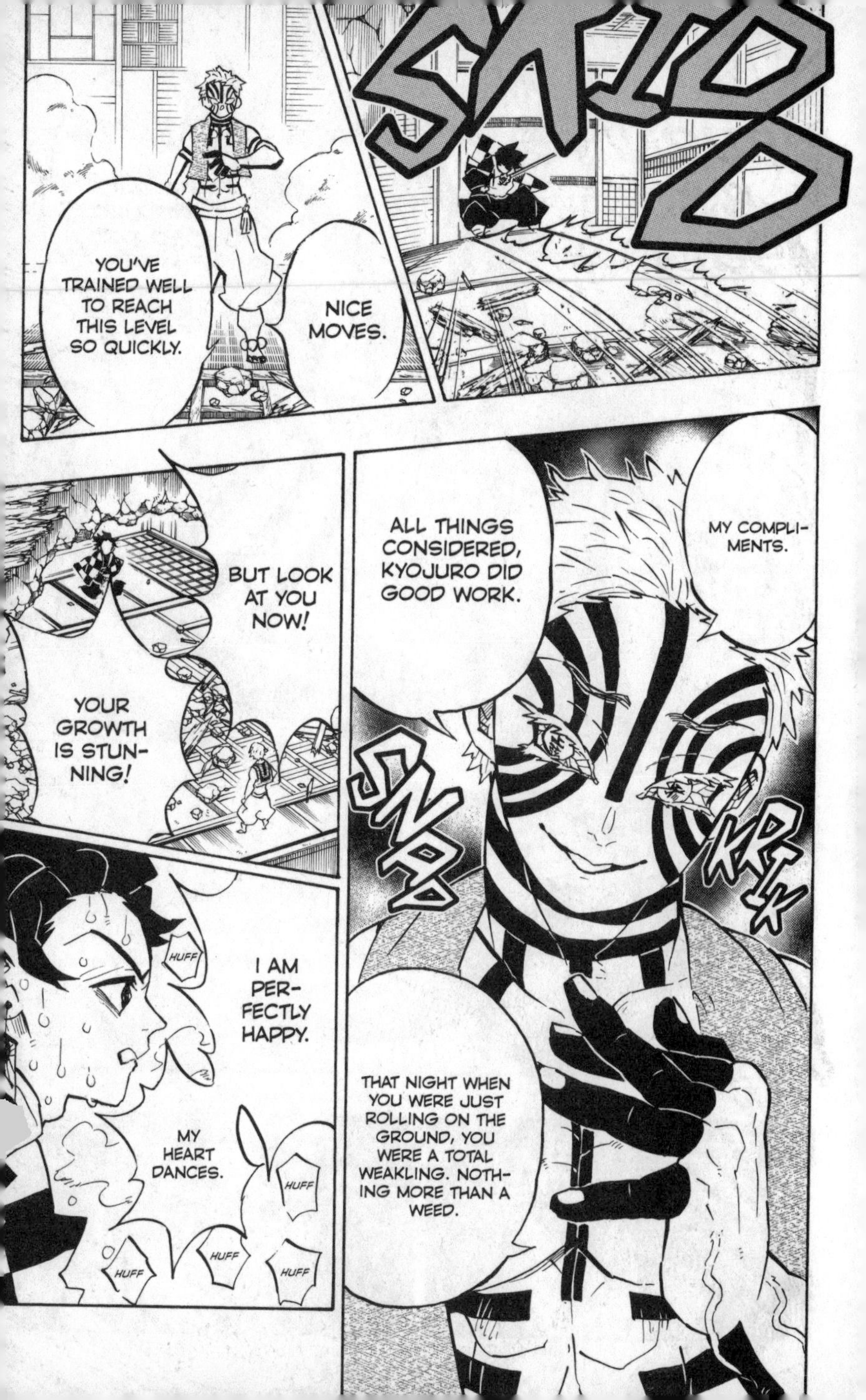
NICE MOVES.
YOU'VE TRAINED WELL TO REACH THIS LEVEL SO QUICKLY.
MY COMPLIMENTS.
ALL THINGS CONSIDERED, KYOJURO DID GOOD WORK.
SNAP
KRIK
THAT NIGHT WHEN YOU WERE JUST ROLLING ON THE GROUND, YOU WERE A TOTAL WEAKLING. NOTHING MORE THAN A WEED.
BUT LOOK AT YOU NOW!
YOUR GROWTH IS STUNNING!
I AM PERFECTLY HAPPY.
HUFF
MY HEART DANCES.
HUFF
HUFF
HUFF
HUFF

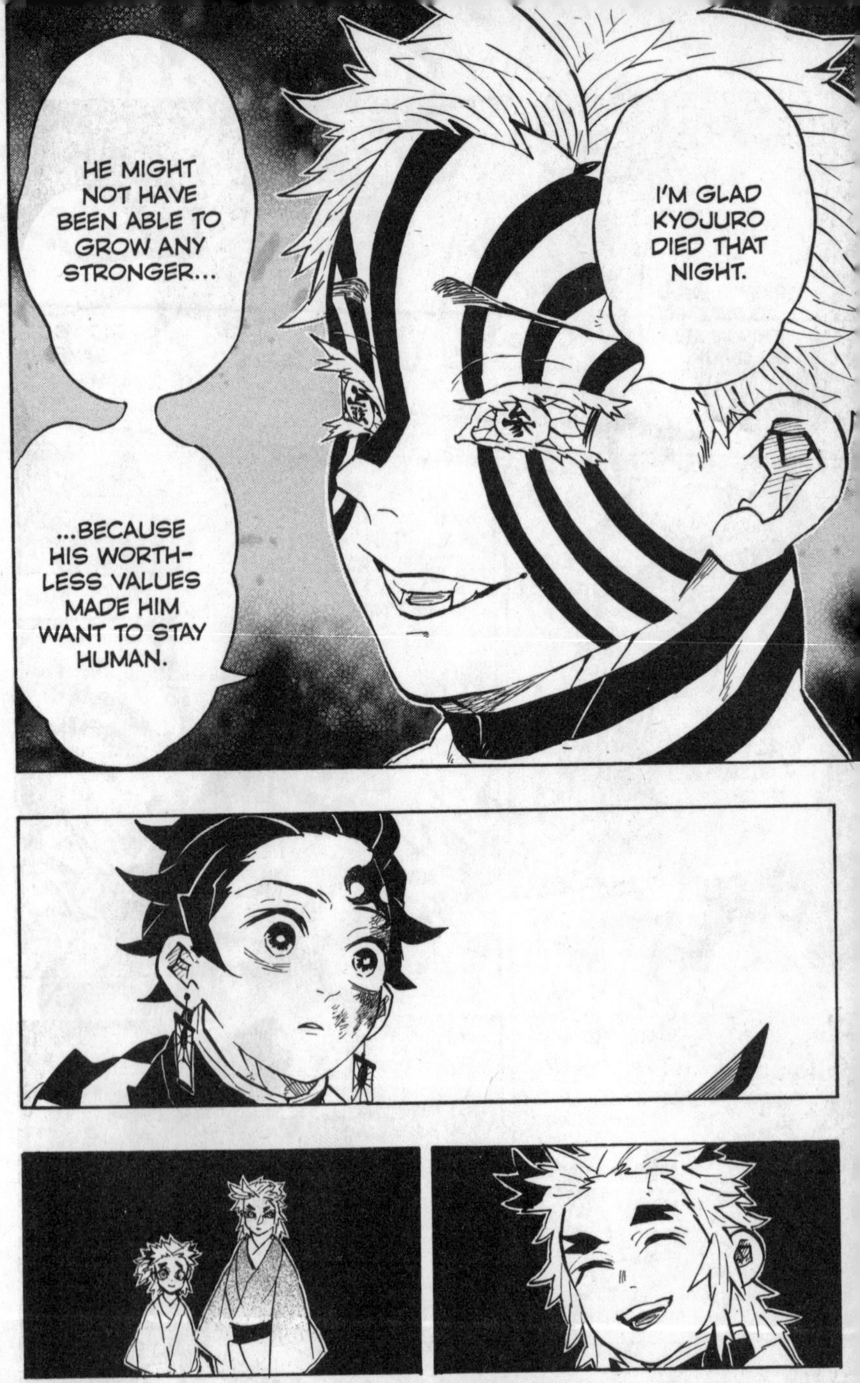
I'M GLAD KYOJURO DIED THAT NIGHT.
HE MIGHT NOT HAVE BEEN ABLE TO GROW ANY STRONGER...
...BECAUSE HIS WORTH-LESS VALUES MADE HIM WANT TO STAY HUMAN.

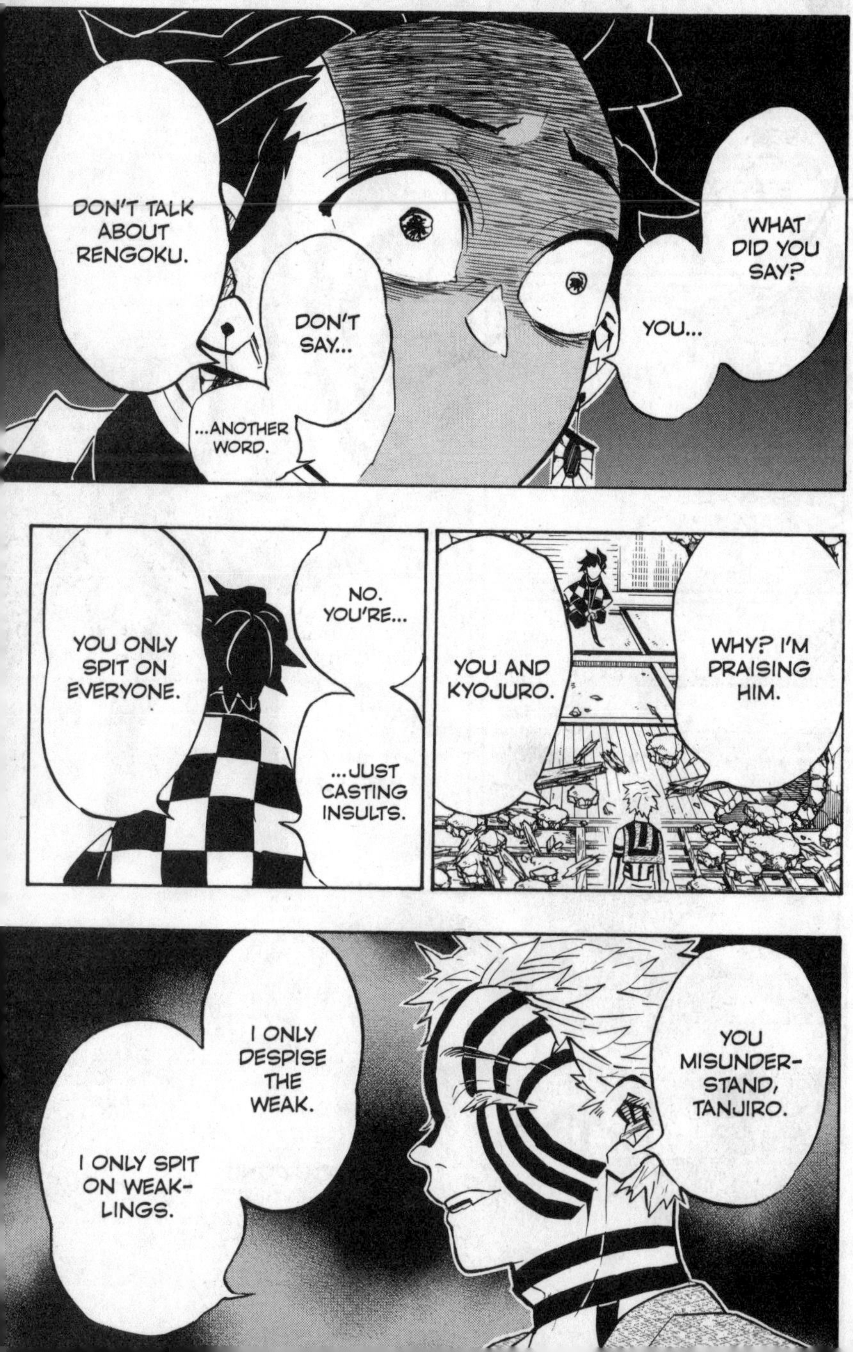
WHAT DID YOU SAY?
YOU...
DON'T SAY...
...ANOTHER WORD.
DON'T TALK ABOUT RENGOKU.
WHY? I'M PRAISING HIM.
YOU AND KYOJURO.
NO. YOU'RE...
...JUST CASTING INSULTS.
YOU ONLY SPIT ON EVERYONE.
YOU MISUNDER-STAND, TANJIRO.
I ONLY DESPISE THE WEAK.
I ONLY SPIT ON WEAK-LINGS.

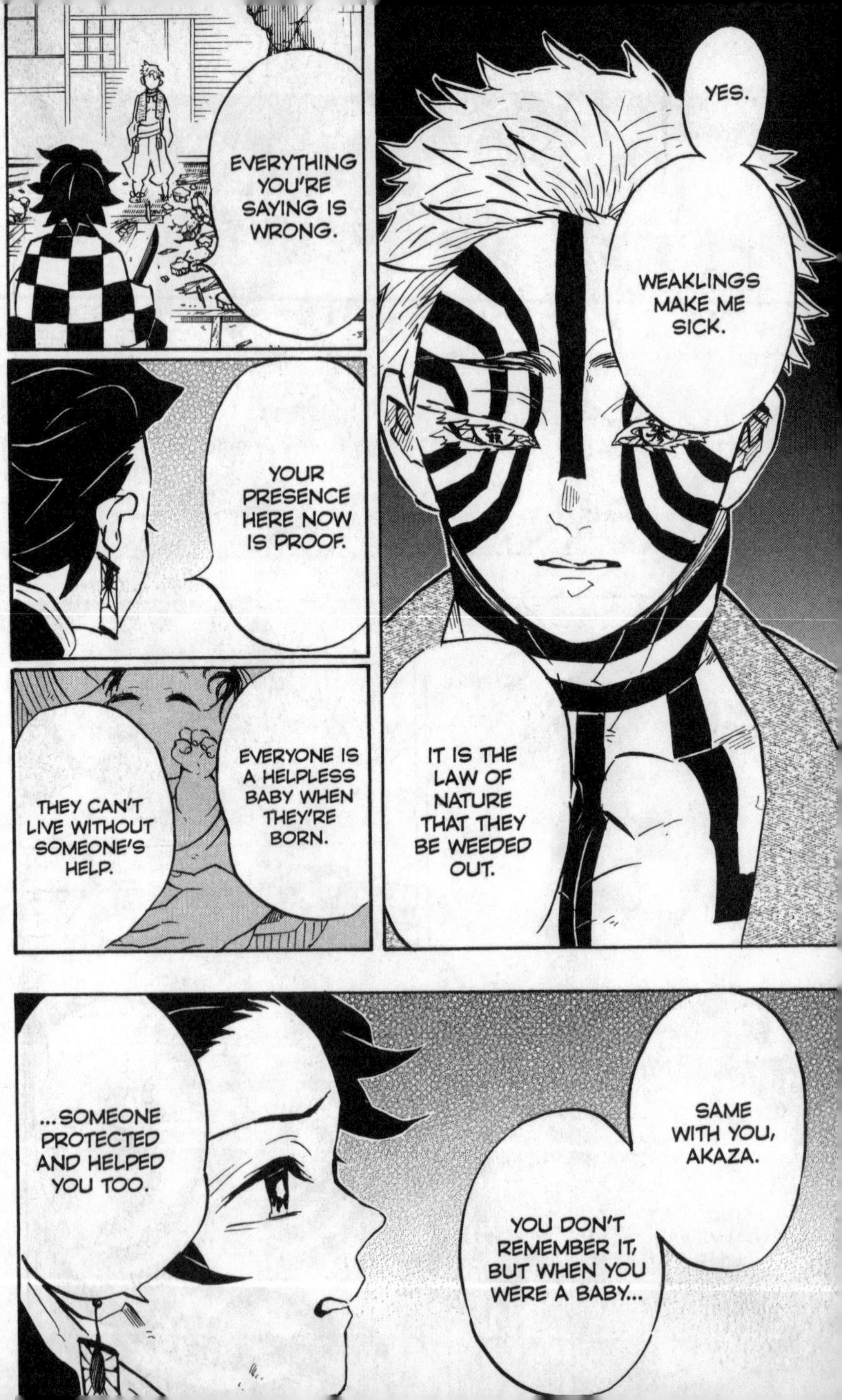
YES.
WEAKLINGS MAKE ME SICK.
IT IS THE LAW OF NATURE THAT THEY BE WEEDED OUT.
EVERYTHING YOU'RE SAYING IS WRONG.
YOUR PRESENCE HERE NOW IS PROOF.
EVERYONE IS A HELPLESS BABY WHEN THEY'RE BORN.
THEY CAN'T LIVE WITHOUT SOMEONE'S HELP.
SAME WITH YOU, AKAZA.
YOU DON'T REMEMBER IT, BUT WHEN YOU WERE A BABY...
...SOMEONE PROTECTED AND HELPED YOU TOO.

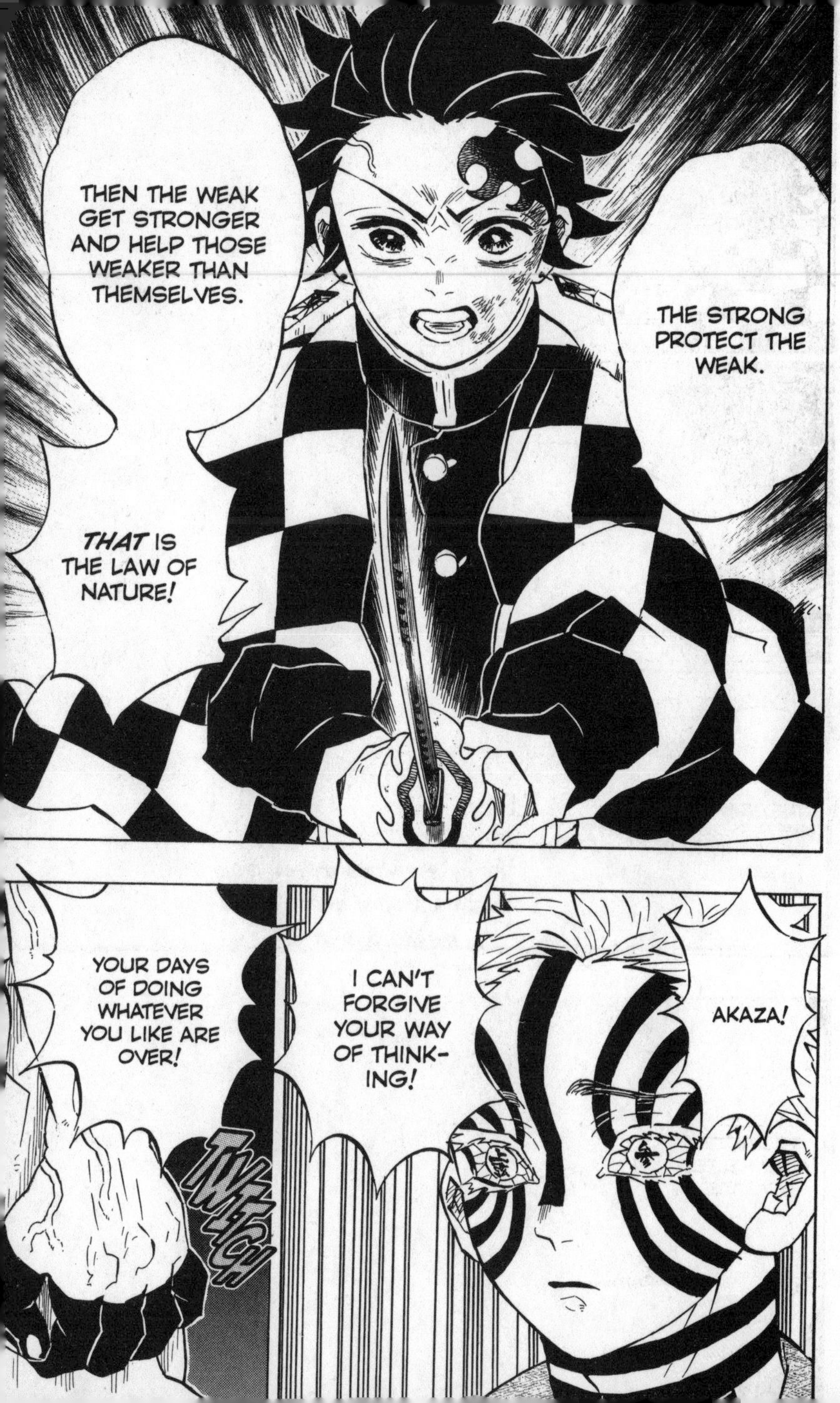
THE STRONG PROTECT THE WEAK.
THEN THE WEAK GET STRONGER AND HELP THOSE WEAKER THAN THEMSELVES.
THAT IS THE LAW OF NATURE!
AKAZA!
I CAN'T FORGIVE YOUR WAY OF THINKING!
YOUR DAYS OF DOING WHATEVER YOU LIKE ARE OVER!
TWITCH!!

Giyu's Crow. He's pretty old,
so he mishears messages,
hobbles around in battle and
makes Giyu worry.

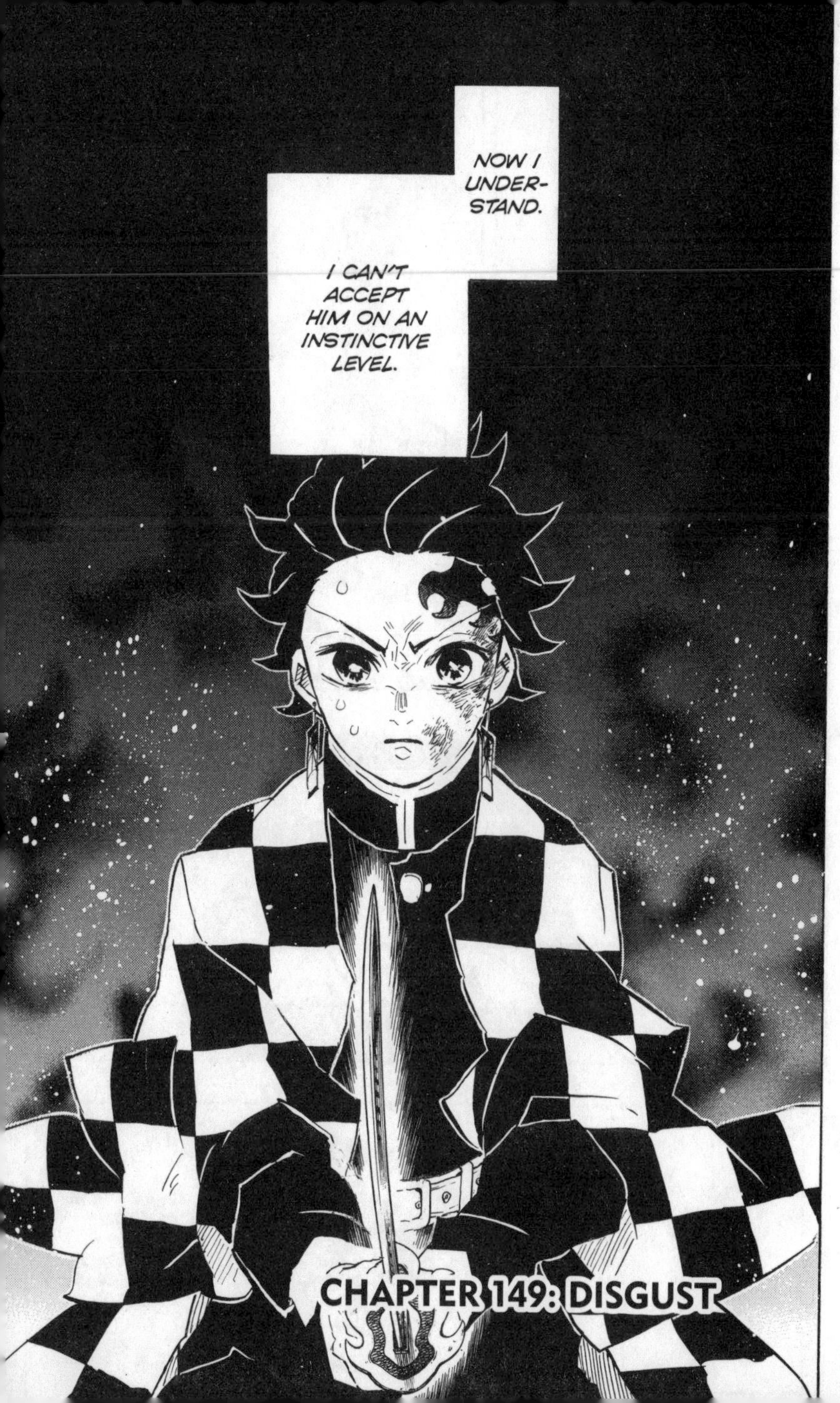
NOW I UNDER-STAND.
I CAN'T ACCEPT HIM ON AN INSTINCTIVE LEVEL.
CHAPTER 149: DISGUST

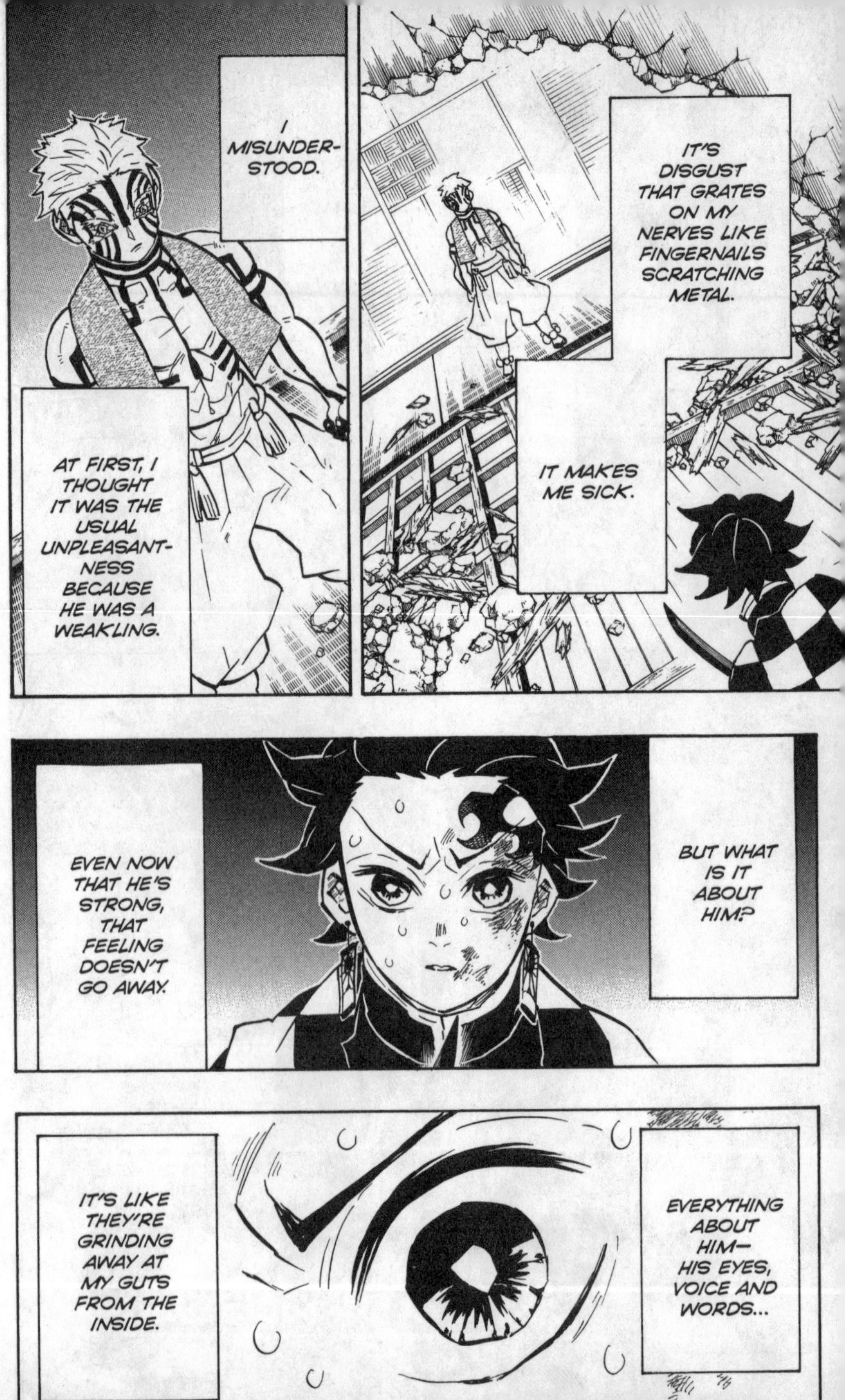
IT'S DISGUST THAT GRATES ON MY NERVES LIKE FINGERNAILS SCRATCHING METAL.
IT MAKES ME SICK.
I MISUNDERSTOOD.
AT FIRST, I THOUGHT IT WAS THE USUAL UNPLEASANTNESS BECAUSE HE WAS A WEAKLING.
BUT WHAT IS IT ABOUT HIM?
EVEN NOW THAT HE'S STRONG, THAT FEELING DOESN'T GO AWAY.
EVERYTHING ABOUT HIM— HIS EYES, VOICE AND WORDS...
IT'S LIKE THEY'RE GRINDING AWAY AT MY GUTS FROM THE INSIDE.

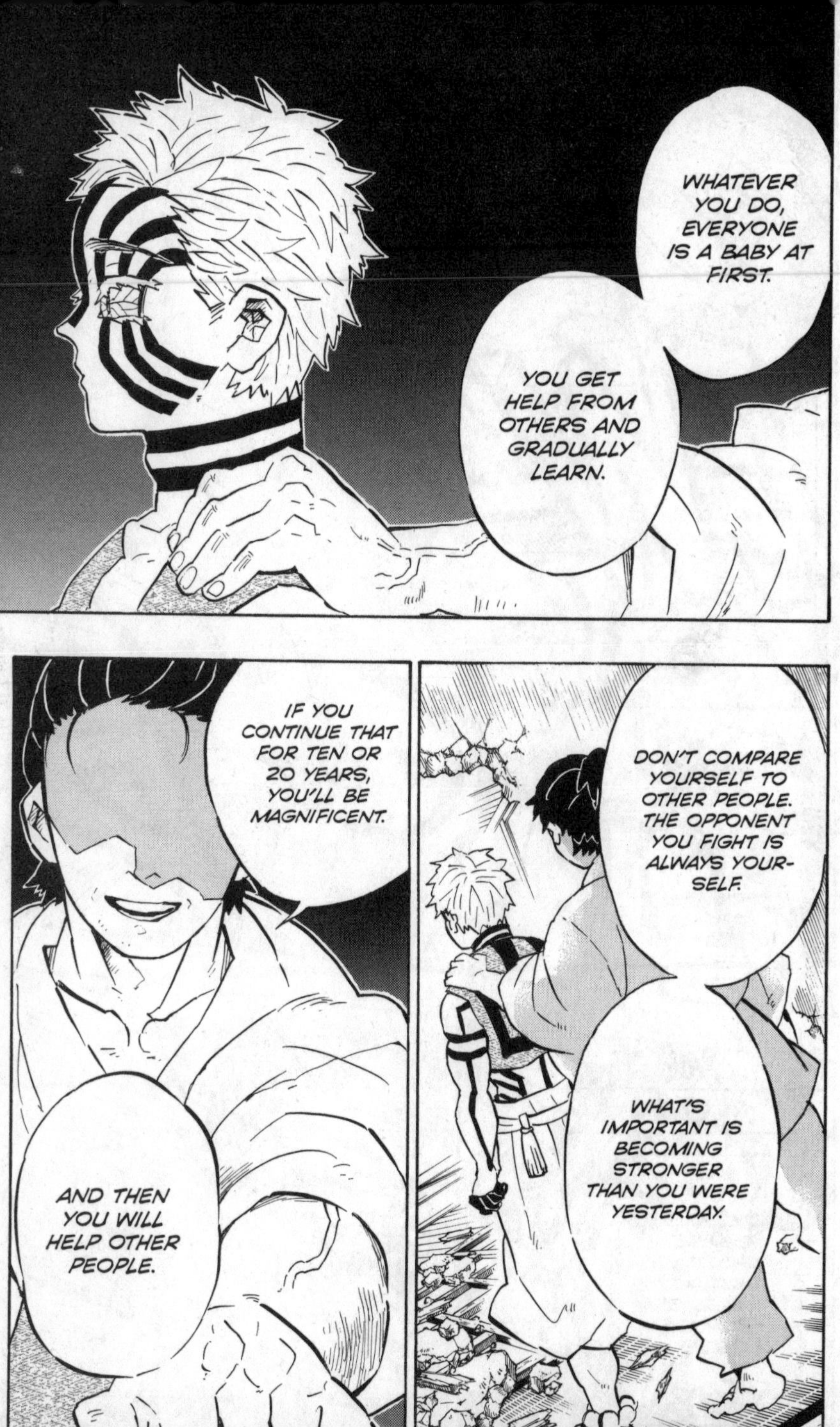
WHATEVER YOU DO, EVERYONE IS A BABY AT FIRST.
YOU GET HELP FROM OTHERS AND GRADUALLY LEARN.
DON'T COMPARE YOURSELF TO OTHER PEOPLE. THE OPPONENT YOU FIGHT IS ALWAYS YOUR-SELF.
WHAT'S IMPORTANT IS BECOMING STRONGER THAN YOU WERE YESTERDAY.
IF YOU CONTINUE THAT FOR TEN OR 20 YEARS, YOU'LL BE MAGNIFICENT.
AND THEN YOU WILL HELP OTHER PEOPLE.

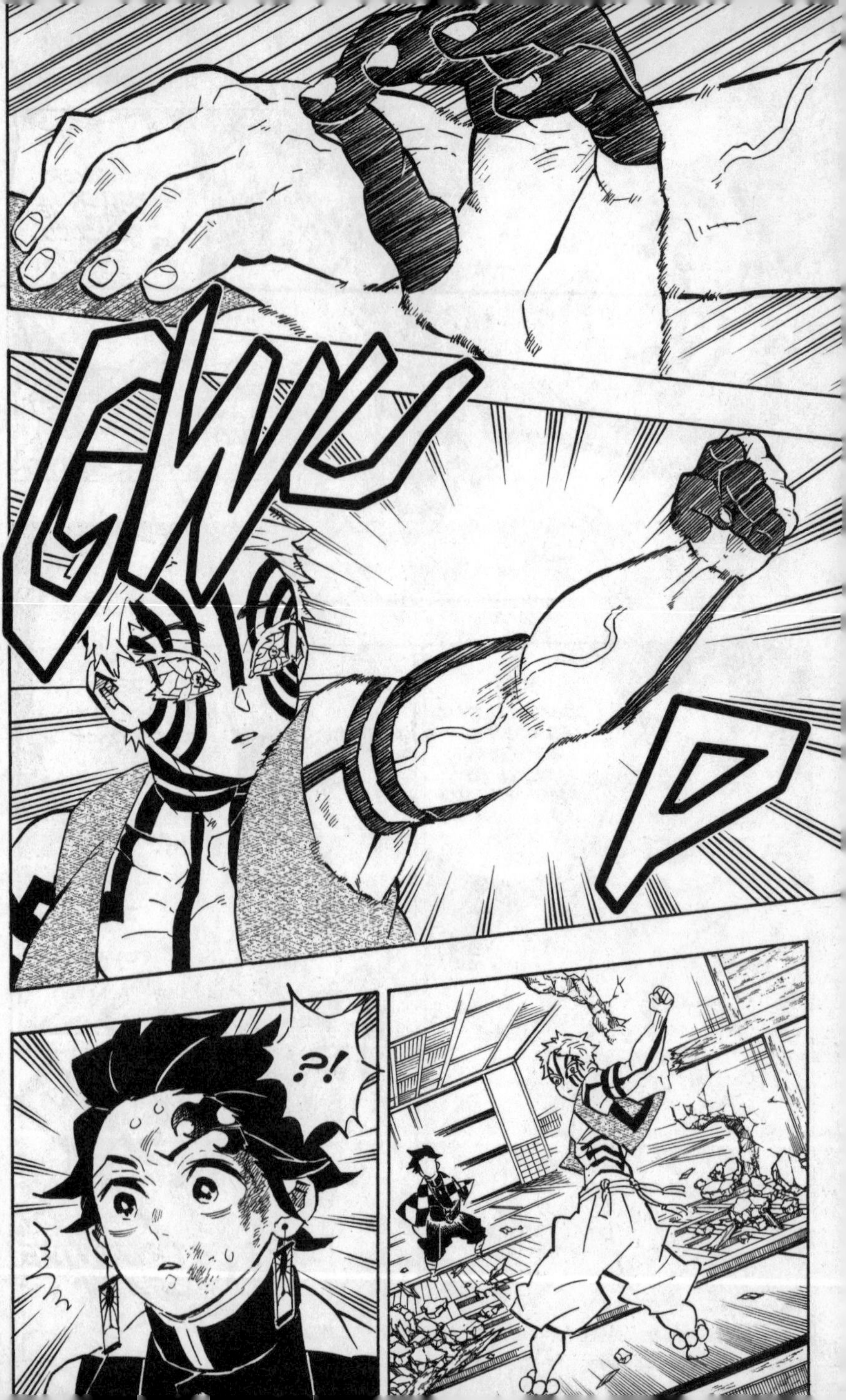
CWUD
?!

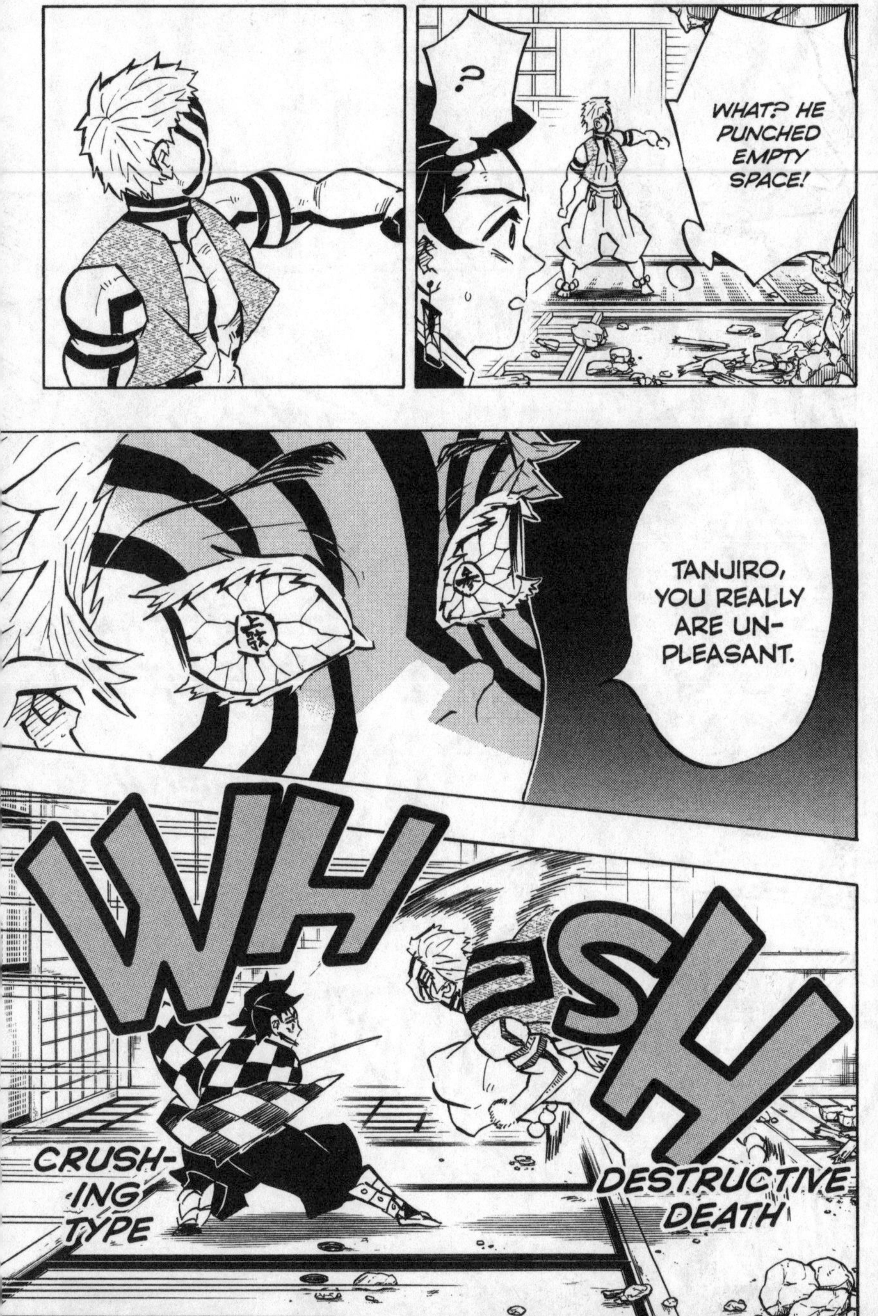
?
WHAT? HE PUNCHED EMPTY SPACE!
TANJIRO, YOU REALLY ARE UN-PLEASANT.
WH
SH
DESTRUCTIVE DEATH
CRUSH-ING TYPE

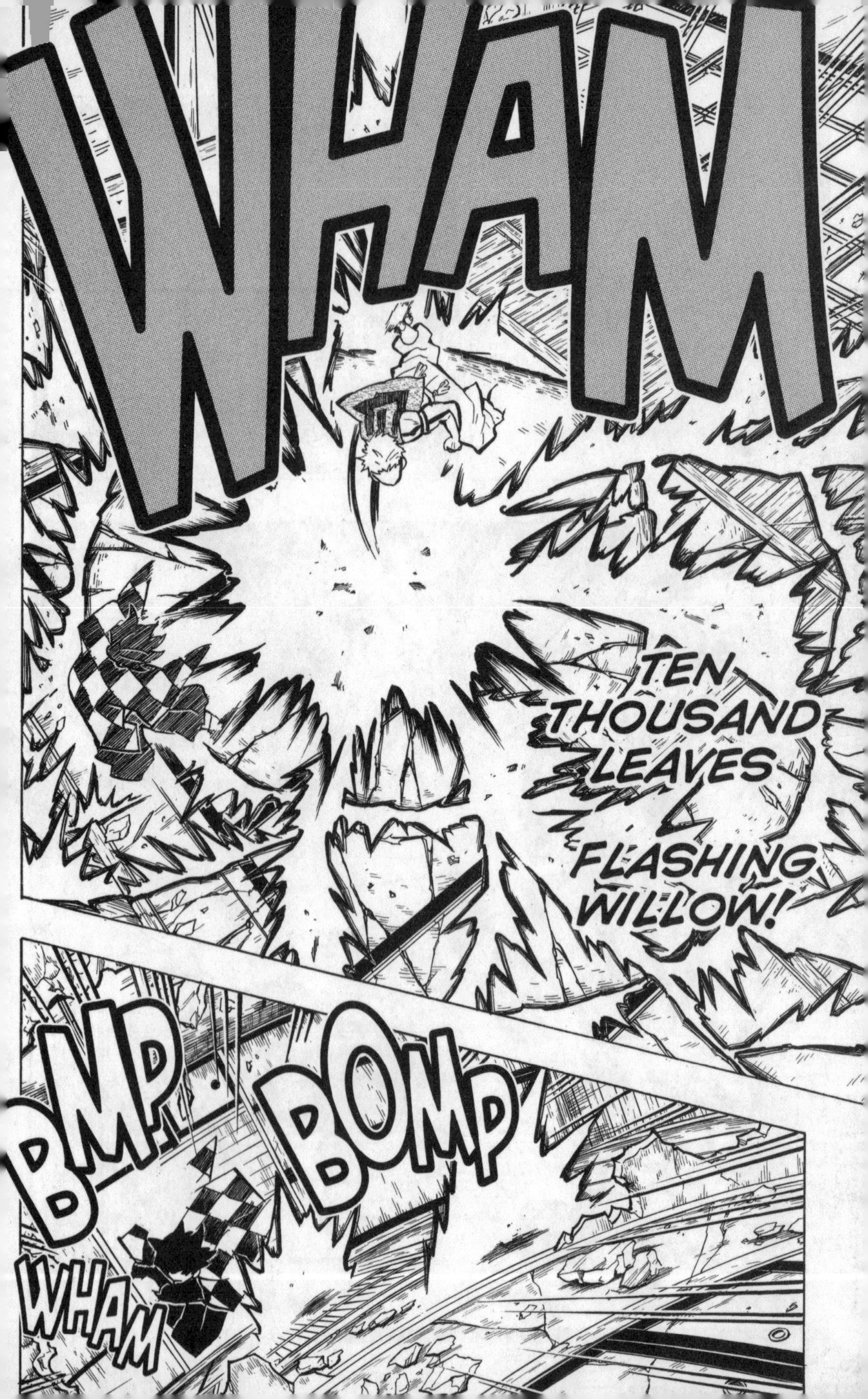
WHAM
TEN THOUSAND LEAVES FLASHING WILLOW!
BOMP
BMP
WHAM

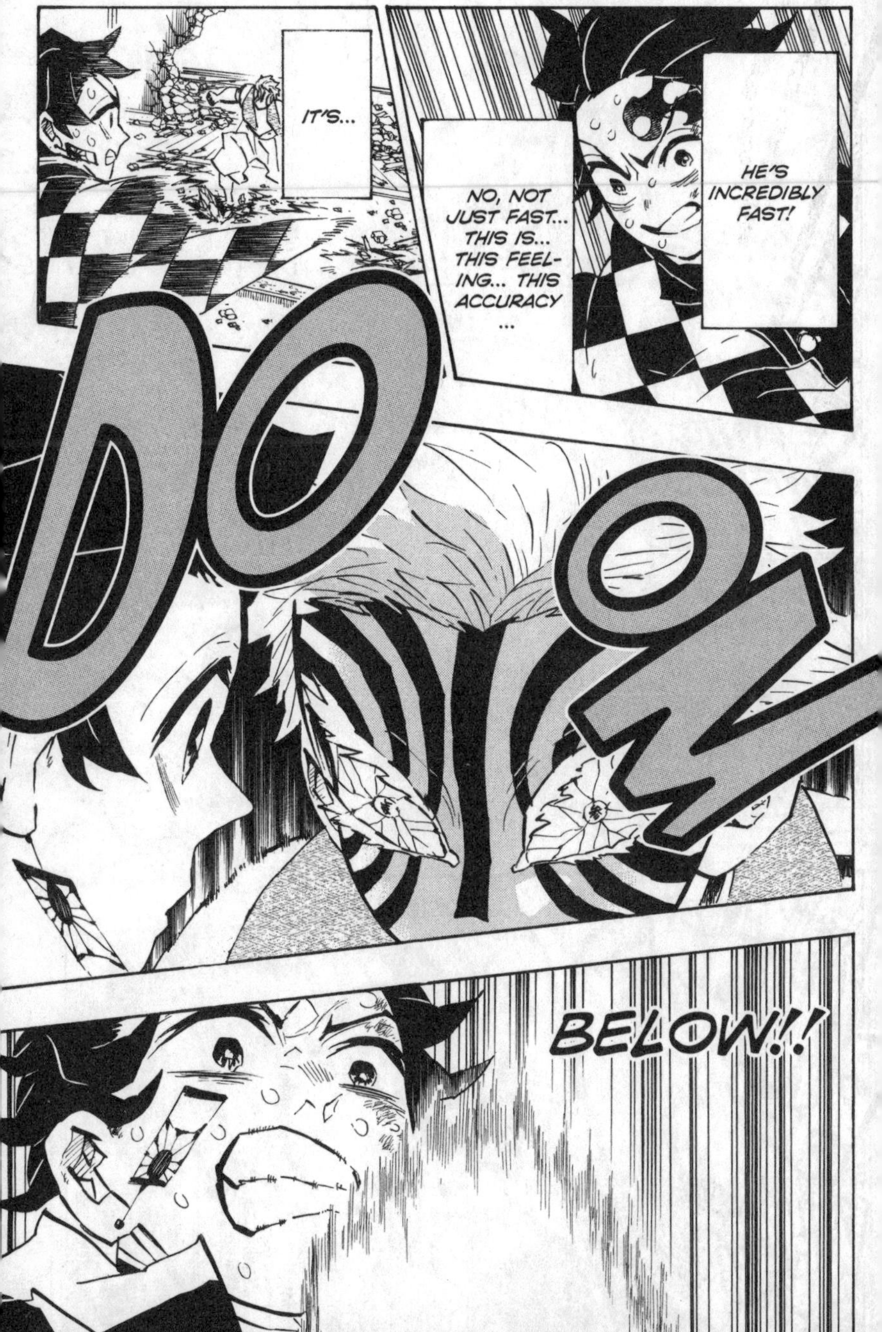
HE'S INCREDIBLY FAST!
NO, NOT JUST FAST... THIS IS... THIS FEELING... THIS ACCURACY ...
IT'S...
DOOM
BELOW!!

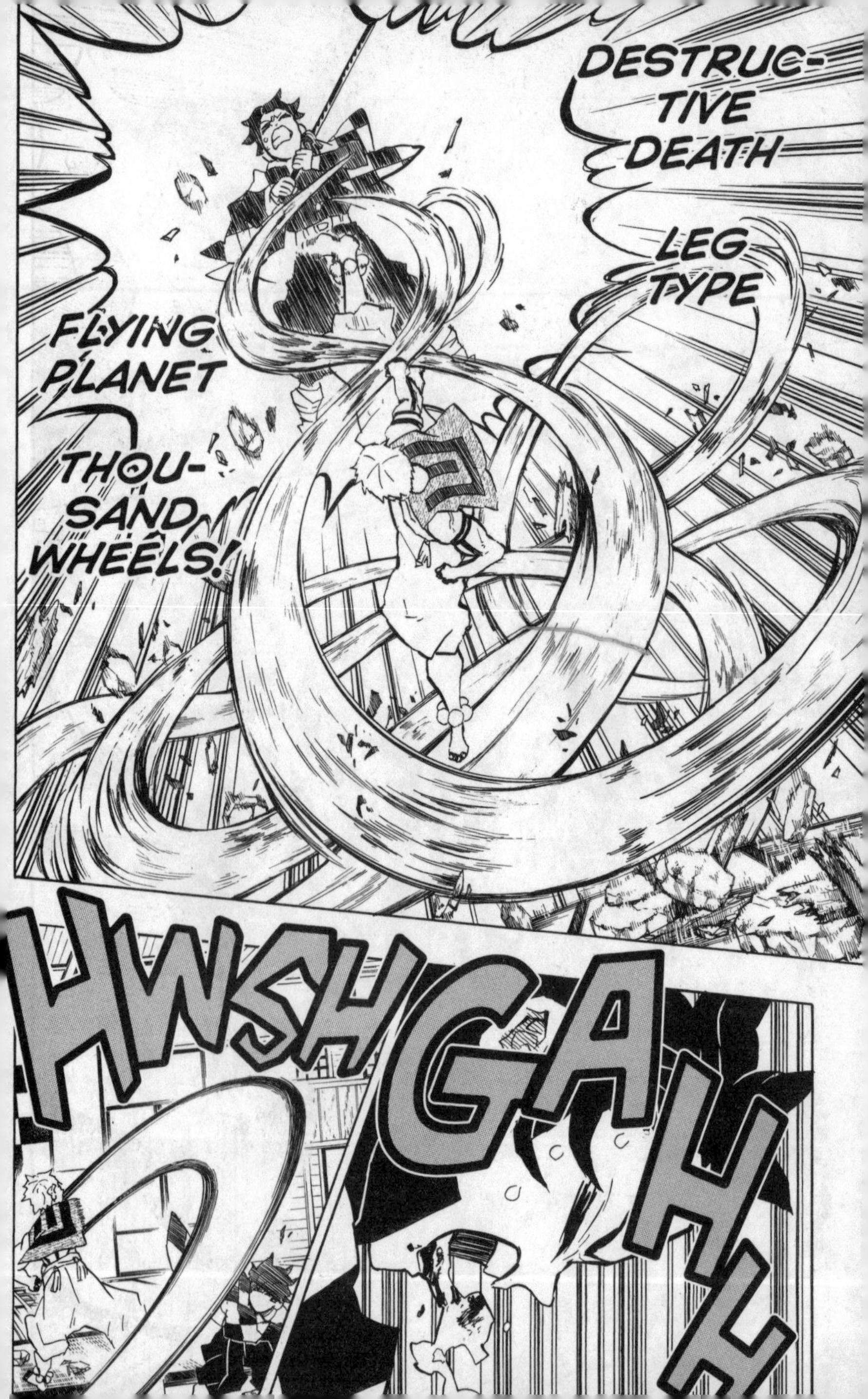
DESTRUCTIVE DEATH
LEG TYPE
FLYING PLANET
THOUSAND WHEELS!
HWSH
GAH

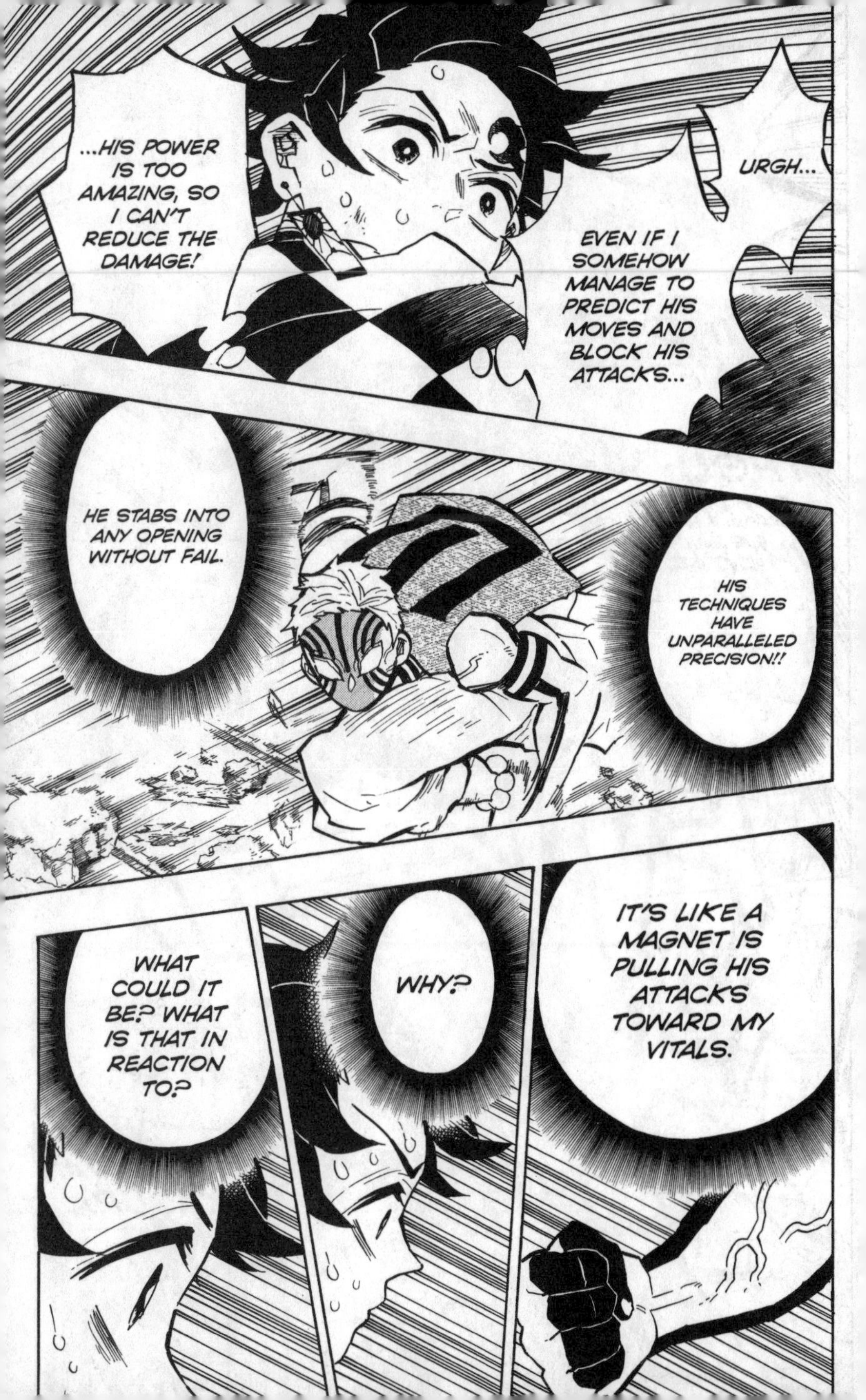
URGH...
EVEN IF I SOMEHOW MANAGE TO PREDICT HIS MOVES AND BLOCK HIS ATTACKS...
...HIS POWER IS TOO AMAZING, SO I CAN'T REDUCE THE DAMAGE!
HIS TECHNIQUES HAVE UNPARALLELED PRECISION!!
HE STABS INTO ANY OPENING WITHOUT FAIL.
IT'S LIKE A MAGNET IS PULLING HIS ATTACKS TOWARD MY VITALS.
WHY?
WHAT COULD IT BE? WHAT IS THAT IN REACTION TO?

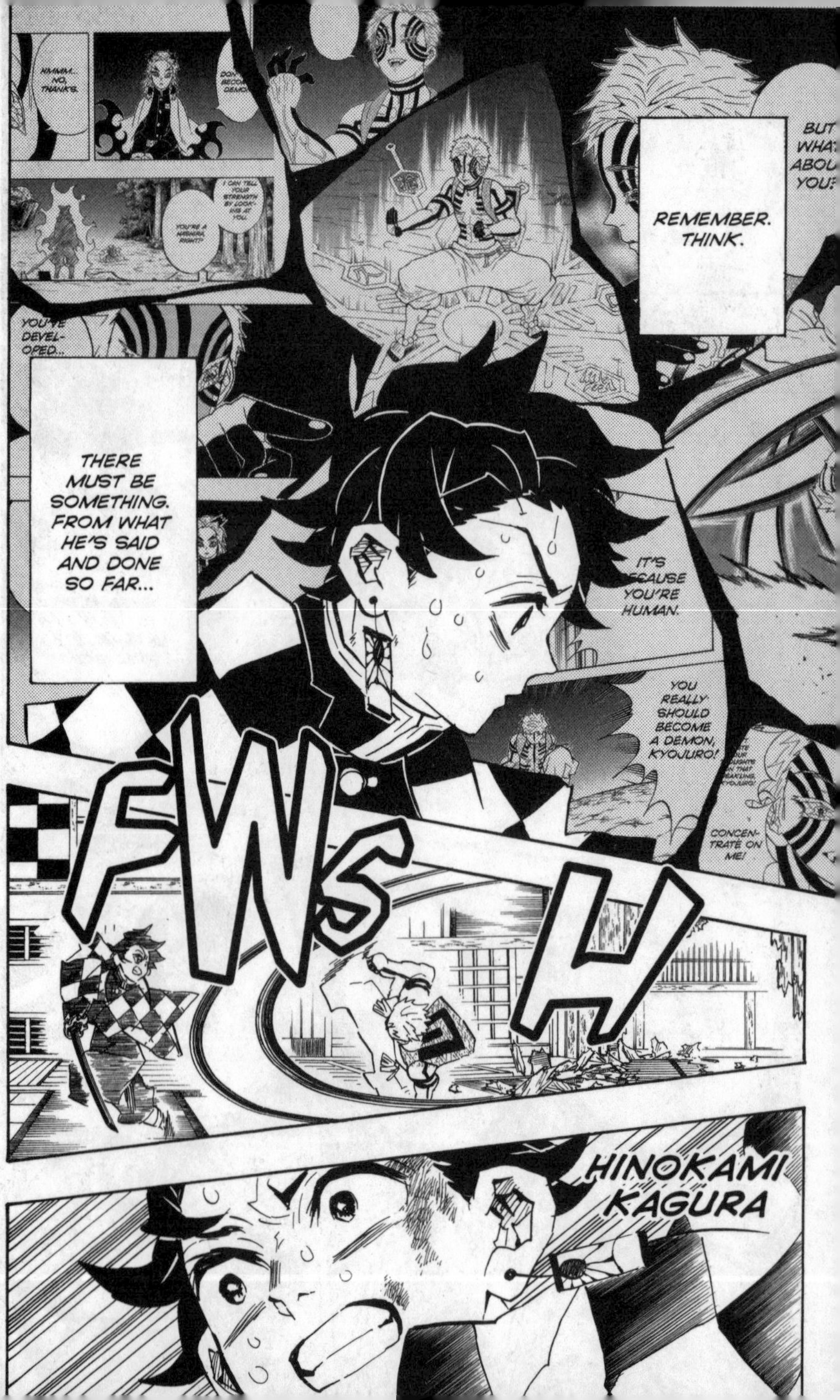
BUT WHAT ABOU YOU?
REMEMBER. THINK.
HMMM... NO, THANKS.
I CAN TELL YOUR STRENGTH BY LOOKING AT YOU.
YOU'RE A HASHIRA, RIGHT?
YOU'VE DEVELOPED...
IT'S BECAUSE YOU'RE HUMAN.
YOU REALLY SHOULD BECOME A DEMON, KYOJURO!
CONCENTRATE ON ME!
THERE MUST BE SOMETHING. FROM WHAT HE'S SAID AND DONE SO FAR...
FWSH
HINOKAMI KAGURA

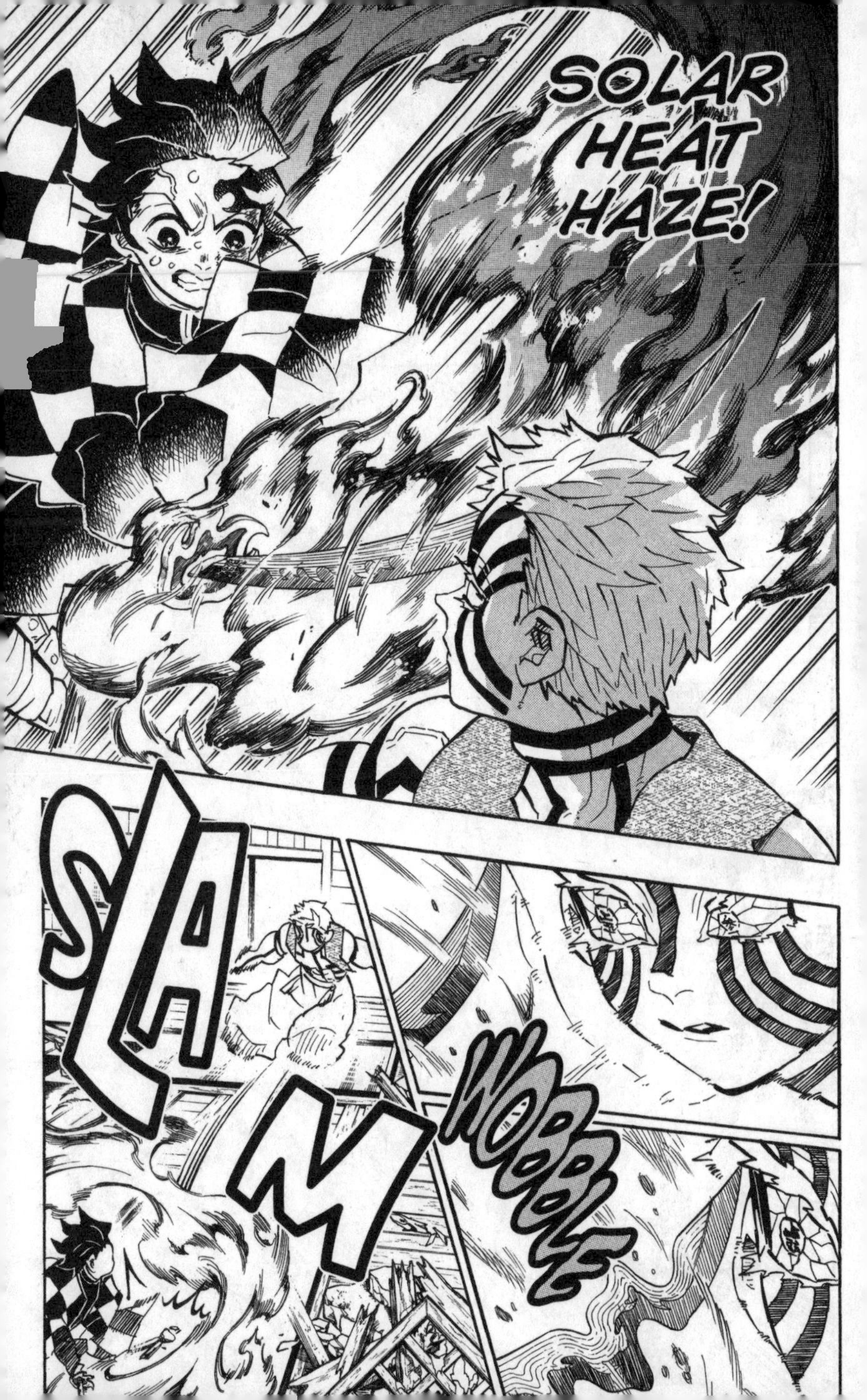
SOLAR HEAT HAZE!
WOBBLE
SLAM

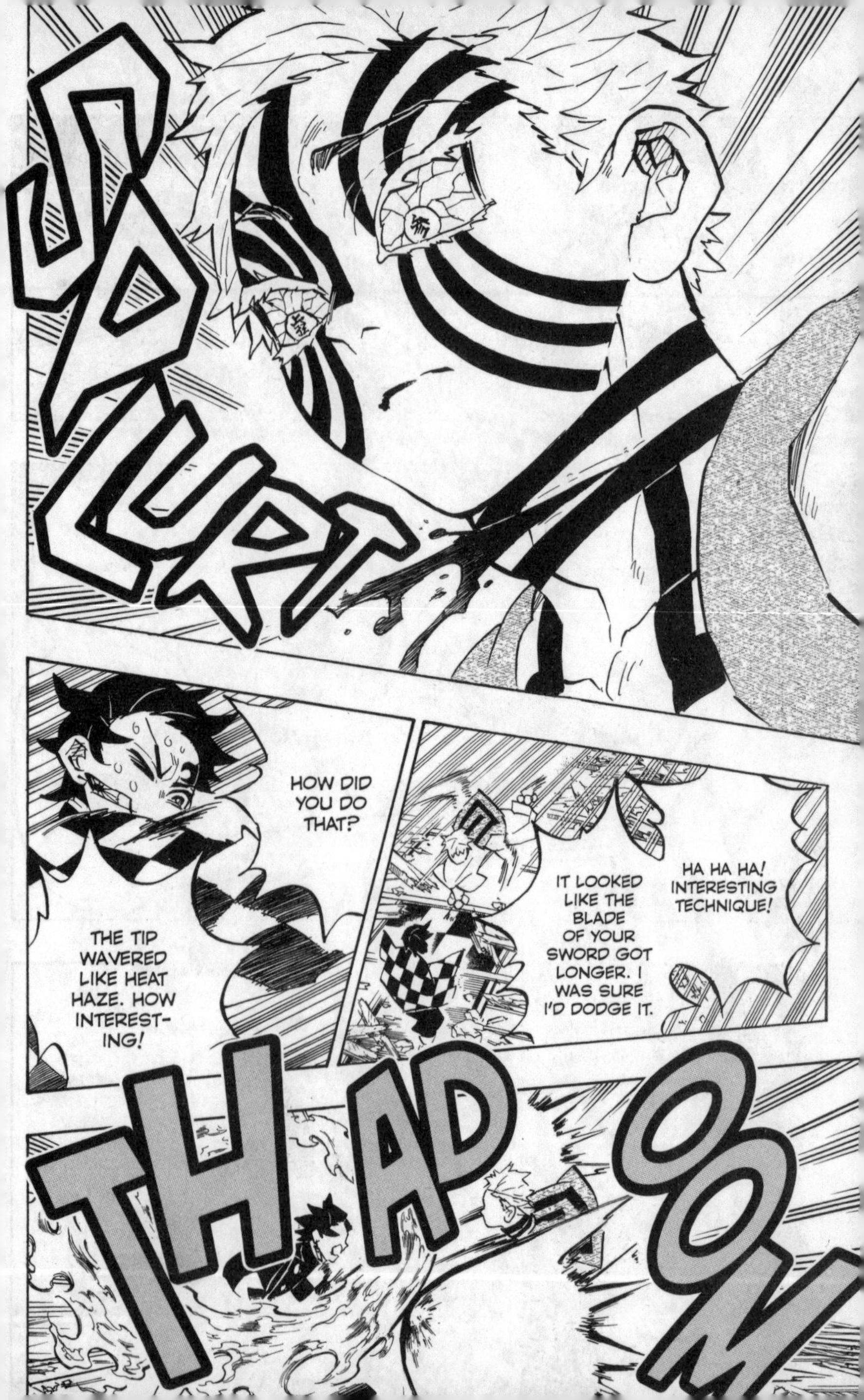
SPLURT
HA HA HA! INTERESTING TECHNIQUE!
IT LOOKED LIKE THE BLADE OF YOUR SWORD GOT LONGER. I WAS SURE I'D DODGE IT.
HOW DID YOU DO THAT?
THE TIP WAVERED LIKE HEAT HAZE. HOW INTERESTING!
THADOOM

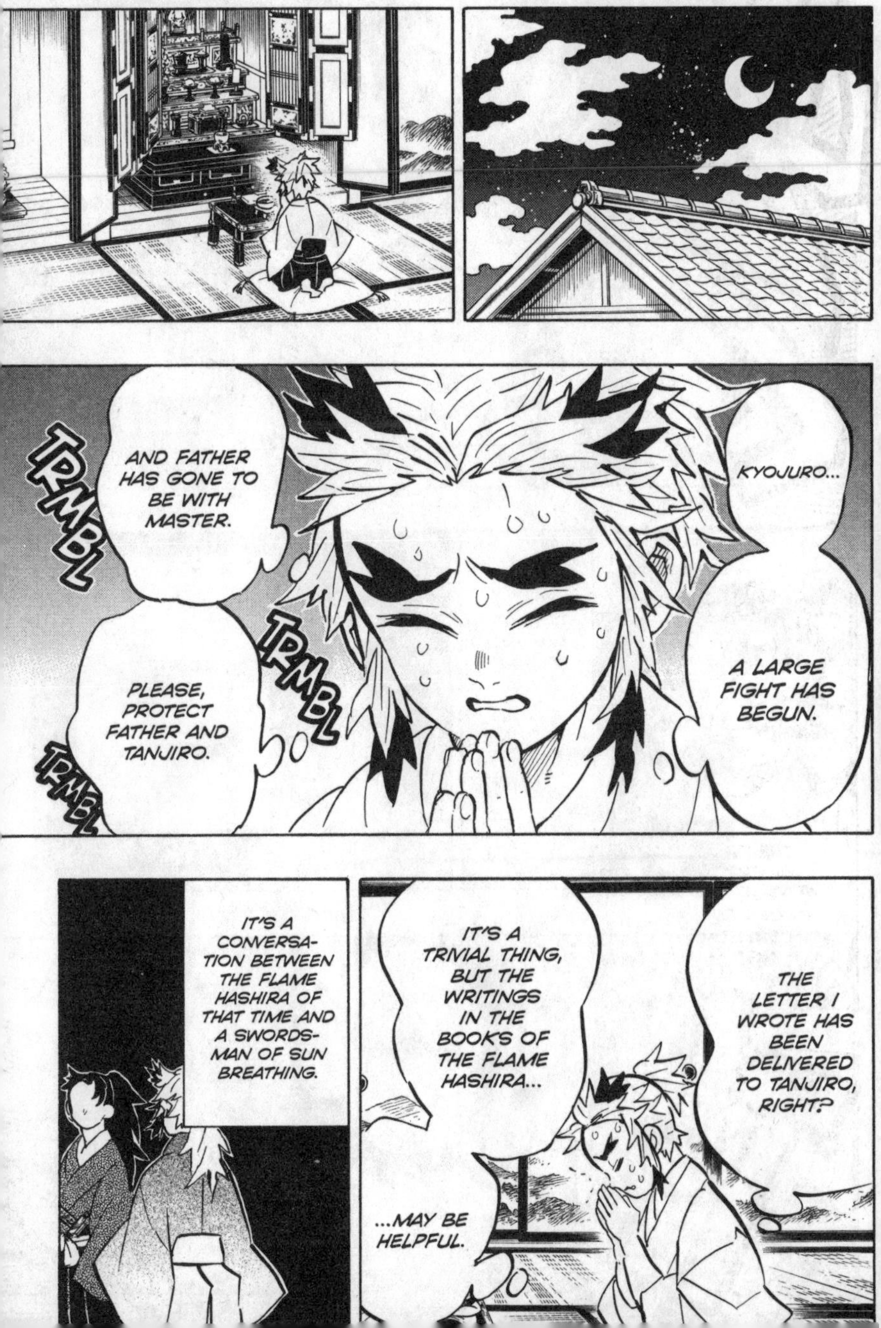
KYOJURO...
A LARGE FIGHT HAS BEGUN.
AND FATHER HAS GONE TO BE WITH MASTER.
TRMBL
TRMBL
PLEASE, PROTECT FATHER AND TANJIRO.
TRMBL
THE LETTER I WROTE HAS BEEN DELIVERED TO TANJIRO, RIGHT?
IT'S A TRIVIAL THING, BUT THE WRITINGS IN THE BOOKS OF THE FLAME HASHIRA...
...MAY BE HELPFUL.
IT'S A CONVERSA-TION BETWEEN THE FLAME HASHIRA OF THAT TIME AND A SWORDS-MAN OF SUN BREATHING.

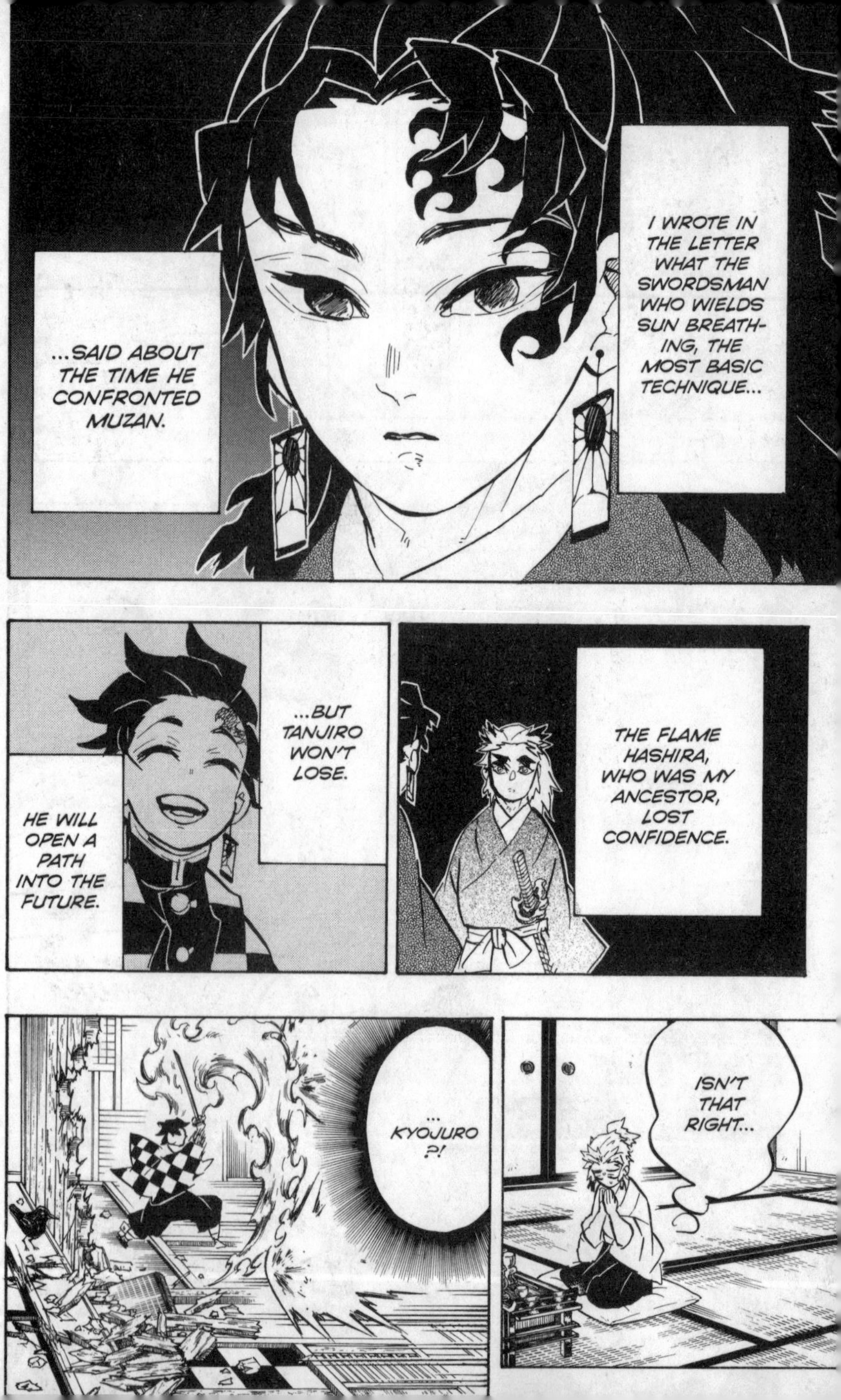
I WROTE IN THE LETTER WHAT THE SWORDSMAN WHO WIELDS SUN BREATHING, THE MOST BASIC TECHNIQUE...
...SAID ABOUT THE TIME HE CONFRONTED MUZAN.
THE FLAME HASHIRA, WHO WAS MY ANCESTOR, LOST CONFIDENCE.
...BUT TANJIRO WON'T LOSE.
HE WILL OPEN A PATH INTO THE FUTURE.
ISN'T THAT RIGHT...
...KYOJURO?!

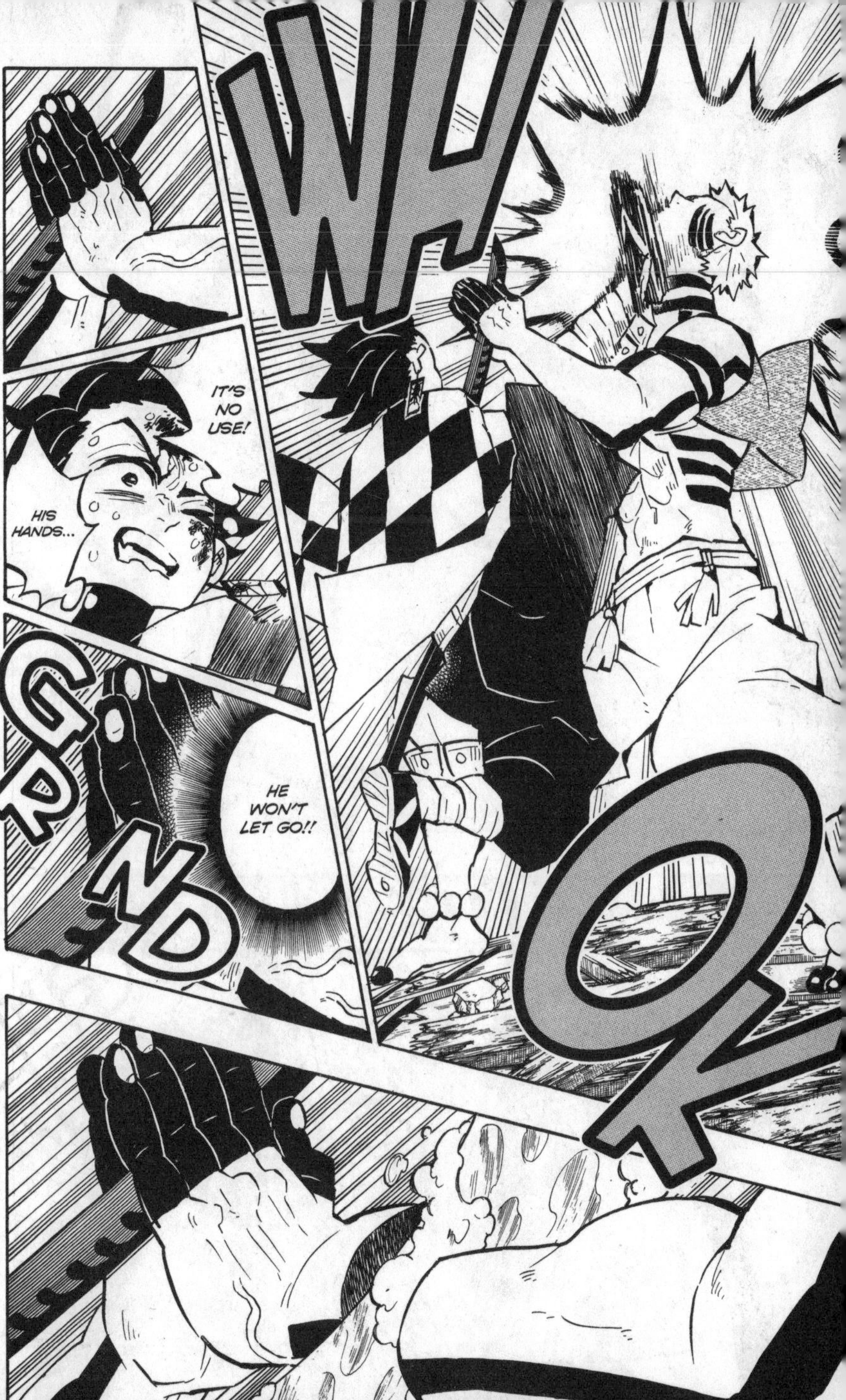
WHO
IT'S NO USE!
HIS HANDS...
HE WON'T LET GO!!
GRND

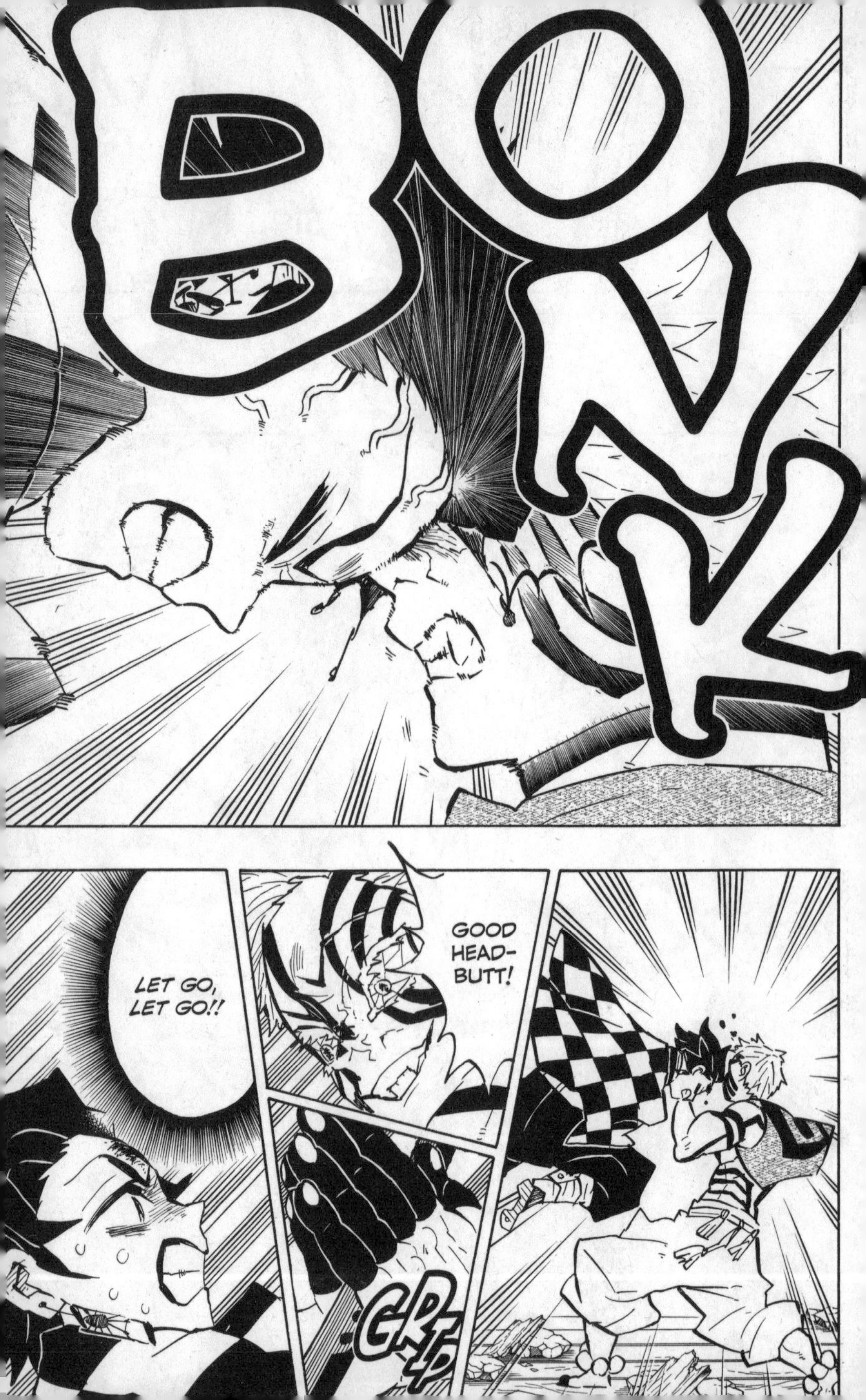
BONK
GOOD HEAD-BUTT!
GRIP
LET GO, LET GO!!

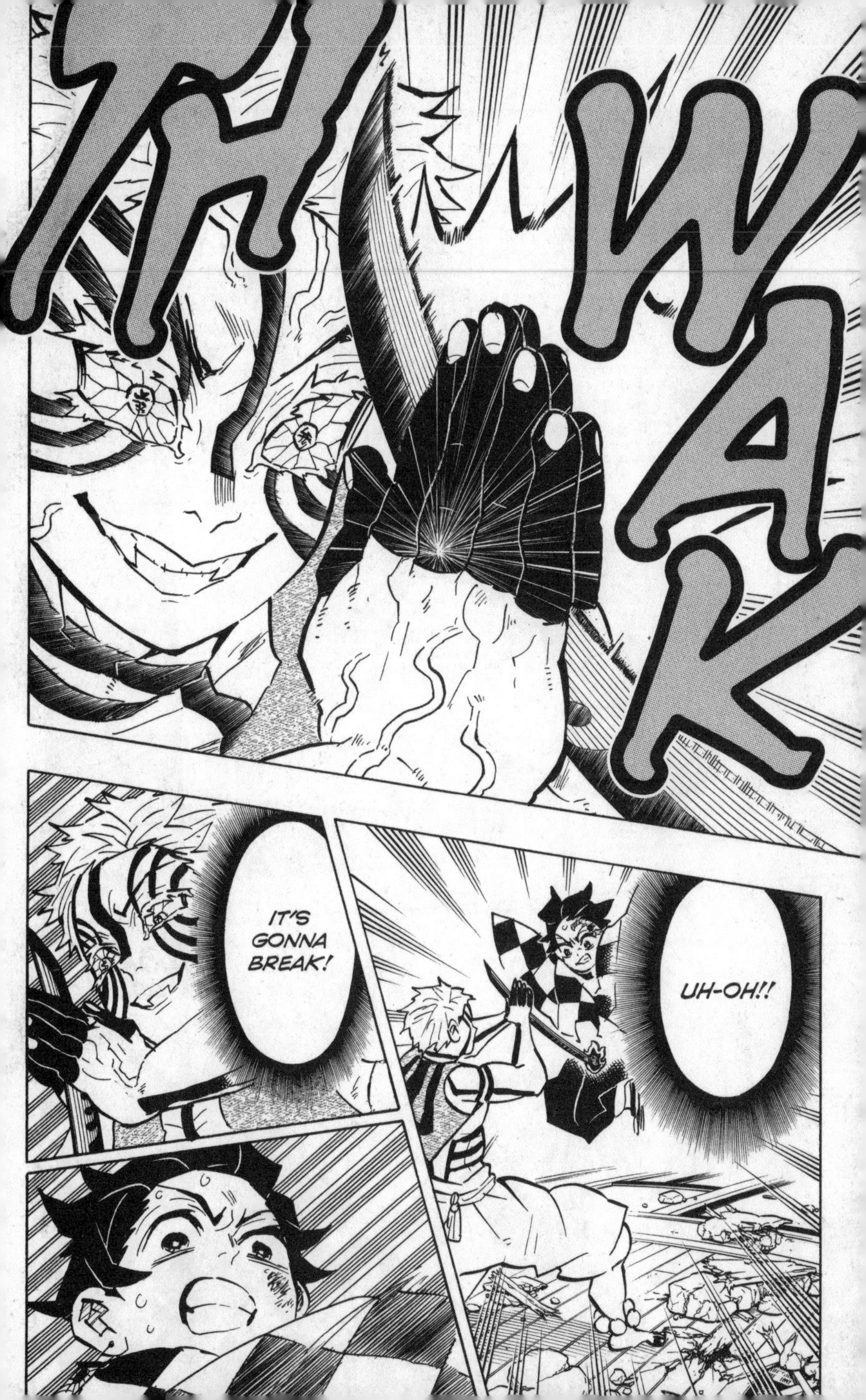
THWAK
UH-OH!!
IT'S GONNA BREAK!

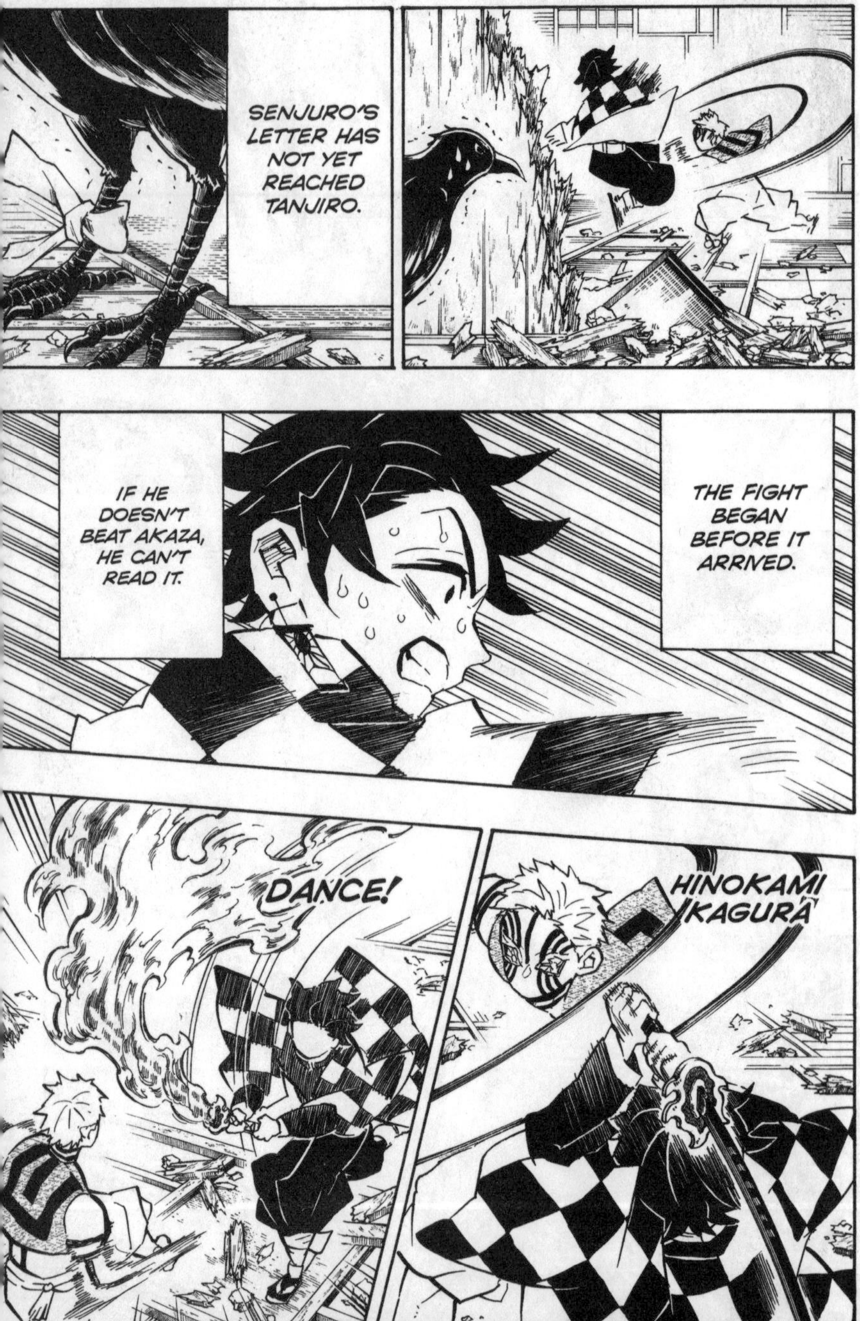
SENJURO'S LETTER HAS NOT YET REACHED TANJIRO.
THE FIGHT BEGAN BEFORE IT ARRIVED.
IF HE DOESN'T BEAT AKAZA, HE CAN'T READ IT.
HINOKAMI KAGURA
DANCE!

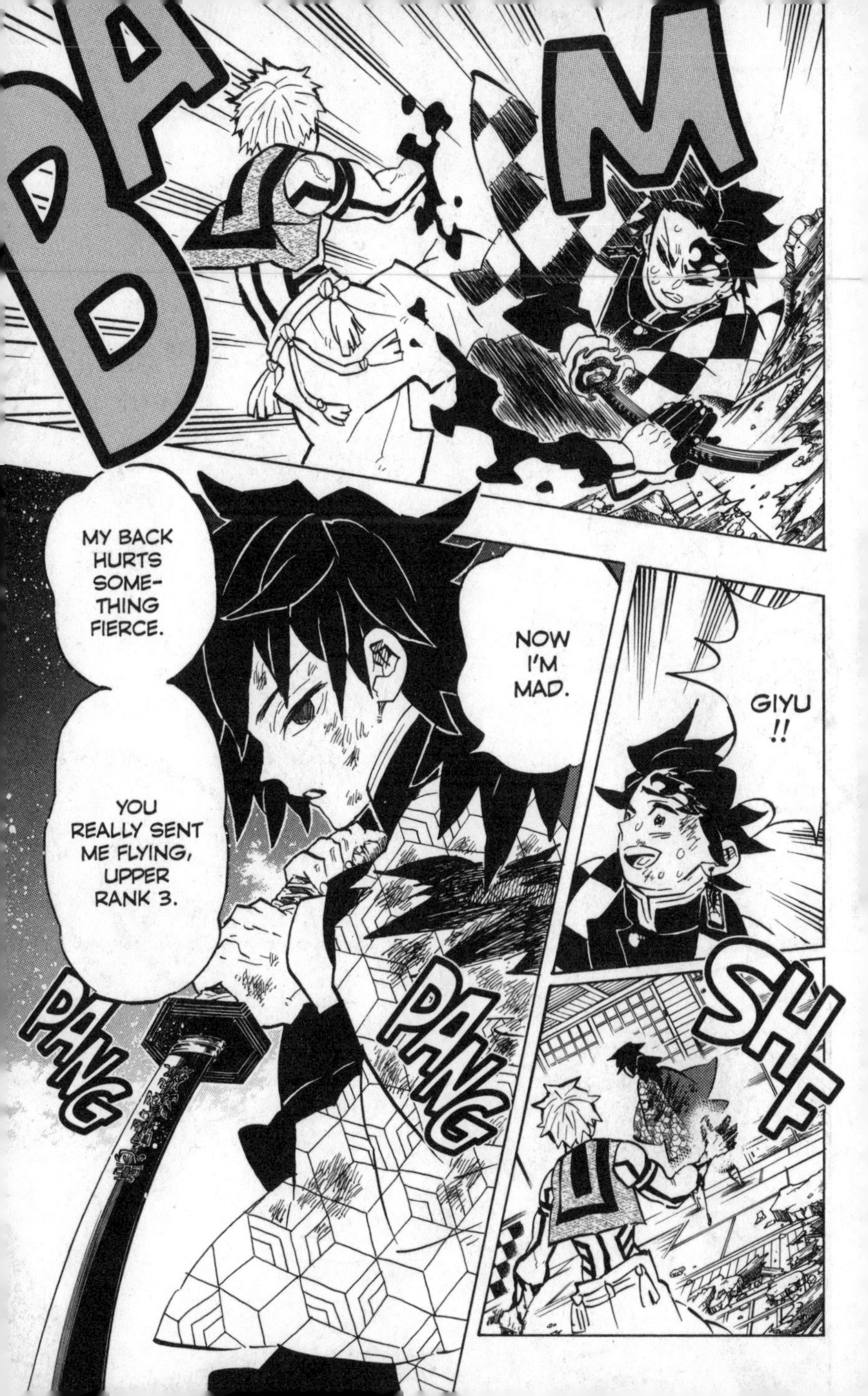
BADAM
GIYU!!
SHF
MY BACK HURTS SOMETHING FIERCE.
YOU REALLY SENT ME FLYING, UPPER RANK 3.
NOW I'M MAD.
PANG
PANG

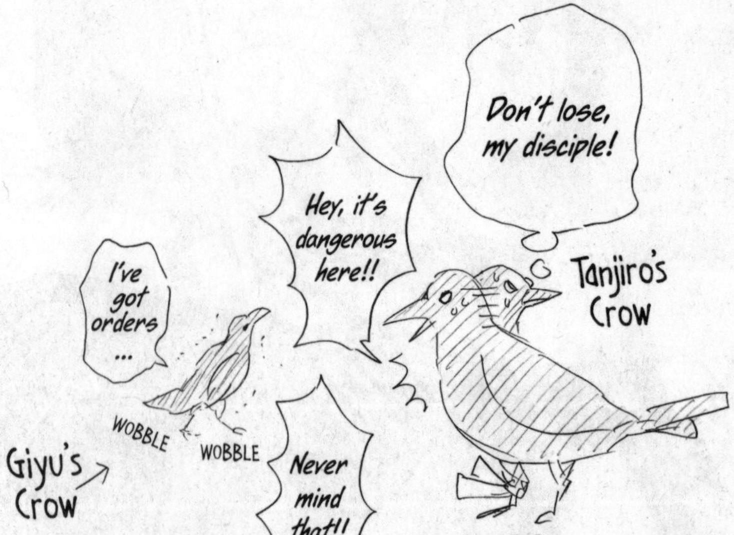
Don't lose, my disciple!
Tanjiro's Crow
Hey, it's dangerous here!!
I've got orders...
Never mind that!!
WOBBLE
WOBBLE
Giyu's Crow
Disciple → Tanjiro

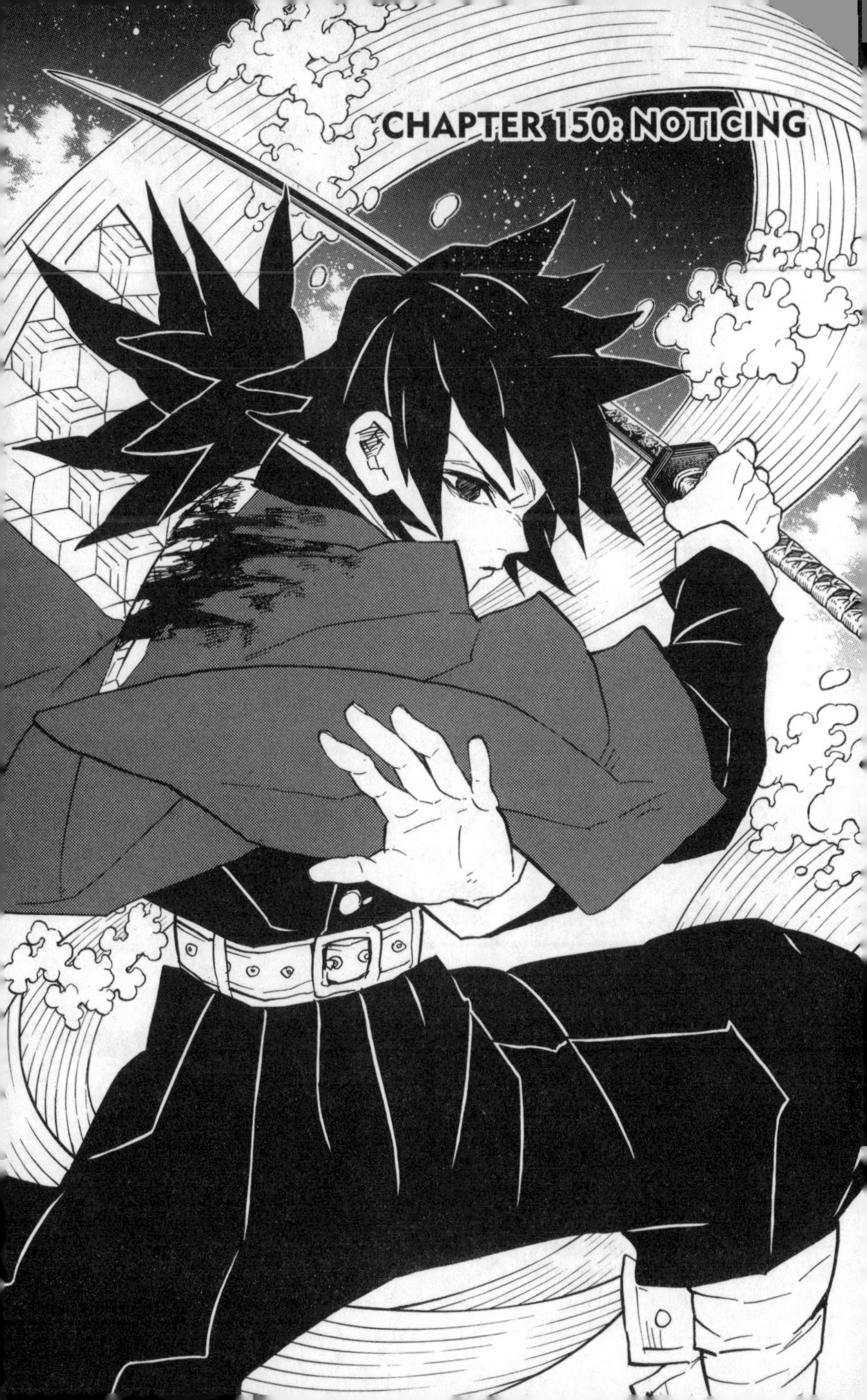
CHAPTER 150: NOTICING

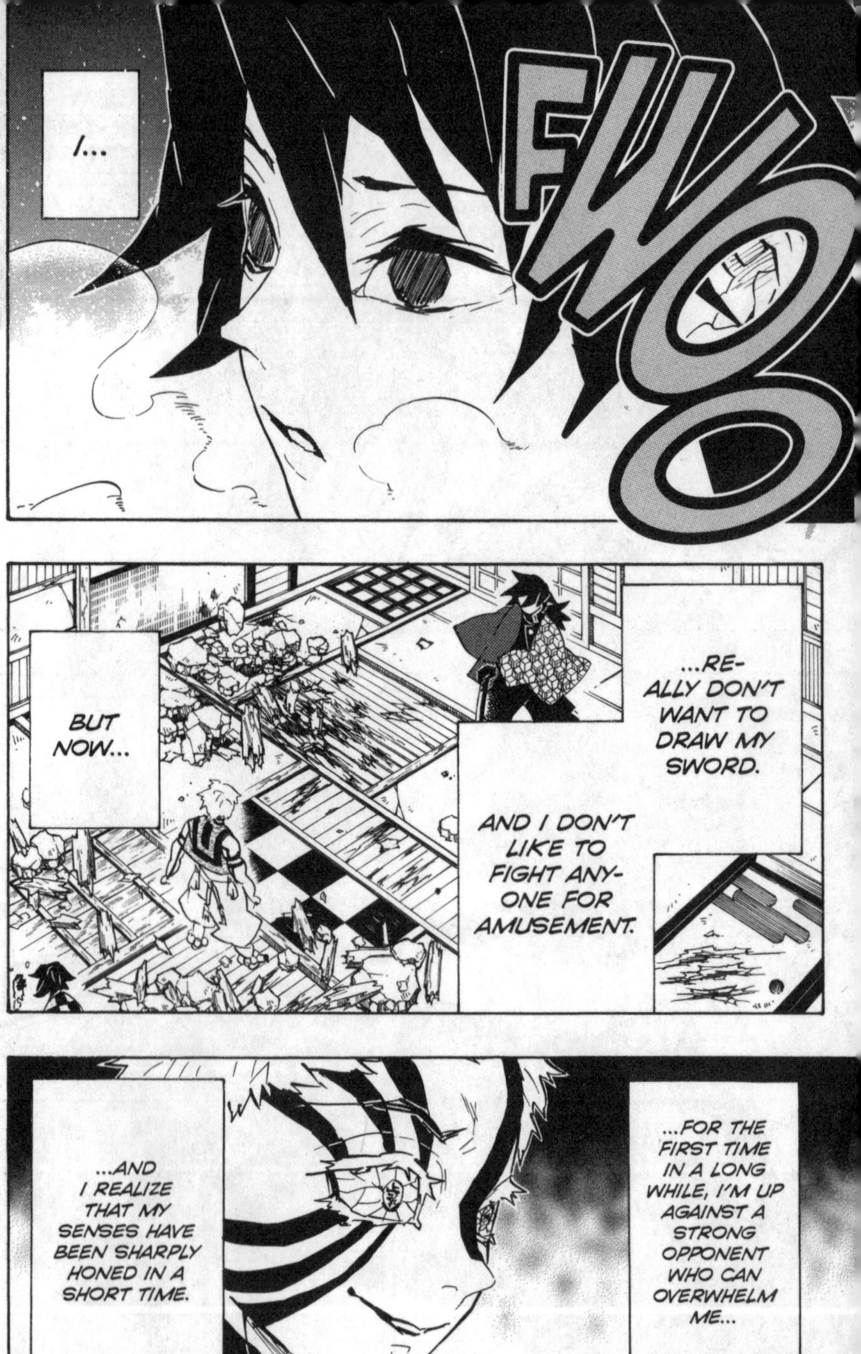
FWOO
I...
...REALLY DON'T WANT TO DRAW MY SWORD.
AND I DON'T LIKE TO FIGHT ANYONE FOR AMUSEMENT.
BUT NOW...
...FOR THE FIRST TIME IN A LONG WHILE, I'M UP AGAINST A STRONG OPPONENT WHO CAN OVERWHELM ME...
...AND I REALIZE THAT MY SENSES HAVE BEEN SHARPLY HONED IN A SHORT TIME.

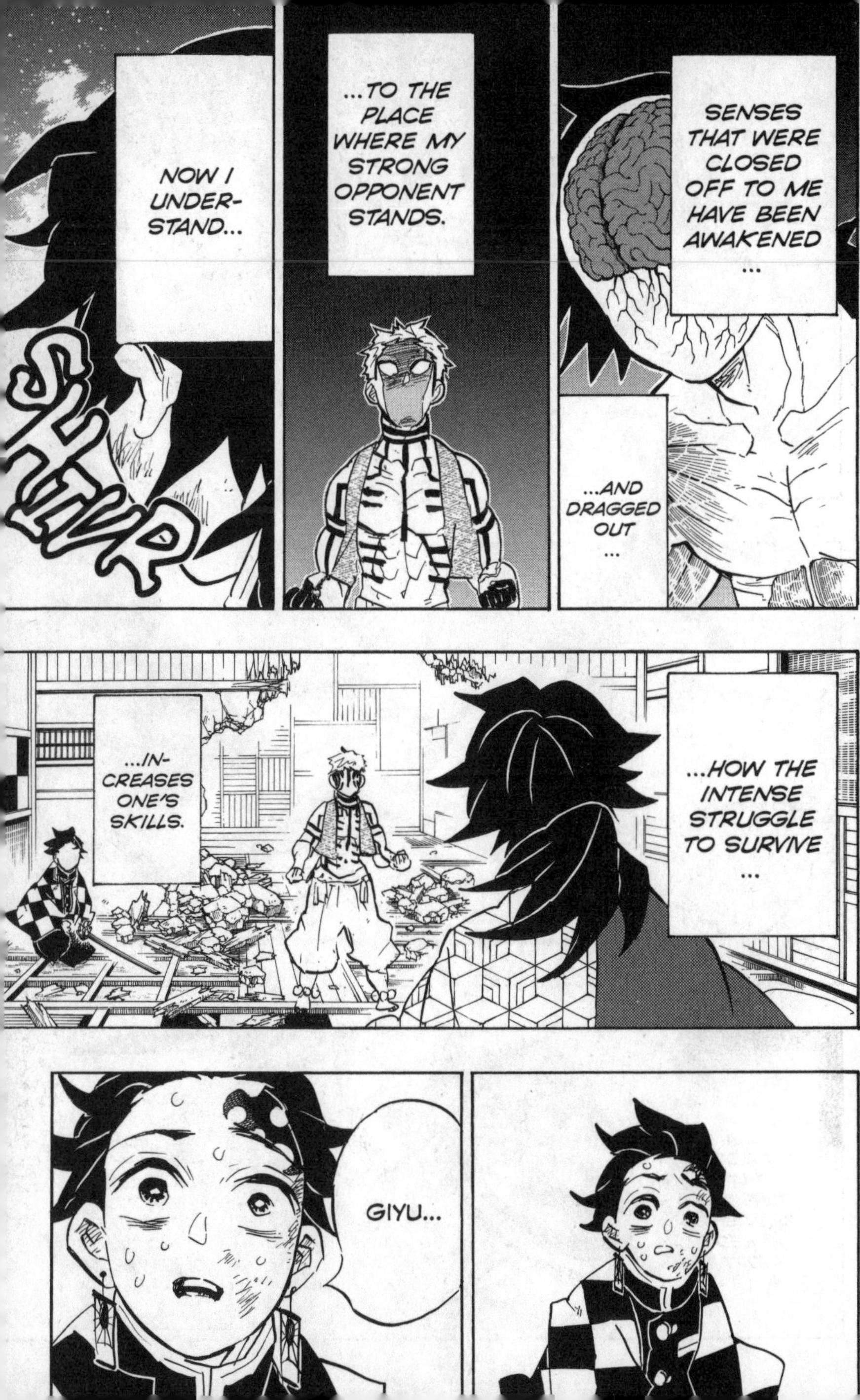
SENSES THAT WERE CLOSED OFF TO ME HAVE BEEN AWAKENED...
...AND DRAGGED OUT...
...TO THE PLACE WHERE MY STRONG OPPONENT STANDS.
NOW I UNDERSTAND...
SHIVR
...HOW THE INTENSE STRUGGLE TO SURVIVE...
...INCREASES ONE'S SKILLS.
GIYU...

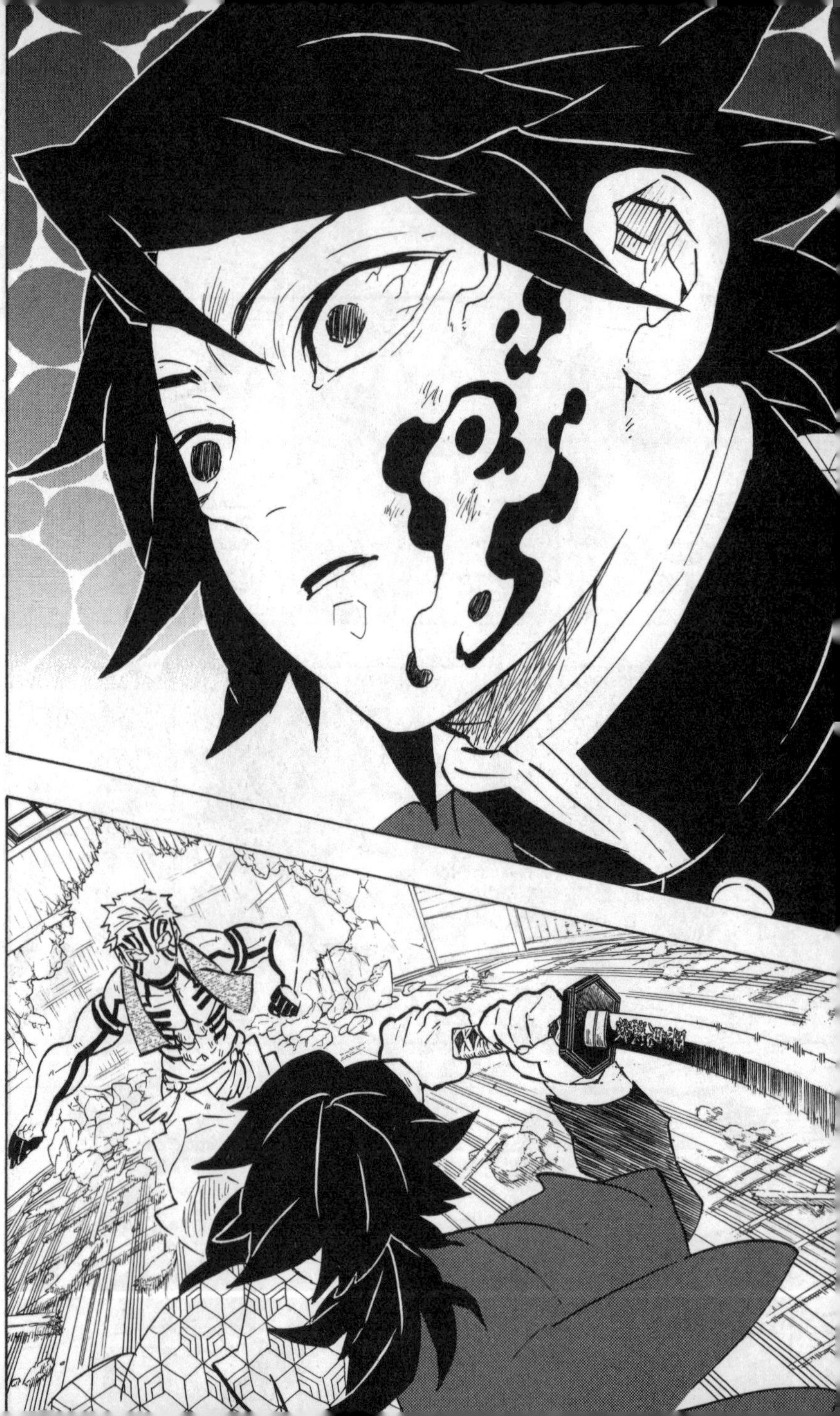

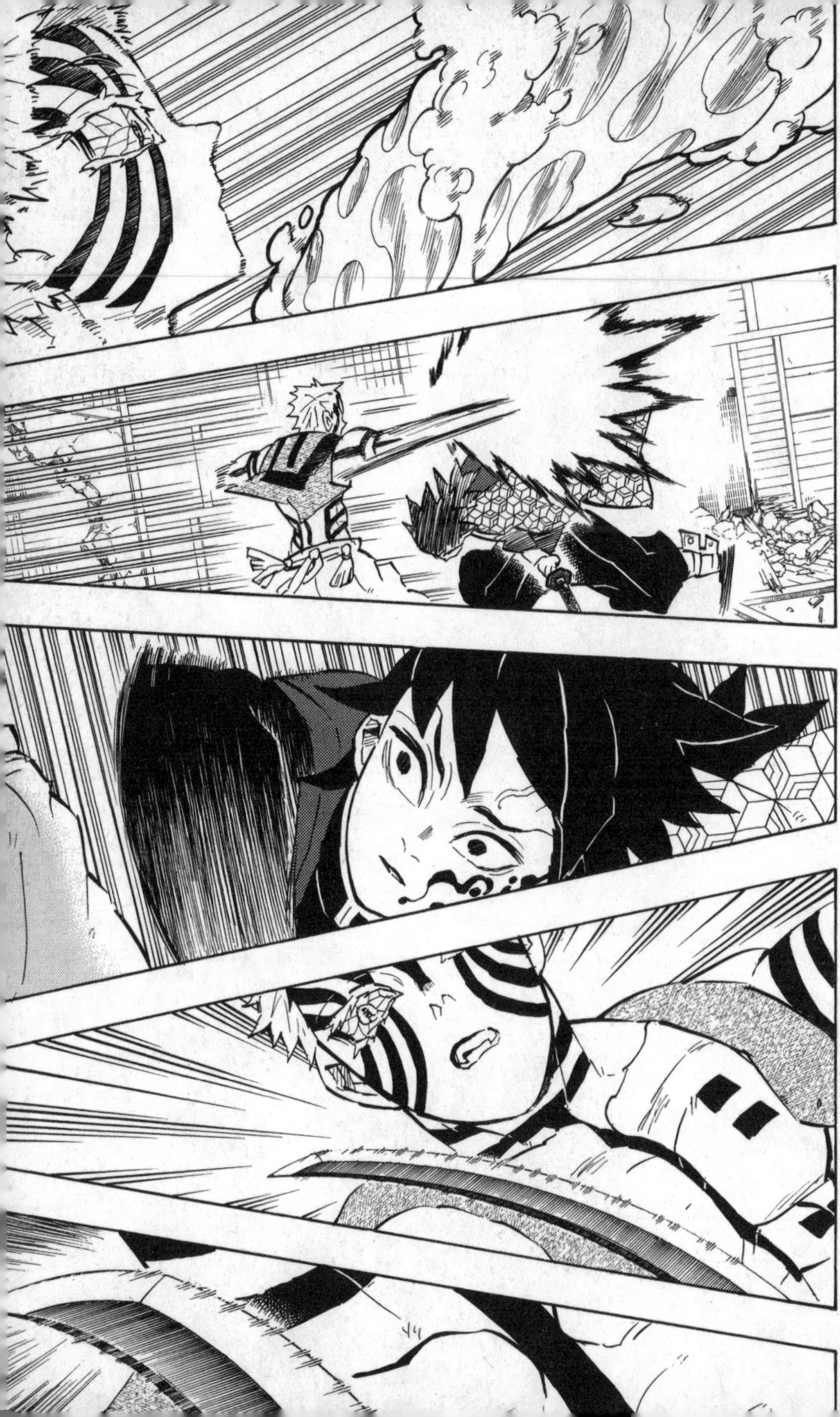

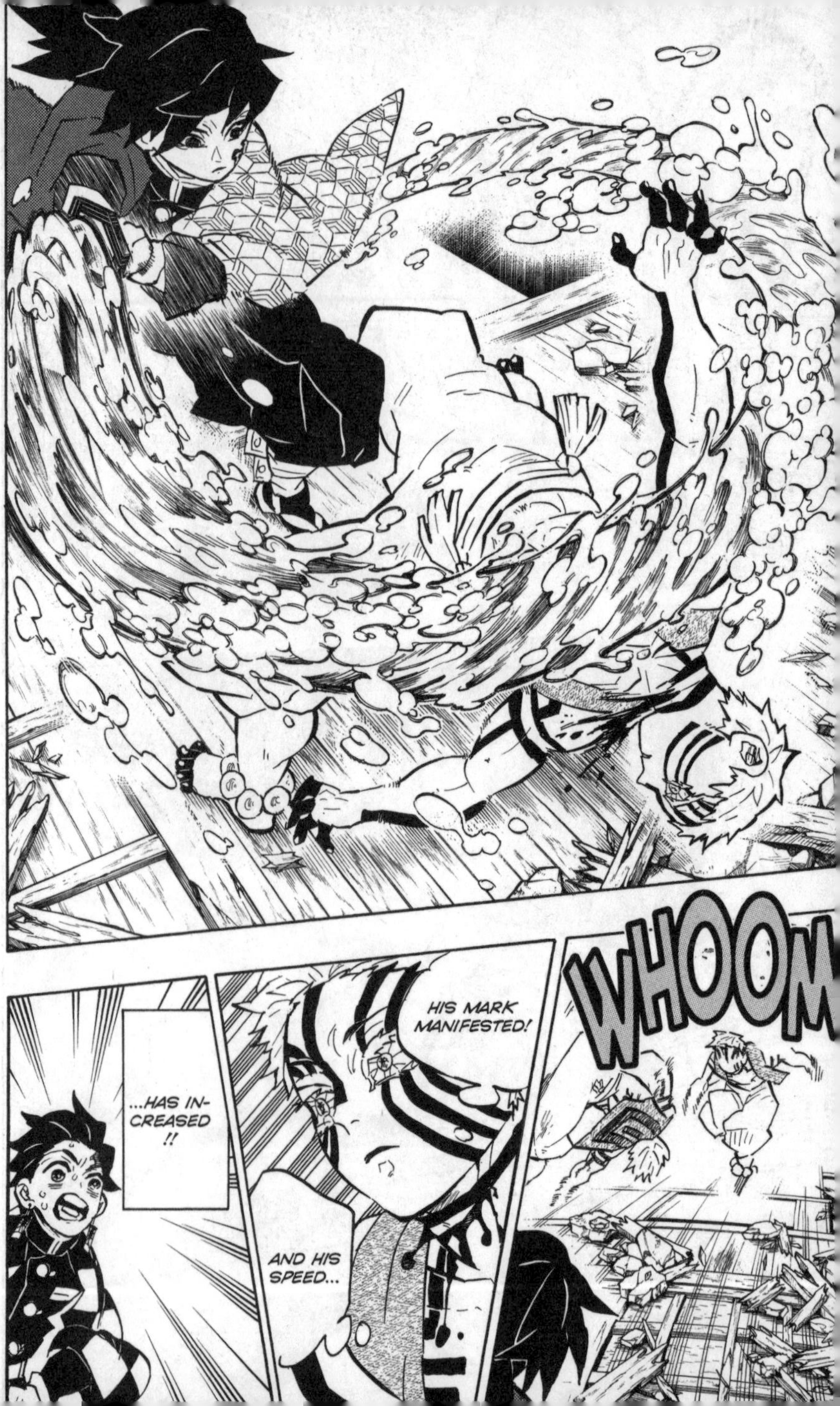
WHOOM
HIS MARK MANIFESTED!
AND HIS SPEED...
...HAS IN-CREASED !!

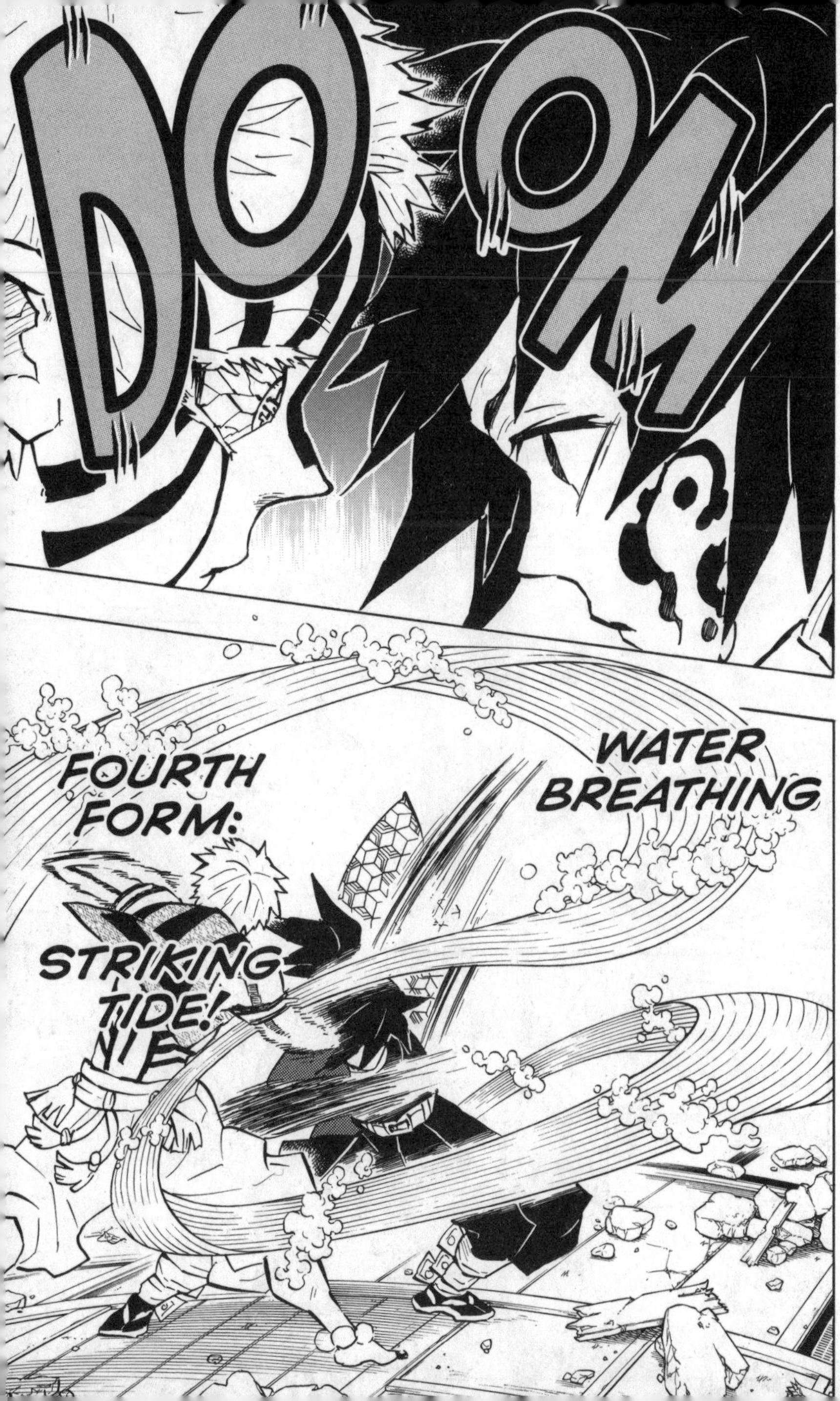
DOOM
WATER BREATHING
FOURTH FORM:
STRIKING TIDE!

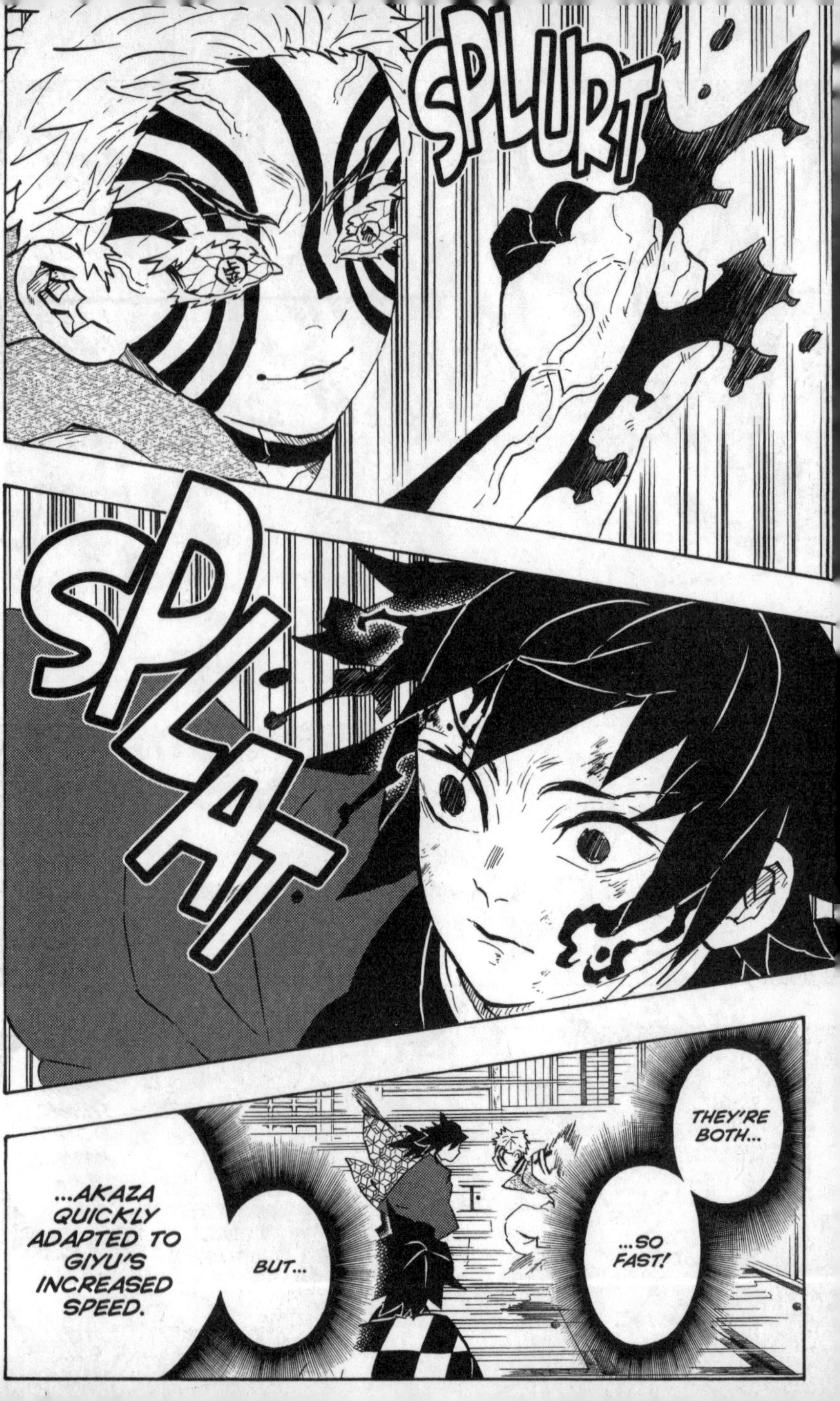
SPLURT
SPLAT
THEY'RE BOTH...
...SO FAST!
BUT...
...AKAZA QUICKLY ADAPTED TO GIYU'S INCREASED SPEED.

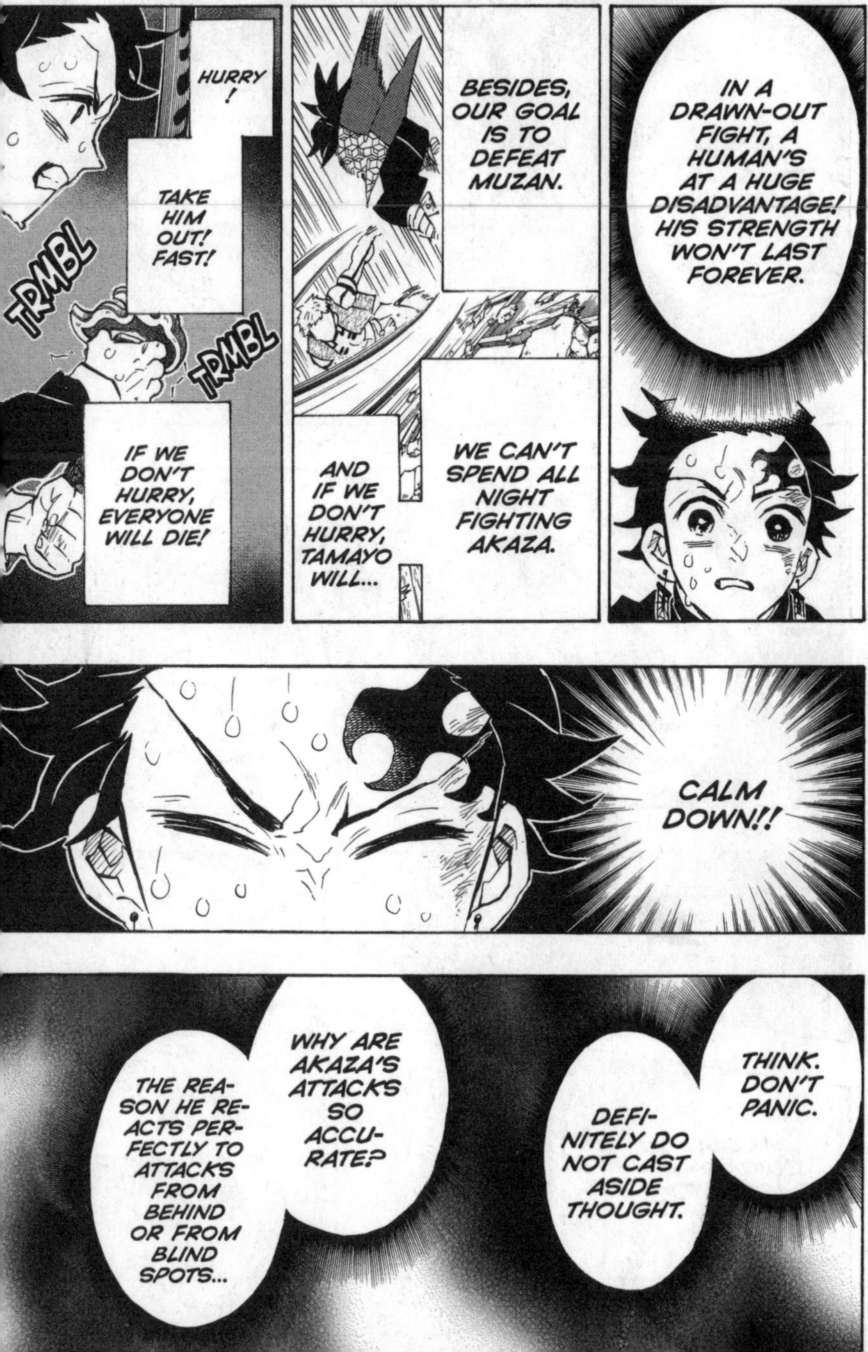
IN A DRAWN-OUT FIGHT, A HUMAN'S AT A HUGE DISADVANTAGE! HIS STRENGTH WON'T LAST FOREVER.
BESIDES, OUR GOAL IS TO DEFEAT MUZAN.
WE CAN'T SPEND ALL NIGHT FIGHTING AKAZA.
AND IF WE DON'T HURRY, TAMAYO WILL...
HURRY!
TAKE HIM OUT! FAST!
TRMBL
TRMBL
IF WE DON'T HURRY, EVERYONE WILL DIE!
CALM DOWN!!
THINK. DON'T PANIC.
DEFINITELY DO NOT CAST ASIDE THOUGHT.
WHY ARE AKAZA'S ATTACKS SO ACCURATE?
THE REASON HE REACTS PERFECTLY TO ATTACKS FROM BEHIND OR FROM BLIND SPOTS...

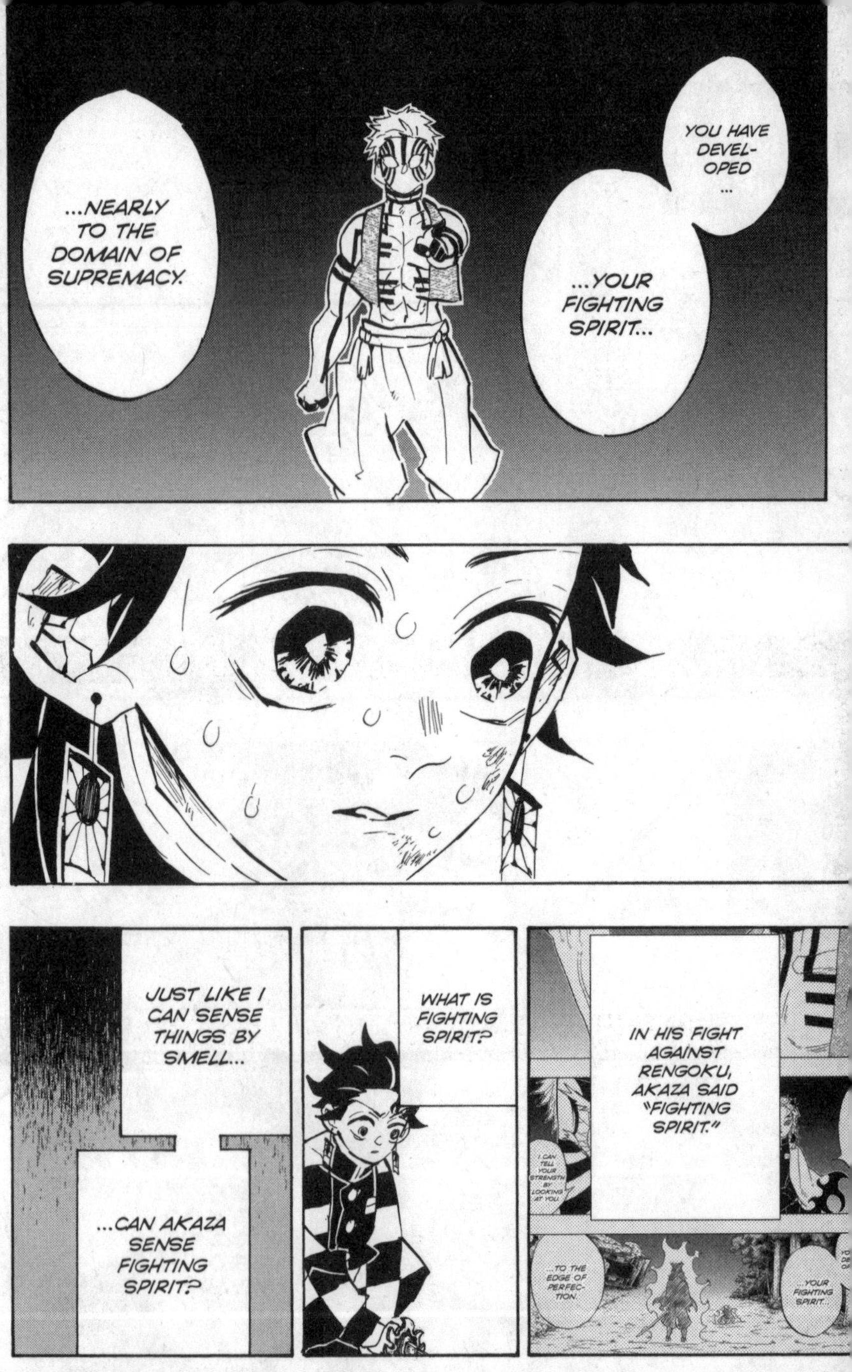
YOU HAVE DEVEL-OPED ...
...YOUR FIGHTING SPIRIT...
...NEARLY TO THE DOMAIN OF SUPREMACY.
IN HIS FIGHT AGAINST RENGOKU, AKAZA SAID "FIGHTING SPIRIT."
I CAN TELL YOUR STRENGTH BY LOOKING AT YOU.
...YOUR FIGHTING SPIRIT...
...TO THE EDGE OF PERFECTION.
WHAT IS FIGHTING SPIRIT?
JUST LIKE I CAN SENSE THINGS BY SMELL...
...CAN AKAZA SENSE FIGHTING SPIRIT?

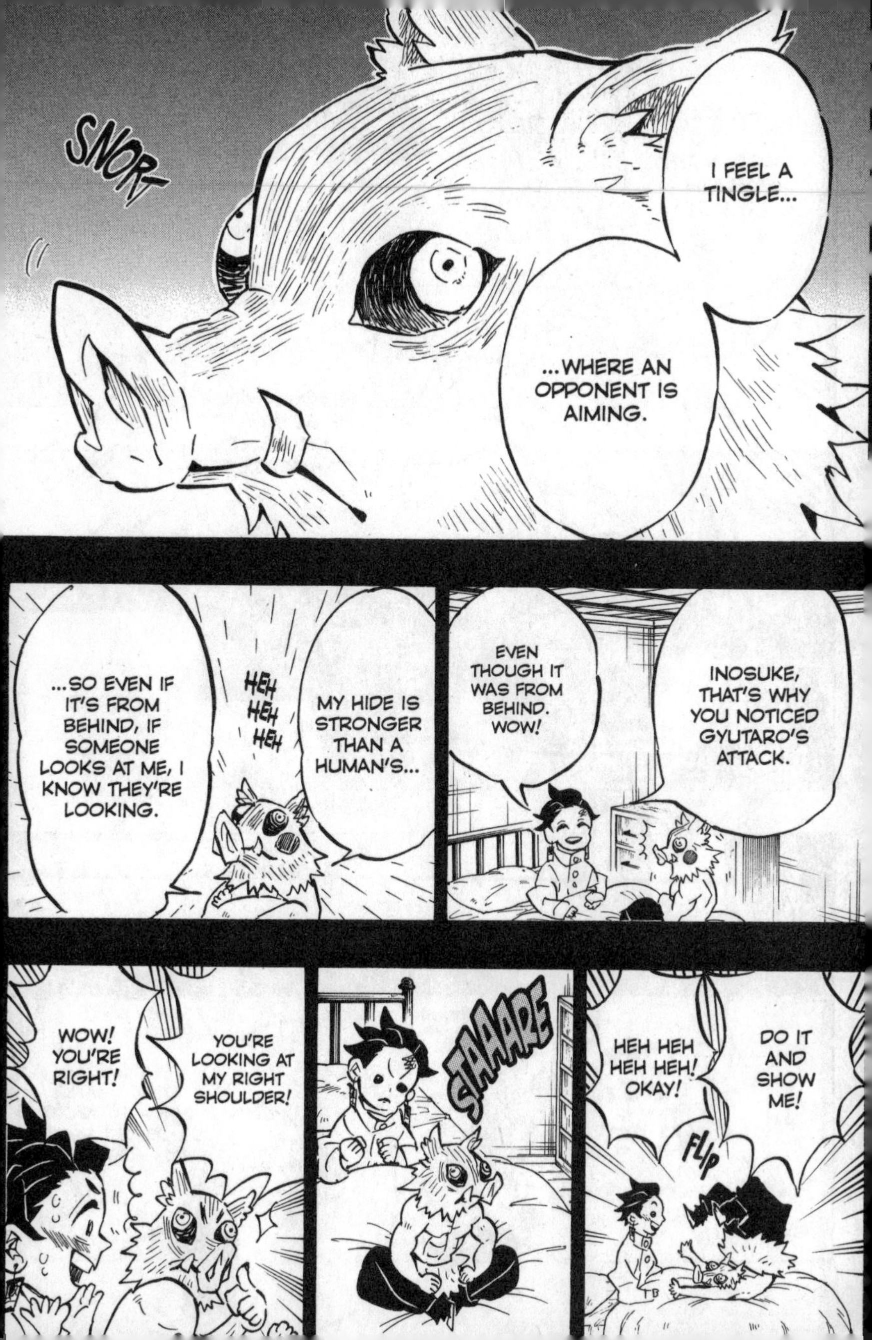
I FEEL A TINGLE...
...WHERE AN OPPONENT IS AIMING.
SNORT
INOSUKE, THAT'S WHY YOU NOTICED GYUTARO'S ATTACK.
EVEN THOUGH IT WAS FROM BEHIND. WOW!
MY HIDE IS STRONGER THAN A HUMAN'S...
HEH HEH HEH
...SO EVEN IF IT'S FROM BEHIND, IF SOMEONE LOOKS AT ME, I KNOW THEY'RE LOOKING.
DO IT AND SHOW ME!
HEH HEH HEH HEH! OKAY!
FLIP
STAAARE
YOU'RE LOOKING AT MY RIGHT SHOULDER!
WOW! YOU'RE RIGHT!

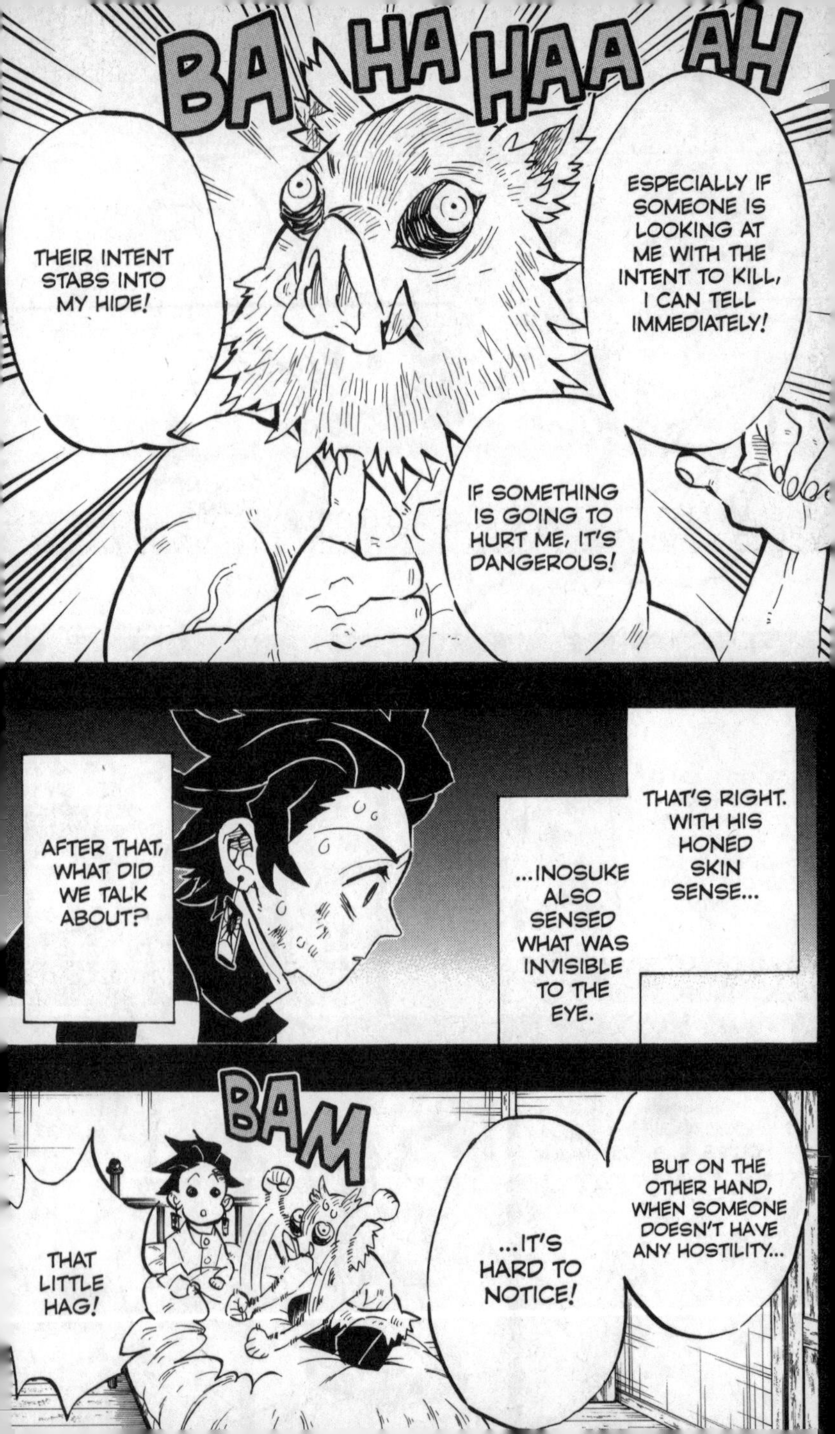
BA HA HAA AH
ESPECIALLY IF SOMEONE IS LOOKING AT ME WITH THE INTENT TO KILL, I CAN TELL IMMEDIATELY!
IF SOMETHING IS GOING TO HURT ME, IT'S DANGEROUS!
THEIR INTENT STABS INTO MY HIDE!
THAT'S RIGHT. WITH HIS HONED SKIN SENSE...
...INOSUKE ALSO SENSED WHAT WAS INVISIBLE TO THE EYE.
AFTER THAT, WHAT DID WE TALK ABOUT?
BUT ON THE OTHER HAND, WHEN SOMEONE DOESN'T HAVE ANY HOSTILITY...
...IT'S HARD TO NOTICE!
BAM
THAT LITTLE HAG!

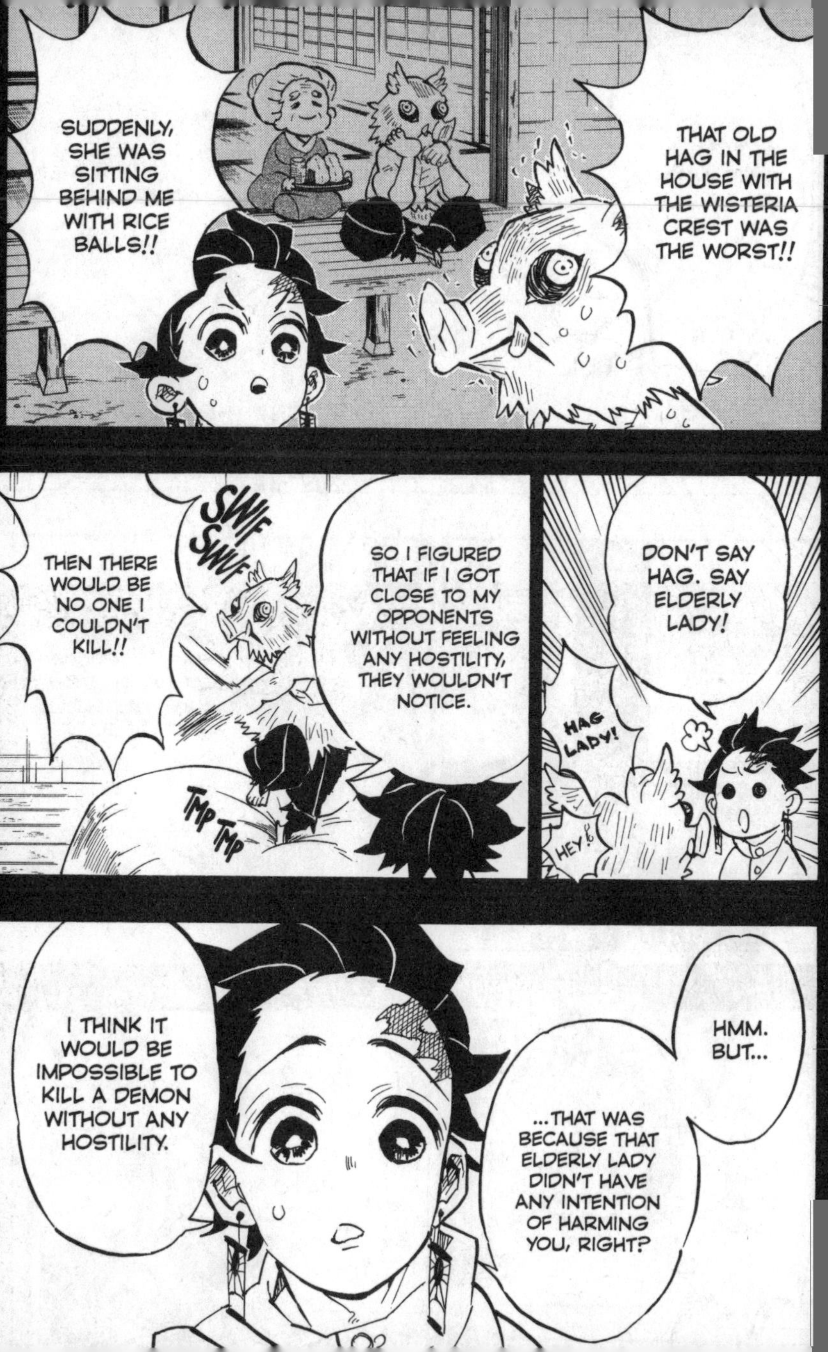
THAT OLD HAG IN THE HOUSE WITH THE WISTERIA CREST WAS THE WORST!!
SUDDENLY, SHE WAS SITTING BEHIND ME WITH RICE BALLS!!
DON'T SAY HAG. SAY ELDERLY LADY!
HAG LADY!
HEY!
SO I FIGURED THAT IF I GOT CLOSE TO MY OPPONENTS WITHOUT FEELING ANY HOSTILITY, THEY WOULDN'T NOTICE.
SWIF SWUF
THEN THERE WOULD BE NO ONE I COULDN'T KILL!!
TMP TMP
HMM. BUT...
...THAT WAS BECAUSE THAT ELDERLY LADY DIDN'T HAVE ANY INTENTION OF HARMING YOU, RIGHT?
I THINK IT WOULD BE IMPOSSIBLE TO KILL A DEMON WITHOUT ANY HOSTILITY.

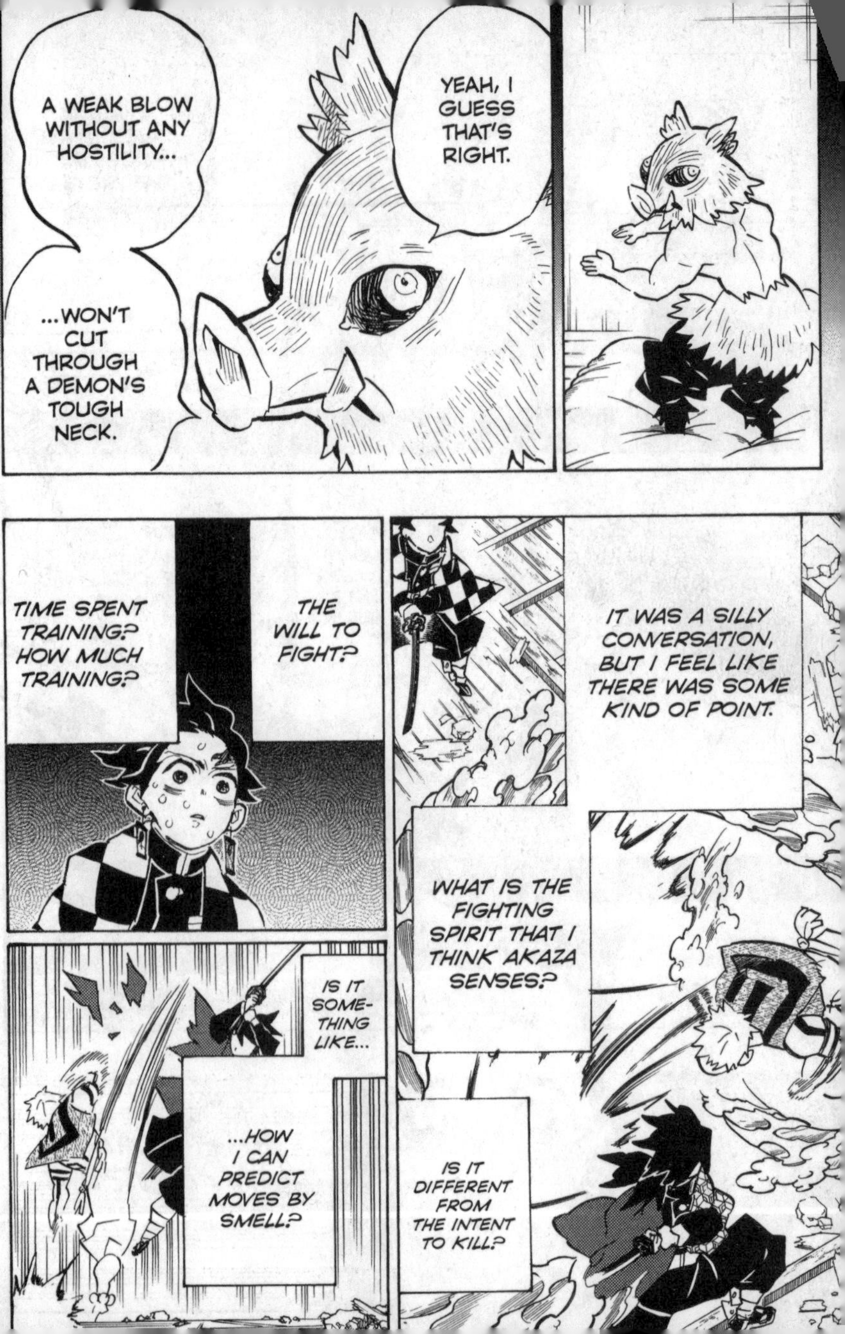
YEAH, I GUESS THAT'S RIGHT.
A WEAK BLOW WITHOUT ANY HOSTILITY...
...WON'T CUT THROUGH A DEMON'S TOUGH NECK.
IT WAS A SILLY CONVERSATION, BUT I FEEL LIKE THERE WAS SOME KIND OF POINT.
THE WILL TO FIGHT?
TIME SPENT TRAINING? HOW MUCH TRAINING?
WHAT IS THE FIGHTING SPIRIT THAT I THINK AKAZA SENSES?
IS IT DIFFERENT FROM THE INTENT TO KILL?
IS IT SOME-THING LIKE...
...HOW I CAN PREDICT MOVES BY SMELL?

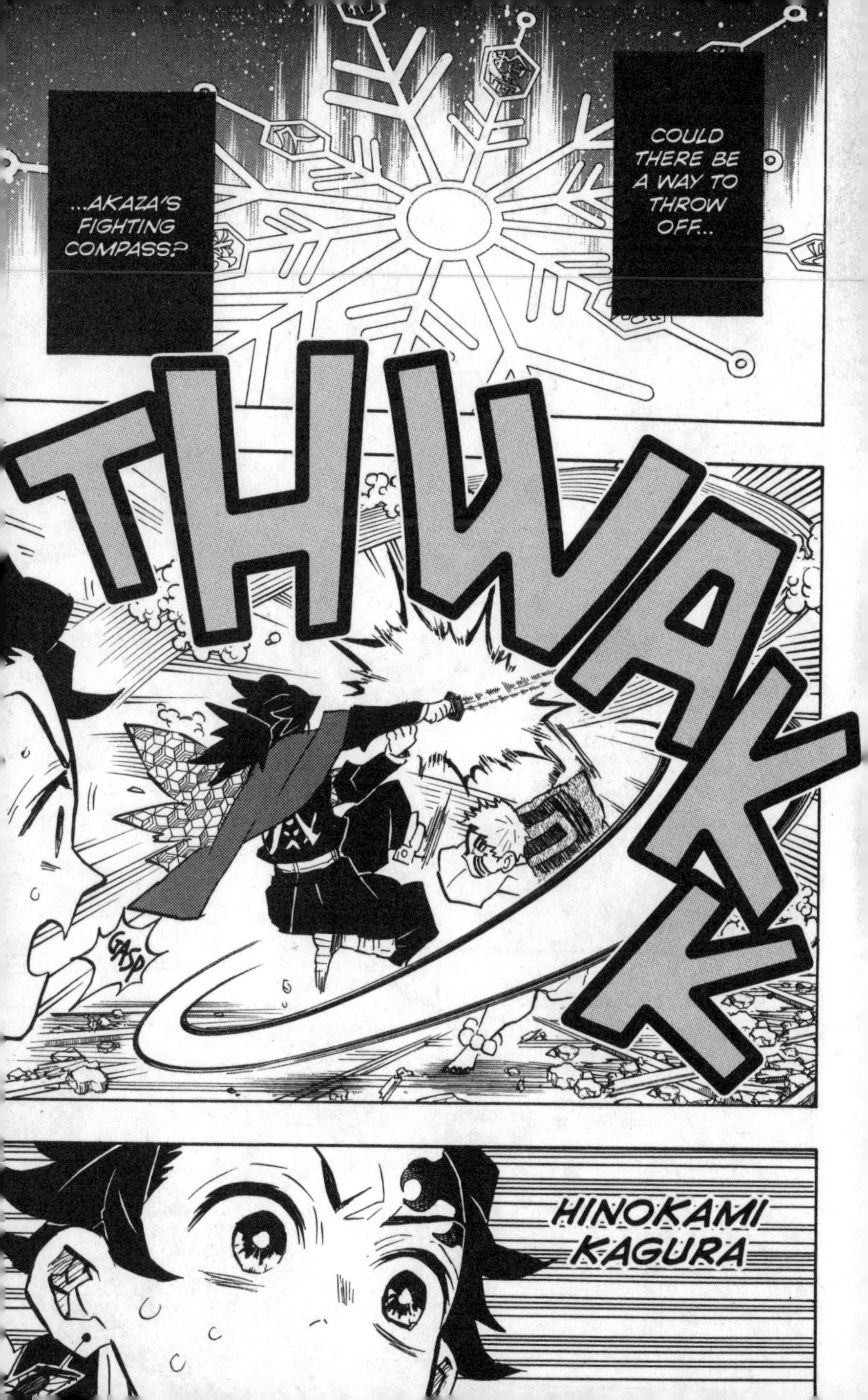
COULD THERE BE A WAY TO THROW OFF...
...AKAZA'S FIGHTING COMPASS?
THWAKK
GASP
HINOKAMI KAGURA

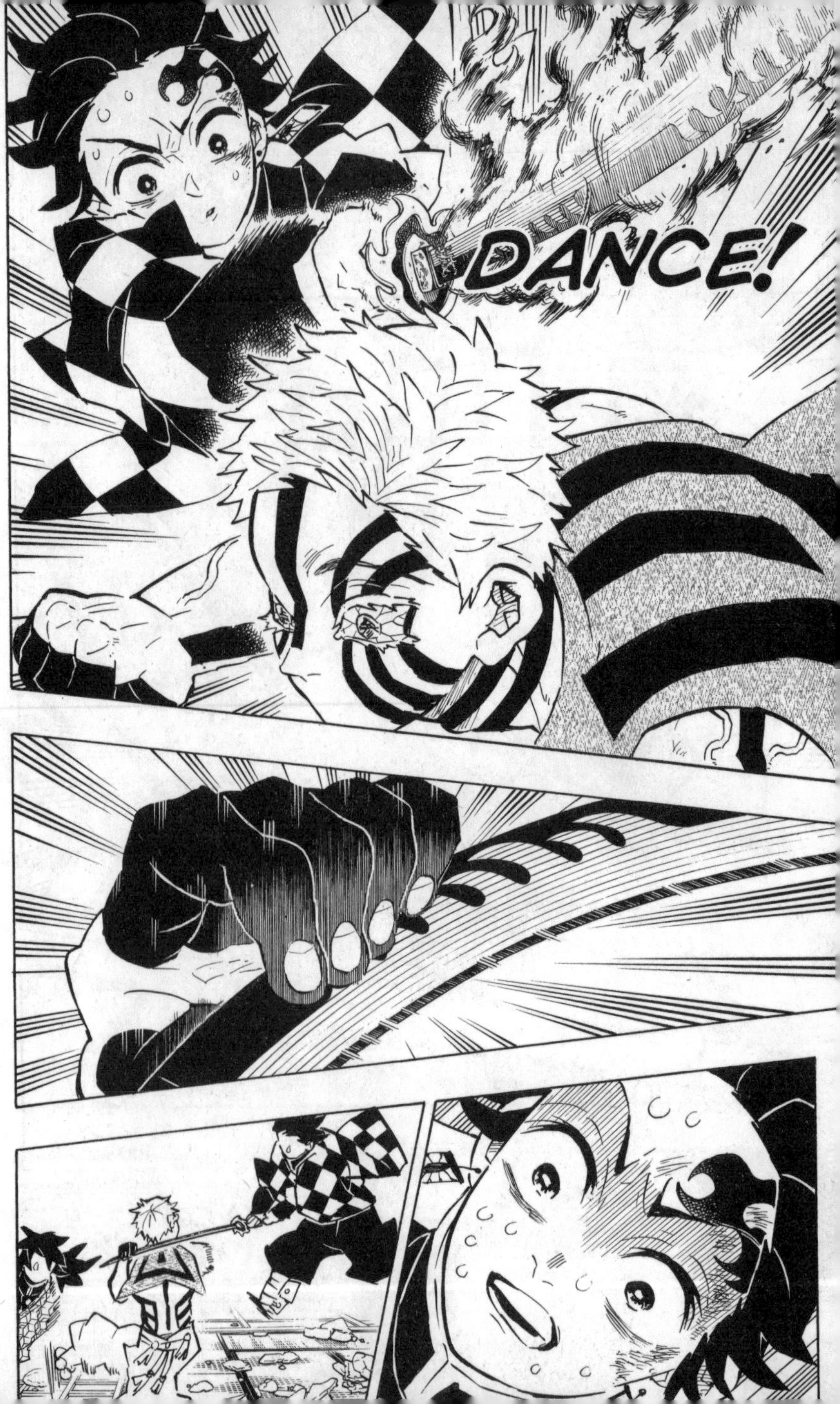
DANCE!

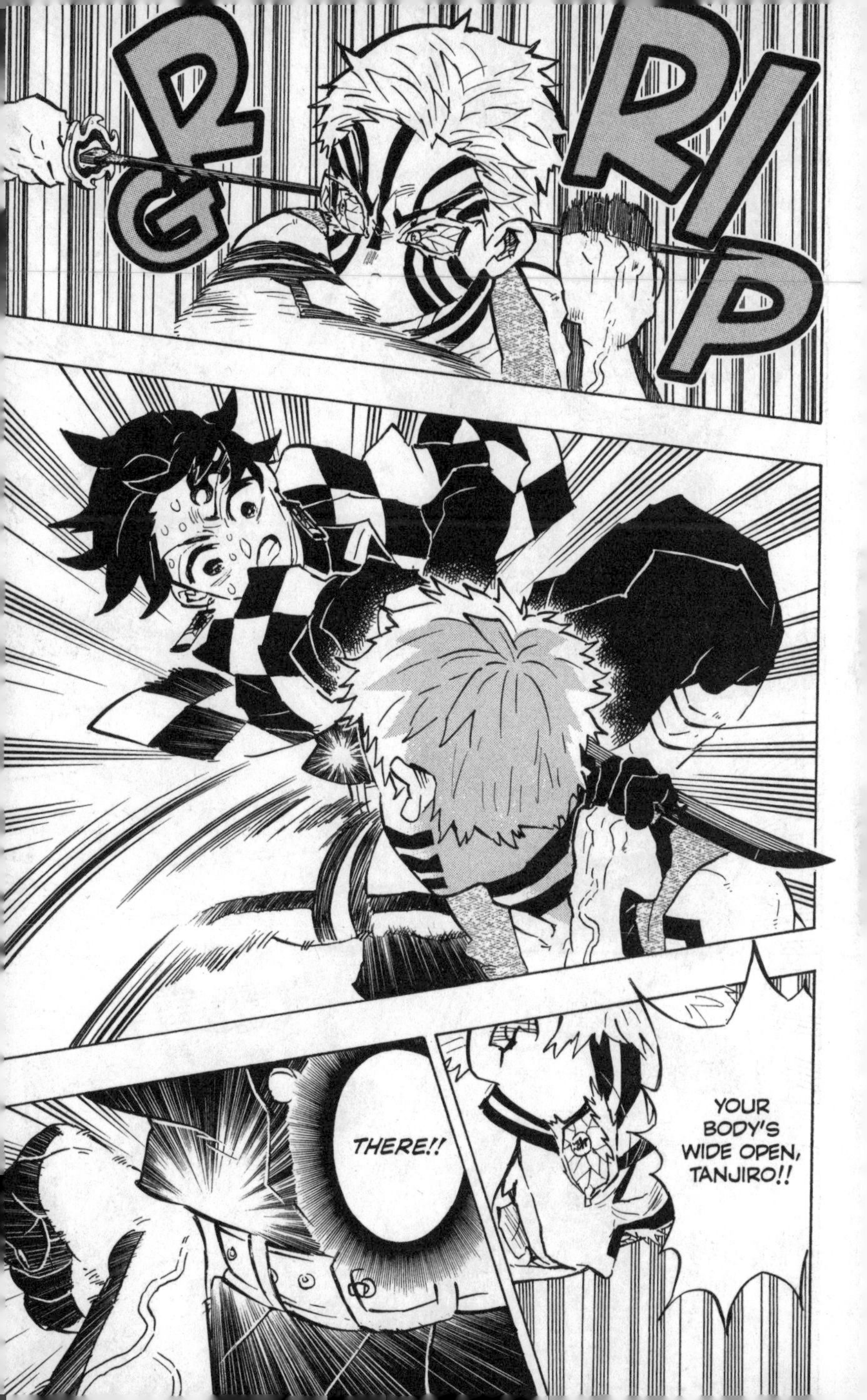
RIP
RIP
YOUR BODY'S WIDE OPEN, TANJIRO!!
THERE!!

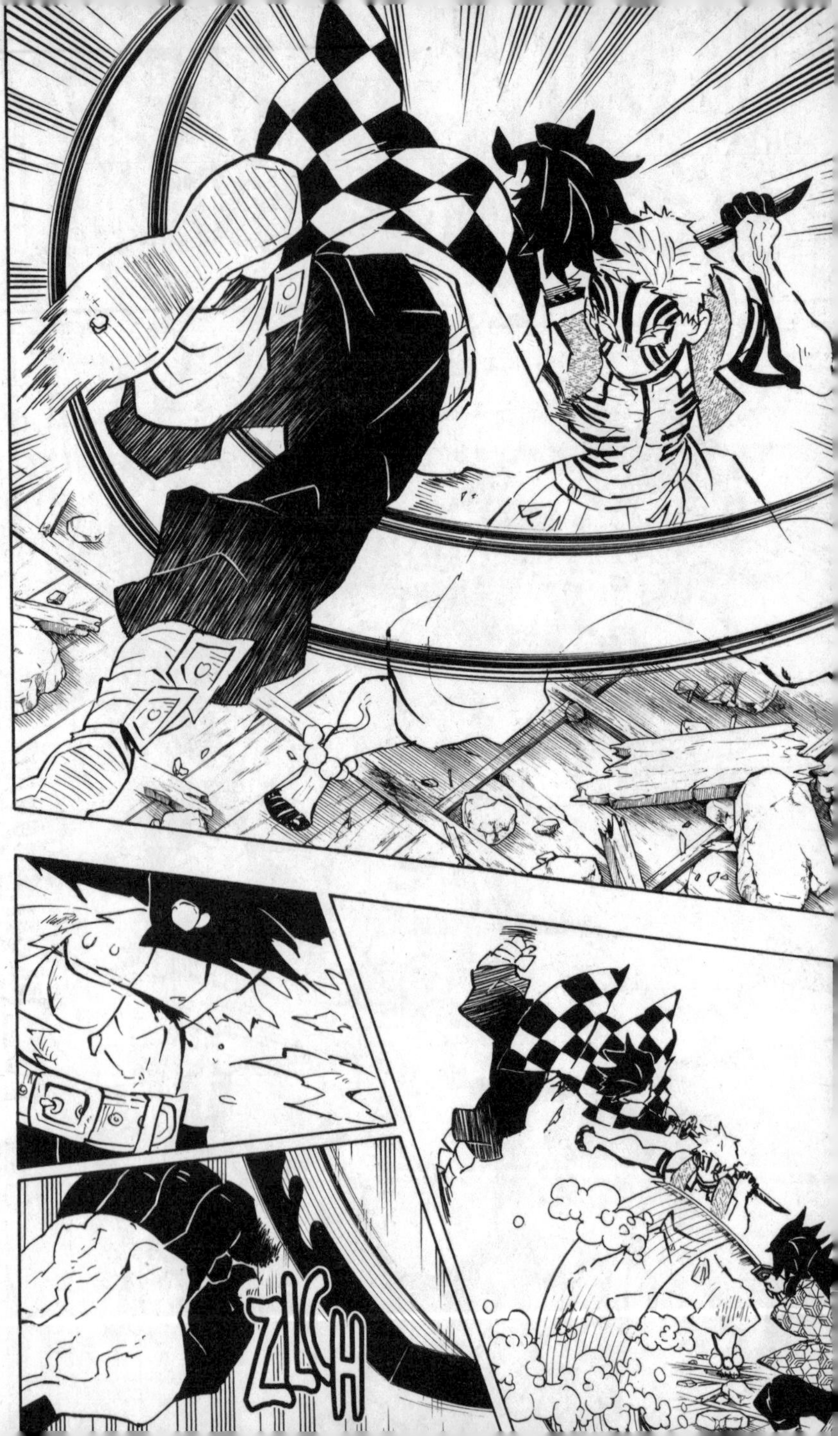
ZLCH

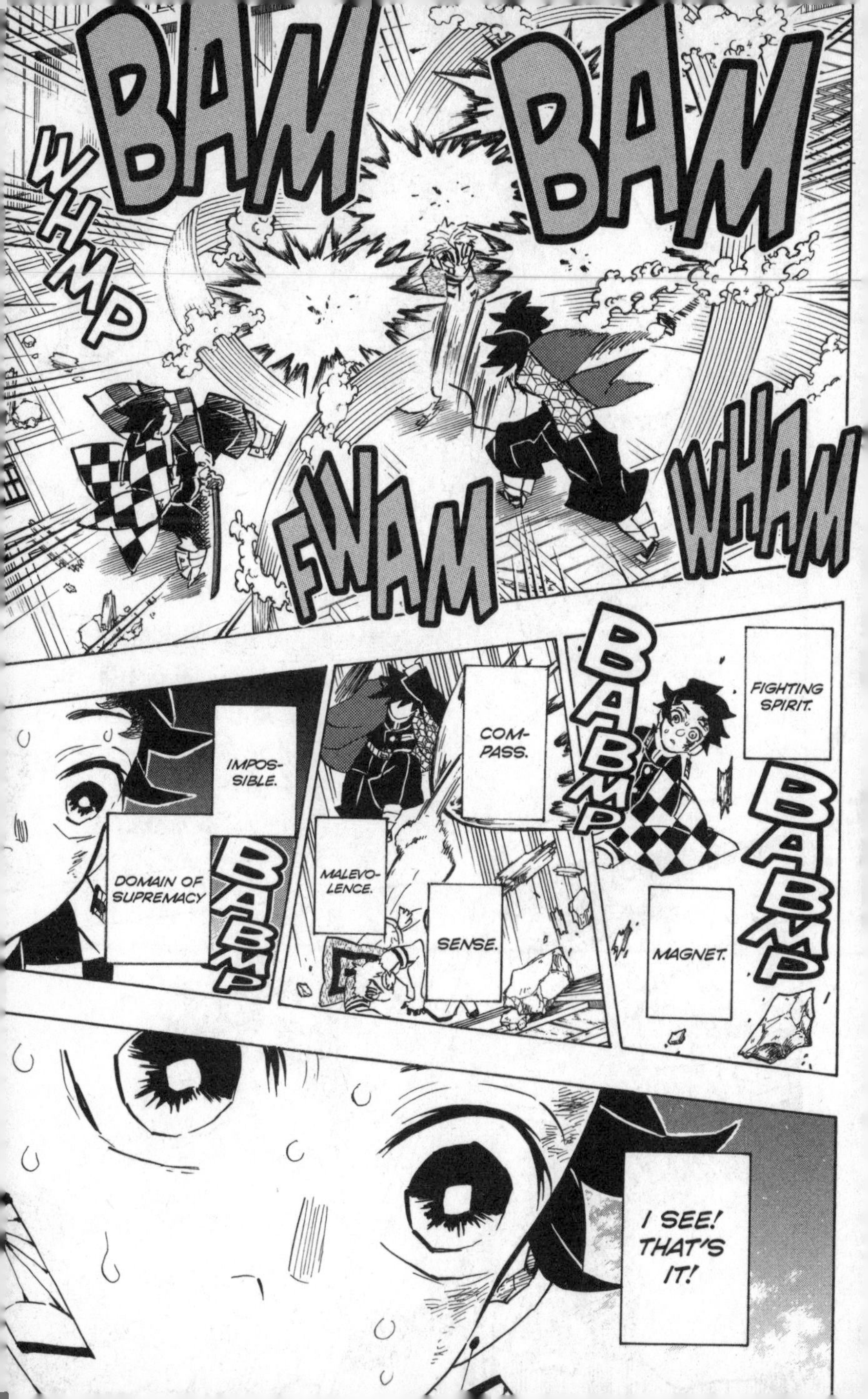
BAM
BAM
WHAM
FWAM
WHMP
FIGHTING SPIRIT.
BABMP
BABMP
MAGNET.
COMPASS.
MALEVOLENCE.
SENSE.
IMPOSSIBLE.
DOMAIN OF SUPREMACY
BABMP
I SEE! THAT'S IT!

Inosuke taking Tanjiro's food. Kiyo set it in front of him, so he thought it was his. He wasn't being mean.

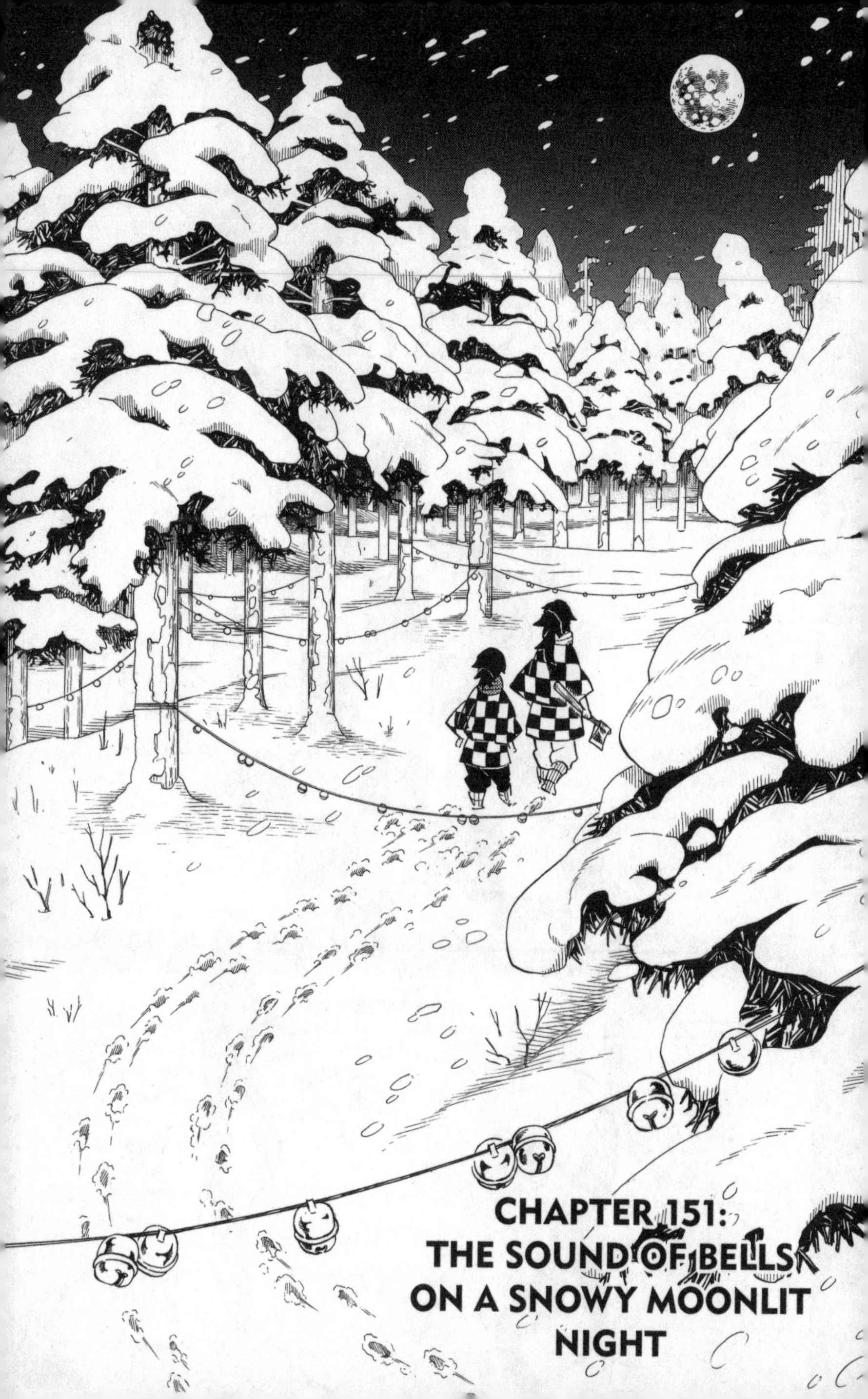
CHAPTER 151:
THE SOUND OF BELLS ON A SNOWY MOONLIT NIGHT

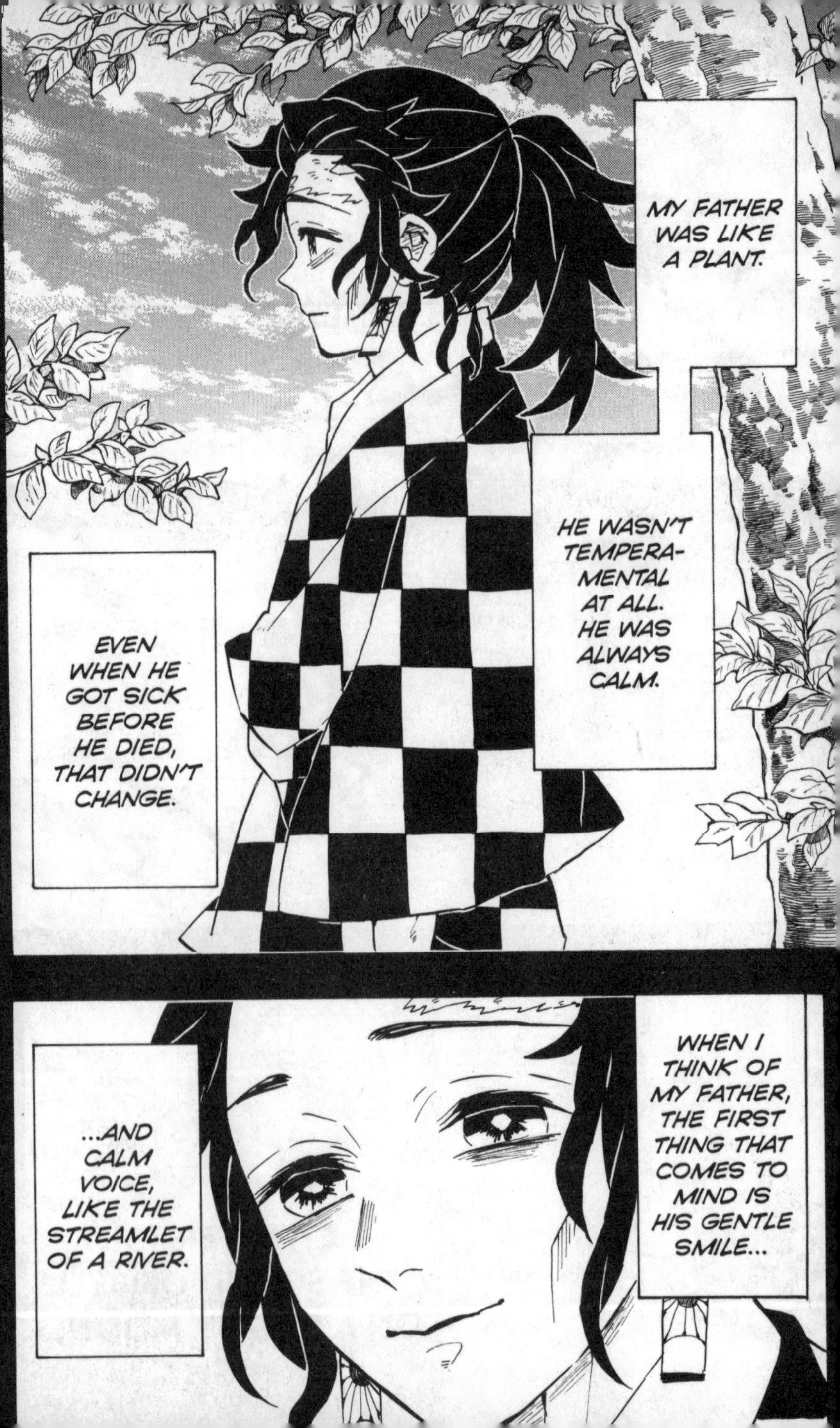
MY FATHER WAS LIKE A PLANT.
HE WASN'T TEMPERA-MENTAL AT ALL. HE WAS ALWAYS CALM.
EVEN WHEN HE GOT SICK BEFORE HE DIED, THAT DIDN'T CHANGE.
WHEN I THINK OF MY FATHER, THE FIRST THING THAT COMES TO MIND IS HIS GENTLE SMILE...
...AND CALM VOICE, LIKE THE STREAMLET OF A RIVER.

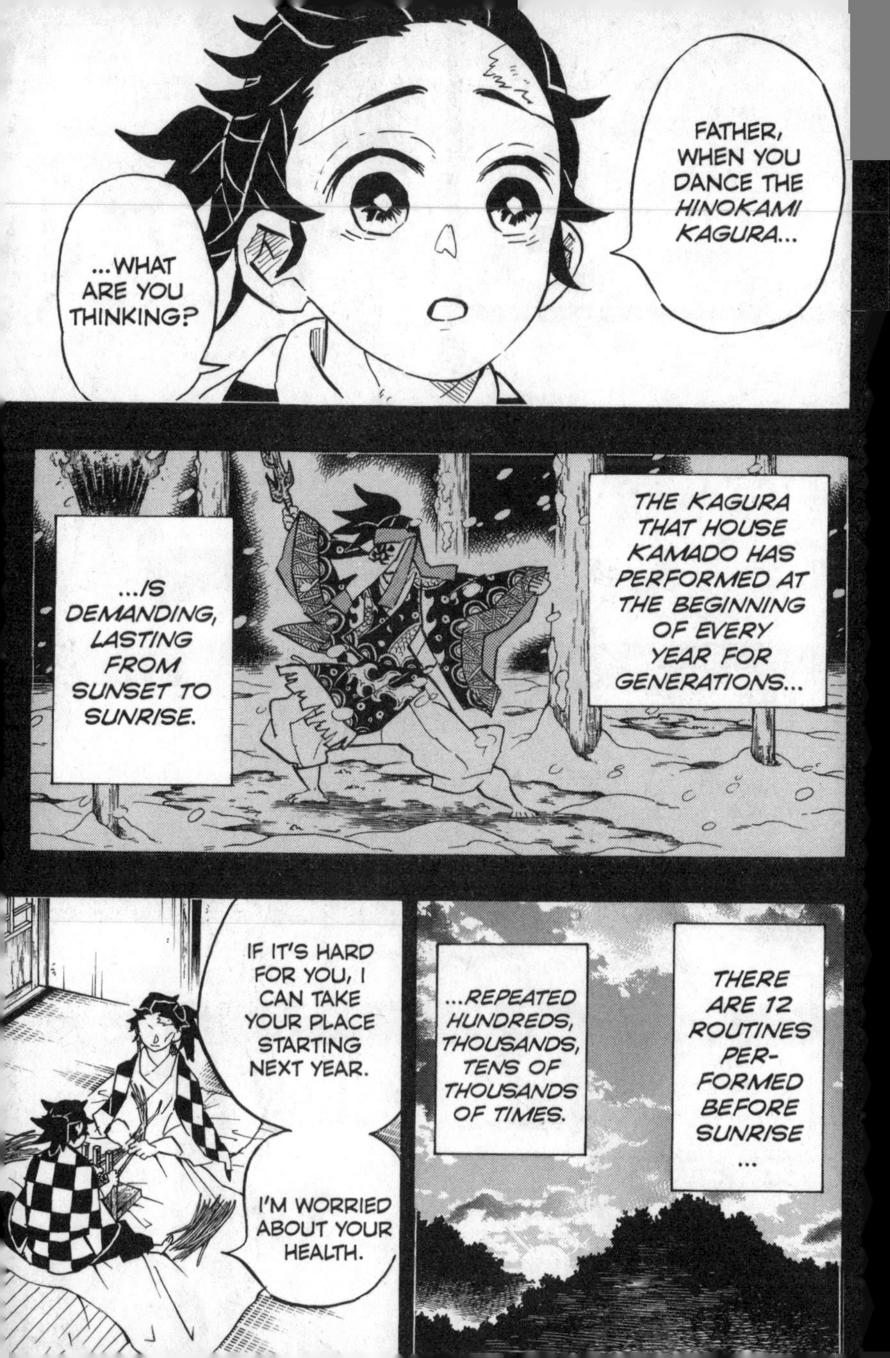
FATHER, WHEN YOU DANCE THE HINOKAMI KAGURA...
...WHAT ARE YOU THINKING?
THE KAGURA THAT HOUSE KAMADO HAS PERFORMED AT THE BEGINNING OF EVERY YEAR FOR GENERATIONS...
...IS DEMANDING, LASTING FROM SUNSET TO SUNRISE.
THERE ARE 12 ROUTINES PER-FORMED BEFORE SUNRISE...
...REPEATED HUNDREDS, THOUSANDS, TENS OF THOUSANDS OF TIMES.
IF IT'S HARD FOR YOU, I CAN TAKE YOUR PLACE STARTING NEXT YEAR.
I'M WORRIED ABOUT YOUR HEALTH.

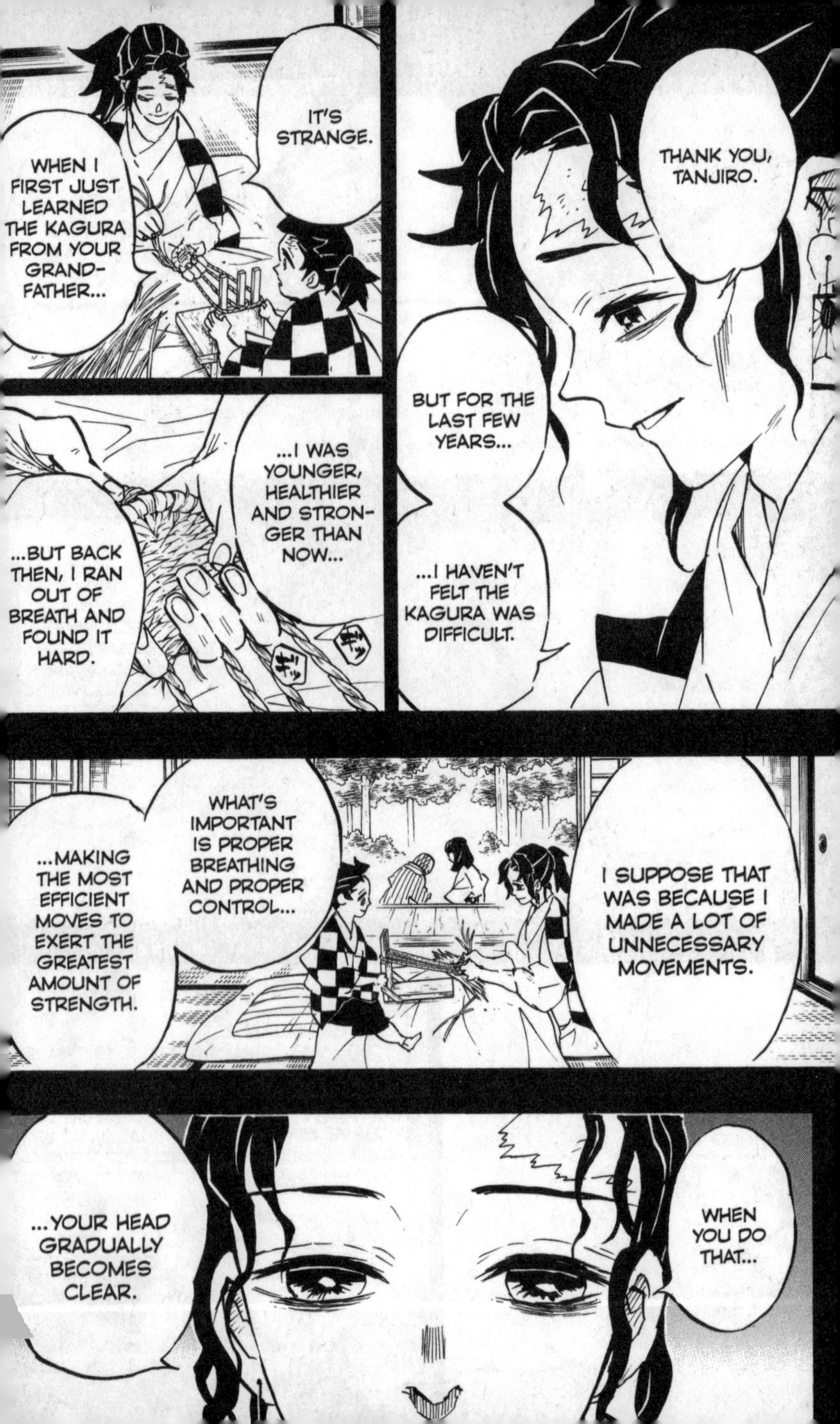
THANK YOU, TANJIRO.
BUT FOR THE LAST FEW YEARS...
...I HAVEN'T FELT THE KAGURA WAS DIFFICULT.
IT'S STRANGE.
WHEN I FIRST JUST LEARNED THE KAGURA FROM YOUR GRANDFATHER...
...I WAS YOUNGER, HEALTHIER AND STRONGER THAN NOW...
...BUT BACK THEN, I RAN OUT OF BREATH AND FOUND IT HARD.
I SUPPOSE THAT WAS BECAUSE I MADE A LOT OF UNNECESSARY MOVEMENTS.
WHAT'S IMPORTANT IS PROPER BREATHING AND PROPER CONTROL...
...MAKING THE MOST EFFICIENT MOVES TO EXERT THE GREATEST AMOUNT OF STRENGTH.
WHEN YOU DO THAT...
...YOUR HEAD GRADUALLY BECOMES CLEAR.

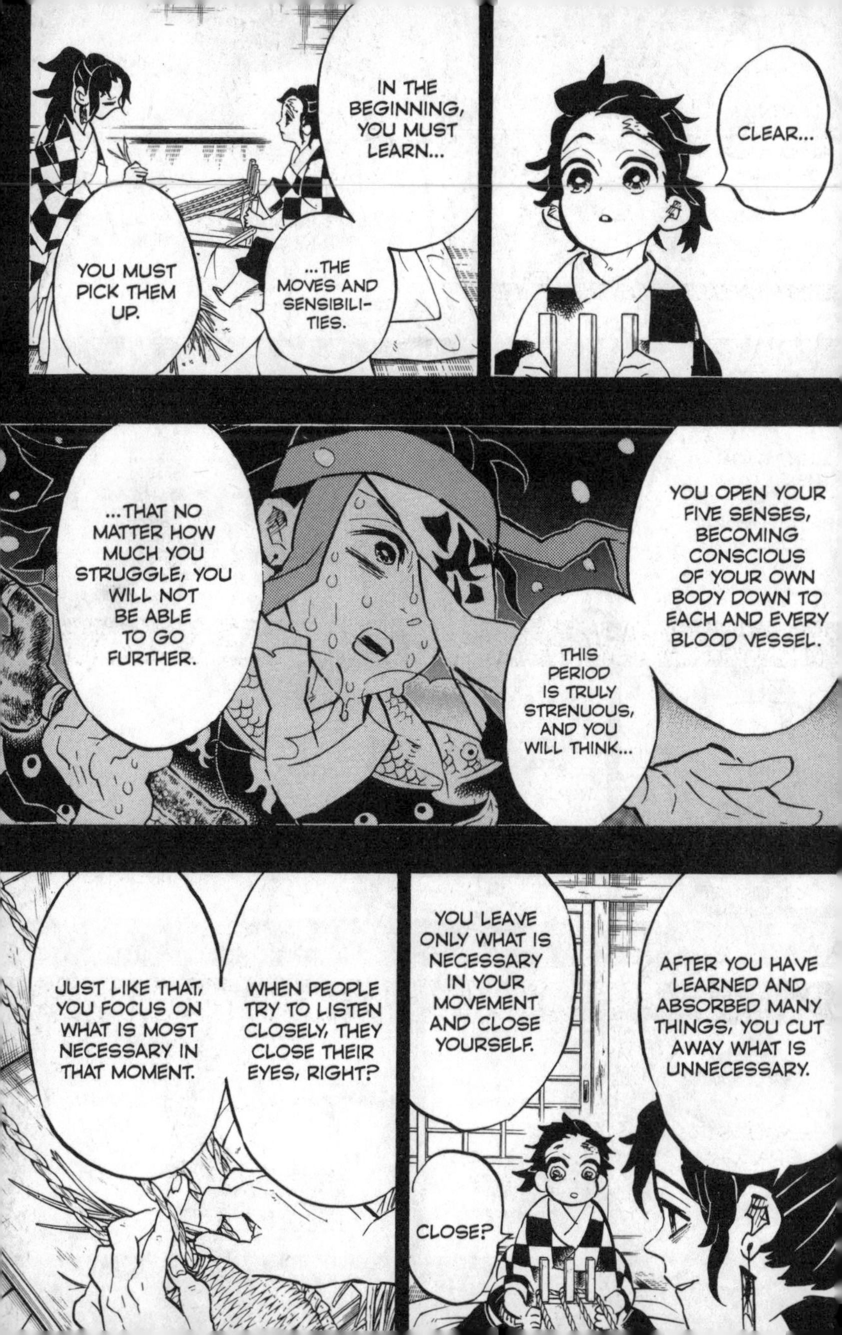
CLEAR...
IN THE BEGINNING, YOU MUST LEARN...
...THE MOVES AND SENSIBILITIES.
YOU MUST PICK THEM UP.
YOU OPEN YOUR FIVE SENSES, BECOMING CONSCIOUS OF YOUR OWN BODY DOWN TO EACH AND EVERY BLOOD VESSEL.
THIS PERIOD IS TRULY STRENUOUS, AND YOU WILL THINK...
...THAT NO MATTER HOW MUCH YOU STRUGGLE, YOU WILL NOT BE ABLE TO GO FURTHER.
AFTER YOU HAVE LEARNED AND ABSORBED MANY THINGS, YOU CUT AWAY WHAT IS UNNECESSARY.
YOU LEAVE ONLY WHAT IS NECESSARY IN YOUR MOVEMENT AND CLOSE YOURSELF.
CLOSE?
WHEN PEOPLE TRY TO LISTEN CLOSELY, THEY CLOSE THEIR EYES, RIGHT?
JUST LIKE THAT, YOU FOCUS ON WHAT IS MOST NECESSARY IN THAT MOMENT.

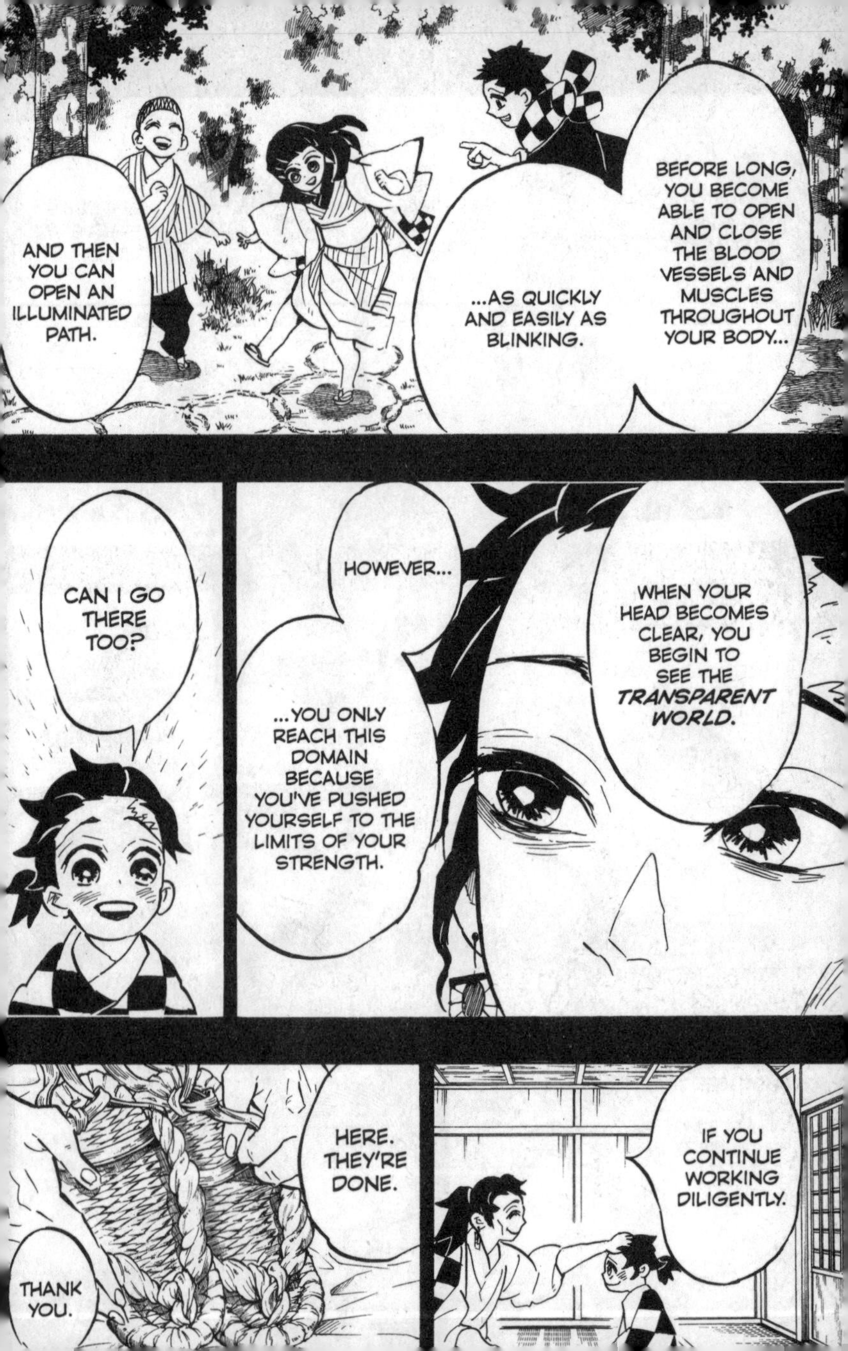
BEFORE LONG, YOU BECOME ABLE TO OPEN AND CLOSE THE BLOOD VESSELS AND MUSCLES THROUGHOUT YOUR BODY...
...AS QUICKLY AND EASILY AS BLINKING.
AND THEN YOU CAN OPEN AN ILLUMINATED PATH.
WHEN YOUR HEAD BECOMES CLEAR, YOU BEGIN TO SEE THE *TRANSPARENT WORLD*.
HOWEVER...
...YOU ONLY REACH THIS DOMAIN BECAUSE YOU'VE PUSHED YOURSELF TO THE LIMITS OF YOUR STRENGTH.
CAN I GO THERE TOO?
IF YOU CONTINUE WORKING DILIGENTLY.
HERE. THEY'RE DONE.
THANK YOU.

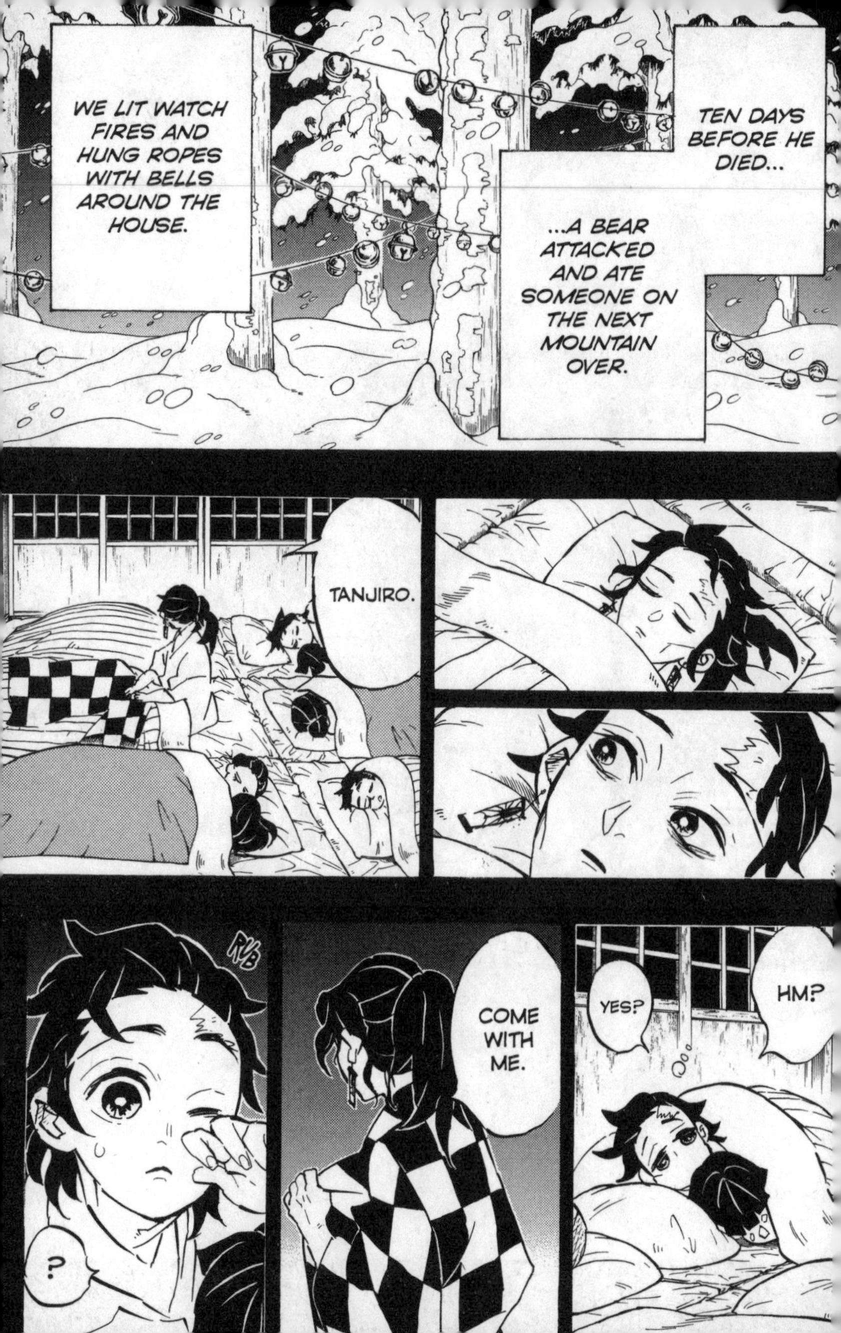

TEN DAYS BEFORE HE DIED...
...A BEAR ATTACKED AND ATE SOMEONE ON THE NEXT MOUNTAIN OVER.
WE LIT WATCH FIRES AND HUNG ROPES WITH BELLS AROUND THE HOUSE.
TANJIRO.
HM?
YES?
COME WITH ME.
RUB
?

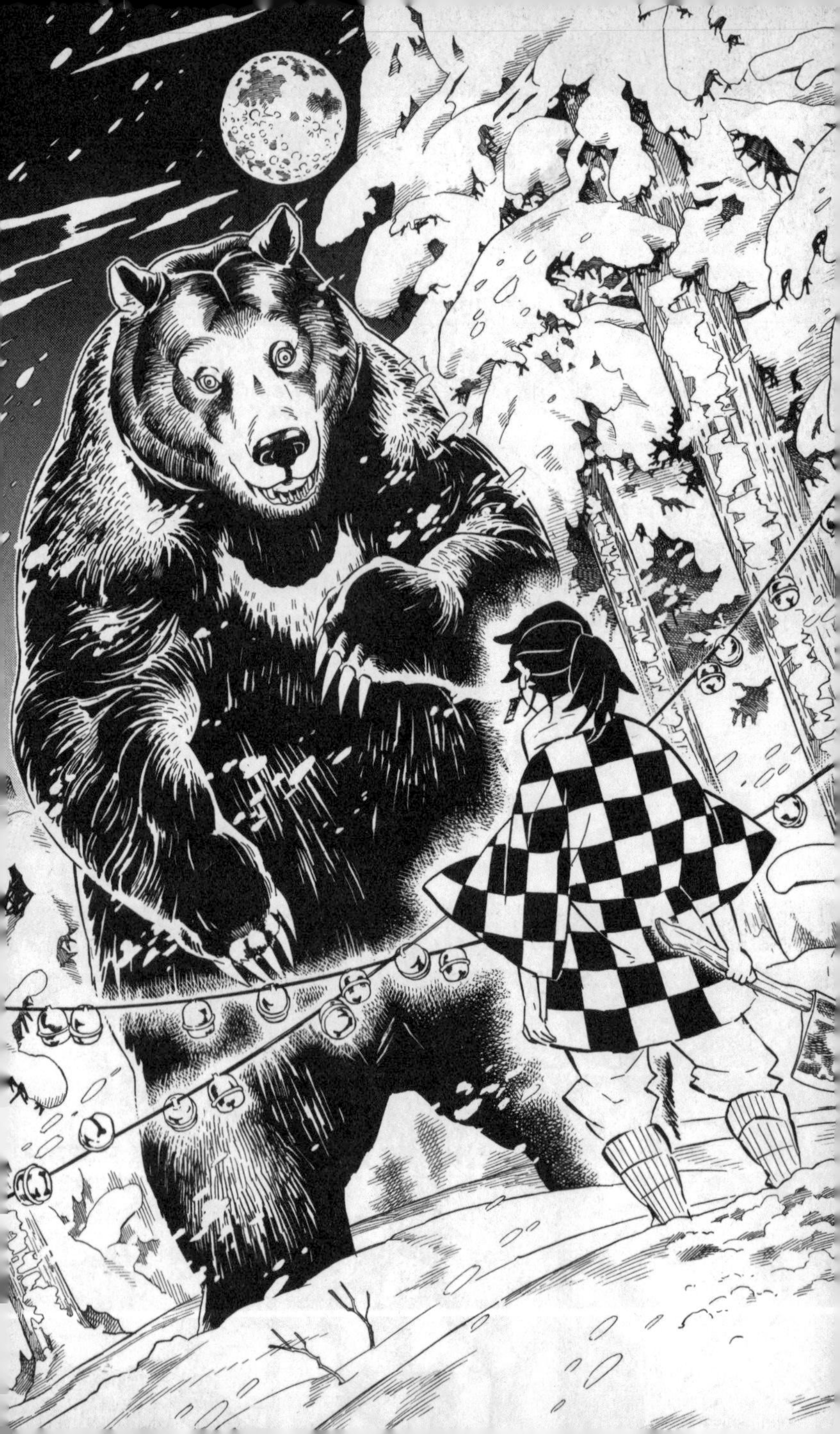

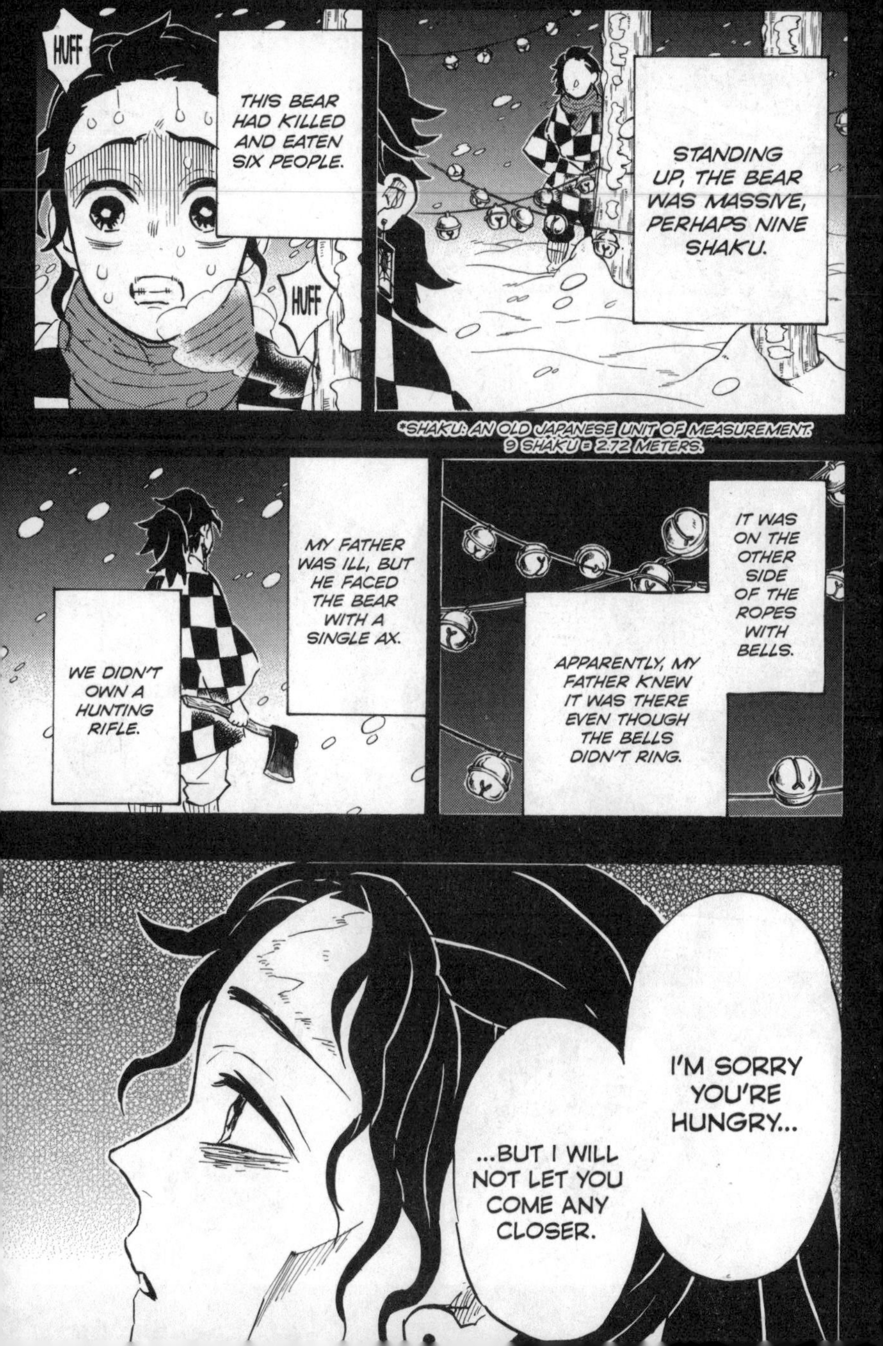
STANDING UP, THE BEAR WAS MASSIVE, PERHAPS NINE SHAKU.
THIS BEAR HAD KILLED AND EATEN SIX PEOPLE.
HUFF
HUFF
*SHAKU: AN OLD JAPANESE UNIT OF MEASUREMENT. 9 SHAKU = 2.72 METERS.
IT WAS ON THE OTHER SIDE OF THE ROPES WITH BELLS.
APPARENTLY, MY FATHER KNEW IT WAS THERE EVEN THOUGH THE BELLS DIDN'T RING.
MY FATHER WAS ILL, BUT HE FACED THE BEAR WITH A SINGLE AX.
WE DIDN'T OWN A HUNTING RIFLE.
I'M SORRY YOU'RE HUNGRY...
...BUT I WILL NOT LET YOU COME ANY CLOSER.

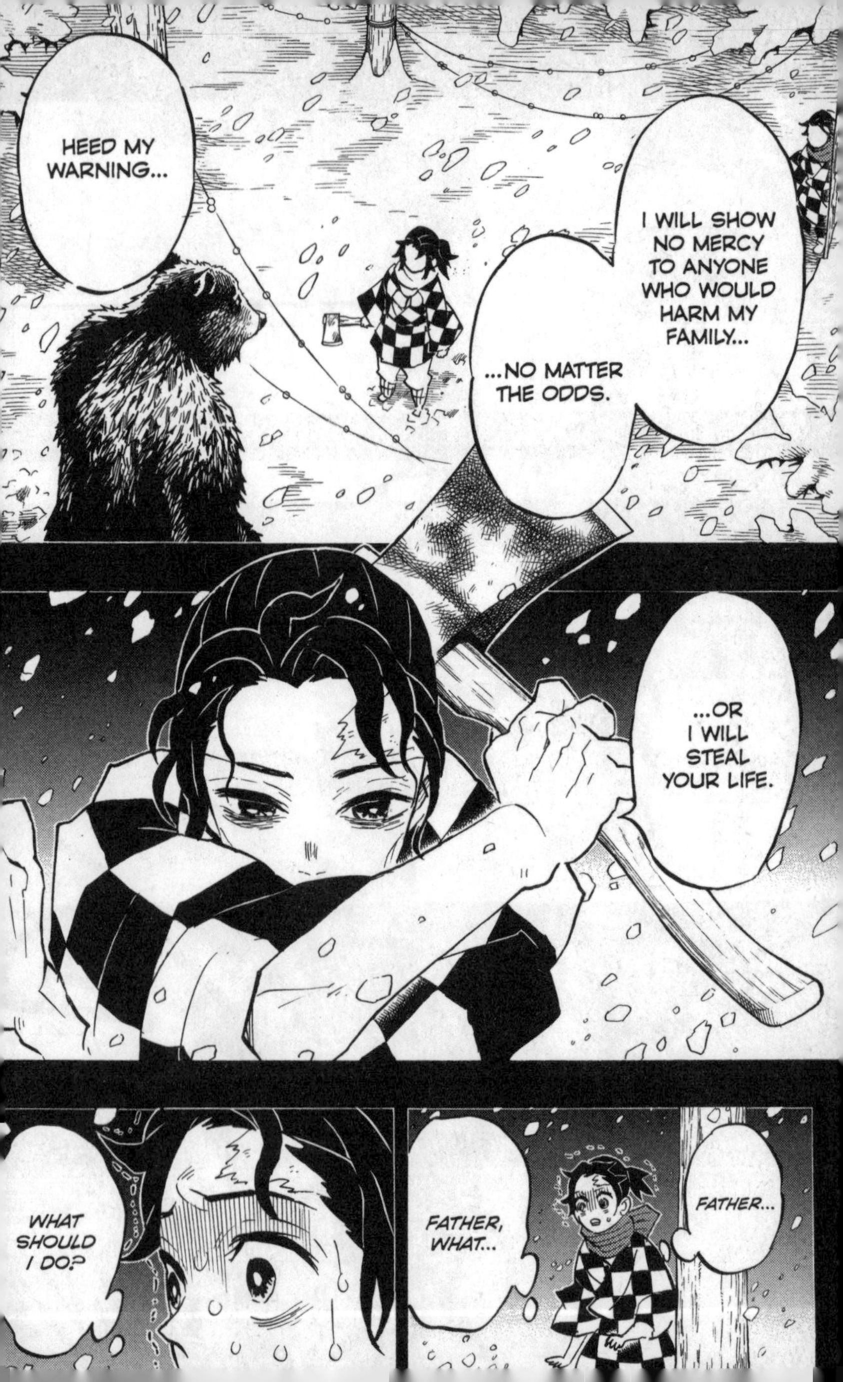
I WILL SHOW NO MERCY TO ANYONE WHO WOULD HARM MY FAMILY...
...NO MATTER THE ODDS.
HEED MY WARNING...
...OR I WILL STEAL YOUR LIFE.
FATHER...
FATHER, WHAT...
WHAT SHOULD I DO?

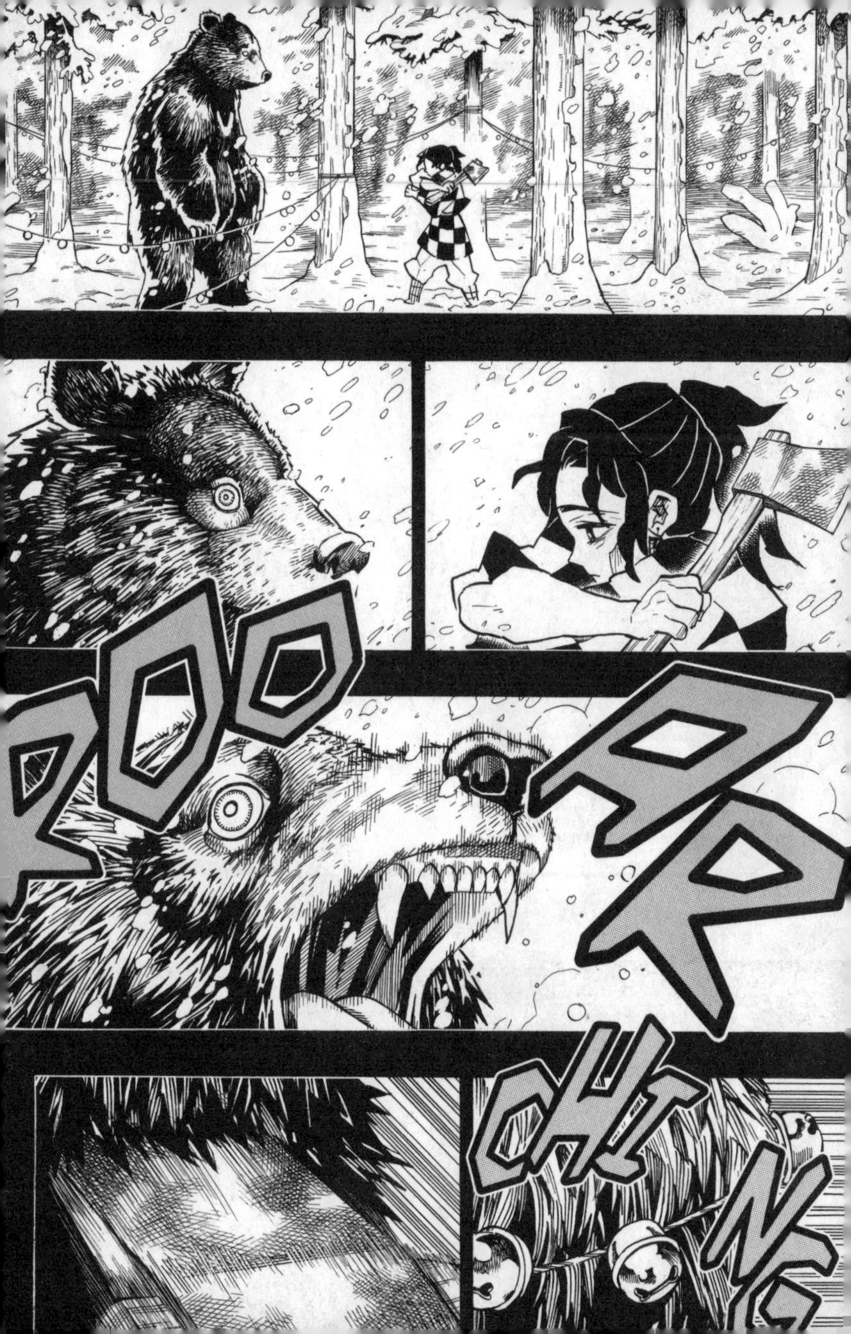
CHIN

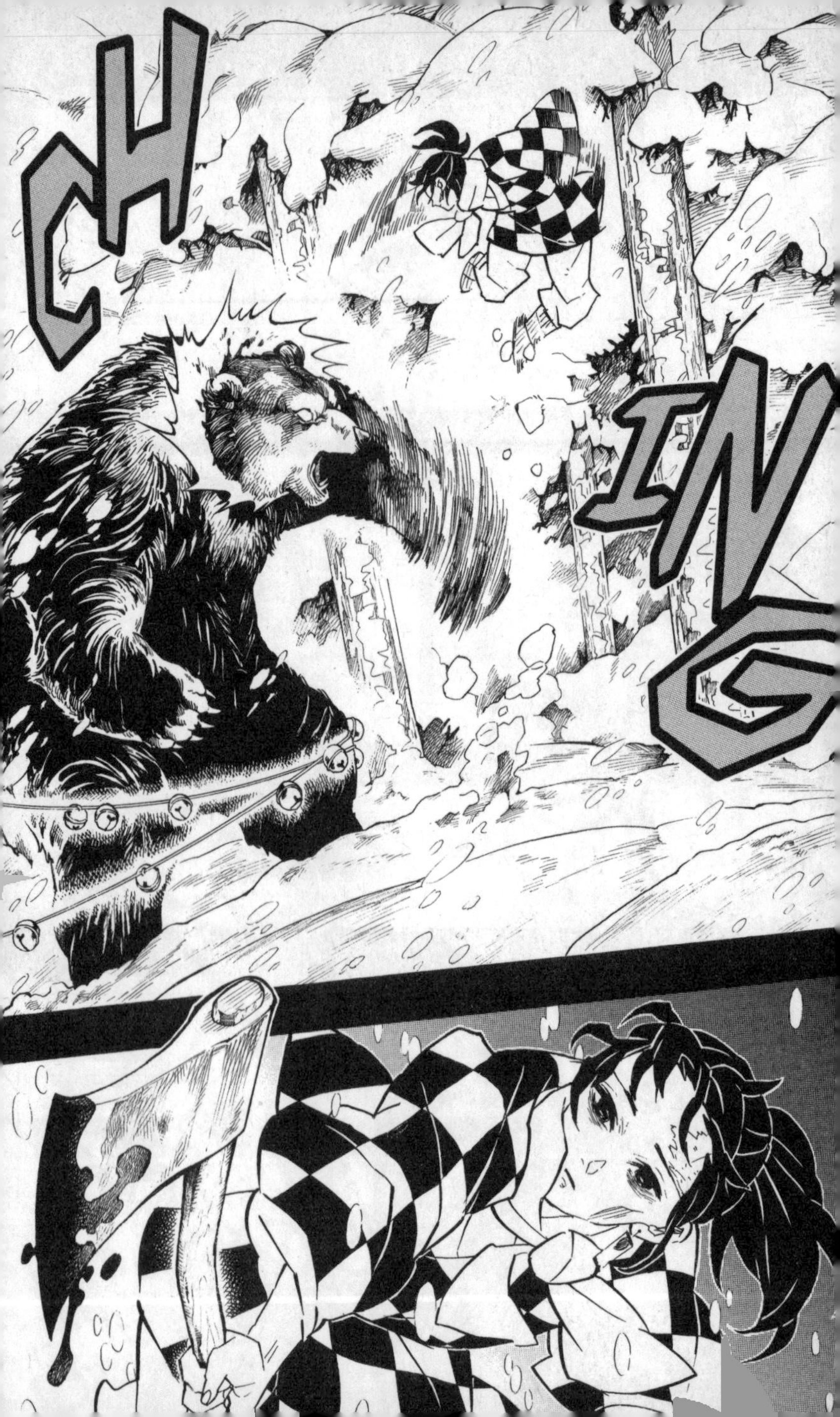
CHING

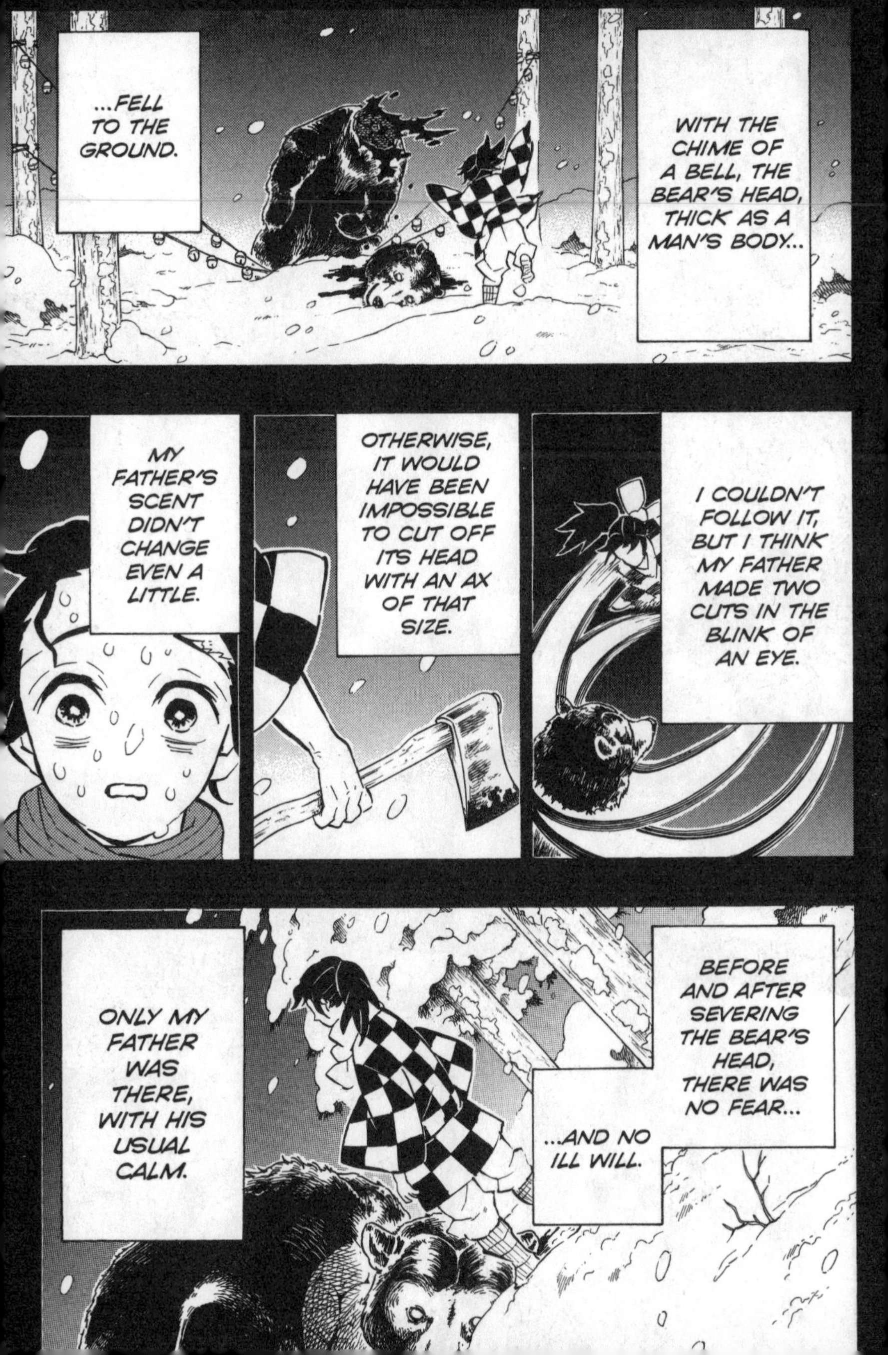
WITH THE CHIME OF A BELL, THE BEAR'S HEAD, THICK AS A MAN'S BODY...
...FELL TO THE GROUND.
I COULDN'T FOLLOW IT, BUT I THINK MY FATHER MADE TWO CUTS IN THE BLINK OF AN EYE.
OTHERWISE, IT WOULD HAVE BEEN IMPOSSIBLE TO CUT OFF ITS HEAD WITH AN AX OF THAT SIZE.
MY FATHER'S SCENT DIDN'T CHANGE EVEN A LITTLE.
BEFORE AND AFTER SEVERING THE BEAR'S HEAD, THERE WAS NO FEAR...
...AND NO ILL WILL.
ONLY MY FATHER WAS THERE, WITH HIS USUAL CALM.

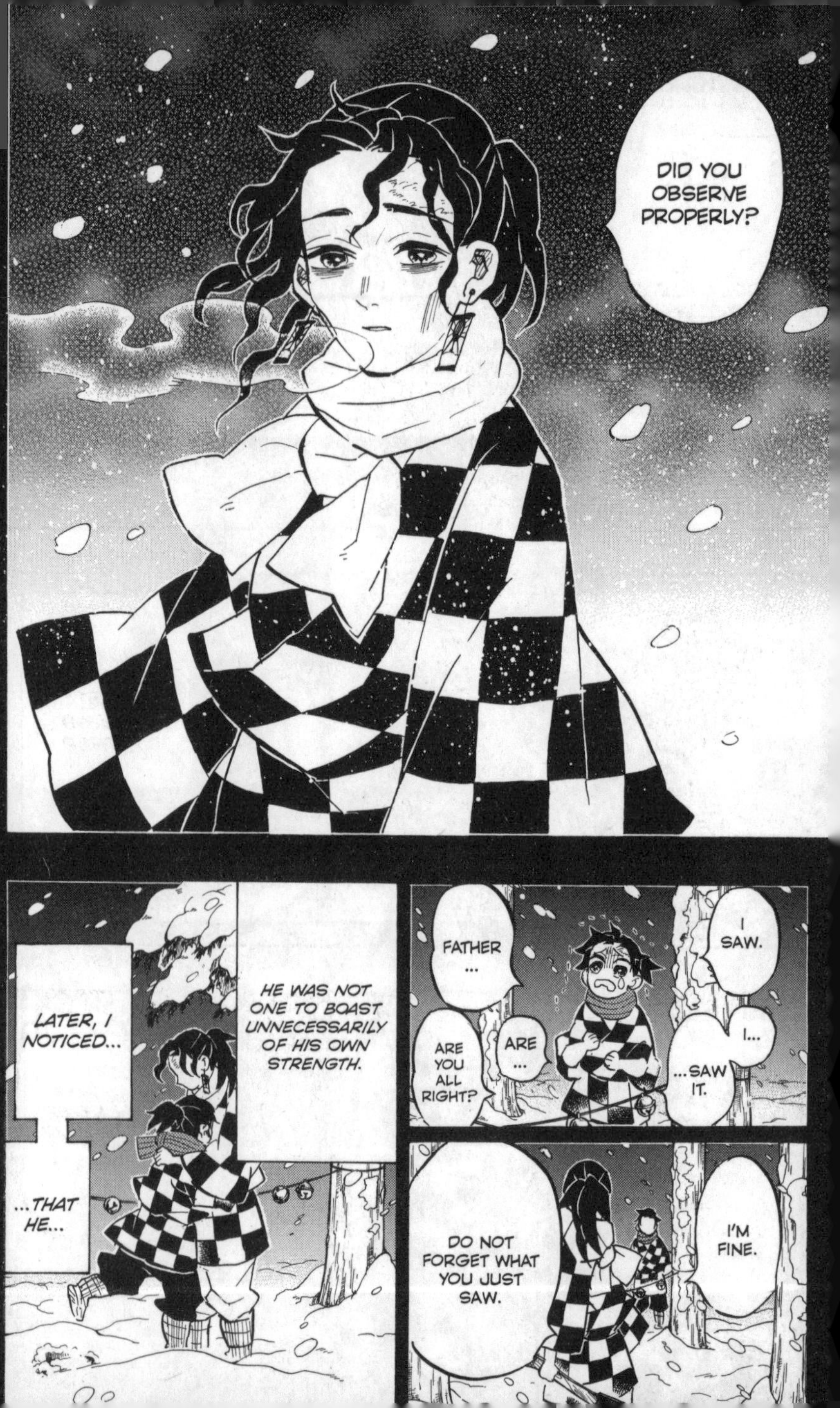
DID YOU OBSERVE PROPERLY?
I SAW.
I...
...SAW IT.
FATHER...
ARE...
ARE YOU ALL RIGHT?
I'M FINE.
DO NOT FORGET WHAT YOU JUST SAW.
HE WAS NOT ONE TO BOAST UNNECESSARILY OF HIS OWN STRENGTH.
LATER, I NOTICED...
...THAT HE...

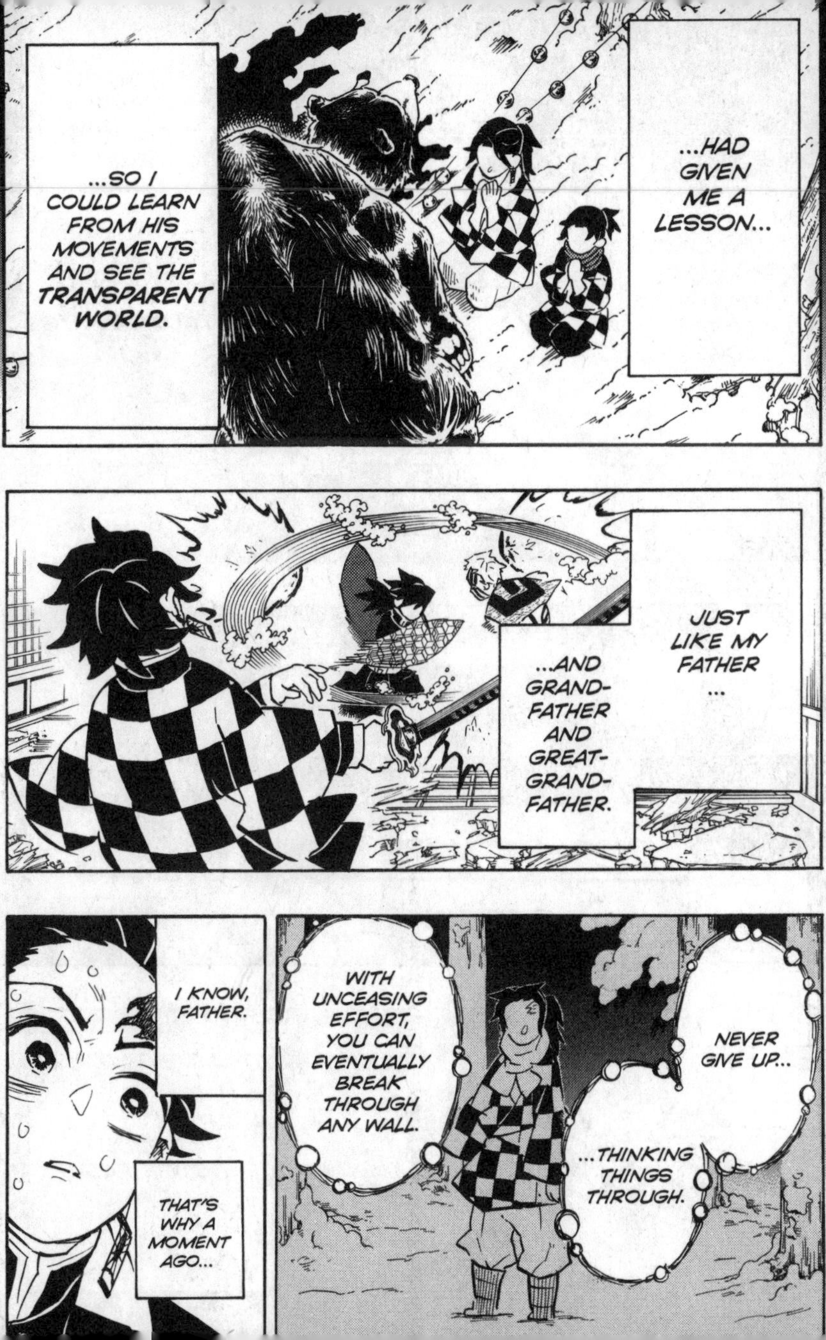
...HAD GIVEN ME A LESSON...
...SO I COULD LEARN FROM HIS MOVEMENTS AND SEE THE TRANSPARENT WORLD.
JUST LIKE MY FATHER ...
...AND GRAND-FATHER AND GREAT-GRAND-FATHER.
NEVER GIVE UP...
...THINKING THINGS THROUGH.
WITH UNCEASING EFFORT, YOU CAN EVENTUALLY BREAK THROUGH ANY WALL.
I KNOW, FATHER.
THAT'S WHY A MOMENT AGO...

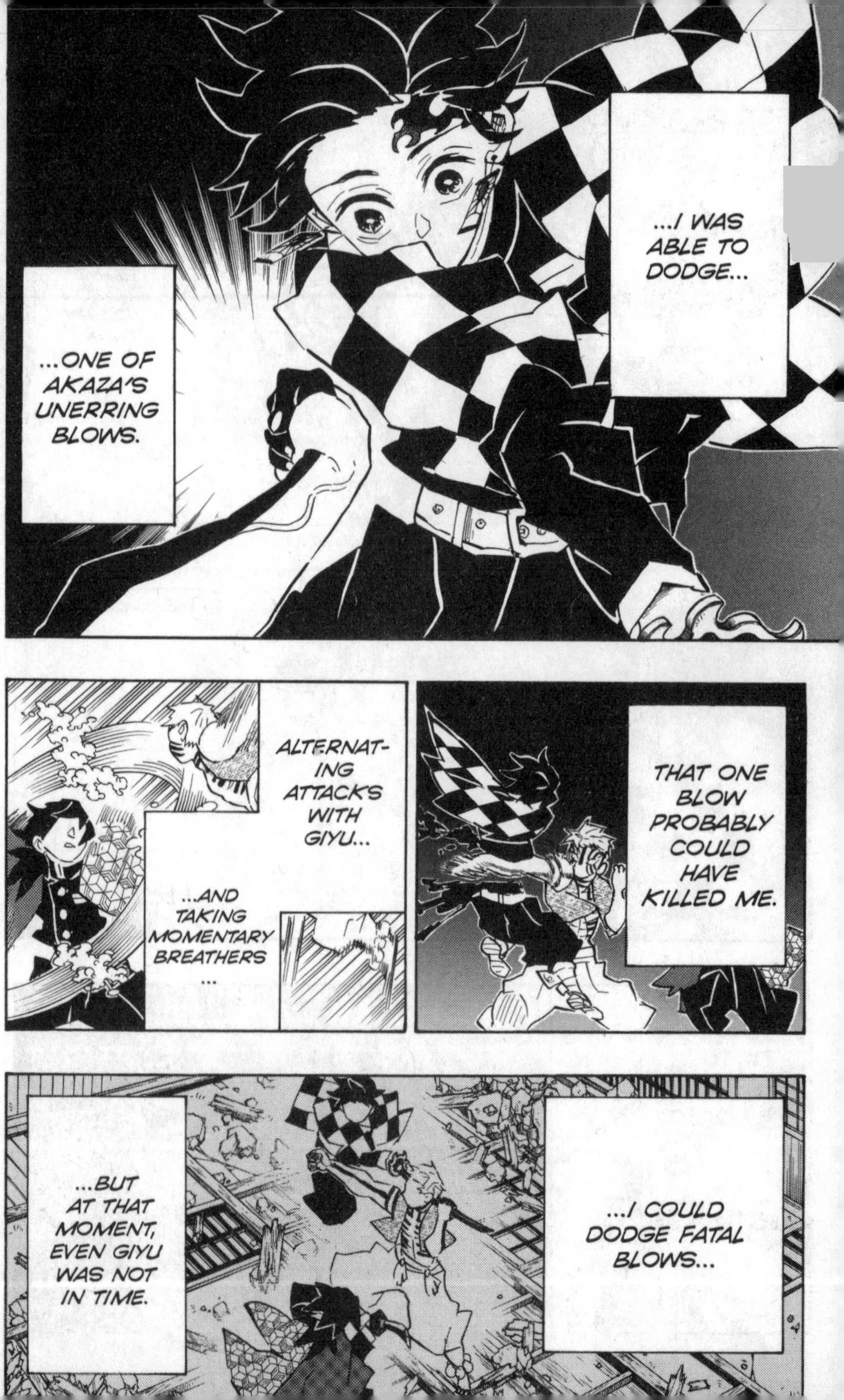
...I WAS ABLE TO DODGE...
...ONE OF AKAZA'S UNERRING BLOWS.
THAT ONE BLOW PROBABLY COULD HAVE KILLED ME.
ALTERNATING ATTACKS WITH GIYU...
...AND TAKING MOMENTARY BREATHERS...
...I COULD DODGE FATAL BLOWS...
...BUT AT THAT MOMENT, EVEN GIYU WAS NOT IN TIME.

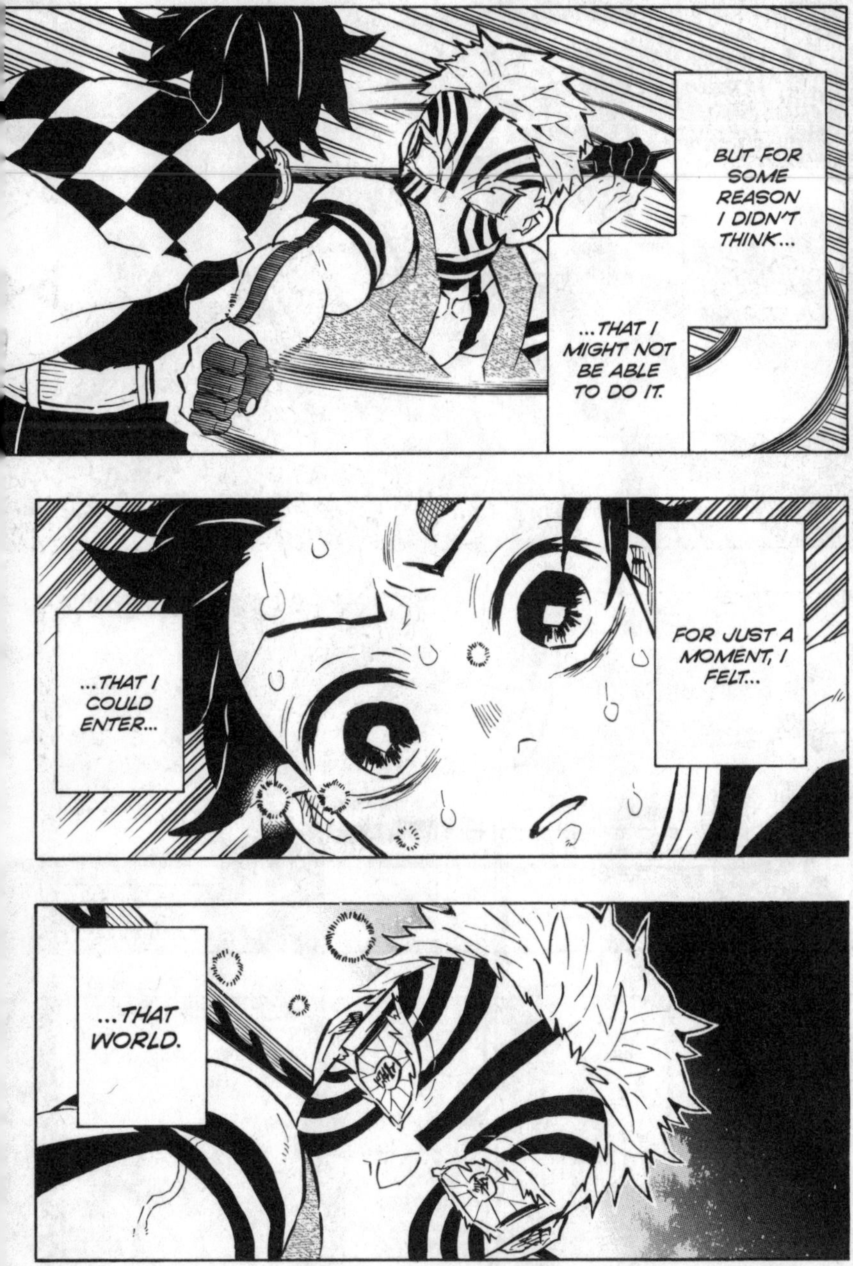
BUT FOR SOME REASON I DIDN'T THINK...
...THAT I MIGHT NOT BE ABLE TO DO IT.
FOR JUST A MOMENT, I FELT...
...THAT I COULD ENTER...
...THAT WORLD.

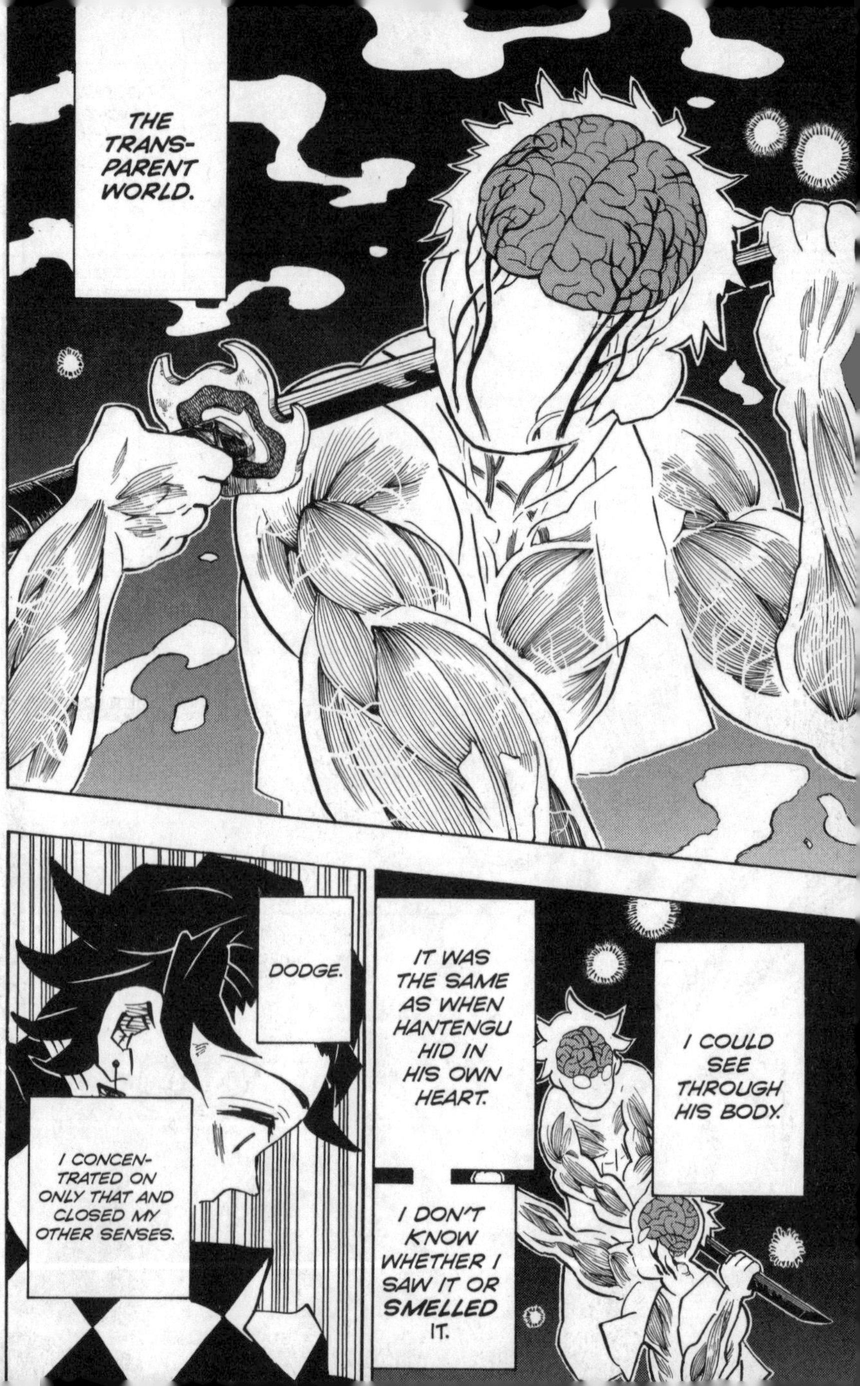
THE TRANS-PARENT WORLD.
I COULD SEE THROUGH HIS BODY.
IT WAS THE SAME AS WHEN HANTENGU HID IN HIS OWN HEART.
I DON'T KNOW WHETHER I SAW IT OR SMELLED IT.
DODGE.
I CONCEN-TRATED ON ONLY THAT AND CLOSED MY OTHER SENSES.

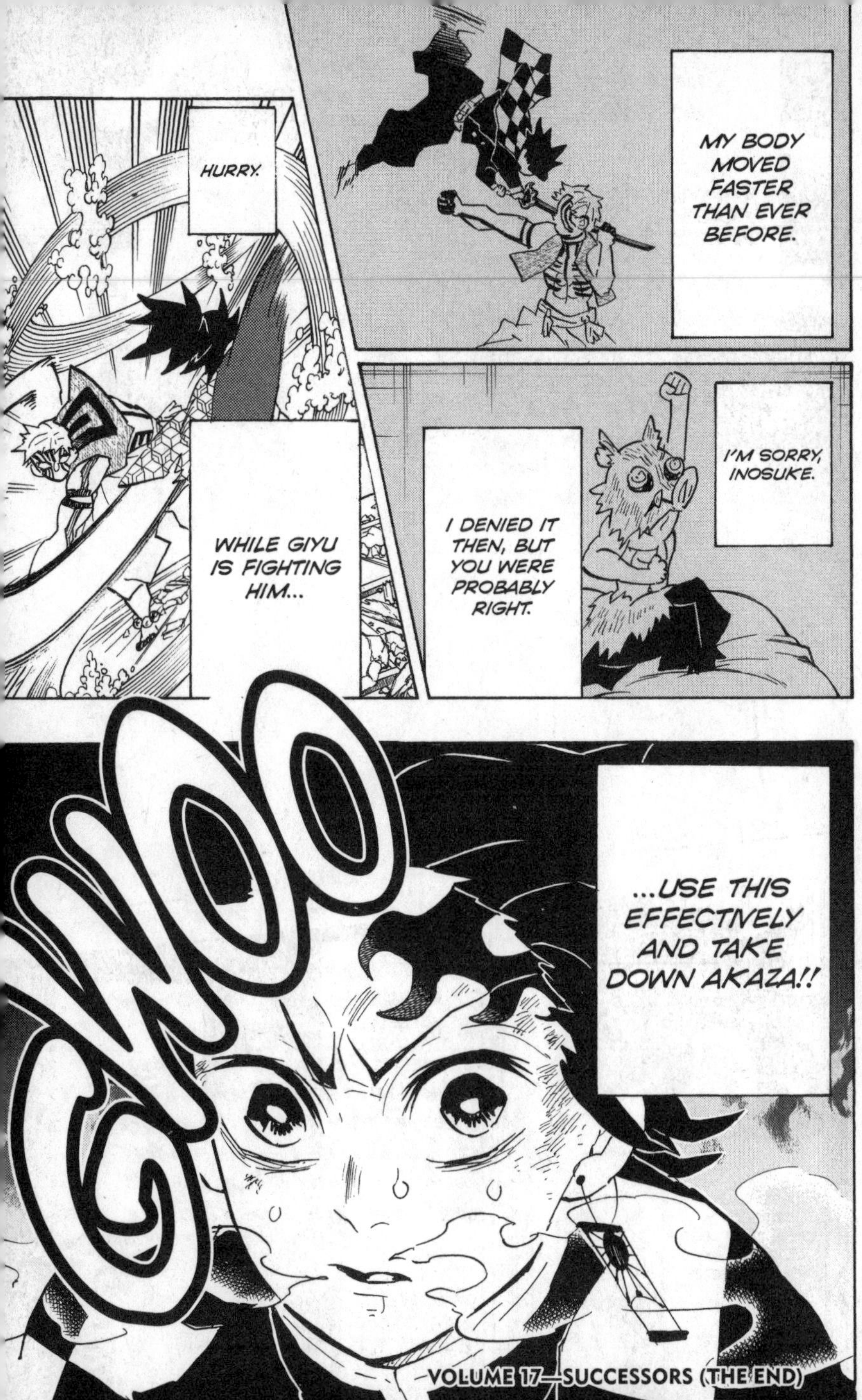
MY BODY MOVED FASTER THAN EVER BEFORE.
I'M SORRY, INOSUKE.
I DENIED IT THEN, BUT YOU WERE PROBABLY RIGHT.
HURRY.
WHILE GIYU IS FIGHTING HIM...
...USE THIS EFFECTIVELY AND TAKE DOWN AKAZA!!
WHOO
VOLUME 17—SUCCESSORS (THE END)

Junior High and High School ☆ Kimetsu Academy

Kanae Kocho. Biology instructor, flower arrangement club advisor.

Kanae Kocho, graduate of Kimetsu Academy. In all three years she attended, people considered her one of the school's top three great beauties. She was disgustingly popular among both girls and boys. Even people who spoke poorly of her looked lovestruck when actually talking to her. She's quiet and mysterious and was once seen throwing a seal at the wall and chanting something like "Rin-pyo-to-sha." Maybe she has spiritual powers?

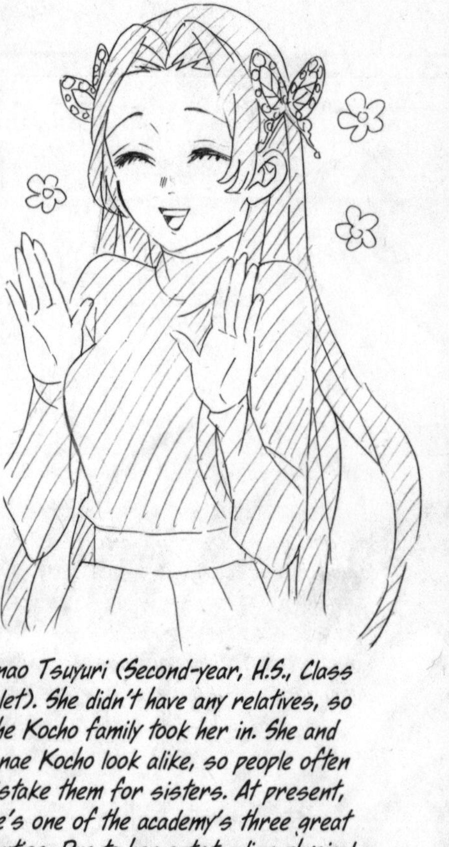

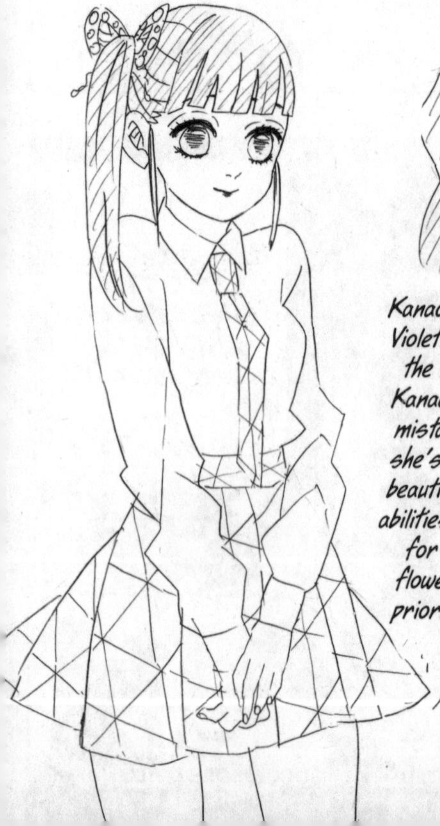

Kanao Tsuyuri (Second-year, H.S., Class Violet). She didn't have any relatives, so the Kocho family took her in. She and Kanae Kocho look alike, so people often mistake them for sisters. At present, she's one of the academy's three great beauties. Due to her outstanding physical abilities, she often gets scouted or asked for help, so she's busy. She's in the flower-arrangement club and wants to prioritize that, so she has a hard time.

Kimetsu Academy Scary Stories

A Pot in the Biology Lab.

Whoever the pot monster's eyes fall upon is subjected to endless condescension. But if you ignore its incomprehensible bragging, it'll tickle you with all its hands, so it's pretty annoying. When Ms. Kanae joined the staff, rumors about it and sightings of it suddenly stopped. Did she exorcise it and send it to the next world?

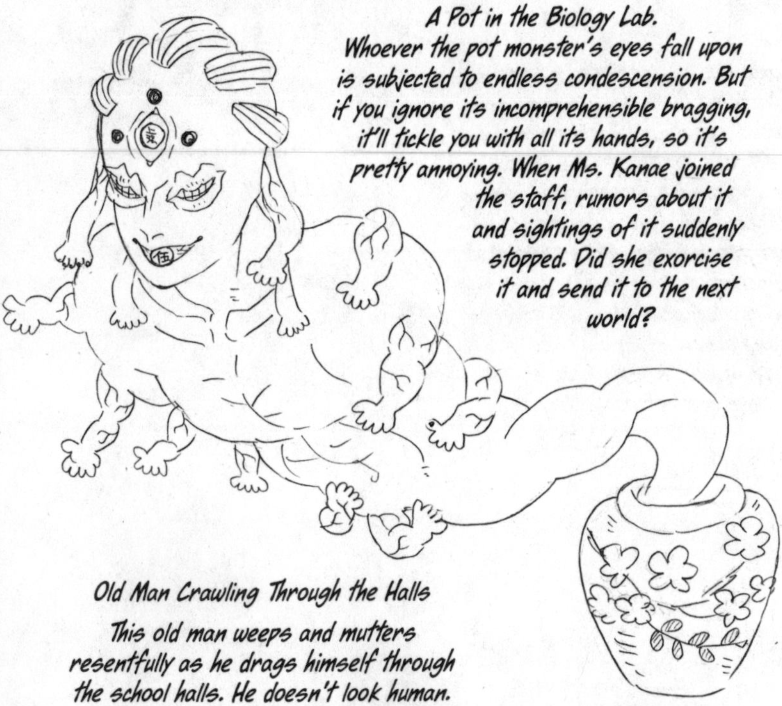

Old Man Crawling Through the Halls

This old man weeps and mutters resentfully as he drags himself through the school halls. He doesn't look human. When he sees someone with a body smaller than his own, he attacks them and steals their belongings. In junior high, Tokito struck him with an axe kick, so his head is swollen.

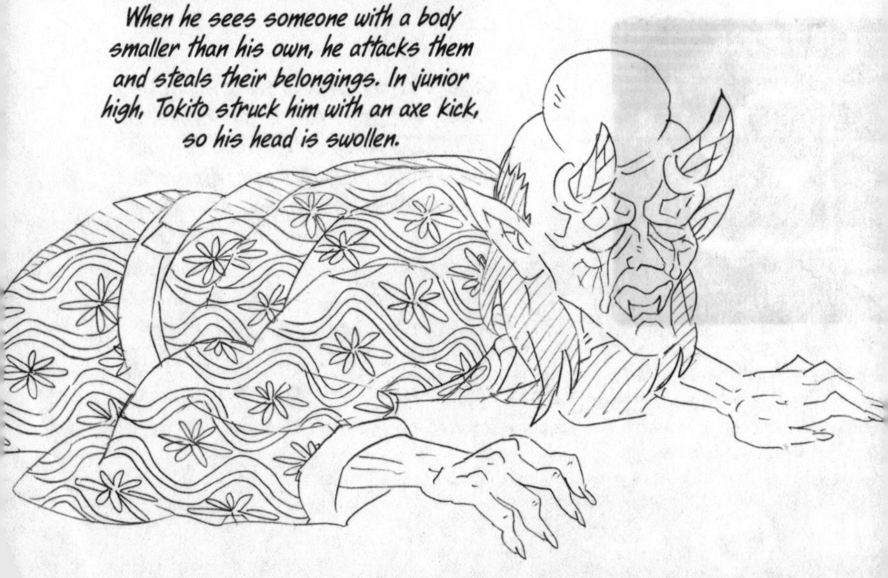

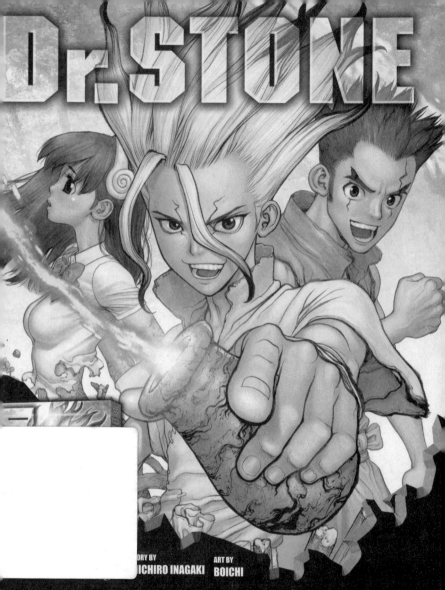

Dr. STONE

STORY BY RIICHIRO INAGAKI

ART BY BOICHI

One fateful day, all of humanity turned to stone. Many millennia later, Taiju frees himself from petrification and finds himself surrounded by statues. The situation looks grim—until he runs into his science-loving friend Senku! Together they plan to restart civilization with the power of science!

Ruby, Weiss, Blake and Yang are students at Beacon Academy, learning to protect the world of Remnant from the fearsome Grimm!

RWBY

MANGA BY **Shirow Miwa**

BASED ON THE ROOSTER TEETH SERIES
CREATED BY Monty Oum

viz.com

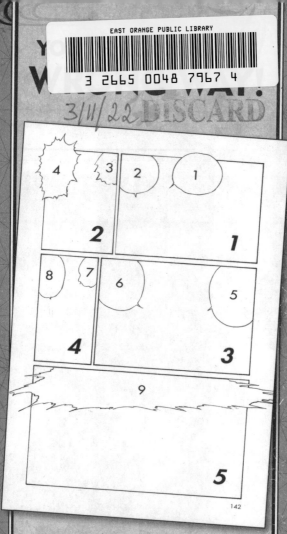

DEMON SLAYER: KIMETSU NO YAIBA
reads from right to left, starting in the upper-right corner. Japanese is read from right to left, meaning that action, sound effects and word-balloon order are completely reversed from English order.